Preface to the Fourth Edition

The first two editions of this book contained a long introductory chapter on philosophy and language. I believed then, and believe still, that philosophical problems can best be clarified, and some of them solved or dissolved, by first discussing the influence of language on the problems we employ language to discuss, and that, far from being an irrelevance or a delay in the philosophical process, such a discussion is a shortcut to the comprehension of philosophical issues.

It is my impression that nonstudents who read the book began with that opening chapter. But most readers were students for whom the book was assigned reading, and apparently very few teachers assigned that opening chapter, with the result that the third edition did not contain it. There were enough complaints about this exclusion, however, that in the present edition the chapter has been restored, in a simplified and abbreviated form.

Many introductory books begin with the topics in which students are already assumed to have an interest, such as religion and ethics. It was tempting to begin with these topics, but in the end this option was rejected. It was essential, I decided, to present basic epistemology first. I have therefore left the structure of the book much the same as it was, although most of the actual words are new. It is hoped that the new treatment is more accessible to introductory readers, and that the use of numerous examples and illustrative dialogues in nontechnical, conversational English will induce the student to read on. Often readers have remembered certain examples long after they have forgotten what points they were designed to illustrate. I hope that what the reader remembers in the present edition will be an admixture of both.

I would like to thank my reviewers: Michael Burke, Indiana University; John Beversluis, Butler University; and Mark Bernstein, University of Texas, San Antonio.

I would also like to express my appreciation to several persons who commented on the previous edition in preparation for the present one: Professor John Dupre of Stanford University; Professor Edward Johnson of the University of New Orleans; Professor Joseph Grcic, Utah Valley State College; and most of all, my colleague and friend, the late Professor Martin Lean.

Preface to the Second Edition

Those who approach philosophy for the first time do so from a variety of motives. Some are drawn into philosophy from their interest in the sciences, some from the arts, some from religion; others come to philosophy without any academic background, motivated by an uneasiness about "the meaning of things" or "what the world is all about"; still others have no motivation more specific than that of wanting to know what people are talking about when they use the word "philosophy." Accordingly, the demands that different people make of philosophy and the questions that they expect it to answer are as diverse as the motives leading them to it; as a result, the books that are written to satisfy these demands are similarly diverse. Often two books professing to introduce readers to philosophy contain little or none of the same material. For these reasons it is impossible to write a book that will satisfy all or perhaps even a majority of readers.

One might try to overcome this difficulty by writing a book so comprehensive that all the problems that anyone considered philo-

sophical would be treated in it, and the readers would have only to select portions in which they are most interested. This, however, is hardly possible in practice: a book of a thousand pages would not begin to suffice. Nor would it be feasible to devote just a few pages to each problem: this would leave only outline summaries of the various issues, which would mean little to the readers; they might learn the meanings of some terms and absorb a few "general trends" from such a presentation, but they would not have been given enough material to make the problems come alive for them. The capsule method is even less successful in philosophy than it is elsewhere. The only apparent solution, then, would be to include not all but only some of the issues in the field. This method has its drawbacks, however, for no matter which problems are included and which are excluded, many readers are bound to object both to some of the inclusions and to some of the exclusions. Yet this is the policy that has been followed in this book, as the one with the fewest all-round disadvantages.

1 Words and the World
LANGUAGE AND REALITY

1. PHILOSOPHICAL QUESTIONS

Why did she die?

She was driving down the highway when another car hit hers. The driver of the other car was going very fast, and a collision at such a speed often kills or maims the people in the vehicles. That's what happened this time. And that's why she died.

I know all that. But, I mean, *why* did she die?

I've just answered that question. She happened to be at that intersection just when the other car hit hers.

But why was she at that place?

She was on the way to the supermarket to go shopping. She would have passed that corner a few minutes earlier, but she was delayed because she had to turn back for something she forgot.

I understand why she was delayed. But I know to know, *why* did she die?

I've given you the cause of her death. But it seems that you don't want to know the cause but the *purpose* of her death.

Yes, I want to know the purpose.

But there may not *be* a purpose. That's why we speak of a "pointless, purposeless death." If God rules all things, then God might have had a purpose in bringing about her death. I don't know what it could be, but at least I know what the word "purpose" means in this context. The woman had a purpose in driving downtown—she wanted to go shopping. And in the same way, God brought about her death and presumably had some purpose in doing so.

But I can't believe that God would want her to die or would do anything to bring it about. Perhaps God's purposes are unknowable, and we can't understand what they are.

Or perhaps there is no purpose to it at all. It just happened.

You mean by chance.

No, not chance—not like when we say that there's a 50-50 chance the coin will turn up heads. Perhaps chance in the sense that neither of the drivers *intended* for their cars to collide with one another. But many things aren't the result of an intention. The planets go round the sun, but not by chance—they follow Newton's laws of motion; yet that doesn't mean that they have a purpose in doing so or even that somebody "up there" has a purpose in making them go round the sun.

I don't see how it could have happened unless there was some purpose in it.

Why do you assume that? The tree falls down in a storm. This event had a cause, but as far as we can tell, no purpose. If something had a purpose, tell me whose purpose it was—that is, who it was that had the purpose.

I guess that leaves God as the one who had the purpose.

In that case, he's the one you should ask. For my part, I can't imagine why anyone would have as a conscious purpose the bring-

1

ing about of the death of an innocent person. So if there was a purpose in it—a divine purpose—I can't imagine what it could have been.

Maybe it isn't the purpose I want to know. I want to know what *meaning* there is in what happened.

Meaning. Do you know for how many different things we use that word "meaning"?

Meaning is meaning; I want to know what meaning there is in her dying.

I'm not trying to underrate the importance to you of this tragic event. But you asked for its meaning, and I can't even try to answer that question without showing you how your question itself can mean so many things.

Such as . . . ?

Well, for one thing, a word has a meaning: the word "cat" means—refers to—cats. It's cats that we're talking about when we use the word. And so on for countless other words.

OK, but that's not what I'm asking for.

There are others. We sometimes use the word "meaning" when we want to know what an event portends. There's a twister in the sky; what does it mean? Tornado coming. Or what does that series of dots and dashes mean? It's Morse code for the word "repeat."

But I'm not asking about natural signs or man-made signals either.

When one nation signs a treaty with another, the leaders of a third nation ask, "What does this mean?" That is, what will be the effects of this action? What may happen as a result? Is that what you mean when you ask, "What's the meaning of her death?"

I don't think so. I'm not asking what effects her death will have. For example, I already know that it will make her loved ones unhappy and that her children will grow up without a mother. I know these things already.

Well, then, what sort of thing *would* be an answer to your question? When one answer after another doesn't suit you, it may be a good idea to consider what *would* be an acceptable answer to the question.

If I knew that, I wouldn't be asking the question.

I don't mean that you should know the answer before you ask the question. I am saying that before you ask the question, you should know what kind of answer would suffice. For example, if I ask, "Where is he?" and someone answers, "He is visiting relatives in Montana," that is the kind of statement that, if true, *would* answer my question. What I want to know is what sort of answer would suffice to answer your question.

I'm not sure. I think I want to know what meaning her death has in the scheme of things.

Do you mean, will it have widespread ramifications in the lives of other people? Maybe it will, and maybe it won't; that depends on how many people she was close to and perhaps on how well known she was in the community.

No, I don't mean just how it will affect other people.

But that *would* be meaning, wouldn't it—if her death inspired those around her to renew their own lives and so on? You could say that her death had meaning for others if it affected them in that way.

Yes, but I mean something more than that. I want to know what importance her death has in the scheme of things, in the plan or purpose of the universe.

OK, if that's what you're asking, you are asking about God's purposes again. I'm not trying to answer the question, you see, I'm just trying to *clarify* the question. I want to know in what area the answer would lie. And it seems that you've told me —you want an answer in terms of divine purpose. Whether such an answer can be given, well, that's another question. We'll have to cover a lot of ground before we get to that.

In this imaginary conversation, we have already found ourselves involved in philosophi-

An Introd
to Philosophical
Analysis

Fourth Edition

John Hospers

Professor Emeritus
University of Southern California

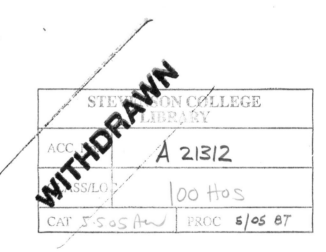

Routledge
Taylor & Francis Group

NEW YORK AND LONDON

First published in Great Britain in 1956
by Routledge & Kegan Paul

Second edition published in 1967

Third edition published in 1990

Fourth edition published in 1997
by Routledge
2 Park Square, Milton Park, Abingdon, Oxon OX14 4RN

Reprinted 2000, 2001, 2003, 2004, 2005

Routledge is an imprint of the Taylor & Francis Group

© 1997, 1988, 1967, 1953 by Prentice-Hall, Inc.
Simon & Schuster/A Viacom Company

Typeset in Baskerville by Compset, Inc.

Printed and bound in Great Britain by
T.J. International Ltd, Padstow, Cornwall

British Library Cataloguing in Publication Data

A catalogue record for this book is available from the British Library

ISBN   0–415–15792–7
        0–415–15793–5 (pbk)

Contents

cal questions. There was a description of some facts about a car accident, but certain words were introduced that are typically "philosophical" words, such as "cause," "purpose," "reason," and "meaning." They all need to be clarified. We use these words in daily conversation, but most people don't use them very carefully or very clearly. In philosophy, we have to use them more carefully; if we do not we often just "talk past" one another and engage in pointless back-and-forth arguments that with some care could easily have been avoided. Let's consider two examples:

1. Philosophy studies reality, but so do the sciences; so in one way or another does every subject we study. And what is meant by the word "reality"? Philosophers have the thankless task of pointing out to those who want "capsule culture in three easy lessons" that such questions are not simple.

Consider the word "real": "That's not a real duck—it's a decoy." "It's not a giraffe out there—it's a configuration of shapes that looks like a giraffe against the sunset sky." "That's not a real pink rat—you're having the DTs, you're hallucinating." "That didn't really happen—it was a dream; or you were misinformed; or you read it wrong; or somebody lied." "That's not a real problem—it's a phony one, you think there's a problem but there isn't." and so on.[1] Each of these uses of the word "real" is different; we can identify what *this* occurrence of the word means when we know what it is being *contrasted* with, and it is contrasted with a variety of different things. For example, an imitation duck is not a real duck. Besides all that, the word "real" is often used merely as an "intensive": "that really happened" is an emphatic way of saying "that happened."

Thus we can't give a simple answer to the question, "What is real?" We have to go through the cumbersome and tiring business of pointing out the various things that the word "real" can mean by contrasting it with what, in that specific context, is not called real (it could change again in a different context). Is a dream real? Well, it's not like the tree out there, but it's a real experience, isn't it? To a beginner this may be bewildering, frustrating, even anger-provoking. People want simple answers to simple questions. But what they don't see is that the question isn't simple. To get them to see this is already to have taken a brief excursion into philosophy.

2. What is the meaning of life? This is often believed to be *the* question that philosophy must answer. But when we ask it at first, we don't see the traps within the question. "What's the meaning of that phone call?" we ask when a voice utters a few hostile words and the line clicks dead. We can be asking various questions—"Who called?" "What does the caller want?" "What does it portend for the future?"—and many other things. "What does 'perihelion' mean?" It means the point on the orbit of a planet when it's nearest to the sun (or of a satellite, when it's nearest to the planet around which it revolves). That's an example of the dictionary sense of the word "meaning"; it tells us how a word is used in a language. "What's the meaning of that remark?"—that is, what did you intend by it? Are you trying to communicate what I think you are? "What's the meaning of a falling barometer?" It means that a storm is on the way; it's an indicator of future events. "If everyone on board the plane was killed, what does that mean?" It means that if your friend was on board, she too was killed; that is, it logically *implies* it; the conclusion is inescapable if you grant the premise.

In these cases we have *multiplicity* of meanings (in this case of the word "meaning" itself): meaning as definition; meaning as in-

---

[1]See J. L. Austin, Sense and Sensibilia (Oxford: Oxford University Press, 1962).

tention; meaning as implication; meaning as purpose; meaning as import for the future; and so on. Thus, when one asks, "What is the meaning of life?," our first task is to try to determine what information the questioner wants supplied. Does she want to know whether her life serves some overall purpose? Why she should continue living? Whether there is a pattern of events in her life that she hasn't discovered but that may be important for her future? Or what she ought to do with her life? Or perhaps whether God has created her for a reason, which she is trying to discover? "Tell me in other words what you want to know," we may say. But doing this, especially for one who hasn't made distinctions like these and who isn't very good at articulating incoherent thoughts and impressions, may be extremely difficult—even impossible—at the start. She may feel that she is being made to go through an uncomfortable effort and concentration that isn't necessary: All she wants to know is, "What is the meaning of life?," and here we are throwing dust in her face, forcing her to choose between alternative formulations before we'll so much as entertain her question. Understandably, this is extremely frustrating.

But until we have cut through the fog we can't get far in philosophy. Our questioner doesn't even realize that she has asked a foggy question, and wonders why we don't answer her with simple directness. Most people at this point stick with their foggy question, obtain somebody's equally foggy answer in some obscure but impressive-sounding bit of pontification ("The meaning of life is to fulfill your destiny"), and then walk away satisfied. But these people have evaded the issues of philosophy.

What Is Philosophy?

Usually, when we begin the study of a subject, we are told what the subject is—what the word naming the subject is supposed to mean. Bi-

ology has to do with the study of living organisms. Astronomy has to do with the study of celestial objects, such as stars and planets. Human history has to do with the study of what people have done and suffered during the centuries.

What then is philosophy? When we open a book with the word "philosophy" in the title, what is the subject on which we may expect it to inform us?

Unfortunately, the word "philosophy" wouldn't give us a very clear idea of what to expect. The word is used very loosely. "What's your philosophy?" someone asks. What kind of answer is appropriate for such a question? If someone responds, "Get whatever you can out of life, that's my philosophy," is this an acceptable answer? If someone asks, "How many planets are in the solar system?" and you reply "Eight," your answer would be incorrect but it *would* be an answer to the question. Is "Get whatever you can out of life" even an answer to the question asked? (It's not even clear what this statement is supposed to mean. Does it mean that one should do whatever one pleases, even if this involves harm to others?)

Everyone seems to agree on one thing, that if a question can be answered *empirically*, by the use of the senses, by seeing, hearing, touching, or the other senses, or setting up experiments, it is not a philosophical question. Thus,

1. Statements of ordinary perception, such as "There are three chairs in this room," and "Most of the earth's surface is covered with water," are not philosophical questions.

2. Questions that the sciences can answer are not philosophical questions. Physics, astronomy, geology, chemistry, biology, and psychology are all empirical sciences, and their discoveries are made through observations and experiments that involve numerous aids for the senses, such as microscopes, telescopes, and spectrometers. If an experi-

ment can settle the question, it is a scientific question and not a philosophical one.

3. Questions about what has happened in the past are not philosophical questions. "When did Abraham Lincoln die?" and "Who lived on the earth a million years ago?" are historical questions. Often we can't answer them except by consulting documents or other evidence contained in rocks, but they are all questions about what could have been observed if someone had been there at the time; sometimes there were contemporary observers (as in the Lincoln example), and sometimes not (as in the question about what occurred millions of years ago). The same considerations apply to questions about the future: we don't know the answers to most of them—not even whether it will rain in this city tomorrow—but it's to these kinds of question that our senses can provide the answers when the time comes.

4. Questions in arithmetic, algebra, and the other branches of mathematics are not philosophical questions. "How much is 600 + 500?" is a question in arithmetic; "Are there bees in this hive?" is an empirical question, to be settled by observation and not by adding, subtracting, and so on. Mathematical questions require calculation, not observation.

What, then, is left for philosophy to consider? Different answers to this question have been suggested; they all take us into much the same areas of thought, although the answers themselves are not the same. Here are the main ones:

1. Philosophy is the study of reality—but not that aspect of reality that is already covered by the various sciences. Whatever questions are not empirical and not mathematical are left over for philosophy to tackle. Not everyone agrees that there are such "leftover" questions, but whether this is so we have yet to consider. The question with which we began ("Why did she die?") at least *seems* to be such a question.

2. Philosophy is the study of *justification;* it is concerned with how we justify the claims we make. How do you know that there is a physical world? That we're not all dreaming? That there is a God beyond the stars? That goodness and beauty really exist? That the mind is separate from the body? That time is infinite?

3. Philosophy is the *analysis* of various concepts that are central to our thought. For example, we speak of causes every day, but what *is* a cause? We use numbers, but what is a number? We speak of justice, but what is justice? We describe things as beautiful, but what is beauty? We speak of before and after in time, but what is time? We describe things as real, but what is reality?

Those who take this last view of philosophy will be most concerned with questions like "What do you mean?," followed by some word or phrase; philosophy analyzes meanings. Those who take the second view are likely to keep asking the question "How do you know?" How do you know that what you say is true? (And what is truth?) How do you know that animals are conscious? How do you know that if Hitler had not existed, World War II would not have occurred?

So many of these questions lead into each other that we won't try to distinguish them further here. But perhaps we should make the traditional listing of the branches of philosophy, although many of them overlap: (1) logic, the study of correct reasoning; (2) epistemology, the study of the justification of claims to knowledge (the constant attempt to answer the question "How do you know?"); (3) metaphysics, the study of reality other than the reality studied by history and the empirical and mathematical sciences (it is also concerned with the categories into which human thought is said to be divided, such as substance, attribute, and number—of which more will be said in due course); and (4) the study of values, principally the good (ethics) and the beautiful (aesthetics).

In all these branches of study, the questions "What do you mean?" and "How do you know?" will be constantly present.

Verbal Issues

Philosophy is full of disagreements. But to clear the decks and make our task simpler, let's first consider one kind of disagreement that, if we're not careful, will get in our way and cause needless confusion. These are *verbal* disagreements, disputes that seem to be about facts but are actually about the words in which the disputes are expressed. The resolution of the dispute depends not on discovering any further facts but only on coming to agreement about the meanings of the words being used in the dispute. Here is a simple example: If a tree falls in the forest and nobody hears it fall, is there a sound? This question has been hotly debated for many years, with one side answering an emphatic "yes" and the other side an equally emphatic "no." The arguments go something like this:

A: Of course there is a sound. Record the tree falling on tape. The tape will record the sounds that were made when you weren't there along with those made when you were there. Sound waves are alternating condensations and rarefactions of air particles, and they occur regardless of whether there is anyone around to hear them.
B: No, there is no sound. If you aren't there, you can't hear the tree falling. The word "sound" refers to the sound *sensation,* and if no one is there, there's no one to have the sensation.

This is surely a verbal dispute—a dispute about words. Once we are clear about the meaning of the words we are using, there is nothing left to dispute.

Many disagreements aren't that easy to resolve, but they still are—or at least seem to be—about the meanings of words. Here are a few cases involving the phrase "the same":

1. All things change, yet we call something the same thing in spite of the changes. If someone scratches this table, it's still the same table. If someone paints it red, we still call it the same table—it's a different color, but the same table. If someone saws off its legs, we might say it is no longer a table but a table top. But if we chop it up for firewood and burn it, we can no longer call it a table at all. It no longer has the shape of a table, and it can no longer serve the function of a table. The same chemical elements are still around—the wood has oxidized and the smoke from it is still in the air—but the table no longer exists. The word "table" is no longer used to label it.

2. Is this train here in the station the same train my sister took to Chicago yesterday?

One might say no; that set of cars is now in Chicago, and what is sitting here in the station is a different set of cars. So it can't be the same train.

But that isn't what makes it the same train. We say it's the same train if the same name of the train is on the daily schedule and if it leaves the station at approximately the same scheduled time every day.

Thus it is and it isn't the same train—not in the same sense, of course. The phrase "same train" is ambiguous, and what we do to resolve the dispute is to point out the ambiguity.

3. "These two hair samples are the same," testified witness Douglas Dietrick at the O. J. Simpson trial.

"What," asked attorney F. Lee Bailey, "do you mean by 'the same'?"

"I mean that there are no significant differences between them."

"Then," said Bailey, "you disagree with Webster when his dictionary defines 'the same' as 'exactly alike.' And these two were not exactly alike, were they?"

"No, not exactly. When we examine hairs and fibers we call them the same if there is no discernible or significant difference between them."

4. Is this the same creature we saw last week when it was a tadpole? No, now it's a frog. But it is one continuously existing physical organism. If an organism undergoes quick changes like this, we don't use the same word for it anymore—we call it a frog now. With most species, however, this doesn't happen—this is the same dog, the same deer, the same tree, as we saw yesterday, although they all have changed since we last saw them. Some of their qualities are different now, but in spite of this, we continue to use the same thing-word (noun).

5. There is Bill Brown. Would he be the same person if he had been born of different parents? If he had been born in the nineteenth century? If he had been born ten minutes earlier than he was?

It might be possible that Bill was born before 1900 and is still around. Suppose he just changed his name; would he still be Bill Brown? Well, he wouldn't any longer be called Bill Brown, but he would still be the same man who was called that before. Would he still be Bill Brown—that is, the person who now carries the name "Bill Brown"—if he had been born of different parents?

Of course not, we say; then he would be a different person. If his mother had had an abortion, she wouldn't have had *him;* she might have had another son later who looks about the same, but he wouldn't be this Bill. To be the same person, he would have to come from that sperm and that egg.

But would he be the same Bill Brown if he had been born two weeks earlier? He could be. His mother might have given birth prematurely. But he would still be the Bill to

whom she gave birth. But he would not be if he had been born a year earlier, when he hadn't even been conceived.

Not everyone would agree that this last case is a verbal issue. Some would say that it's a metaphysical issue about the nature of the self. We shall consider this matter after we have first clarified some other concepts that lead up to it, such as the mind and the body (Chapter 6). At any rate, these issues are all closely bound with the words that are used to describe them.

2. WORDS AND THINGS

Animals communicate with one another through sounds, gestures, and body language to indicate that danger is near, that they want something, that they are ready to mate, and so on. Human beings also communicate with each other in these ways. But the distinctive way in which human beings communicate is by means of words. Some animals, such as chimpanzees, can understand some words and even sentences, although apparently they can't invent them. Human beings, however, not only invent them but use many thousands of them to communicate thoughts and questions so complex or abstract that no other kind of animal is able to understand them. (Just ask your cat what she thinks about the meaning of life.)

If a word is spoken, it is a noise; if it is written, it is a set of marks on paper (or a blackboard, etc.). But many noises and written marks are not words. Grunts and laughs are not words, and pictures and drawings are not words. Sometimes they can convey more than words can: a photograph can show what a thing looks like more accurately than any words can. But to describe situations, real and imagined, we need words; and every tribe, no matter how primitive, has a vocabulary of many words with which to describe aspects of the world around them as well as their inner feelings and fantasies.

But now there is a problem: the number of things in the universe is, if not infinite, at least indefinitely large, greater than we can count. There are billions of stars and millions of galaxies (star cities), each containing millions of stars. Now consider how many quadrillions of atoms of matter are contained in each star and each planet. There seems to be no limit to them.

The number of qualities that things have seems to be limitless as well. We have a few words for various shapes: "square," "rectangular," "octagonal," and so on. (When we are talking about the *thing*, square, we use no quotation marks around the word; but when we are talking about the *word*, "square," we use quotation marks, so as to distinguish the word from the thing that the word stands for. For example,

Cats have tails.
"Cats" has four letters.)

But for most shapes we have no words that are specific enough to describe them. Take a piece of glass and break it into pieces; what is the word for the shape into which this piece of glass shatters, and for the shape of any number of such pieces that result from subsequent shatterings of the glass? We would need thousands of words for these thousands of shapes.

Or consider the way things feel to the touch: the way a hot iron feels when it touches the skin, then a lukewarm iron, then a piece of ice. Consider how bamboo feels, then cedar wood, then elm leaves, then heather, and so on. There is an endless array of these qualities that we can distinguish from one another yet for which we have no words.

The number of words in a language is finite. The English language contains more than forty thousand words—more than most of us can remember, but still not enough to enable us to tell these infinitely various things and qualities apart.

But we want to be able to use words to talk about anything we wish—any of the limitless array of things, any of the limitless array of qualities. So we group the individual things and qualities into *classes* or *kinds*. No two dogs are alike, but they have certain resemblances among one another.

Words and things.

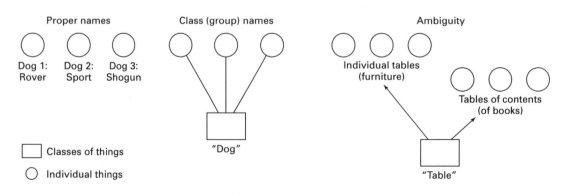

We *abstract* these qualities—having four legs, having a long nose, having the ability to bark, and so on—from the individuals that possess them; that is, we take these aspects of individual dogs and consider them separately. Individuals are similar to one another in countless ways, and we can take any of these similarities and make them the basis of membership in a class. Dogs are creatures that have certain features or characteristics in common; cats have a different (but overlapping) set of features in common; and so on.

Thus, instead of having one word for one thing, we have one word for many things. When a word stands for one thing only, like "Abraham Lincoln," it is the name of a certain individual, not a class of individuals. Such words are called *proper names.* Thus "Abraham Lincoln" is the name of the sixteenth president of the United States. But most nouns refer to *classes* of things: "man," "dog," "tree," and so on. (See figure.)

Heracleitus and General Words

The early Greek philosopher Heracleitus (540–480 B.C.) said—or is reported to have said—that you can't step into the same river twice, because the drops of water that are in the river when you cross it today are not the same drops that were there when you crossed yesterday.

Why, we are inclined to ask, should the fact that the drops are different today keep us from saying that it's still the same river? Don't we already know that the drops of water are not the same? Why can't we use the label "same river" even though the drops are admittedly not the same?

Let's assume that Heracleitus wasn't blind, or even colorblind, when he looked out of his window, and that he saw pretty much the same scene we would have seen if we had been there. Isn't the only difference

between his scene and ours in the *description* and not in the scene itself? Isn't the whole issue a verbal one—of how he uses language versus how we do?

Heracleitus said that everything is constantly changing, that nothing ever remains the same. If asked whether we could step into the same *pond* twice, presumably he would have said no, even if the pond *does* contain the same drops of water today as yesterday. Since everything is in constant flux, and nothing remains the same, even from one moment to the next, it isn't the same pond that we put our feet in now as we did one minute ago.

But surely, we say, if everything is constantly changing, there must be *things* that exist to do the changing–things that precede and outlast the changes that occur in them. Doesn't change require something that does the changing?

But Heracleitus wouldn't admit that much. There isn't a thing at all, not even a thing that changes. We should stop talking about things and talk only about successive momentary states. Here are successive states of what we call the table: there is table-at-state-A, a moment later there is table-at-state-B, and so on. Since no two of these successive states are exactly alike (since everything constantly changes), we should have a different *word* for each one of them. Since each state is different from every other, each state should have a different word (label) to stand for it.

Of course, if we tried to do this, we would soon run out of words. Our language would become infinitely lengthy, and our memory would soon be taxed beyond endurance in trying to recall all those millions of words. In fact, each word would be a proper name for one momentary state.

In our daily lives we don't take this linguistic turn; we don't make up a different word for each momentary state; we don't even use a different word for each individual thing (that's done only in the case of proper names). We use a different word for each *group* of things, based on similarity: one word for dogs, another word for foxes, and so on.

But Heracleitus would remind us, there is a danger in this: it's the same-word-same-thing fallacy, sometimes called the "collectivist fallacy." If she's had bad luck twice dating bankers, she turns down the next opportunity: "Another banker," she says, neglecting the fact that not all bankers are alike. Neither are all Native Americans alike, nor all wolves, nor all amoebas; each one is an *individual.* Perhaps if we had different names for each of them we wouldn't be so likely to put them all in one mental package and think of them as all having the same qualities. Having the same label makes us inclined to forget their many individual differences. One could construe Heracleitus as trying to stamp out the collectivist fallacy by giving every thing, indeed every state of every thing, a different name.

What then was Heracleitus doing? Was he pointing to any empirical difference between his world and ours? No, it seems to be a verbal difference, a difference in the descriptions. Then what's the big deal? Apparently Heracleitus was trying to *dramatize* the differences among things; everything is in a constant state of change, even if our language does not reflect this fact. Because language tends to ignore these differences, it tends to make us guilty of the collectivist fallacy. Therefore (he would say) language is an imperfect way of dealing with the world.

There is another side to the coin, however: we need general words, and not merely for the sake of linguistic economy. Probably no two things in the world are exactly alike, but they do have some characteristics in common, and we need general words to refer to them. If there were only proper names, there would be no general term "man" that links the Boston aristocrat to a primitive tribesman; they are both human beings, and the general term "human being" (or "man") helps to remind us of what they have in common.

Classification

A group of a hundred things may have characteristics A, B, and C in common, and may be called an X (X being anything that has A, B, and C); but the group may also have D, E, and F in common, and may be called a Y (Y being whatever has D, E, and F). You thus could classify an object in the group as an X or as a Y, with equal correctness.

How we classify the object depends not only on its characteristics but also on our interests. There is a practical interest in classifying snakes as poisonous or nonpoisonous, but no particular interest in classifying them as more than eight inches in diameter or less than eight. Animals are classified in one way by zoologists, in another way by the fur industry, and in still another way by the leather industry. Houses are classified in one way by an architect, in another way by a gas inspector, and in still another by the fire department.

There are as many possible classes in the world as there are common characteristics or combinations thereof that can be made the basis of a classification. We could classify animals by their color if we chose, but it would not be a very fruitful classification. If animals always bred true to color but offspring of the same parents had a chaotic variety of shapes, sizes, and number of legs, then we might consider classification by color to be more "natural" than classification by any other means.

We speak of "natural" classes in biology, when (for example) one organism has features A, B, C, and D and its offspring also have A, B, C, and D (although perhaps differing in G and H). Dogs give birth to other dogs and cats to other cats. The features that are transmitted are (in general) the features that we take to be defining of the class—bone structure, for example, but not color.

There are also man-made classes, such as bicycles and cars. Each number of the first class has common features not possessed by members of the second class.

Classes exist "out there" in the sense that the characteristics things have in common exist in the world, waiting (as it were) to be made the basis for a classification. But they are man-made in that the *act of classifying* is the work of human beings, depending on their needs and interests. From the infinite reservoir of nature we could have taken different groups of common characteristics as the bases of classification from those we did select.

When we want to give a name to a class of things that is like—but not *quite* like—one for which we already have a name, we have a choice. Shall we extend the old name to include the different but related things, or shall we keep the old name and devise a new one for the new class? Shall we call the new antitank weapons "guns" (with a qualifying adjective in front) on the basis of their similarity to the things we already call guns, or shall we call them by a new name, "bazookas," because of their differences from most of the things we call guns? Shall we call communism a religion because of certain qualities of devotion, fanatical loyalty, and submergence of the self in a common cause that it shares with ways of life and thought we already call religions, or shall we deny it the word "religion" because communism professes no belief in a supernatural? What of a chemical element that possesses every characteristic usually associated with a name, except its atomic weight? Shall we consider it a different class and distinguish it with a new name, or shall we retain the old name and say that they all belong in the same class, and then distinguish this group from the rest of the class by using the word "isotope"?

We can, of course, do either. If we use the same word for both, we shall be calling attention to the similarity between the new class and the old; but at the same time we shall be obscuring the differences between them, and many will assume that they are alike because they have the same name. But if we use a new word we shall be in danger of losing sight of the features they have in common. Sometimes the decision is made in the interests of preserving an entire system of classification: Mendeleef's Table of the Elements was an immensely fruitful basis for classification of the chemical elements, and we tend to classify in such a way as to preserve a system of classification that has already proved its worth.

Words as Tools

Just as we use nouns to stand for kinds of things (not individual things, except in the case of proper names), so we use adjectives to stand for *kinds* of qualities: "sweet," "sour," "dark," "heavy," "smooth," "reticulated," and so on. "Dark" may be dark brown, dark blue, dark green, or dark red, but the adjective "dark" applies to them all: we have one word and many different qualities united by a certain similarity.

Adverbs are words that are used to describe *ways* of behaving or doing: "swiftly," "greedily," "hastily," "lovingly," "haltingly," "slowly," "deliberately." Again, each of these adverbs is used not only to describe the manner of *this* particular action but the manner of countless others that have some similarity to it. "Slowly" can describe how a person walks, how she pronounces her words, how she eats her food, and so on.

Prepositions refer to certain *relations* that things have to one another: "above," "below," "inside," "outside," "between," "beyond."

Verbs stand for different kinds of action or initiation of change: "eat," "run," "slide," "accelerate," "fly," "stop."

Conjunctions do not describe any features of the world but indicate how various clauses in a sentence are related to one another: "He and she will go" has a different meaning from "He or she will go." "Stop or I'll scream" is the same as "If you don't stop, I'll scream," but different from "Stop and I'll scream."

Interjections are used to express a person's attitude toward something—they don't describe the thing, they express how we feel toward it: "alas," "hurrah," "dammit," "whoopee." (We can express our feelings in many other ways as well, as we shall discuss in Chapter 8.)

When a word is used to name a class of things, the word is like the label on a bottle. The label tells you what's in the bottle, and if two bottles have different kinds of contents, it is important not to use the same label for both of them. The label has no importance in itself; it only indicates what is in the bottle. Labels, of course, can be written in different languages yet still be labels for the same kind of thing. They can also be either heard (if oral) or seen (if written). Either way, having words saves us enormous labor: instead of going to the thing, giraffe, we can mention the word, "giraffe," and other people who understand the English language will know what we mean.

"A word is only a sign." But it isn't a natural sign, the way a twister in the sky is the sign of a tornado or falling barometric pressure is the sign of an approaching storm. These signs occur in nature, and human beings had to discover what they are and act accordingly. We could not turn them around or change them, since they are not man-made. But words, like the notes on a musical staff, are *conventional* signs: this word stands for this class of things, this note on the staff stands for this class of sound pitches. In natural signs, A signifies B regardless of what human beings believe or decide; in conventional signs, human beings decide which A's will be used to stand for which B's.

As we have seen, however, not all words are the names of classes of things (nouns) or even classes of actions (verbs) or classes of qualities (adjectives). Every word in a language has some job to do, but no two of them have exactly the same job or even the same *kind* of job. Words are like *tools* in a tool kit. Just as each tool is used to do a different job—you don't do with a hammer the same thing you do with a wrench—so different kinds of words perform different tasks. Pronouns, for example, are substitutes for nouns, except that "I" always refers to whomever is speaking and "you" refers to whomever is being spoken to. To know the meaning of a word is to know what kind of job it does, what its function is in the language.

When do we know the meaning of a word or phrase? When we know the *rule for its use*—that is, when we know under what conditions the word is to be used, when the word is applicable to a given situation, and when it is not. Usually when we ask for the rule for the use of a word, we are asking for the *definition* of the word.

3. DEFINITION

Do you know what an isotope is? a vitamin? a cold? DNA? a tectonic plate? a nebula?

"Well, if you don't know, define it." But people who aren't working in the special discipline involved wouldn't usually be able to do this. How many people outside chemistry would be able to say that an isotope of a chemical element is "a species of atom with the same atomic number and the same position in the periodic table and nearly identical chemical behavior, but with differing atomic mass." But without such a definition, we wouldn't know under just what circumstances we are entitled to use the word, would we?

Still, we often have *some* idea: we can toss around the word "vitamin" for years and seem to communicate with other people in using it, although if asked for a definition we would be quite blank. For that matter, what would you say if someone asked you to define words you use constantly, such as "chair," "tree," "trot," or "run"?

Ordinarily we don't attempt to give the definition of a word unless some dispute arises involving its use. "No, that's not a table, that's a desk." "I wouldn't call her a neurotic, she's a psychotic." "No, that's not a truck, it's a van." And then we try to isolate the characteristic that is the object of dispute.

A definition of a word tells us what characteristics (features, qualities, properties—all these words are used, and philosophers often draw distinctions among them) something has to have in order for the word to apply to it. The word "triangle" means any plane closed figure bounded by three straight lines. It is defined in terms of these three features. Each of the three is a *defining* feature: that is, something wouldn't be a triangle if it lacked any one of them. And the three together give us the definition: the word is applicable to whatever has these three characteristics and to nothing that does not have them.

How can we tell whether a certain characteristic, A, is defining of class X? Ask yourself whether you would call it an X, or whether other users of the language would call it an X, if it did not have A. Would it still be a triangle if it didn't have three sides? No; then having three sides is a defining feature—a *sine qua non* (literally "without which not"). Would it still be a triangle if the three sides were unequal? Yes, that feature is defining only of equilateral triangles.

"Would it still be an X if it didn't have A?" is not the same question as "Would it still

have A if it weren't an X?" Could it still be a plane figure if it weren't a triangle? Of course: it could be a square, a parallelogram, a pentagon, and so on. Having A is essential to being an X, but being an X is not essential to having A: Y and Z may also have A. This wouldn't be stone if it weren't solid (as opposed to liquid or gaseous), but it could be solid without being stone—it could be iron, wood, ice, and so on.

A word is said to *designate* the sum of the characteristics that something must have in order for the word to be applicable to it. The word "triangle" designates the properties of being three-sided, closed, and two-dimensional. These three are sufficient to define the word, as it is used in the English language. This definition distinguishes triangles from everything that is *not* a triangle.

In daily life, when we call something by a certain name we don't usually bother to say which features are defining (at least as we are using the word) and which ones are not. Would you still call this a table if you painted it a different color? Of course; so the color is not defining. Would you still say it was a table if you could petrify it (turn it into stone)? Yes, as long as it continued to have a top and legs to support it. Would you say it was still a table if you cut off the legs? Here we might not be sure; but if it had no legs but hung by a chain from the ceiling, and we could still use it to read and write by, and to serve meals on, probably we would still call it a table; in that case, having legs would not be a defining feature of a table. Often we can't make up our minds whether this thing is an X, because we're not sure whether we would call a certain feature of X a defining feature. Consider:

Steel is an alloy of iron.
Steel is used in construction.

The first sentence states what in English usage would be a defining feature: if this weren't an alloy of iron, it wouldn't be steel (the word "steel" would not be applicable to it). But the second sentence doesn't state a defining feature: this would still be steel even if it were no longer used in construction. The first sentence states part of the meaning of the *word* "steel," and the second sentence asserts a fact about the *thing*, steel.

If someone says that all swans are white, is she giving us (part of) the meaning of the word "swan" or informing us of a fact about the *thing*, swan? People came to dispute about this when black swans were discovered in Australia. Biologists called them swans because they were just like the other swans except for their color. Some insisted, however, that if it isn't white it isn't a swan (that is, being white is a defining feature of swans), so the black creatures in Australia therefore aren't swans.

How could this dispute be resolved? It could have been resolved either way, by a fiat about whether being white was or was not defining of swans. It was quickly settled, however, in the biologists' favor: since color is traditionally a variable, it had not been used as defining of any species. Being white is therefore an *accompanying* feature of most swans, although not of all swans. (There can also be *universally* accompanying features, in which *all* X's have A but A is still not defining. That would have been the situation if no swans other than white ones had ever been discovered. Or if steel were *always* without exception used for construction, this feature would still be accompanying and not a part of the meaning of the word "steel.")

Definition and Existence

When you have stated a definition, you have not given any information one way or the other as to whether anything described in the definition actually *exists*. The word "horse" *denotes* many things—that is, there are many horses in the world. But the word "centaur" (in Greek mythology, a creature that is half-man and half-horse) denotes no things at all, since no centaurs exist. Centaur-*pictures* exist, and since people imagine these creatures, centaur-*images* exist, but as far as anyone knows, no centaurs exist. The class of centaurs is a *null class*.

But don't say, on that account, that the word "centaur" means nothing, since it stands for no existent thing. We have a clear enough idea of what a centaur would be like, and we could identify it if we saw one; the same is true with unicorns (horses with a horn in the middle of their foreheads), brownies, elves, dragons, gremlins, and so on. All these words designate some combination of characteristics, but no instances exist of any class of things having these characteristics.

Scope of Definitions

If you defined "telephone" as an instrument for communication, this definition would be too broad to fit our actual usage of the word: there are many instruments for communication besides telephones. But if you defined "tree" as a plant with green leaves and a trunk, this definition would include only deciduous trees and would exclude evergreen trees—and we do use the word "tree" so as to include evergreens; thus the definition would be too narrow. We want to get into the definition all those features that we take to be defining, and none that are not defining.

Even if the definition were neither too broad nor too narrow, it might still not correctly state how the word is actually used. Suppose someone says that an elephant is an animal that draws water up its trunk and squirts it into its mouth. Suppose that every elephant does this, and that everything that does this is an elephant (that is, nothing *but* elephants do this). But we can still ask, "Couldn't a creature do this and still not be an elephant? Might some new species be discovered, for instance? And couldn't a creature *fail* to do this and still be an elephant— one whose trunk is permanently stopped up, perhaps?" An elephant who couldn't use its trunk would still be an elephant, surely. Here we have to consider not only what we would call creatures that do exist, but what we would say *if* a creature had a certain characteristic, even if it didn't actually have it: that is, what we want to know is what are the characteristics whose presence would entitle something to be called an elephant and whose absence would prevent us from calling it an elephant. To know this, we must go beyond the range of the *actual* things to which the word is applied. The philosopher John Venn put it this way:

> The practical test in fact, when we wish to know whether any proposed definition is a true one or not, is to try whether by conceivable variation of circumstances we can cause it to break down, by its exclusion of what we are resolved to retain, or its inclusion of what we are resolved to reject.[2]

Thus, if every round thing in the world were red, and if every red thing in the world were round, the words "red" and "round" would have the same *extension:* a complete list of red things would also include all the round things, and a complete list of all the round things would also include all the red things. The one quality would never be found without the other. And yet they would *not* be the same quality. The two words would still have a different meaning: "red" would still be the name of a color, and "round" would still be the name of a shape. No sameness of ex-

tension would ever make them have the same meaning.

Truth and Definition

When we define a word, we indicate to someone what the word means. But a word doesn't just "mean" by itself: it is we, human users of language, who give words the only meaning they have. By themselves, they are just noises or strange-looking marks on paper. What then are we doing when we "indicate what a word means"? We are making one of two things:

1. *Stipulative definition.* We seldom stipulate new meanings for words already in existence. Occasionally someone does so, perhaps because she believes that a word already in existence doesn't have a clear enough meaning, and she stipulates a more precise one. "And *this*," she says, "is what I am going to mean by the term from here on. I stipulate for the sake of clarity." Or she may find no word in existence that carries the shade of meaning that she wants to convey. Since she doesn't use an old word to carry a more precise meaning, she invents a new one. "What would you call the number ten to the tenth power?" the mathematician Edward Kastner asked his small grandson, and the grandson, who of course didn't understand the question, uttered the noise "googol." And that is what the noise "googol" has since then been used to mean.

A stipulation is neither true nor false. It is like a suggestion—"Let's use the word to mean . . ."—or a statement of intention—"I hereby stipulate that this noise shall be used to mean . . ."

2. *Reportive definitions.* But most definitions of words already in use are *reports* of how a word is actually used. The word "father" is used to refer to a male parent. That's what the word "father" means in English. And it's a true definition, in the sense that

[2]John Venn, Empirical Logic (New York: Macmillan, 1899), p. 304.

it's a *true report* of how people in our language group use the word "father."

Can a definition then be true or false? Yes, it is true if it correctly reports how a word is used, and false if it does not. Isn't it true (one might ask) that a father is a male parent? Isn't that what a father is? And we can reply, "Yes, that is what the word 'father' is used to mean. We could have used the same word to mean something else, or another word to mean what we mean by this one. But throughout centuries of history the noise 'father' came to mean what it does now, and it's *true* that that's what it means."

Some philosophers have believed, however, that definitions can be true or false, not just as true or false reports of how language is used, but true or false in a much more profound way. One principal task of philosophy, thought Plato (428–348 B.C.), is to *discover* true definitions. Plato devoted most of his famous dialogues to the attempt to find true definitions. In the *Laches* he tried to find the definition of courage; in the *Meno* he tried to discover the definition of piety; in the *Republic* he attempted to find the definition of justice.

"What is the true definition of courage?" he asked. And Socrates (470–399 B.C.), in the dialogues, kept hammering away at this, prodding the other person to provide a definition, then picking away at it critically by finding cases to which it did not apply. Is it courage when someone acts with reckless disregard of danger? No, that is not courage, it is only recklessness. Is it courage if an army commander waits till he has a larger number of forces before he attacks? No, Socrates decided, that's caution more than it is courage. Is the foolhardy man then courageous? No, for courage requires the use of intelligence, not merely brute strength. And so, on and on, with one suggested example of courage after another, none of them sufficing (in Socrates' view) to provide a true definition

of courage. Most of the time Plato never arrived at his goal of finding a true definition; but, if we could but find it, it *is* "out there," waiting to be found. Anything other than that is not true courage. The true definition is something to be discovered—it isn't invented or dreamed up by human beings.

Are definitions invented or discovered? This question has been much disputed:

A: Definitions are discovered, not invented.
B: We do discover them—we weren't born knowing them. But what we discover is nothing more than how other people who use the language already use the word. Socrates was trying to discover the *criteria* that his protagonists used for deciding when a word applies to a given situation and when it does not. He knew that it is very difficult for most people to state such criteria; hence, he asked, "Would you call it courage in situation X? Then how about situation Y?" He was assuming that there was *one* definition to be found—not (what we say today) that we may have various and overlapping meanings for the same word. The one thing that he sought, he thought of as "the true definition." He thought he was discovering something out there in the world, as we might discover gold or diamonds. Actually he was only finding out in more detail how we actually use the words we employ: would you use it in situation X? No? Then how about another one, Y, that's similar to it? and so on. It's a detailed inquiry into verbal usage, not an inquiry into the nature of the world. When we discover what some newly found species of animal is "really like," we look at it closely over a period of time; but what is there to look at closely when we "discover true definitions," other than our own usage of words in a language?

A: But what Plato was doing was not defining *words;* he was interested in defining *things.*

B: Now what exactly is it to define a *thing?* I know what definition is if it's words or phrases we're defining; we are describing the criteria that are used for applying (or withholding) a certain word to certain situations in reality. I don't understand what the phrase "defining a thing" is supposed to mean.

A: What it means is trying to discover the *essence* of a thing—what the thing essentially is. We can't just stipulate that, we discover it. That's why if someone says that jumping into the fray is an example of courage, Socrates says, "No, that's not true courage; it's something else, namely recklessness."

B: All that means is that we don't use the *word* "courage" to describe a different quality, recklessness.

A: We don't use the word "courage" for it because it *isn't* courage. If we say that jumping into the fray is courage, we haven't yet discovered the essential nature of courage.

B: I think that what you call "essence" is just *defining characteristics.* What is the essence of a triangle (or triangularity)? Being a three-sided closed plane figure. And that's how we define the word "triangle." The definition is a true report of how we use the *word* "triangle"—that's all. There's no essence out there in the world; there are only the characteristics we *make* defining by our use of the word. The characteristics of a thing are out there in the world, but it is we (human beings) who make some of them defining (in our use of a word) and others nondefining. We can say that a bachelor is a man who has never been married, or that he is a man who is not married *now.* It depends on which way we define the word "bachelor." What

reality is like, we discover; what we use our words to mean is up to us.

A: You dismiss essences too easily. We do discover the true nature of things, and these true natures are then embodied in true definitions. Let me give you an example. People have seen lightning from time immemorial, but they didn't know what lightning really is until modern science started talking about streams of electrons. People have been around water for thousands of years, yet only after the discoveries of modern chemistry did chemists discover the true definition of water, H_2O.

B: Hold it. People knew all along what lightning is, in the sense that they knew how to *recognize* it, how to *identify* it, how to *distinguish* it from other things. Only with modern science did they come to know the *scientific explanation* of this phenomenon, lightning. People knew all along what water is: they drank it, washed in it, bathed in it, saw it in lakes and rivers. What was discovered was the chemical formula for water.

A: Yes, and that chemical formula provided the *true definition* of water.

B: You can call that the true definition if you like, but saying it obscures the facts. The facts are these: for centuries people knew how to distinguish water from other things; they could identify it, recognize it, use it. Then a discovery was made in chemistry, and as a result people knew something else about water, namely its chemical formula. This was an additional *fact about* water, which came as new knowledge.

A: Yes, and that new knowledge provided the true definition.

B: You can say, if you like, that people started to use the word "water" in a different way than before. Once "water" just meant the liquid we find in lakes and rivers. I think that's what it still means, but if you like you can say that people now use the word "water" in a different way, to mean H_2O. You say that English usage has now shifted, so the word "water" now means something different than it did before?

A: Yes. The characteristic of being in lakes and rivers was how people identified water, but they didn't know what water really is. They know it now, or at least scientists do.

B: And the rest of mankind, ignorant of chemistry, don't know what water is, and never did?

A: That's right.

B: But if you can identify something by means of certain features and thereby distinguish it from all other things, that is surely what we mean by definition. That is how people have used the word all along. Do you really mean that when they drank water, they *didn't know what they were drinking?*

A: They didn't know the true definition of water. Now we do know what it is.

B: No, there is no true or false way of using a word. What is true is that people use a word in one way at one time and may use it in a different way at another time—that's just a fact about the users of a language. People once used the word "aggravated" to mean the intensification of a condition already present; now they usually use the word to mean just "annoyed" or "vexed." But there's no "true definition" in all this. People just use words in certain ways, that's all; don't make it more complicated than that.

A: It's a matter of discovering, not inventing. Suppose that for centuries seafarers identified whales by means of certain distinguishing features, A, B, and C. But then it was discovered that whatever had A, B, and C had another feature: they

were not fish but mammals. Let's call that feature D. And so the true definition of a whale was discovered: A, B, C, and D.

B: The discovery was that the creatures having A, B, and C also had D. We didn't have to incorporate D into the definition. But we did, because the classification of animals into mammals, reptiles, birds, and so on, was already so well established. Being a mammal was a pretty important characteristic. And so it became defining. The definition of "whale" shifted from A, B, and C to A, B, C, and D.

A: And shifted in the direction of truth, wouldn't you say? Whales *are* mammals, after all. Putting this feature into the definition was essential in getting at the truth.

B: One truth about whales is that they are mammals. We can either incorporate this feature into our definition or not. For various reasons of classification that I've already described, we chose to incorporate it.

A: The advance of science helps us arrive at true definitions. Sometimes it replaces old definitions with better (truer) ones. Once syphilis was identified by the presence of certain recurring symptoms. Then the cause—the spirochete—was discovered through microscopes. Whenever the spirochete was present, the other symptoms always followed. So "syphilis" came to be defined, as it is now, solely by the presence of the spirochete. We now have the truth about syphilis, as we did not before.

B: The truth about the disease, yes. We discovered that when there is A, there is also, shortly thereafter, B, C, and D. But we didn't *discover* the definition. We made a *decision* about the definition. We could have continued to use the word "syphilis" to refer to the symptoms and then called the spirochete the *cause* of syphilis. Or, we could have used the word "syphilis" to refer to the cause only, the presence of the spirochete. In this second alternative, we could then say, "The presence of the spirochete *is* syphilis."

A: Yes, this is what syphilis *is*. We discovered another true definition.

B: No; we discovered another fact about nature. Whether we choose to incorporate such facts into our definition is up to us.

What Is Man?

In the generic sense of the word "man," meaning all human beings, male and female, adults and children, what is man?

A: I think Aristotle provided the true definition: man is the rational animal. Rationality includes at least the ability to think, to form concepts, to reason, to weigh alternatives, and to initiate actions.

B: But not all human beings do these things. Infants don't. They may have rational potential, but the potential is not yet actual. There are also people who are human vegetables and kept alive through being hooked up to machines. There are others who are barely aware of anything, and don't know who or where they are. There are people with advanced Alzheimer's disease, once rational but no longer having any such potential. Surely these are all human beings, although they are not in any clear sense "rational."

A: Aristotle could say that they're not really human beings, only physical organisms that look like human beings. Or he could say (as he did) that it is our *nature* to be rational—and that this could be true even though not everyone exempli-

fies or fulfills that nature to the same degree.

B: There is a problem about the phrase "the nature of." Suppose someone says that it's the nature of dogs to bark and of cats to meow and hiss. But not all dogs bark and not all cats meow. When we speak of "the nature of" something we are referring to certain *dispositional* traits that it has—of how it *tends* to respond to certain kinds of stimuli. We speak of a thing's nature when we observe its *pervasive* traits, which are widespread but need not be universal—not every member of the class may have them. (We may say, "I used to think that his extreme hostility was a passing phase, but now I think it's his nature," but here we are taking "his nature" to mean *his* pervasive traits, not those of people in general.)

   People say all kinds of things about "human nature," most of which are false: "All people are selfish," "All people are predators," "All men are evil," "All people are potential criminals (or potential saints)." These are all *generalizations* about people—they are not definitions.

A: How then would you define "man" ("human being") if not as a rational animal?

B: How do we identify a living creature as a human being? I can't give you an exact verbal definition, but I can show you instances and photographs, and describe some salient characteristics—not all of which have to be present in every instance. Typically a human being walks upright, has two arms, two legs, two eyes, and two ears, and the various parts are spatially related to each other in pretty definite ways—the chest is above the stomach, the stomach above the thighs, and so on (unlike most mammalian species, which walk on four legs). Even if a leg or arm or eye is missing, we can still identify the creature as human. Looking through a biological picture book, we may say to a child, "That's a man. No, that is a chimpanzee. No, that over there is a monkey." The child quickly sees the pattern (Gestalt) and makes no more mistakes in identification. The child already knows how to distinguish human beings from all the others. True, there may be borderline cases: is Neanderthal man close enough to today's man to be counted as being of the same species? We tend to say yes, but we aren't sure. But that's because the Neanderthal physiognomy is borderline, somewhere between humans and apes, just as a certain color is between red and orange.

A: You haven't identified humans by their most important feature, rationality.

B: Rationality is doubtless the most important feature, but in practice this is not how we distinguish humans from nonhumans. If you walk into a meeting room, you can quickly identify all the organisms sitting on the chairs as human beings, and not monkeys or chimpanzees. But you haven't spoken yet with any of them, and you haven't had time to check their rationality. Still, you call them human beings, and so do we all. We can distinguish the human from the nonhuman *without* any reference to language or intelligence. I identify that creature as a human being *before* I know whether he or she possesses rationality. I submit that this is a true report of how we use the phrase "human being."

A: I don't see why you couldn't say that a human being is the *aesthetic animal*—the only creature with a sense of beauty; doesn't that distinguish humans from all other species just as well?

B: No, because I can know whether someone is a human before I can know whether the person has any aesthetic sense. And the same with "man is the *laughing* animal." A person who never laughed would still be a human (and would still be even if *no* human ever laughed). A hyena who laughs is still not a human. Chimpanzees as well as humans make tools—so *tool-making* capacity won't do either. Nor will talking: a parrot who talks is still not human—it doesn't understand the language it is using. And even if it did, it is still a bird and not a human. No, I insist that what I gave you just now is a true reportive definition of the word "human" as it is actually used.

A: But it doesn't capture the essence of man, man's rationality.

B: You call that the essence because you choose to define "man" in terms of it. I have tried to show you that it doesn't reflect the way we use the word in daily practice. I could call my definition "the essence" too if we wanted to play language games; but I've told you what that comes to—a contest between definitions. I've given you the one we actually use every day of our lives. You say, "It isn't the true definition," and I can reply only that there isn't any such thing.

A new type of truck is invented, different enough so that people use a different name for it: "that's not a truck, it's a van." Is there a true definition of the word "van"? Surely it's a matter of what we choose to call it: we can say it's a truck with a difference, or that it belongs to a different "mechanical species," a van. We take the difference as being important enough to justify devising a new classification. That's all. There's no more "true definition" of human than there is a true definition of "van." Don't sanctify this dispute about language (about what to call it) by elevating it into a dispute about "the real essence of a van" or "the true definition of a van." There is no such thing, not of a van, not of a human.

A: Which definition you choose, however, can make an enormous practical difference. Suppose one physician says that a patient doesn't have a disease unless there's some identifiable physical entity such as a germ, a virus, a malfunctioning organ. But a psychiatrist insists that this isn't necessary for there to be disease or illness: a person can be utterly incapacitated and unable to function if she's deeply depressed for months at a time, or catatonic (barely moving for days), even if there is not (or not yet) any known physical disease-entity that could be seen by means of an x-ray or a microscope.

Now, should we just take our pick between these definitions? If you are a psychotherapist, and insurance policies cover only diseases, and you have patients who are as totally incapacitated by some mental condition as they would be by cancer, you'll favor the second definition, for only in that way can your patients receive the needed insurance coverage. Surely the second definition is preferable under these conditions.

B: It's true that it makes a lot of practical difference which definition is adopted. Probably the consequences of adopting the second definition are preferable— though it may also encourage some phonies and malingerers. At any rate, using one definition rather than another doesn't mean that either of them is *true*.

A: But isn't it *true* that a disease is a condition that inhibits normal functioning, regardless of what caused it?

B: Only if you already *define* the word "disease" to mean that!

4. VAGUENESS

So far, we may have the impression that the relation between words and the world is fairly neat and tidy. Here is a definition of a term,

"X"; these are its defining characteristics: A, B, and C. And these are the characteristics that often go along with the defining ones but that aren't part of the definition: D, E, and F.

But the situation is far from neat and tidy. We have already considered *ambiguity:* the use of a word to mean more than one kind of thing, as in "bank of the river" and "bank of Manhattan." Most words are ambiguous in one way or another—they are used with more than one meaning, as you can see by consulting any dictionary. But there is another feature that is even more prevalent and less likely to be recognized, namely *vagueness*. Vagueness plays havoc with our neat classification of defining versus non-defining characteristics.

The U.S. Constitution guarantees all of us "due process of law." But what exactly is due process? If you are convicted without a trial, that is clearly not due process; but what if you are tried by a jury that's prejudiced against you? That isn't due process either— but what jury is really impartial (unprejudiced)? If Smith had an expensive defense lawyer, and Jones had only a public defender, is there a difference in due process?

The Constitution prohibits what it calls "cruel and unusual punishment," but doesn't say what this is. Presumably torture and flogging are cruel, and so is a year of solitary confinement. But what about capital punishment? Throughout most of American history, it was not considered cruel, and was surely far from unusual, except for a brief period in the late 1960s when it was outlawed by the Supreme Court. Some consider it exactly the appropriate punishment for murder; others say that since it involves the taking of a life, it is the cruelest of all. There are some punishments we would say are definitely cruel and others that are definitely not, but in between we can't be sure: the word is vague.

"You've been hanging around this street corner for several hours," the officer says, "and you don't seem to have any aim or purpose. So I'm arresting you for vagrancy." "But I'm not a vagrant," says the man; "I had an appointment and the person never showed up."

The term "vagrancy" is *vague*—fuzzy at the edges; its *range of application* is not clear. The officer is supposed to arrest vagrants and doesn't quite know what to do in this case. So later the law is changed: a vagrant is now defined as anyone who remains in the same city block for at least three hours and has less than five dollars on his or her person. Now the definition of "vagrant" is more precise ("vague" is the opposite of "precise"), and the officer knows what to do. But now we have a different problem: the definition doesn't cover what we want it to cover. Many people with less than five dollars on their person may for various reasons walk a city block for three hours and yet, we believe, not qualify as vagrants. The new law thus seems quite *arbitrary*.

Sometimes the information we can give is not very precise: "Yes, I know he was running fast, but I don't know how fast." If you are a witness in court you may be asked for more precise information, but vague information may be all you can give. (One witness, asked how far the door of the building was from her at the time of the robbery, replied "18 feet, 7¼ inches." "How did you know?" asked the astonished attorney. "I was sure that some fool would ask me, so I measured it!")

In daily life we need vague words, but for special purposes, such as science, they are too vague to be useful; for example, we want to know exactly how long a column of mercury is. If the U.S. Bureau of the Census wants to draw a distinction between a town and a city, it draws the line at 5,000 inhabitants, and when a child is born, what was a town of 4,999 is now a city. The borderline is arbitrary, but any other borderline would be just as arbitrary. Yellow shades into orange

and orange into red, and there is no clear break to divide one color from another. Any place we want to draw the line—"That's yellow; no, that's orange"—is arbitrary.

To be convicted, a defendant must be "guilty beyond reasonable doubt." But the phrase "reasonable doubt" is vague; two jurors watching the same trial might disagree as to whether there is reasonable doubt. A person's life might depend on where the line is drawn. Yet to make the phrase more precise seems to be even worse; circumstances differ greatly from case to case, and we can't anticipate which ones should induce doubt. If we were to say "beyond all possibility of doubt," there might be no convictions at all. Other legal terms, such as "due process," are similarly vague.

Sometimes a word is vague not because there is no single cutoff point, but because there are *multiple criteria* for its application. A term may be associated with characteristics A, B, C, D, and E. But if a thing has A, B, and C, the term may apply without D or E. Or, it can have B, C, D, and E but not A and still apply. As long as it has some of the features, the term is applicable. But there may be no one feature that *all* members of the class have in common; the term may be applicable no matter which feature is absent as long as all or most of the others are there. And the others needn't have the same *weight:* having D may count more heavily than having E. In a famous passage, the philosopher Ludwig Wittgenstein (1889–1951) said:

> Consider for example the proceedings that we call "games." I mean board-games, card-games, ball-games, Olympic games, and so on. What is common to them all?—Don't say, "There *must* be something common, or they would not be called 'games,'—but *look and see* whether there is anything common to all.—For if you look at them, you will not see something that is common to *all*, but similarities, relationships, and a whole series of them at that. To repeat: don't

think, but look!—Look for example at board-games, with their multifarious relationships. Now pass to card-games; here you find many correspondences with the first group, but many common features drop out, and others appear. When we pass next to ball-games, much that is common is retained, but much is lost.—Are they all "amusing"? Compare chess with noughts and crosses. Or is there always winning and losing, or competition between players? Think of patience [solitaire]. In ball games there is winning and losing; but when a child throws his ball at the wall and catches it again, this feature has disappeared. Look at the parts played by skill and luck; and at the difference between skill in chess and skill in tennis. Think now of games like ring-a-ring-a-roses; here is the element of amusement, but how many other characteristic features have disappeared! And we can go through the many, many other groups of games in the same way; we can see how similarities crop out and disappear.[3]

All this may offend our sense of logical rigor—"When we use a word we should know exactly when it applies to something in the world and when it doesn't"—but language is not built that way. A word comes into common usage whose boundaries of application are not precisely delineated; we can say that it applies in certain standard or typical cases ("This definitely is a cat") and that it doesn't in others ("No, that's definitely not a cat"), but even in a seemingly simple case like this, things might happen that would make us doubt whether the word was applicable. What if your cat suddenly swelled to twenty times its present size, before your eyes and in the presence of witnesses, and started to grow feathers?

Or if it showed some queer behavior usually not to be found with cats, say, if, under certain conditions, it could be revived from death whereas normal cats could not? Shall I, in such a case, say that a new species has come into being? Or that it was a cat with extraordinary properties?

Again, suppose I say "There is my friend over there." What if on drawing closer in order to shake hands with him he suddenly disappeared? "Therefore it was not my friend but some delusion or other." But suppose a few seconds later I saw him again, could grasp his hand, etc. What then? "Therefore my friend was nevertheless there and his disappearance was some delusion or other." But imagine after a while he disappeared again, or seemed to disappear—what shall I say now? Have we rules ready for all imaginable possibilities? . . .

Suppose I come across a being that looks like a man, speaks like a man, behaves like a man, and is only one span tall—shall I say it *is* a man? Or what about the case of a person who is so old as to remember King Darius? Would you say he is an immortal? Is there anything like an exhaustive definition that finally and once for all sets our mind at rest? "But are there not exact definitions at least in science?" Let's see. The notion of gold seems to be defined with absolute precision, say by the spectrum of gold with its characteristic lines. Now what would you say if a substance was discovered that looked like gold, satisfied all the chemical tests for gold, whilst it emitted a new sort of radiation? "But such things do not happen." Quite so; but they *might* happen, and that is enough to show that we can never exclude altogether the possibility of some unforeseen situation arising in which we shall have to modify our definition.[4]

Finally, we should notice that the words by which we define a term are *themselves* vague. Consider the definition of "adolescence" as the time between childhood and adulthood (or as some have said, between childhood and adultery). Both these last words are vague: there is no definite point at which childhood ends or adulthood begins. But just because these words *are* vague, they con-

---

[3]Ludwig Wittgenstein, *Philosophical Investigations*, trans. G.E.M. Anscombe (New York: Macmillan, 1953),

[4]Friedrich Waismann, "Verifiability," in Antony Flew, ed., *Logic and Language*, 1st ser. (Oxford: Blackwell, 1953), pp. 119–120.

vey quite well the meaning of the original word, "adolescence." A more precise definition would not give us information about how the word is actually used.

Countless disputes arise because one or more of the terms is vague in a way crucial to the argument. For example, the income tax law requires you to pay taxes in a state if you reside in that state. But what is it to reside or to be a resident? Is he an inhabitant of Montana if he works there? If he owns a home there (even if he owns another home in California)? If he spends more of his time in Montana than in California? If his company's home office is in Montana? In ordinary usage at least, the term "resident" doesn't tell us how to answer these questions.

Constant disputes arise about whether the use of tobacco is addicting: "Of course it is," or "No, it isn't—you can get hooked on it but it isn't addicting." Assuming that cocaine is addicting, how much like that must the use of alcohol and tobacco be? Must there be withdrawal symptoms? Must there be a change in the person's work habits? Must there be physiological changes in, for example, blood pressure or heartbeat? What if it has such effects on some people but not on others—should we call it addicting then? Doubtless the word is and will remain vague, but this fact is seldom recognized. People argue, "Yes, it is," or "No, it isn't," without asking, "What do you *mean* by calling it addictive?" Before they embark on questions of truth, they should first be clear about questions of meaning. In an abstract discipline such as philosophy, such confusions are even more prevalent than they are elsewhere.

5. CONNOTATION

A snake is a legless reptile; that is, that's what we mean when we use the word "snake." At least that's what we mean when we use the word "snake" in its primary meaning. But we also use the word in a sense that is derivative from that: because most people are repelled by snakes, the word has an unfavorable association in people's minds. They think of snakes as slimy (which they are not) and revolting (which they are to many or most people); these are popular *connotations* of the word "snake." Does the word "snake" have this connotation for people who are fond of snakes? Apparently it does. Much as he may like snakes, he knows that he is not being complimented when his wife says to him, "You snake!"

Many such connotations of a word are fairly universal. "He is a wolf." "He's a weasel." "He is a tiger." Machiavelli wrote that the prince must be both a lion and a fox. (Don't we know that this means he must be both strong and clever?) An assistant dean is "a mouse aiming to be a rat." We don't need an explanation of that one either, do we? If the connotation varied greatly from person to person, we wouldn't be able to infer what a person meant by using these animal-words to talk about people.

Is the connotation of a word part of its meaning? One might say, "No, it isn't; the meaning of the word 'snake' is one thing, and what associations people have with it are another." But if the association is fairly universal, it is also plausible to say that the connotation *is* part of its meaning—and usually the dictionary lists it in reporting what the word means. Some have called this *secondary* meaning, because it presupposes the primary sense. Some have called it *metaphorical* meaning, because there is an implicit comparison between the man who is called a wolf and the quadrupeds who are called wolves. (A metaphor is an implicit comparison between two unlike things.) Either way, one hasn't explained how the word is actually used unless one explains this secondary meaning as well—you wouldn't send a person into the world who was familiar with only the primary meanings of words, for she would make too many mistakes. She wouldn't understand what was meant when another woman was described to her as a "cat."

The secondary meaning of a word includes the full range of what it *suggests* to the hearer or reader:

> The word "sea" *designates* certain characteristics such as being a large body of salt water; this is its primary word-meaning. It also *connotes* certain other characteristics, such as being sometimes dangerous, being changeable in mood but endless in motion, being a thoroughfare, being a barrier, and so on. These are its *secondary word-meanings*.[5]

Thus, Hamlet's "Canst thou not minister unto a mind diseased?" can be said to mean "Can't you wait on a lunatic?" But the secondary meanings of these words are vastly different. Is Macbeth's "[Life] is a tale told by an idiot, full of sound and fury, signifying nothing" reducible to "Life is meaningless"? Far from it: "idiot," "sound," "fury," and so on are so rich with secondary meanings that they cannot be translated without loss. "To the last syllable of recorded time" is not reducible to "To the last minute of recorded time"—the connotation of "syllable" is quite different from, and much richer than, that of the literal word "minute." Just try to translate the following lines from Shakespeare in such a way as to involve no loss of connotation:

> Where is a tide in the affairs of men
> Which, taken at the flood, leads on to fortune.
> Omitted, all the voyage of their life
> Is bound in shallows and in miseries.
> On such a full sea are we now afloat;
> And we must take the current where it waves,
> Or lose our ventures. (*Julius Caesar*, Act 4, scene 3)

There is a richer array of connotations in these lines than in the line "If we don't go ahead with the project now, when the time is right, we may lose it entirely."

Emotive Meaning

Among the associations that words have in people's minds are the *feelings* and *attitudes* that their utterance tend to evoke. When the word tends regularly or universally to evoke a certain kind of feeling or attitude, it is said to have "emotive meaning." The emotive meaning of a word consists of the aura of favorable or unfavorable feeling that hovers about a word. "Gorgeous" has a favorable emotive meaning—the person using this word is expressing her own attitude toward the person or thing she is describing and/or is trying to evoke a similar attitude in others. "Nasty" has, correspondingly, an *un*favorable emotive meaning.

These words don't so much *describe* the object in question as to register the speaker's *reaction* to it. There are emotively neutral ways of referring to certain racial groups, for example, "African American," but there are also emotively loaded ways of referring to them, such as the "n-word" frequently used in the O. J. Simpson trial. The first word raises no one's blood pressure, whereas the second word can be used as an occasion for riot and murder. There are also emotively loaded negative words for Italians, Jews, Irish, and so on. Racial epithets are all emotively loaded words.

The emotive effect that certain words have upon hearers is immense. But should it be called *meaning*? No one would deny that the utterance of these words has an enormous *effect*—but why say it is meaning? If you call someone a dirty rat, this certainly has an unfavorable effect on hearers (at least you intend it to), but is this a part of the meaning of these words? Shall we say that "Italian" and "Wop" have the same meaning but different effects, or shall we include the in-

---

[5]Monroe C. Beardsley, Aesthetics (New York: Harcourt Brace, 1958), p. 125.

tended emotional effect as part of each term's meaning and say therefore that the meaning of the two terms is different?

The answer depends on whether the emotive effect of the word is the main determinant for its use. Thus, using the word "communist" to refer to anyone who believes that the state should own the means of production, including real estate, has emotive effects, and to most people in the United States the word elicits a feeling or attitude of disfavor. But a person could call himself a communist and mean by it only that he believes that the economy should be controlled by the government (including ownership of homes, factories, etc.) and *not* intend this to have an unfavorable effect. And in doing so he would not be using the word incorrectly; we can understand what a communist is *without* the use of the word having any emotive effect one way or the other.

However, if you called a person a stool pigeon, you would not be saying *only* that she was a police informant. You would be conveying an *unfavorable attitude* toward her. If, in using the phrase, you didn't intend to convey an unfavorable attitude, you wouldn't have called her a stool pigeon (which by its very use conveys the attitude); instead, you would have called her an informant for the police. In the case of "stool pigeon," the unfavorable attitude is *built into* the use of the phrase, and it *could not* be used neutrally: if you wanted to speak neutrally you would not use that phrase. And thus since, in this case the negative emotive effect is part of the meaning of the phrase, it deserves to be called "emotive meaning."

6. OSTENSIVE DEFINITION

A dictionary tells you what a word is used to mean by members of a given language group. In doing so, it always uses *other* words.

If you don't already know the meanings of the words in the definition, you can try looking them up.

But a baby who knows no words at all can't learn the meanings of words in this way. Babies and children learn their first words *ostensively* (from the Latin *ostendere,* or "to show")—by being shown examples of how they apply to the world. They learn the meanings of "Mama," "Daddy," "doll," "eat," "shoe," and countless other words by being shown examples of what they apply to and also of what they don't apply to: "That's a book; that's not a book but a magazine," and so on. We all learned ostensively many word meanings that we could later have learned verbally.

There are limitations to ostensive definition, however. Defining a word ostensively doesn't tell the hearer its *limits of application.* If all the things the parent has pointed to and called "tables" have legs, it isn't yet clear whether an object would still be called a table if it looked like the others but had no legs. You might not be able to *show* examples of any, but the hearer might wonder if such an object would still be a table. Would this animal still be a rabbit if it had a tail? (The teacher said, "The rabbit has a tail, but not to speak of," and the child wrote, "The rabbit has a tail but you mustn't talk about it.") Verbal definitions can accomplish these tasks more easily.

Ostensive definition is limited to what you can show. You can show the difference between walking and running, but not the meanings of "time," "infinity," or "property." You can't show people's inner feelings, for example, joy, frustration, peacefulness, despair, and so on, although you can show the behavior and body language of people who are experiencing these various feelings, and of course the child will one day come to know their meanings in her own personal experience.

Still, ostensive definition is a fairly rapid method of learning the meanings of new words:

> Let us say that we are playing golf and that we have hit the ball in a certain way with certain unfortunate results, so that our companion says to us, "That's a bad slice." He repeats this remark every time our ball fails to go straight. If we are reasonably bright, we learn in a very short time to say, when it happens again, "That's a bad slice." On one occasion, however, our friend says to us, "That's not a slice this time; that's a hook." In this case we wonder what has happened, and we wonder what is different about the last stroke from those previous. As soon as we make the distinction, we have added still another word to our vocabulary. The result is that after nine holes of golf, we can use both these words accurately—and perhaps several others as well, such as "divot," "number-five iron," "approach shot," *without ever having been told what they mean*. Indeed, we may play golf for years without ever being able to give a dictionary definition of "to slice": "To strike (the ball) so that the face of the club draws inward across the face of the ball, causing it to curve toward the right in flight (with a right-handed player)."[6]

Are there words that *can't* be defined? That depends on what we mean by "define." If to define a word is to indicate *in some way or other* what it means, the answer is surely no: if there were no way of indicating to another person what you mean by a word, you could not communicate its meaning to others, and the word could never become a part of a public language. But if by "define" you mean only *verbal* definition (defining by other words), then it does seem that some words are indefinable.

When we give a verbal definition, we place the thing (or activity, process, quality, etc.) in a wider class under which it falls: dogs are

---

[6]S. I. Hayakawa, Language in Thought and Action (Fort Worth: Harcourt Brace, 1942), p. 45.

mammals, triangles are plane figures. Then we *distinguish* this thing or class of things from other members of the same class: triangles are three-sided whereas squares and octagons are not. But there are reasons why we sometimes can't do this:

1. Sometimes the class is already so wide that there is no wider classification under which it falls. Highly abstract words like "being," "existence," "time," and "space" are examples. We can distinguish some things that exist, like dogs, from other things that do not exist, like centaurs. But how would you give a general definition of "existence," other than by using words that are its synonyms and that present the same problem again?

Don't we all know what time is? We can say that this happened before that or after that, or that we can remember back twenty years, and so on. We all know how to use temporal words. But how would you define "time"? We can distinguish what's called phenomenal time (a lecture seems very long when it's boring) from physical time (how much time-by-the-clock it occupied). But that is to make a distinction within time, not to define "time" itself. We do have experience of time; in fact, *all* our experiences occur in time. But about all we seem able to say about time itself is metaphorical: for example, "Time is a river," or "Time is a moving shadow of eternity." However, as a definition these are quite useless: if you didn't already know what time is, how could you know what "moving shadow of eternity" means?

2. Consider now the least abstract words, like "red," "shrill," "pungent," "bitter," "anger," and "pain." Someone may be able to state the physiological conditions under which people experience fear, but this is not the same as telling us what the word "fear" itself stands for. A scientist may state, correctly, that red is the color we see in response to any wavelength of light of the span of 4,000 to 7,000 Angstrom units. But that tells us only

with what the experience of red is *correlated*. It wouldn't enable a person who was born blind to see or imagine the color that you and I see. (In fact, if we see red spots before our eyes after a blow on the head, are these wavelengths of light at all?)

Suppose again that everything in the world that is red is round and that everything round is red. Then a person born blind could always correctly identify red things by touching them and discovering that they are round. But the moment that this correlation failed, this person's identification of red things would be mistaken. It would hold only as long as the correlation holds. Exactly the same would be true of the person who identified red by means of wavelengths of light. And even if her *identification* of red things never failed, this person still wouldn't know "what red is" in the most fundamental sense: she still wouldn't know what red *looks like*. That can be known only be someone who can *see* red. A man born blind may have a wide knowledge of optics; he may even specialize in the physics of color. But he can still have no idea of what sighted people *see*. (Don't say, "At least blind people see black." They don't see black or any other color; they don't *see* at all.) Similarly, a person born deaf can have no idea of what a bell or a human voice sounds like. A person who has no experience of love can't know what being in love feels like, and a person who has never experienced jealousy can have no idea what experience others have in mind when they use the word.

Impressions and Ideas

All knowledge, wrote David Hume (1711–1776), is derived from what he called *impressions*. Some of our ideas come from the "external" senses—sight, touch, hearing, smell, and taste. Other ideas have an internal source, such as pain, pleasure, exhilaration, depression, anxiety, anticipation, joy, and sorrow. We would have no idea what these emotions are if we had not first experienced them. Just as we would have no idea of colors if we had been born blind, so we would not have any idea of fear if we had not experienced fear.

However, we have ideas of many kinds of thing of which we have no impressions. We have the idea of a golden mountain, said Hume, because we have seen mountains and seen things colored gold. So we put these two ideas together in our minds and get a *complex* idea. Once we have acquired simple ideas from sense-experience, we can put them together in whatever way we please to form new ideas. The idea of a centaur is the idea of a creature with the head of a man and the body of a horse. We can imagine green dogs and brown clouds without ever having seen them. Our ability to imagine seems quite unlimited. But it is not, as Hume pointed out in a famous passage:

> Nothing, at first view, may seem more unbounded than the thought of man, which not only escapes all human power and authority but is not even restrained within the limits of nature and reality. To form monsters, and join incongruous shapes and appearances, costs the imagination no more trouble than to conceive the most natural and familiar objects. And while the body is confined to one planet, along which it creeps with pain and difficulty, the thought can in an instant transport us into the most distant regions of the universe. . . .
>
> But though our thought seems to possess this unbounded liberty, we shall find, upon a nearer examination, that it is really confined within very narrow limits, and that all this creative power of the mind amounts to no more than the faculty of compounding, transposing, augmenting, or diminishing the materials afforded us by the senses and experience. When we think of a golden mountain, we only join two consistent ideas, gold and mountain, with

which we were formerly acquainted. . . . In short, all the materials of thinking are derived either from our outward or inward sentiment; the mixture and composition of these belongs alone to the mind and will.[7]

How do we tell which ideas are simple and which are complex? Presumably the simple ones are ideas we could not have had if we had not had impressions of them. We could not imagine red without having seen it, although we can imagine red cats without having seen them ("red cats" being a complex idea). But the limits of this aren't quite clear. If we have seen a hundred shades of blue but not one missing shade somewhere in the middle, could we imagine it without having seen it? (Hume thought we could, by imagining the shade just lighter and the one just darker and then "putting them together" in our minds.) Could we imagine orange if we had never seen it, but had seen red and yellow? Could we imagine green if we had seen only blue and yellow? Green surely doesn't look like either blue or yellow, so the answer here might be no. (We can get green paint by mixing blue and yellow paints, but that doesn't tell us whether we could imagine green without ever having seen it.) Could we imagine a sweet taste if we have experienced only sour and bitter? Can we imagine a polygon with a million sides?

What images we can have, one might say, depends on who is doing the imagining. Some people may be able to conjure up an image of a two-hundred-sided polygon, others may not. Perhaps some people can have an image of orange even if they have seen only red and yellow, whereas others are unable to do so. Does it really matter? The im-

portant point, some critics of Hume have suggested, is that we can have *concepts* for which no images at all are available. We have no image of ultraviolet: bees can see it (we can't imagine what it looks like to them), but since we human beings haven't seen it, we can't imagine it. Don't say that it's a very deep violet, for that is still a visible color.

We have no ultraviolet images. Yet scientists deal with ultraviolet all the time, and can use spectrometers and other devices to discover facts about that span of the spectrum. We may *know as much about* ultraviolet as we do about violet; it's just that we can't see it. The same considerations hold true, of course, for sounds of higher pitch than any that human beings can hear. Dogs respond to whistles and other sounds at higher pitches than we can hear, but we have no idea what it sounds like to *them*. We wonder in vain what the sounds are that get them so excited, and what the smells that lead them to chase their quarry smell like to them.

When, then, do we have a concept of X? When we can *define* the word "X"? Most of us can't do that even for our most familiar concepts, such as trees and tables. Perhaps then when we can *apply* the word "X" correctly? But can't we have a concept of X without knowing the word for it? Can't a child have the concept of a candle without having ever heard the word?

One might say that you have a concept of X if you can distinguish X's from non-X's. The child can distinguish dogs from everything that is not a dog; isn't it plausible to say that the child has the concept of a dog? For that matter, the cat can distinguish very well between dogs and everything else—other cats, wolves, lizards, radiators, and so on. And in that case, isn't it reasonable to say that the cat has the concept of a dog, just as human beings do? Similarly, the dog can dis-

---

[7]David Hume, An Enquiry Concerning Human Understanding (1751), Section 2, Paragraphs 4 and 5.

tinguish bones from all other things in the world and can respond appropriately to them—that is, bury them, chew on them, eat them—in a way that it responds to no other kind of thing.

But we have a *criterion* for deciding when something is an X and when it is not; and isn't this essential for having a concept? One could say so, but in that case the dog still has the concept of a bone. It is surely no accident that the dog can unfailingly make the distinction. We may not know what criterion the dog uses, but isn't it reasonable to assume that it has one?

Human beings have many concepts that other animals lack. We have a concept of liberty, of equilibrium, or reciprocity, of fairness, of triangulation (to mention only a few at random), and hundreds of others. We have no images of these; they are not things that can be pictured in any of the senses. They all involve an ability to make distinctions among items that are not data of the senses. Let's say we have the concept of liberty—we may not all agree on quite what it is, and the word "liberty" itself may be ambiguous: is it freedom from something? freedom to do something? Whichever it is (or both, or neither), there is no sensory image of it. It's true that we could have no concept of liberty unless we had some experience of the world, although there is *no specific kind of experience* (perhaps of seeing people released from chains) that we would have to have in order to have the concept. We would surely have to have the experience of seeing people doing what they want to do, as opposed to doing what others compel them to do. But most of the concepts that human beings have that other creatures don't have are on a fairly abstract level, often quite a few steps removed from sensory experience.

One version of a traditional epistemological theory called *empiricism* says that all con-

cepts are in some way derived from experience. *Rationalism,* by contrast (in one of several meanings of that word), says that not all concepts need be thus derived. Some concepts may be "built into" our brains, so that we need to have no examples of them in our sense-experience in order to have the concept. Perhaps the concept of God is one of these; then we can have the concept of God without having had any sense-experiences at all. (Empiricists would say that the idea of God is a complex idea, combining the idea of a person, or personhood, with that of great power and benevolence, and that we can have such an idea whether the object exists or not.) Perhaps other concepts, such as that of causation, are "wired into" us and don't need any basis in sensory experience. In any case, there are other issues of greater importance to which the terms "rationalism" and "empiricism" have historically been attached, which we shall consider in Chapter 5.

We also have concepts of, for example, equality, infinity, implication, and deductibility. How are they all to be connected with sense-experiences like seeing red or feeling pain? To achieve this connection,

> one must not only know the meanings of nouns, verbs, and adjectives, one must also understand the significance of the syntactical form of the sentence; and for many sentences, one must understand various kinds of words that serve to connect nouns, adjectives, and verbs into sentences so as to affect the meaning of the sentence as a whole. One must be able to distinguish semantically between "John hit Jim," "Jim hit John," "Did John hit Jim?" "John hit Jim!" and "John, please don't hit Jim." This means that before one can engage in conversation one must be able to handle and understand such factors as word order, "auxiliaries" like "do," "shall," and "is"; and connectives like "is," "this," and "and." These elements can neither get their meaning by association with distinguishable items in experience nor be defined in terms of items

that can. Where could we look in our sense-perception for the object of word-order patterns, pauses, or words like "is" and "that"? And as for defining these elements in terms of words like "blue" and "table," the prospect has seemed so remote that no one has so much as attempted it.[8]

7. MEANINGLESSNESS

All words have meaning—although, as we have seen, many words do not stand for any things, qualities, or relations. "Whoopee" and "ouch" do not name anything; they express one's feelings, yet they have meaning. Without meaning, a word would be merely a strange noise or a peculiar set of marks on paper.

Words can be combined so as to form a meaningless sentence (or clause, or phrase). "Walking sat eat very" consists of words, but they fail to add up to a sentence. "The theory of relativity is blue" is a sentence, but in any usual meaning of the words at least, it conveys no meaning.

Grammatical incompleteness. Sometimes a sentence is grammatically incomplete: it fails to contain an element required to complete its meaning. Suppose someone says "The lamp is above," and we say, "Above what?" And she says, "Not above anything, just above." But if A is above, doesn't it have to be above something? (Ordinarily, "A is above B" means that A is further from the center of the earth than B—though when we say "This moon of Mars is above the other moon," we may mean that it is further from the center of Mars. It depends on what stellar or planetary object is our center of reference.)

We do say things like "She's above all that" ("She won't 'lower herself' to do something

just for money"), where we aren't using "above" literally, in its ordinary spatial sense, but in a nonliteral or figurative sense. Still, literally or not, being above requires an A and a B. If someone said merely "She's above" and elaborated by saying only "Not above anything—just above, that's all," what would we make of it? Wouldn't it be meaningless?

Being above is a relation that requires two terms. Some require more than two. Here are two posts, A and B, and a horse, C, standing between them. What would it mean to say that the horse stood between the post, A—not between one post A and another one B? Doesn't being between require two things that C is between? If someone kept saying "C is between A," shouldn't we respond that the sentence being uttered is meaningless?

Sometimes the B-term is left unstated. "A is better." Better than whom or what? "A is large." Larger than what? Such terms are *comparative:* they compare one person or thing with another with regard to some quality. (If there were only one object in the universe, would it be large? What would it mean to say so?)

Category mistakes. Some meaningless sentences involve what are called category mistakes, or type crossings. "The theory of relativity is blue." "Quadratic equations go to horse races." "Saturday is in bed." "The number 5 died yesterday." What's wrong with these sentences? They aren't merely false, like "Snow is black" and "Mice are larger than elephants." We at least know what these mean, and because we do, we can say they are false. But what does it even mean to say that Saturday is in bed?

"Who's this guy Saturday?" one might ask. "Oh, you mean it's the name of a person." "No, I mean Saturday, the seventh day of the week. I'm saying that the day of the week is in bed." What can we say now? How can a day of the week be in bed? A bed is an object in

[8]William Alston, *Philosophy of Language* (Englewood Cliffs, NJ: Prentice Hall, 1963), p. 68.

space. Is a day the sort of thing that can be in a bed or in any other position in space?

Why not say that such statements are merely false? "Quadratic equations go to horse races." "Well, they don't, do they? So it's false." But there is something else wrong here. We know what it would be for an elephant to be in bed (we can describe it or draw it), but a day of the week? We know what a horse race is and what a quadratic equation is; but of what situation is "Quadratic equations go to horse races" the description?

One might suggest that the sentence has meaning, but that we can't imagine the situation that it purports to describe—that we just can't conceive of it, that our powers of conception are limited. But there seems to be a different kind of mistake here: Although we can't imagine a hundred billion light-years of distance, we can understand the astronomer who says that a certain galaxy is that far away. But we don't understand what situation is being described in the sentences "Saturday is in bed" and "The number 5 has died."

Why is this? Many philosophers have said that everything that exists falls into certain general categories. Numbers are one kind of thing; they are timeless objects—they don't have a history, and temporal terms such as "before" and "after" do not apply to them. They are "abstract entities" and not particular things. Terms like "light," "heavy," "red," and "green" apply only to particulars (individual things). If we said that a number was born or died, we'd be mixing incompatible types of entities. (We can erase the *numeral* 2 from the blackboard, but that doesn't change the fact that the sum of the *numbers* 2 and 3 is 5.)

It's not always clear, however, exactly when two kinds of thing belong in different categories. Numbers and animals do, but ants and anteaters don't. (They're both particulars.) Suppose a person drinks a beer, smokes a cigarette, and eats a sandwich. If someone said, "He ate his beer," "He drank his cigarette," and "He smoked a sandwich," is she trespassing on category boundaries? If so, the categories are very narrow compared with the wide categories of particular things and abstract entities. Perhaps we should say merely, "If you can tell me what it's like to smoke a sandwich, I'll grant that the sentence has meaning. Could you describe it please?"

"He sprained his ankle." We all know what that means. What about "He sprained his liver"? What would that be like? Doesn't "sprain" involve bones and joints, and if there are not bones or joints, can there be a sprain? What about "She sprained her brain"? We might say this if she had studied very hard and couldn't concentrate anymore, but then wouldn't we be using the word "sprain" in a different meaning?

We are all acquainted with the differences between standing up, sitting, and lying down. Now suppose we say that the book is lying on the table. What does "lying" mean here? Well, the book isn't exactly lying down, but its position is *more like* lying than like sitting or standing. When it's upright on the shelf, we might even say, "The book is standing there." We can also say "The book is sitting over there," but it's not very clear what position is being described by someone who says this. It's not the same relation of parts that we refer to when we say that a person is sitting.

Metaphor. Finally, we often use words in *metaphorical* senses. We may at first take them to be meaningless, but they are not, although we may have to "dig" a bit to grasp the meaning. Macbeth's "Life's but a walking shadow" may seem meaningless at first ("Shadow of what?"), but it isn't that unlike the ordinary expression "She's only a shadow of her former self." In a metaphor, a word or phrase that usually names one kind of object or idea is used to name another kind of object or idea so as to bring out the similarity between them. Dylan Thomas' lines "The force that through the green fuse drives the flower / Drives my green age" can be paraphrased in this way: "The same forces that operate in the development of a flower also operate in human events." To call a stem a fuse is to call attention to the explosive quality of young growing plants, and to call an age green is to point out the relation between greenness and immaturity: green fruits are growing and not yet ripe. If we could discern no relation between greenness and immaturity, we wouldn't know what to make of the phrase "green age."

Poets often use language to suggest a similarity that may not have occurred to most readers before. Metaphor, said Aristotle (382–324 B.C.), is the ability to discern likeness among unlike things. Metaphor is not merely a linguistic adornment or decoration. In *Measure for Measure,* Shakespeare speaks of dying as "to lie imprisoned in the viewless winds," which is a far cry from saying only that a person died. Saying that he died doesn't "pack the punch" of the original passage.

But can't metaphor get out of line and lapse into meaninglessness? We may be able to make sense of Shakespeare's "sleeping temples" (*The Tempest*), but what about combinations of nouns and adjectives we might concoct at will, such as "mathematical bathrooms," "participial bipeds," "supine idioms," "aggressive vases," "stipulated refraction"? What can we do, for example, with "mathematical bathrooms"? Shall we interpret "mathematical" to mean geometric, and say perhaps that they are bathrooms with regular figures like squares and triangles as well decorations? We might find many other far-out interpretations never intended by the author.

We can construe e. e. cummings's "rubber questions" as questions that bounce back at you when you ask them. Can we do the same with "aggressive vases"? But what about the expressions made up at random by dropping a set of nouns in one hat and a set of adjectives in another, such as "man-eating quadrilaterals"? We can always *stipulate* some meaning of our own that is not embedded in the text, but that hardly makes it a meaningful expression in a public language. But let's continue:

A: Nothing is "embedded in the text." It's all how you prefer or choose to interpret a word or phrase. A sentence may be meaningful to one person but not to another.

B: Of course. If you understand French and I don't, a French sentence will be meaningless to me though not to you. Is that all you mean?

A: What I mean is that we can attach any meaning we choose to an existing expression, just by stipulation. If by the word "Saturday" you mean your friend George, then it's perfectly meaningful to say that Saturday is in bed.

B: You are just playing a word game. Sure, we have freedom of stipulation—we can mean what we like by a word. But we can't render "Saturday is in bed" meaningful, if we mean *what we now mean* by these words.

A: Usually, if we don't understand what a person is trying to say, we can ask him to restate his meaning in other words.

B: Yes, and what if he explains "Saturday is in bed" by saying "The seventh day of the week is in bed." Will that do?

A: No. You can't just give synonyms; if the one expression is meaningless, its alleged translation will be meaningless also.

B: And sometimes there's just no other way to say it. If I say there's a tree out there in front of us, and you say you don't know what it means to say that, I don't think I can say the same thing in other words. I can try to explain to you what a tree is, consult the dictionary, show pictures and so on; but once that's all done I don't know what more I can do. It's about as basic as I can get. If you don't understand it, I'm sorry, there's nothing more I can do.

A: And if I say "Saturday is in bed" and you say you don't understand, won't I please say it in other words, and I can't think of any other words for saying it, then what? I will insist that the meaning is clear to me and that no other sentence will make it clearer, and you will say that what I'm saying is meaningless.

B: Or at least that I can't fathom what you could possibly mean, if you use the words in the sentence in accord with English usage.

A: And how do we decide who is right? Is there a test for determining when a sentence has meaning and when it doesn't?

B: Not one that everyone would agree on.

A: A philosopher was once criticized for sleeping too long, and after being chided repeatedly about this he said, "I don't really sleep longer than other people, I only sleep more slowly." Doesn't that have a meaning?

B: I doubt it, but I would have to ask, is sleeping the sort of thing a person can do fast or slowly? Isn't "He sleeps more slowly than others" just another way of saying "He sleeps longer than others"? Aren't they two ways of saying the same thing? If they're not, I must say I have no idea what is meant by saying that he slept more slowly.

A: And what if I say that I do know what it means?

B: I would say, Give me an example of someone sleeping more slowly but *not* longer. What can you say to differentiate

them in meaning? If there's nothing to distinguish them, I'd say that these are just two ways of saying the same thing. Or that if they're not, the one expression—"sleeping more slowly"—is meaningless. Or if it's some far-out metaphor, explain *that* to me, please.

A: And what if I said that they do have different meanings and you just don't understand the difference?

B: I'd say you have said nothing that would distinguish them from each other. I'd have to translate the expression into something I can understand. Suppose a theologian says, "The physical world is not real at all, human beings are only half-real, and only God is fully real." I just don't know what could be meant by this. I would say that the person had better first clarify what he means by the word "real."

A: Surely he means that what we take to be trees and mountains are only delusions or fantasies. You may say he is mistaken, but don't therefore conclude that what he says is meaningless.

B: I don't. I'm always willing to try to understand what a person means by the words he uses. Before I say that some sentence is flat-out meaningless, I would *probe*—carefully inquire what he means by it. Could it be this, could it be that? That is the main problem in verbal communication. Currently the local history channel on television has a byline, "History is you." Now what in the world does that mean? Is it just a bundle of words, or perhaps a category mistake? Perhaps it's supposed to mean "History is *in* you." But then, of course, what does *that* mean? Perhaps that your genes are the product of millions of your ancestors' genes, and without their being as they are you wouldn't be you, or you wouldn't be here at all, or some such thing. I don't know. Why don't the people who say these things tell us what they mean by them, instead of making us do all the work? I'd say, "Clarify your meaning; you're the one who invented the phrase, so you're the one who'd better make it intelligible, instead of slinging a bunch of words together to make us feel a sense of awe and mystery, as if something profound is being said. They think they're saying something profound, or at least give you the impression that that's what they're doing, but all the time it's a bunch of words they've put together which tell us nothing. Much of what passes as philosophy is nothing but that, and we should be onto this game at the outset.

After all, history is not a person, so it can't be you. With that said, we either put it down as the nonsense that it is, or we try to eke some meaning from it that relies on some strange, far-out use of words—in which case the speaker owes us an account of what he's talking about. Let him put up or shut up, and show us that what he's concocting is something more than verbal garbage.

A: But there doesn't seem to be any general agreed-on criterion of when it is verbal garbage and when it isn't.

B: Granted. But let's consider some philosophical problem in the coming chapters. Perhaps they will shed some light on this vexed issue of meaninglessness.

EXERCISES

1. Is the following a verbal issue? If so, how would you resolve it? A squirrel, clinging to a tree, goes round and round it, always on the opposite side of the tree from a man it is trying to elude. Thus the squirrel goes around the tree, and the man goes around the tree (at some distance from it). But does the man go around the squirrel?[9]

2. You replace a defective part in your car. The next day you do the same with another part, and then do so each day until you have replaced every part with a new one. Is what you have at the end of this process the same car (with new parts), or is it a different car? And, if it is different, when did it become so?

3. Jack said to his brother Dick, "When I die I'll leave you all my money," The next day he changed his mind and decided to leave it all to his wife instead, and he wrote in his will, "All my money I leave to my next of kin" (his wife). But unknown to Jack, his wife had died. Next day Jack himself died, and his money went to his next of kin, his brother Dick. Did Jack keep his promise to Dick?

4. Is a tomato a fruit or a vegetable? What kind of question is this, and how would you resolve it? Now do the same with the question, "Is music a language?"

5. Is this the same cold I had last week, coming back after five days, or is it a different one? Does it make any difference whether you answer yes or no?

6. Death was long defined as the cessation of heartbeat. Later the definition was changed to the cessation of brain waves. Assuming that what's wanted is a condition from which one can't recover (we don't say, "He was killed twice last year"), is the second definition better than the first? Would you call the second a true definition?

---

[9]Adapted from William James, Pragmatism (New York: Longmans Green, 1907), pp. 43–45.

7. Assume that A is a defining characteristic of class X, and that B is an accompanying characteristic. Which of the following statements is/are true?

a. This wouldn't be an X if it didn't have A.
b. This wouldn't be an X if it didn't have B.
c. If it weren't an X, it wouldn't have A.
d. If it weren't an X, it wouldn't have B.

8. Consider the following issues, using your knowledge of defining and accompanying characteristics to clarify the controversy in each case?

a. Is this a table if I cut off its legs? If I cut it up for firewood?
b. Is it still water even if it's not liquid now?
c. Is it still wood after I've burned it?
d. Is he an adult before he is twenty-one years old?
e. Is this still the same train, even though it's a different set of cars?
f. Is this still the same train, even though it leaves the station at a different time each day?
g. Is this iron, even though it's not magnetic?
h. Is this a zebra, even though it has no stripes?
i. Am I the same person as I was ten years ago, even though all the cells that were then in my body have been replaced by others?
j. Is it still grass after the cow has eaten it?

9. Evaluate the following definitions, with reasons:

a. Bird: feathered vertebrate.
b. Fanatic: one who redoubles his efforts after he has forgotten his aim.
c. Sage: a spice used in turkey stuffing.
d. Tree: the largest of all plants.
e. Liberal: one who values liberty.
f. House: a building designed for human habitation.
g. Twilight: the period between day and night.
h. Motion: change of position with respect to the earth's surface.
i. Wastebasket: a basket used for containing discarded trash.
j. Book: anything containing paper, covers, and print.
k. Equator: an imaginary line extending around the earth, midway between the poles.
l. Marriage: legalized prostitution.

m. Left: opposite of right.
n. Religion: what you do with your leisure time.
o. Wednesday: the day that follows Tuesday.
p. Pump: an instrument used for drawing water from under the earth's surface.
q. Eat: ingest through the mouth.
r. Heart: the organ that pumps blood through the body.

10. Try to formulate a satisfactory definition of the word "act" in the light of the following considerations and questions.

"In law, there must be an act." Attempted murder is considered an act; but intended murder is not. However, what is involved in being an act? If you shoot someone and the victim dies, what was your act: the crooking of your finger around the trigger? the crooking of your finger around the trigger plus the bullet leaving the gun? these two plus the bullet entering the victim's body? these three plus the bullet entering the victim's heart? these four plus the death of the victim? Which count as part of your act, and which as consequences of your act?

Which of the following would count as acts, and why?

a. You kill someone while sleepwalking.
b. You stab a person to death but have no recollection of having done so.
c. You do something unthinkingly, from sheer force of habit, without any reflection or premeditation.
d. You do nothing at all, but let someone die of starvation when you could have fed him, or let him drown when you could have rescued him.
e. You fail to take care of your car, so when the brakes fail to function your car hits a pedestrian who dies as a result.

11. Could you imagine what a sweet taste was like if you had experienced only sour and bitter tastes? Could you imagine the taste of a tangerine if you had tasted only lemons and oranges, or the taste of a nectarine if you had tasted only plums and peaches? Could you tell in advance what the experience of sadness at the death of a loved one would be like, if you had experienced only sadness in other contexts, such as sadness at the cessation of enjoyment and at the theft of a prized possession? Could you tell in advance what the sadness of a Mahler andante would be like if you had experienced only andantes by Mozart? Can you know what it is to be greedy if you had never experienced greed? If Mr. X were described to you as greedy, would you have any idea what his feeling-states were like or what to expect from him?

12. Can you have any idea of the following without having experienced them firsthand? Would you consider the ideas of them simple or complex? State whether you are using "idea" in the sense of image or of concept.

a. space
b. bookends
c. nothing
d. motion
e. swimming
f. life
g. novelty
h. regret

13. Can you state in what way(s), if any, the following concepts are based on experience? What experiences or kind of experiences must a person have in order to have an idea of each of these concepts?

a. doorknob
b. racial integration
c. morally deserving
d. welcome
e. probability
f. economic opportunity
g. infinity

14.

Somebody told her [Karen, the librarian] that the library's bookshelves contained form-

aldehyde. Soon she was suffering from a headache, aching joints, and labored breathing. . . . But then Karen heard that there was no formaldehyde in the shelves. Suddenly the symptoms disappeared. A colleague later told me that it turned out that the shelves contained formaldehyde after all, but Karen remained blissfully ignorant of this and hence free of symptoms.[10]

A: I think this so-called disease isn't real at all. It's phony.
B: But she really does feel all these symptoms. She isn't lying; she really has those pains and discomforts.
A: Still, it isn't real. There's no germ or microbe in her body that causes such a condition.
B: Maybe not, but it's real *to her.*

Continue or resolve this dispute.

15. Do you consider the following sentences to be meaningless? Why?

a. She saw a noise (or heard a color).
b. She drew a line that was –2 inches long.
c. "Life, like a dome of many-colored glass/ Stains the white radiance of eternity" (Shelley).
d. "We are the eyelids of defeated caves" (Allen Tate).
e. What happened before time began?
f. Beyond the horizon; beyond space; beyond reality; beyond reproach.

SELECTED READINGS

ADLER, MORTIMER. *Some Questions about Language.* LaSalle, IL: Open Court, 1976.
ALSTON, WILLIAM. *Philosophy of Language.* Englewood Cliffs, NJ: Prentice Hall, 1963.
AUSTIN, JOHN L. *How to do Things with Words.* New York: Oxford University Press, 1965.

---

[10]Michael Fumento, "Sick of It All," Reason, June 1966, p. 20.

BLACK, MAX. *Language and Philosophy*. Ithaca: Cornell University Press, 1949.

BROWN, ROGER. *Words and Things*. New York: Free Press, 1958.

CHAPPELL, V. C. *Ordinary Language*. Prentice Hall, 1964.

COHEN, JONATHAN. *The Diversity of Meaning*. London: Herder & Herder, 1963.

DRANGE, THEODORE. *Type Crossings*. The Hague: Mouton, 1966.

ERWIN, EDWARD. *The Concept of Meaninglessness*. Baltimore: Johns Hopkins University Press, 1970.

HIGGINBOTHAM, JAMES. *Language and Cognition*. Boston: Blackwell, 1990.

HUME, DAVID. *An Enquiry Concerning Human Understanding*. 1751. Many editions.

JOHNSON, ALEXANDER B. *A Treatise on Language*. Edited by David Rynin. Berkeley: University of California Press, 1947. First published 1836.

KATZ, K. JERROLD. *The Philosophy of Language*. New York: Harper, 1966.

MARTINSON, A. *The Philosophy of Language*. New York: Oxford University Press, 1990.

MILL, JOHN STUART. *A System of Logic*. Book 1. London: Longmans Green, 1843.

NAGEL, THOMAS. *What Does It All Mean?* New York: Oxford University Press, 1987.

PLATO. *Euthyphro; Laches; Meno*. Many editions.

QUINE, WILLARD V. *Word and Object*. New York: Wiley, 1960.

ROBINSON, RICHARD. *Definition*. New York: Oxford University Press, 1950.

SANDERS, STEVEN, and DAVID CHENEY, eds. *The Meaning of Life*. Englewood Cliffs, NJ: Prentice Hall, 1980.

SUPPES, PATRICK. *Language for Humans and Robots*. Boston: Blackwell, 1991.

WAISMANN, FRIEDRICH. *Principles of Linguistic Philosophy*. London: Macmillan, 1965.

WITTGENSTEIN, LUDWIG. *Philosophical Investigations*. Translated by G. E. M. Anscombe. New York: Macmillan, 1953.

Note: Most of the items in the reading lists are books rather than essays or articles. Articles in philosophical periodicals are usually less readily available and more technical, and are usually cited in the reading lists only when they are included in an anthology that is also listed.

2 *What Can We Know?*
KNOWLEDGE

1. WHAT IS KNOWING?

What can we know? Can we know the future? Can we know that things exist that we can't perceive? Can we know that there are aliens somewhere in the universe? Can we know that God created the universe or guides its history? Can we know that there is life after death? Can we know that animals have minds? Can we know that killing is wrong?

All these are questions in epistemology, the theory of knowledge. The questions can become quite complicated, as we shall see. But first it's rather important to know what knowledge is—what it means to know something. Our first question, accordingly, will be "What is knowledge?"

We can use the word "knowledge," like any other word, to mean anything we choose. But, as the word is already used, what is it used to mean? What conditions have to be fulfilled before we are prepared to say that a person knows something? It isn't enough to believe it; it isn't enough just to guess it. But what *is* enough?

We don't always mean the same thing by the phrase "to know something." Here are the main ones:

1. *Knowing how.* Do you know how to ride a horse? to swim? to use a welding torch? to scuba dive? Such questions have to do with an *ability* to engage in a certain activity. Usually it is a learned ability, like knowing how to walk, but sometimes it is not, like knowing how to cry.

Animals know how to do many things that people don't, and often—more often than with human beings—they know how to do something without having to learn it. Almost all creatures know how to swim (and they haven't been given lessons). Chickens know how to hide and conceal themselves from passing hawks only a day after being hatched. Animals know how to select foods that they can digest: dogs will eat meat but not (usually) leaves, and rabbits will eat leaves but not meat. They are sometimes said to "know by instinct" or (more usually) to have been "genetically programmed" to engage in these activities.

2. *Acquaintance.* "Do you know that man?" "Yes, I recognize him." This is not the same as, "Do you know any facts about him?" "Do you know that old country lane near the red house a mile south of town?" "Yes, I've been there—I'm acquainted with it." You know Yosemite Falls (in this sense of "know") if you have been there and seen it, if you have confronted it through your senses in some way. This is not the same as knowing *facts about* it. A person who has never been there but has read all about it in an encyclopedia may know many more facts about the place than the person who has seen it but has never learned any facts about it.

Philosophers have sometimes called this "knowledge by acquaintance." Others say, however, that this is acquaintance, not knowledge. If you have seen Yosemite Falls you can hardly escape knowing a few elementary facts about it, such as its geographical location, but just "drinking it in," or staring at it, doesn't provide knowledge. Knowledge comes, they would say, only when you have before your mind some statement that is either true or false. You couldn't have knowledge (knowing that) without acquaintance with *something,* perhaps just the letters on a page, but still, acquaintance isn't knowledge; it only provides the material for knowledge. You don't have knowledge until you are in a position to claim something as true or false. In short, knowledge is *propositional.*

We distinguish propositions from sentences. A sentence may contain the word "the" twice; it may contain eight words; it may be translated into another sentence in another language. Here are two sentences: "An elephant is larger than a mouse," and "A mouse is smaller than an elephant." The first sentence begins with the words "an elephant," the second does not. They are two different sentences. But they both have the same *meaning,* that is, they state (express) the same proposition. A proposition has to do with the meaning of a sentence: same meaning, same proposition. Sentences are linguistic vehicles through which people express propositions.

This difference is important when we need to emphasize the difference between the meaning and the vehicle that is used to express that meaning. Philosophers are most interested in meanings, and they tend to speak of propositions. But the word "proposition" is not customarily used in daily discourse (except in a different sense, as in "I have a proposition to put to you"). The more common word "statement" is generally used instead, although "statement" is ambiguous: it can mean either the proposition that is expressed or the sentence that expresses it.

3. *Knowing-that.* Most of the time, when we use the word "know," we are referring to knowing-*that:* "I know that I am now sitting

down," "I know that the earth has existed for many years," "I know that I care about you," and so on. Knowing-that is knowing that some situation or state of affairs actually occurs or exists.

But what *is* knowing-that? What conditions must be fulfilled in order for us to be justified in saying that we know something?

Belief

Take *p* to stand for any proposition. In order to know *p,* it's necessary for you to believe *p.* Believing it isn't enough, since people can believe many propositions that aren't true. But if you didn't at least believe it, you wouldn't be said to know it.

People can *say* they believe something even if they don't. They may lie, of course, or they may delude themselves into thinking they are sincere even when they're not. It's often difficult to tell: does she really believe she's the great-granddaughter of a distinguished nobleman? After all, she's said it so many times, she may not even ask herself any more whether she really believes it. She would *say* she believed it if you asked her, but does she?

Suppose you've just won the million-dollar jackpot. "I know it's true," you say, "but I still can't believe it." But you do believe it, don't you? Intellectually you may believe it, but you've been disappointed so many times in the past that your emotions haven't yet caught up with your intellectual realization. You haven't yet "digested" the information. Or, a woman knows that her husband is dead—she has seen his body lying in state—but she has not yet come to terms with it emotionally, and she says, "I know it but I still don't believe it."

"If you really believe something," it has been said, "you must be willing to act on it." But what if it's not the kind of statement one could act on because it has no consequences for us? You believe that Saturn has twelve moons and would say so if asked, but there's not much you can do about it to prove your sincerity, other than to say "yes" if asked whether you believe it.

Belief can also be a matter of degree: you can believe something but not very strongly. You have beliefs you would stake your life on, and others on which you would stake very little. You may believe something because a friend told you, but you aren't quite sure whether your friend can always be trusted to give you correct information. Still, if you didn't believe it at all—if you positively disbelieved it—could you claim to know it?

Belief is sometimes said to be the *subjective* condition of knowing. We turn now to the *objective* condition: if you know it, it must be *true*.

Truth

To know it is to know it to be *true*. If I know I am sitting on a chair, I know that the statement "I am sitting on a chair" is true. I may *believe* what isn't true, but I can't *know* what isn't true. If what I believe turns out not to be true, then I didn't know it; I only *thought* I knew it. If you say, "I knew she was in the room next to me all the time," and it turns out that she was a thousand miles away, then you didn't really know she was in the next room, since she wasn't.

Knowing isn't the same as being certain. You were certain that she was nearby, but she wasn't. People feel absolutely certain about lots of things that aren't so. They were certain for thousands of years that the earth is flat. They were certain that certain people were witches. A woman on a recent television talk show was certain that she had visited both Venus and Mars during the past few months. She claimed to know it, as surely as she knew she was sitting there. During religious wars people on one side claim to know

with certainty ("with certainty" is redundant—if they know, don't they know with certainty?) that their side has the truth, and those on the other side also claim to know that *they* have the truth, even when the two beliefs contradict one another. People can have a very intense *feeling of certainty* ("We will win the war," "She's going to recover") about many things that are far from certain and in fact may not be true at all.

In daily life we don't have much trouble with the concept of truth. We may disagree on *how we discover* that a statement is true; this will be our subject in the second half of this chapter. But even a small child knows the difference between lying and telling the truth. "Johnny, tell the truth! Did you really call Jane's mother a bitch?" Johnny may or may not answer the question truly, but unless he has a sudden lapse of memory he knows whether he is giving a truthful answer. It is only when people have been tainted by a little philosophy that they ask questions such as the following:

1. "I don't believe there's any such thing as truth." "Not even the statement you just made?" one might ask. Does the person mean that all statements are false? That not only "Snow is black" is false but also "Snow is white"? Does the person really mean to say that no statements that are made are ever true—not even that he was born, or had a childhood, or had parents, or is now alive?

2. "I mean that there is no *absolute* truth." What exactly does the word "absolute" add? What is the difference between "It's true that snow is white" and "It's absolutely true that snow is white"? The word "absolute" gives the utterance a certain emphasis, but what does it add to the meaning of the statement? And when someone protests, "What you say is absolutely false," how is this different (except in emphasis) from saying, "What you say is false"? Don't both sentences label the same situation?

3. "All truth is relative." "Absolute" is the opposite of "relative." If someone says, "All truths are relative," what does *that* mean? Relative to what? "I am now sitting in a chair." How is this statement relative? And what does it mean to say so?

A person might say, "If I am sitting on one side of the desk and you on the other, the vase that to you is on the right side of the desk is to me on the left side. It's relative to one's position." "Right" and "left" are indeed relative terms, but is the truth they express relative? "From where Mary sits the vase is on the right," and "From where Jerry sits (on the opposite side of the desk) the vase is on the left"—aren't both of these propositions just true, period?

Or, one might say, "If I'm facing north, east is to my right; but if I'm facing south, east is to my left." Is that statement relative to anything? Isn't it just true (without qualifications)? If someone objects that "east is to the right" is a relative truth, one can reply that the statement itself is *incomplete;* you can't know whether it's true till you know what direction the speaker is facing. If the speaker is facing north, the statement is true—that is, the statement "East is to your right if you're facing north."

4. But doesn't the truth of a statement depend on who it is that's speaking? If one person says, "Calculus is interesting," and another person says, "Speak for yourself—it may be interesting to you, but it's boring to me," what is it that's true? Is calculus boring or not? Clearly what interests one person bores another. "X interests you," and "X bores me," can both be true, and often are. There are many statements of this kind: "I find her fascinating." "Well, I don't." They are not contradicting one another; they're each stating how they feel, and they feel oppositely.

A statement isn't true-for-you and false-for-me even when it's *about* you or *about* me.

It may be a truth about you that you like to handle snakes, and it's a truth about me that I do not. It's not just true-for-you that you like to handle snakes but true, period.

5. One can respond in the same way to the charge that truth is relative to time. Isn't the statement "New York City has over 6 million inhabitants" relative to the time about which the statement is made? Isn't it true at one time and not at another time? But again the relativity disappears when we include the information that's needed to complete the statement. "New York City had more than 6 million inhabitants in 1896" is false, and "New York City had more than 6 million inhabitants in 1996" is true. Neither is relative to the time; the time is included in the statement, and must be if we are to give an accurate report about New York City's population.

6. Suppose someone says, "*As far as I'm concerned,* it's true." What exactly does the phrase "as far as I'm concerned" add? Is the statement true? If a member of the jury says, "As far as I'm concerned, the man is guilty," doesn't that translate into "*I think* he's guilty"? Isn't "it's true as far as I'm concerned" a confused way of saying "I believe it's true"? And of course what one person believes, another may not.

Two people are arguing, and one of them says, "As far as I'm concerned, there are aliens from other worlds on the earth now," and the other says, "As far as I'm concerned, that's not so." Well, are there or aren't there? Isn't that the question? Isn't the "as far as I'm concerned" just a way of getting off the hook in case the proposition turns out not to be true?

All this may seem too plain and obvious to mention. Still, people say this sort of thing constantly and it may be important to point out when their assertions are inaccurate. They do say things like, "As far as I'm concerned, what he says is true"—but that leaves open the question as to whether what he says *is* true. If a person is asked in court, "Is it true that you killed that woman?," what is the judge or jury supposed to conclude if she says, "Well, as far as I'm concerned, I didn't"?

If one person says of a proposition *p,* "It's true," and the other says, "It's not true," and it's the very same proposition in both cases, then surely one of them is mistaken. But if one says, "*I believe* it's true," and the other says, "*I believe* it's not true," both statements may be true: one believes it and the other does not. And if one of them says, "*To me* it's true," and the other says, "*To me* it's not true," one must ask them what the "to me" adds to the statement, whether the phrase can be dropped without loss of meaning, or whether it means only that the speaker *believes* it's true.

7. "But what if it's partly true and partly false?" If you are confronted by a mass of statements, in which you can discern a few that are true, you may say, "There's some truth in what you say." Perhaps with a few corrections a few true statements can be extracted from the mess.

Can one and the same statement be partly true and partly false? Yes, if it's a compound statement: "Snow is white and grass is white" is false because one of its component statements is false—as every student is supposed to be aware when taking a true-false test.

But what of a simple statement such as, "She is a scheming, selfish brat"? Such a statement is extremely vague, and it isn't clear what the limits of application are for words like "selfish," "brat," and so on. But even apart from this, what is said may be true of this person, but other things of a different kind may also be true of her: she may on occasions be outgoing, helpful, and generous. Both can be true as long as neither statement claims to be the *whole truth* about her. "She is nothing but X" may not be true, but "She is sometimes X and sometimes Y" may be true.

Or, "She is always X" may be false, although "Part of the time she is X, and part of the time she is Y," may be, as we say, "All too true."

8. What if someone says, "It may be true, or it may be false, or it may be neither: its truth may be *unknown.*" This is mixing truth with our knowledge of truth. A statement may be true but not known to be true and false but not known to be false. If unknown, it's still true or false but we don't know which. It's either true or false that there is an intruder in the house next-door, but since the family is gone for the weekend, the truth or falsity of the statement is unknown.

The truth of a statement should not be confused with someone's knowledge of its truth. More truths are being discovered all the time, and many are still unknown, but are no less true for the fact that we do not yet know them.

Criteria of truth. "What is truth?" asked Pontius Pilate, who did not stay for an answer.

But what is the question? If it's true propositions we are talking about—not some other sense of "true" such as, "She's a true friend," or "This is a true plumb," or "This is a true diamond" (that is, it is a diamond and not something else), the question asks when a proposition is true. Well, a proposition is true when it tells us what *is.* Aristotle devoted one sentence to answering the question: "To say of what is that it is not, or of what is not that it is, is false; while to say of what is, and of what is not that it is not, is true."

Or one could put it even more simply: The statement that snow is white is true, if and only if snow *is* white. "The earth is round" is true if and only if the earth is round. Or, we could say that a statement is true if it reports the way some aspect of reality is, and false if it misreports reality.

1. *Correspondence.* What has just been described is sometimes called the "correspon-

dence theory of truth." A statement is true if it corresponds to reality (or as is sometimes said, to a fact). Someone says there are five trees in the courtyard, and I look, count them, and say, "That's true"—that is, the statement corresponds with the fact.

Philosophers have given themselves headaches speculating on what the word "correspond" means in the sentence. (Do we need the word at all?) If I match color charts to cans of paint, the colors on the chart resemble the colors of the paint in the cans; they correspond in being alike. There is no such resemblance between words and facts. But correspondence doesn't require any such similarity.

We speak of a one-to-one correspondence between two things, for example, between the books in a library and the cards in the card catalog. Is there such a one-to-one correspondence between a sentence and a fact? Surely not, for the sentence can be translated into other languages and still express the same fact. It's the meaning that counts, not the sentence per se.

The correspondence theory applies easily to empirical statements. Are there five books on this desk? Just check the statement against the alleged fact. But suppose someone says, "If Cleopatra's nose had been half an inch longer, Egypt would not have become part of the Roman Empire" (because Marc Antony wouldn't have been attracted to her). Historians may dispute whether this statement is true. But where is the situation to which it corresponds? There is no such situation, since it never occurred. "If X had happened (which it did not), Y would not have happened (although it did), is an example of a contrary-to-fact hypothetical (conditional) statement. Where is the reality to correspond with the statement?

There are other types of statements as well, which we have not yet considered: statements in mathematics ("2 + 2 = 4") and logic ("If A is larger than B, B is smaller than A").

These are surely true, but what kind of truths are they? Do they correspond to any fact of reality?

Anyway, a statement by itself corresponds to a fact only if the speaker intends it for that purpose. An instructor may say, "The moon is in syzygy," not to state a fact but to give an example of how the word "syzygy" is used. And so on. A seemingly simple issue has suddenly been riddled with complexities, of which only small hints have been given here. Meanwhile, we turn to a second conception of truth.

2. *Coherence.* Not correspondence but coherence, it has been suggested, is what decides whether a statement is true. Coherence with what? With other statements. Its truth consists in its coherence with a body, or system, of other statements.

What is meant by "coherence"? One meaning is, "A proposition is coherent with a body of other propositions if it is logically *consistent* with them; that is, if it doesn't *contradict* any of them." A proposition, *p,* is not coherent with another proposition or set of propositions if anywhere within the set there is a not-*p*, the negation (denial) of *p*. But this is a very loose kind of requirement. "There is a vase on this desk" is consistent with "Saturn has twelve satellites." In that sense they are coherent with each other, but what has this to do with their being true? If Saturn had thirteen moons instead of twelve, would that be any less coherent with there being a vase on this desk?

One could make the coherence requirement stronger by saying that the propositions must *entail* (logically imply) one another: "This is a square" entails "This has four sides." But "This is a square" entails nothing about Saturn's moons or my vacation last year or just about any other proposition we believe to be true.

Rather, coherence among propositions has to do with a body, or system, of propositions that are not only consistent with each other but that *mutually support* one another; they don't logically entail one another but they provide *evidence* for each other. Suppose we suspect that Mr. Jones killed a certain person. There were no witnesses, but blood with the victim's DNA was found on Jones's jacket, Jones was seen leaving the victim's house a few minutes after the established time of death, Jones abruptly left his home a mile away an hour before the killing took place, and so on. The statement that Jones committed the murder is coherent with all these other statements; the other statements provide evidential support for it.

If I can't find my pen, I say, "It must be somewhere," even though I search every place where I think I might have lost it. Its disappearance remains a puzzle to this day, yet it never occurs to me to say, "Perhaps it was annihilated—one moment it was a collection of molecules, and the next moment, pfft! no molecules, nothing." Yet we dismiss this possibility because there is such a huge array of beliefs, garnered through long effort over many years, that is not coherent with the belief in annihilation, although my continued inability to find it *is* coherent with belief in its annihilation. (Maybe it could happen in a black hole, but, we say, not on earth.) "The pen suffered total annihilation" doesn't fit with—is not coherent with—a great mass of other statements that we already consider to be true.

Suppose I am alone in the house, and I keep hearing what seems to be a toilet flushing upstairs. I go and find no one. Perhaps I am not alone after all, but I check every room and closet, and there's no one. I hear the sound again and go to the bathroom: the tank fills with water and then the sound stops. I don't know how it could have happened, but after a while it happens again. Perhaps it was a genie or some incorporeal spirit; I didn't consider that possibility before, but now I am not so sure. So I situation myself in the upstairs bathroom again and

wait. Sure enough, it happens again; I see the lever move and the water flow out of the tank, but nothing and nobody can be seen pressing it. Well, perhaps the event depends on some other factors I haven't considered, some strange condition inside the tank that a plumber might be able to explain. Meanwhile I take a video picture of the whole thing, to prove to others that I really saw all this.

I do call in a plumber, and he observes what I did, but he can't explain it either. Neither of us rests very easy with the idea that some immaterial spirit has pressed the lever. What if something "from the spirit world," wherever that is, is doing this? If such things started to happen frequently, we might give up our belief that only a physical force can cause a physical effect and conclude that the science of mechanics is not up to explaining what it claims to explain—events as simple as the pressing of a lever.

Still, we would accept the spirit hypothesis only with great reluctance—not because we are stubborn, not because we don't want to admit any reality in the universe except the physical, but because what we see and hear on these occasions is *not coherent* with the whole body of knowledge we already have. The complex and interconnected network of principles of applied mechanics, which every would-be plumber spends many months learning, seems to be put in question. It's as if a monkey wrench had been suddenly thrown into the machinery of our thought— as if we had achieved a coherent system of mechanical laws and now something turns up that threatens the structure of principles we have so laboriously built. We tend to discard the "spirit world" explanation because it is not coherent with the vast mass of other things we know, or believe we know.

Isn't it the lack of coherence that leads us to reject it? If only this new discovery were coherent with what we already believe, it would be so much easier to accept it. But there are (as we shall see) many examples in science of discoveries, such as x-rays and electricity, that were not coherent with a body of propositions already accepted, that opened up new and hitherto unsuspected areas of investigation, and that exhibited a wider coherence (coherence with more propositions already accepted) than anything that had been thought of up to that time.

Coherence is of great importance in the sciences, where there is a large body of propositions that are mutually dependent on one another. In scientific theory, the only means available for choosing among competing theories is their degree of coherence with other propositions already accepted (see Chapter 4).

But what of the statements on which the theory is based? The spirit hypothesis about the flushing toilet is not coherent with propositions already accepted about plumbing, but what of the statements that led to the hypothesis in the first place, such as that I kept hearing the sound upstairs and that it had no assignable cause for it? Was the statement "I heard what sounded like a toilet flushing upstairs" itself accepted because of its coherence with other statements? (Could coherence be defined without already presupposing—assuming—the concept of truth?)

3. *The pragmatic theory.* "The truth is what *works.*" The first question to be asked is, "What does it mean?" We know well enough what it is for a mechanical object to "work." Don't you know when your car works? You turn on the ignition, and the car fails to start; you check the battery, the carburetor, the wiring, and so on, and everything looks all right, but still the car won't start. A friend who is a mechanic makes a few changes under the hood, the car starts, and you drive it to your destination. There is no doubt that the car "works." The functioning of mechanical objects is the "home base" for our use of the word "work."

But what does it mean for a *belief* to "work"? You believe you are now reading a book. Let's say you are, but does this belief "work"? What does it mean to say that it does or that it doesn't? Does your belief that the car works, itself work? Can propositions be tested by whether they "work"?

A *program* or a procedure may work, that is, it may have its intended effects. A diet program may work in this sense; in fact it may work for one person and not for another. An exercise program may "work" in the sense of making you feel more vigorous and healthy. But what if someone says, "Christianity works for me"? Does this mean that it makes her feel better? That she is now happier or more hopeful than before? In this sense one might say that Christianity "works," at least for her (but perhaps not for others).

But what has its "working" in a specific case to do with its *truth?* If it "works" for you but not for me, is it then true for you but not for me? What exactly is the relation between its being true and its "working"? Surely they aren't the same thing?

If a king who wanted to put an end to religious strife within his kingdom passed an edict saying that everyone was from that moment on required on pain of death to believe in Isis and Osiris, he might succeed, if he had a large squad of enforcers. Doubters would be put to death, and everyone else would either believe or keep quiet about it. Parents would teach their children about Isis and Osiris, and no other religious belief would gain a foothold, until finally there would be no competition, and no more strife or even argument about religion. Did the belief "work"? It did in the sense that it put a stop to religious wars. But what has that to do with the belief being *true?*

The contemporary philosopher Karl Popper has written, in defense of truth as correspondence, that there is no doubt that correspondence to the facts is what we usually call "truth"—that in ordinary language it is correspondence that we call "truth," rather than coherence or pragmatic usefulness. A judge who admonishes a witness to speak the truth and nothing but the truth does not admonish the witness to speak what he thinks is useful either for himself or for anybody else. The judge admonishes a witness to speak the truth and nothing but the truth, but he does not say, "All we require of you is that you do not get involved in contradictions," which he would say were he a believer in the coherence theory. But this is not what he demands of the witness.[1]

Evidence

Believing isn't enough for knowing—a person may believe what isn't true, and truth isn't enough—a proposition may be true although you may not know that it is. If you are ignorant of it, you can hardly be said to know it. Neither can you be said to know it if you only *guess* it.

A player predicts that the next throw of the dice will be double-sixes. And as it turns out, that is what it is. "I knew it!" he exclaims in triumph. We feel mildly irritated, because we are convinced that he didn't really know it—he only guessed it, and the guess turned out in his favor. "He didn't really know," we say, "he only guessed." People often say that they knew when it was only a lucky guess. What is lacking?

What is lacking is *evidence.* To know it, he had to have *good reason* to believe it. His statement can't be just a "shot in the dark." You say you know that the earth is round because you've seen the curvature from airplanes, you've flown around the earth yourself, and before that you read this fact in countless books and magazines. All this gives you good reason to believe it.

Why do you say you know that this is your sister's child? The child looks like her, she says it's her child (and you've never known her to lie), and you went with her to the hospital when she was eight-and-a-half months pregnant. But does all this entitle you to *know*? Couldn't there still have been some slip-up? How strong must the evidence be? considerable? incontrovertible? conclusive? And what do these three words mean—aren't they all somewhat vague?

Let's consider a few examples of how we actually use the word "know."

1. While driving I hear a familiar thumping sound and say to myself, "I've got a flat tire." I get out of the car and look, and behold, the left rear tire is flat. Before I got out of the car I had strong reason to believe the statement, but now that I see it for myself, surely I *know*. This is a standard kind of knowing that we use every day.

2. I say, "I know that this man next to me is Ryan Carter. I've known him most of my life, and I recognize him clearly." But what if, unknown to me, he has an identical twin who just came into town? Then to my surprise I was mistaken in saying this man is Ryan. I have every reason to identify him as Ryan; my evidence is extremely strong. Ordinarily I'd say I was absolutely sure. Yet my identification of him as Ryan turned out to be mistaken—I didn't *know* that this man was Ryan, since he wasn't.

3. "Do you know that your desk and books are still in your office?" "Of course I know," I say, "I left the office only five minutes ago, and they were all there." "But how can you be sure that in those five minutes some movers didn't come in and take all the things out?" "I was right next-door, and I would surely have heard some sounds of scraping and so on. And I didn't see any movers around; the place was quiet. Anyway, how could they have done it in five minutes?" "Do you mean that if someone were offered a mil-

---

[1]Karl Popper, *Objective Knowledge* (London: Oxford University Press, 1979), p. 317.

lion dollars to see to it that the stuff was moved out quietly in five minutes, they couldn't have done it? Would you stake your life on it?" "Well, perhaps not my life—but still, I know." Just to be sure I go back to the office, and all the things are still there. I was right—so I knew, didn't I?

Should I say that the evidence was conclusive? No, not quite—at the time I was questioned about, I wasn't in the room, so there was a possibility that I didn't have some evidence. Should I say that I didn't know, or didn't quite know, because of that improbable but possible contingency? Or should I say that I knew, although I did know that I might have been mistaken (but if I had been mistaken, then of course I didn't know)?

4. I open a certain book to page 100, and I see that the first word on the page is "upon." To make sure, I look at the page and at the same printed word again—it's still the same. I ask other people, and they all say the word is "upon." I take a Polaroid picture of the page and develop it: the first word is still "upon." Surely, I would say, I don't just believe this—I know it.

But I run into a "perpetual doubter"— someone who on leaving her house goes back and forth to the front door to make sure she's locked it. "You have to make absolutely sure," she says. So I look again and yet again; the result is still the same. Isn't that the end of the matter? If someone asked me what I was doing, and I said, "I'm making sure that the first word on this page is 'upon,'" wouldn't my statement be a bit ridiculous? I can continue to stare at the page, but what more could I do that would be called "making sure what the first word on the page is"?

It could be that if I stare at the page for a long time I would see, or seem to see, a different word. But then, someone might object, I would be seeing this at time t-2; but it would still be true that at time t-1, I *did* cer-

tainly see the word "upon" there. Or would what I saw at time t-2 cast doubt on what I saw, or was sure I saw, at time t-1?

Strong and weak senses of "know." One might say, "As long as there was any evidence I might have had that I didn't actually have, I didn't really know, because the missing bits of evidence *might* have turned out negatively. During those few moments I left my office, if I *had* been there I might have found the bookshelves empty! As long as that's a possibility, however remote, I can't say that I *know* that the books were there."

This is too rigorous a requirement for the needs of daily life. "In the ordinary way of speaking," I would surely say that I knew that the books were there on the shelf even when nobody saw them, and that the word "upon" was the first word on page 100. We would say that although the evidence was not conclusive, it was sufficient for knowing.

Philosophers have sometimes distinguished what they call the *strong* sense of "know" from the *weak* sense. In the strong sense, I don't know until I have conclusive evidence. The evidence is conclusive when there is *nothing more* that I or anyone could discover that would cast the slightest doubt on the statement. All the evidence must be in; there can be nothing lacking. In the weak sense, the "daily life" sense, we know when we have a preponderance of evidence in favor of it and (even though we have tried to find it) no evidence against it. In this sense, it *might* have turned out that books weren't on the shelf during those intervening minutes, and if this *had* turned out to be so, then I didn't know because I can't know what is false. But it turned out as expected, so I did know. I knew in the weak sense that the books were still on the shelf during my absence from the room. I know those true propositions that I believe with good reason. (Did I know in the *strong* sense that the first word on page 100 was "upon"? It would surely seem so, but let's wait; philosophers are ingenious at devising previously un-thought-of situations in which one might still have doubt. We shall consider some of these in Chapter 3.)

1. When do you *know* that the accused man is guilty? Not guilty beyond a reasonable doubt, which is all that the law requires, but guilty beyond *any* doubt. He may have con-fessed, but that doesn't prove his guilt: there are false confessions all the time. If someone testifies that she saw him doing the killing, you still can't be sure: many witnesses per-jure themselves—they may not be lying, but they may make an innocent mistake in iden-tification. They are certain that suspect num-ber 3 in the police line-up is the man, but they don't recollect very accurately; some time has elapsed, and their memory image of the man doesn't resemble the man all that much any more. In all these cases you have evidence but not knowledge. Suppose fur-ther that someone recorded the whole mur-der on tape and that the tape shows this man wielding the knife. Can't we now say that we know that the suspect was guilty?

Still, isn't it possible that what the camera shows is a look-alike, someone with so strong a resemblance to the suspect that even his mother wouldn't be able to tell the differ-ence? Couldn't it have been the look-alike who did it? But then there's the DNA evi-dence, which indicts the original culprit by a million-to-one margin. We've sent men to their deaths on less evidence than this, but in this case don't we *know* he's guilty? Not in the strong sense—not if we demand that nothing that might yet be discovered would make any difference; not if we demand that all the evi-dence be "in" so that there is no chance that any yet-to-be-discovered shred of evidence, however slight, would turn up to cast the slightest doubt on our claim to know. Of course we don't ordinarily use the word "know" in the strong sense; but if we do, even

this case won't meet the requirement. Some evidence could still turn up that goes the other way. We are still entitled to doubt, to say, "We don't know—not quite!"

2. Let's try one more: I can understand how you might doubt that I have a hand if you look in a bad light or in a dense fog or if there's something wrong with your eyes. But in this case we are sitting a couple of feet apart in this well-lighted room. I raise my hand and say, "Here is my hand." And you say to me, "I doubt that that's a hand." And I say, "What more do you want? Here it is, you can see it; come closer, touch it. You still aren't satisfied? Take a picture of it; call other people in as witnesses if you like. After all that, what more do you want? What more evidence is there that I can give you?" I could understand your doubt as long as some of the conditions of knowing were unfulfilled; but I've fulfilled them all, and you still doubt. What is it that you're doubting? What test is there that, if performed, would *resolve* your doubt? You want to touch it again? Go ahead; here it is. You keep on saying, "I doubt," but every time I give you the means of resolving your doubt, you perform the test and you still say, "I doubt." What test is there whose negative outcome you fear?

You may say, "I doubt that *if* I were to reach for your hand a minute from now there would still be anything there." So we wait a minute, and you still touch the hand. Do you want another minute? Do you really think that if I don't remove it, it may not still be there? Doubting is a game with you. You *say*, "I doubt," but these are now empty words. You're not really doubting anymore.

We have distinguished the daily-life sense of "know" (the weak sense) from the philo-sophically stringent sense (the strong sense), which admits no possibility of uncertainty. But we have still not reached the end of the issue. A *skeptic* about knowledge could still say that in stating the examples we have already *assumed* too much. In giving the example of the flat tire we assumed that we *really did see* the flat tire and didn't just imagine it. In the hand example, we assumed that there really was a hand there, that you weren't dreaming it. The skeptic would doubt everything, even that there is a physical world. The skeptic's doubt is more all-encompassing than any we have yet presented. Thus far all we have done is to "get the show on the road." We shall do more with it in the next chapter.

2. THE SOURCES OF KNOWLEDGE

How do we acquire knowledge? Numerous answers to this question have been suggested, but they come under two main headings, *reason* and *experience*. Of the two, experience seems the more obvious: we know there's a tree out there because we can see it and touch it; that is, we know it by means of our senses, that is, through sense-experience. But there are also occasions when we say, "I figured it out"—we reasoned that it must be that way; for example, if all the people in the class went to the picnic, and Alice was in that class, then Alice too went to the picnic. In arithmetic, algebra, trigonometry, and calculus, we don't "look and see"; we reason and figure it out.

Reason

An early Greek philosopher, Parmenides (515–440 B.C.), held that reason is the sole judge of what is true. And reason, he said, leads to the conclusion that there is no such thing as change in the universe. How did he arrive at this strange conclusion?

There is no such thing as *nothing*, he said. If there were empty space in the universe, that empty space would be nothing. (In fact, by the word "nothing" he meant empty

space.) The universe could not have been created, because then prior to its creation there would have been nothing—and nothing cannot exist: what exists is always something. If what existed had parts, between the parts there would be empty space (nothing), and nothing cannot exist. Also, what exists must be indestructible, for if it were destroyed, then it (or whatever was destroyed) would no longer exist—it would be replaced by nothing, and there can be no nothing.

Therefore, reasoned Parmenides, change is an illusion. Reason says that change cannot exist, and reason is decisive. If we respond that experience tells us that change does exist, then experience deludes us—experience is mistaken. Parmenides claimed to have proved that no change can ever occur, and if this is so, everything that contradicts it is in error.

We might attack him mockingly, saying, "'There is no change,' said Parmenides, and then he walked away." But Parmenides would say that even his walking away was an illusion, since walking away involves change. In fact, since all coming-into-existence is an illusion, Parmenides' own temporal life is an illusion. But this would not faze Parmenides: the universe is unchanging, and change is impossible, so his coming-into-being is also impossible, including his own life history and his walking away.

We could say, of course, that Parmenides has not reasoned *correctly*. His critics have been unanimous in saying that his reasoning was wrong at several points. For example, why should "nothing" mean the same as "empty space"? We use the word "nothing" in many other ways. Thus, we say, "Nothing would please me more than to hear from you"; that surely doesn't commit us to denying empty space. Or we could take the old argument, "Nothing is better than wisdom; dry bread is better than nothing; therefore dry bread is better than wisdom." But there is an equivocation here (using a word in one sense in an argument, then using it in another sense in the same argument): "Nothing is better than wisdom" means that wisdom is the best thing there is (here we needn't use the word "nothing" at all); "Dry bread is better than nothing" means that if you have dry bread, that's better than having no food at all. So the conclusion doesn't logically follow. There are also other mistakes. "Nothing" doesn't mean merely "empty space"—we have just gone through a couple of other meanings for it.

Still, if a person *has* reasoned correctly, hasn't she proved her case? And if her conclusions contradict those of experience, who wins—reason or experience? We'll return to this question after we've considered deductive reasoning.

The word "reason" does not always carry the same meaning. One clear meaning that it does have is reason*ing,* and we shall begin with that. Surely we can arrive at truth through reasoning—but, like Parmenides, we don't always reason correctly. Are there any criteria for when we do and when we don't? The name for the discipline that tells us this is *logic.* Logic is the study of correct reasoning. It is a separate study, and many courses in colleges and universities are devoted to it. Logic has about the same relation to philosophy that mathematics has to physics and astronomy.

Logic. Suppose someone were to reason this way:

All cows are green.
I am a cow.
    Therefore,
I am green.

"That's not true!" someone may say. "Yes, it is," another person says, "the reasoning is perfectly OK."

Both are correct in what they are asserting. The first person is saying that cows aren't green and so on, and that the statements are all false. The second person is saying that although the statements are false, the reasoning is *valid*—that *if* all A is B and all B is C, then it logically follows that (and one is entitled to conclude that) all A is C. Logic is the study of valid reasoning. It doesn't matter whether the premises (the statements that precede the "therefore") are true; what matters is that *if* you grant the premises, you must logically grant the conclusion.

Now consider the following:

All cows are mammals.
All mammals are living things.
    Therefore,
All living things are mammals.

In this instance, both premises are true, but the conclusion doesn't logically follow; the reasoning is invalid. (The conclusion that would follow is, of course, "All cows are living things.")

Arguments are valid or invalid because of their *form,* regardless of their *content.* It doesn't matter what premises you use; what matters is whether the premises logically yield the conclusion (whether the conclusion logically follows from the premises). Thus, any argument of the form "All A's are B's, and all B's are C's, therefore all A's are C's," is a *valid* propositional form—no matter what A, B, and C are, the argument is valid.

Examples of valid propositional forms include:

1 If no A's are B's, then no B's are A's. (If no dogs are cats, then no cats are dogs.)
2 If A is larger than B, and B is larger than C, then A is larger than C.
3 If some A's are B's, then some B's are A's. (If some dogs are white creatures, then some white creatures are dogs.)

Here are a few examples of invalid forms:

1   If all A's are B's, then all B's are A's. (If all dogs are mammals, then all mammals are dogs.)
2   If some A's are not B's, then some B's are not A's. (If some clocks are not things that give correct time, then some things that give correct time are not clocks.)
3   If *p* implies *q*, and *q* implies *r*, then *r* implies *p*. (If being a square implies being a rectangle, and being a rectangle implies being a quadrilateral, then being a quadrilateral implies being a square.)

If you get your monthly bill from a department store and check only whether the addition is correct, you will not have completed your examination of the bill; the arithmetic may be correct, but the items added may not be—you may have been billed for items you never purchased. To know that the bill is correct, you have to know (1) that the addition is correct; and (2) that the items listed are indeed items you purchased (at the price listed).

An argument is said to be *sound* if (1) the reasoning is valid; *and* (2) the premises are true. But logic won't tell you whether the premises are true. Logic will only take whatever premises you please and tell you whether you can validly infer your conclusion from them.

"But how then can logic provide us with new information? Whatever appears in the conclusion (of a valid argument) is already contained in the premises of the argument." This is true, but it depends on what we mean by the word "contained." The conclusion is not literally contained within the premises, as a marble is contained in a bag. Nor is it contained in the sense that it *occurs* in the premises; in the argument "All persons have heads; John Stewart is a person; therefore John Stewart has a head," the statement "John Stewart has a head" does not occur in the premises. The conclusion is, however, contained in the premises in the sense that it is *logically deducible from* the premises. The question, then, still faces us: when the conclusion is deducible from the premises, are we learning anything from the conclusion that we did not already know in stating the premises?

We can answer this quite simply: sometimes we do, and sometimes we don't. It all depends on the complexity of the argument and the intelligence of the individual. The question "Do we learn through deductive reasoning what we did not know before?" is a psychological question, the answer to which varies from person to person. In the case of the argument about John Stewart, the conclusion probably does not give us any new information; before we get to the conclusion we already know what it is. Sometimes, however, the conclusion does give us new knowledge—we had not put the premises together before to draw the conclusion.

> Mr. X, a man of high reputation and great social standing, had been asked to preside at a big social function. He was late in coming, and so a Roman Catholic priest was asked to make a speech to pass the time till his arrival. The priest told various anecdotes, including one which recorded his embarrassment when as confessor he had to deal with his first penitent and the latter confessed to a particularly atrocious murder. Shortly afterwards, Mr. X arrived, and in his speech he said: "I see Father ———— is here. Now, though he may not recognize me, he is an old friend of mine, in fact I was his first penitent."[2]

The audience of course remembered the premises—the first penitent was a murderer, Mr. X was the first penitent—and validly drew the conclusion, which probably came to most of them as a surprise.

In a deductive argument of any complexity, the conclusion probably *will* come as a

---

[2]Alfred C. Ewing, *The Fundamental Questions of Philosophy* (London: Macmillan, 1951), p. 29.

surprise to most people. Consider this argument:

> If the guard was not paying attention at the time, the car was not noticed when it came in.
> If the witness's account is correct, the guard was not paying attention at the time.
> Either the car was noticed or Jones is hiding something.
> Jones is not hiding anything.
>   Therefore,
> The witness's account is not correct.

To a person with perfect reasoning powers, who could instantly see the implications of every statement or combination of statements; no conclusion would come as new information; but since human beings are not thus gifted, there are many conclusions of valid deductive arguments that do come as new information, in spite of the fact that "the conclusion is contained in (deducible from) the premises."

Proof. Whenever we discuss an issue with others, we are constantly confronted by the demand, "*Prove* it." To prove something is presumably to establish it beyond a doubt (or, sometimes, beyond a reasonable doubt). But how you prove something depends on what kind of situation you are talking about.

1. In the most commonly used sense of "prove," you can prove something by giving very strong evidence for it; "I'll prove my case in court," a defendant says. "Prove to me," says the prosecuting attorney, "that you were in Atlanta the night of the murder." (If the murder was committed in Chicago, that would let the defendant off.) He may then provide evidence. His parents testify that he was indeed in Atlanta that night; friends claim that they saw him in Atlanta; someone saw him board a plane from Chicago earlier in the day. Of course that doesn't *prove* that he didn't commit the murder, for all these people might be lying to protect him or be mistaken in their identification (the person

they saw might have been his identical twin). In court cases the evidence is almost always circumstantial, but a large body of evidence nevertheless is well on the way to proof—particularly if police find someone else's fingerprints on the gun and in the house where the murder took place. Indeed, the prosecution is not required to prove its case beyond all possible doubt, but only "beyond a reasonable doubt."

2. In the sense in which the term "proof" is used in mathematics and logic, to prove something is to deduce it validly from true premises. Merely to perform a valid deduction isn't enough, as long as the premises from which the deduction is made can still be questioned.

Sometimes in a deductive argument, we use as premises certain propositions which are called *axioms*. Axioms are "assumed to be true" for purposes of the argument; they are *posited*—accepted in the context of the argument—and that which is posited may not be known to be true. One can carry out elaborate and valid deductions, while yet not questioning the axioms that constitute the premises of the argument; these will perhaps be questioned later. Thus, much of the Euclidean geometry can be deduced if you assume Euclid's Axiom of Parallels: "taking a straight line and a point outside the line, only one straight line can be drawn through that point which is parallel to the first line." The premise seems plausible enough—many would consider it to be obviously true—but a problem for geometers has been that the Axiom of Parallels has never been proved. But if you assume this axiom, then (together with other premises) many propositions can be deduced that are of relevance to geometry, surveying, and engineering.

Systems of geometry begin with certain axioms and definitions and proceed from there to deduce theorems, which (using more axioms and definitions along the way) yield more theorems and so on. Assuming there are no errors in deduction, the conclusions are valid. But are they true? That depends on whether the premises (in this case the axioms) are true. The Axiom of Parallels is part of the Euclidean geometry we all learned in high school. But in the newer geometrical systems of Georg Riemann and Nicolai Lobatchevsky, the Axiom of Parallels is not included, and different conclusions are validly drawn. The premises of the Euclidean system seem to most people to be obviously true; but geometers tell us that while they suffice for ordinary finite distances, they will not do for the millions of light years of outer space, because of the curvature of space.

At any rate, whether premises are *true* is something that must be discovered empirically, by observation and measurement. Whether deductions are *valid* is discovered by following the rules of deductive logic. *Pure* geometry is concerned only with the validity of deductive systems; *applied* geometry (as in surveying and engineering) is concerned also with whether the premises from which the deductions are made are true.

What can we say, thus far, about the problem posed by Parmenides? Logic tells us that *if* certain premises are true, then a certain conclusion necessarily follows. It doesn't tell us that the premises themselves are true. Even if Promenides' reasoning were valid, this wouldn't show that his premises were true.

Logic alone doesn't tell us which premises are true. It doesn't tell us what actually *exists*. How then do we find out whether we have true premises?

That depends on the premises. Most of the premises in arguments are in one way or another statements about experience (someone's, not necessarily yours), such as "All swans are white." In Parmenides' case, the premises are questionable—for example, he

was assuredly mistaken about the meaning of "nothing"—but so is the reasoning: from his premises it doesn't follow that nothing ever changes.

There is no conflict, then, between reason and experience. Deductive reasoning tells us what conclusions we can *validly* draw from certain premises. Inductive reasoning, as we shall see, tells us what conclusions are *probable* on the basis of given evidence. In general, we turn to experience to tell us whether the premises themselves are *true*.

The word "reason", however, has a broader meaning.

Reason as a faculty. Thus far we have discussed *deductive* reasoning—general criteria that we can use to determine when a conclusion of an argument logically follows from the premises. In *inductive* reasoning the conclusion does not logically follow from the premises—one can assert the premises and deny the conclusion without inconsistency. Reasoning in the sciences is usually of this kind, and we shall discuss inductive reasoning in Chapter 4 on the philosophy of science. In inductive reasoning the premises provide evidence for the conclusion without logically implying (entailing) the conclusion.

The word "reason," however, is used more widely than is "reasoning." Human beings have the *faculty* of reason: reason involves the capacity to form concepts and understand them, to learn and use language, to acquire beliefs about the world, and to act on those beliefs. We not only have the concept of a lion, we recognize it as a lion, and we respond in action (or inaction) to that recognition. All this is involved in the broad use of the term "reason" that is used in philosophy and the humanities. When it is said, for example, that "people use reason to find solutions to their problems," it is not only deductive reasoning that is meant, but the whole array of abilities just described. When it is said that the ancient Greek philosophers were among the first to try to solve ethical problems through reason rather than through religious faith, it is again this array of abilities that is generally referred to.

Do only human beings have these faculties? Animals surely perceive things in their environment and take them into account when they act. Surely they do not use propositional reasoning, since they do not have that system of conventions that we call language (chimpanzees can understand some words but apparently cannot invent a language). Some animals figure out solutions to problems, like getting a banana out of a tree. They possess some of the attributes that are vaguely called "reason," although they do not possess them to the degree that human beings do.

The "Laws of Thought"

We use logic to get from one proposition to another: it tells us whether, *if p* is true, *q* must be true, false, or neither. But what about the propositions by themselves?

The truth or falsity of most propositions— "Snow is white," or "I am sitting on a chair"— is determined by *experience* of one kind or another. We shall examine these in the next section. But first, there are propositions that have seemed to many philosophers to be *self-evident;* sometimes they are called *truths of reason.* They are, it is said, so obviously true that no sane person could possibly doubt them. For example:

I am here.
I am alive.
1 + 1 = 2.

What seems obviously true to one person may not seem obvious to another. It once seemed obvious to most people that the world is flat and that the sun and stars re-

volve around the earth. Yet these are far from obvious, and most people who have learned even a little geography or astronomy don't believe they are true at all.

Let's consider "I am here." What does "here" mean? Presumably "here" means wherever I am. "I am here" then becomes "I am where I am." And this is a *tautology* (from the Greek *tautos,* or "the same"): the predicate just repeats all or part of what is said in the subject of the sentence.

What about "I am alive"? If you assume that this is said by a live human being, the statement becomes "I, a live person, am alive"— which again is a tautology. Without that assumption, however, it is not: the statement "I am alive" could come out of a machine, and in that case it wouldn't even be true.

"1 + 1 = 2" is a tautology if "2" means the same as "1 + 1"—which most of us would say is just what it does mean. We shall discuss mathematical truths in Chapter 5.

We shall encounter other examples as we go along. Meanwhile, let's consider three very important propositions, first stated by Aristotle. They have been called the "laws of thought," but this is a misleading name: these aren't statements about how people think—many people think irrationally and constantly get involved in contradictions. Instead, the propositions constitute the logical *foundations* of thought: principles that are presupposed (assumed) in every statement we make. These three "laws" are:

1 The Law of Identity: A is A.
2 The Law of Noncontradiction: nothing can be both A and not-A.
3 The Law of Excluded Middle: everything is either A or not-A.

Aren't these three statements too obvious to need saying? Besides, they don't seem to be very informative. This desk is this desk. So what? What does this tell us? What do we know that we didn't know before? "A is B" might be informative, but "A is A" seems quite pointless.

Yet Aristotle considered these principles, or laws, to be presupposed in all thought. Try to deny them and see what happens:

A: I deny that A is A.

B: I see. And is your denial a denial?

A: Of course.

B: Then A is A. You presupposed that A is A in what you just said. You can't even *think* about anything without assuming this principle. Take anything at all and call it A; then it is A that you are talking about or thinking about and not something else. How could the A you are talking about also *not* be A? If it's a chair you are thinking about, then it's a chair, not a tomato.

Or suppose that someone says that "A is A" isn't always true, because an A *becomes* a B: "Tadpoles become frogs, and are no longer tadpoles."

But "A is A" doesn't deny that what was an A can become a B. It only tells you that when you have an A, it's an A you have, and when the A has become a B, then it's a B. What things become is an interesting topic in empirical science. But the Law of Identity contains no such "interesting information." It says only that when something is an A, it's an A. Boring perhaps, but true.

Or suppose that someone were to deny the Law of Noncontradiction:

A: This is a table and also not a table.

B: Well, what is it you're talking about—a table or not a table?

A: Both. I'm saying that this is, and is not, a table.

B: You mean that you're using the word "table" in two different senses? This is a

table (piece of furniture) and not a table of contents?

A: No, I mean in the very same sense.

B: What do you mean by the subject-term of your sentence? You first say it's a table, and then in the next breath you say it is not a table. Well, what is it then that you are talking about?

A: A table that is not a table.

B: But when you say it is a table, and then that it is not, you contradict yourself.

A: OK, so I'm contradicting myself. What's wrong with that?

B: A contradiction is unintelligible. Close your eyes and imagine a table. Now imagine something that's not a table, and now try to imagine something that's both a table and not a table at the same time.

A: Whether I can imagine it is irrelevant. I can't imagine a million-sided polygon either.

B: There could be a million-sided polygon, whether you can imagine it or not. There's no contradiction in saying there is. But at least we know what we're talking about; we have a concept even if not an image. But in the case of the table, we have to decide *what* it is that we're talking about. If it's a table, OK. If it's something else, OK. But it can't be both the table and something else.

Suppose I invite you for dinner at seven o'clock tonight, and you say, "I accept." Then a moment later you say, "I don't accept." I say, "Have you changed your mind?" and you say, "No." "Do you accept or not accept?" "Both." "You mean you're coming and you're not coming?" "That's right."

What am I to expect now? Shall I prepare dinner for you or not? I can't both prepare it and not prepare it. I say, "I don't understand." You say, "You may not understand it, but I do. I am 'beyond' the Law of Noncontradiction." "Well, in your 'beyond' realm, are you accepting my invitation or not?" "Both. I'm sorry you don't understand that." "No!" I say, "*you* don't understand it either. Can you both exist and not exist, both be here and not be here?"

Aristotle's principle is that *reality contains no contradictions*. "This is X" and "This is not X" cannot both be true.

A: But reality does contain contradictions. People behave in contradictory ways. She is a dynamo of energy at one time, and very soon afterward she can't be bothered. She is gracious and loving, and also she is spiteful and cruel. Opposite characteristics reside in the same person.

B: She is full of energy at time *t*-1 and passive at *t*-2—no contradiction there.

A: But she is at the same time both loving and cruel. There are many such people.

B: She may have both *potentialities* in her at the same time, but she can't *do* X and also not-X at the same time.

A: A person may have opposite feelings toward the same person. A man may love his wife and hate her at the same time. He may love her for her warmth and attractiveness, and hate her for her shortsightedness and stubbornness—both at the same time.

B: What Aristotle said was that nothing can be A and not-A at the same time *in the same respect*. He may like her characteristics A and B and dislike her characteristics C and D. Because of such ambivalent attitudes we often say such things as, "Well, I like her and I don't." This sounds like a violation of the Law of Noncontradiction, but it isn't. He can't both like feature A and not like it at the same time and in the same respect. Two

contradictory propositions can't both be simultaneously true. What you have given me is just a case of mixed feelings. You haven't given me any proposition that is both true and not-true.

A: I suggest that there are lots of cases. If someone asks me, "Do you like oysters?," I may think a moment and then reply, "I like them and I don't."

B: That is, you like them in one way but not in another; you have a mixed attitude toward them.

A: If I taste a new casserole, I may simultaneously like *and* dislike it in the same respect—that is, with respect to its taste.

B: Then surely there is something about its taste that you like, such as its tartness, but something else about its taste that you don't like, perhaps its spiciness. You like its taste in one way (one respect) but not in another.

The Law of Excluded Middle is the one that has come in for the most criticism. It says that between A and not-A there is no middle ground—whatever something is, it is either A or not-A.

1. "But that isn't so," one may say. "Something need not be either hot or cold. A car need not go either fast or slow. The liquid may be neither hot nor cold but lukewarm; the car may travel neither fast nor slow but at a moderate speed."

But this objection is a confusion of *negatives* with *opposites*. The Law of Excluded Middle does not say that the car is going either fast or slow. Nor does it say that a given temperature is either hot or cold, or that an examination must be either easy or difficult. Each of these is a pair of opposites, and there may be a middle ground between them. The temperature of a liquid may be neither hot nor cold but lukewarm; an examination may be neither easy nor difficult; a car may go at a medium speed that is neither fast nor slow. The Law of Excluded Middle does not say that there is no middle ground between *opposites* (hot and cold), for of course there is. It only says that there is no middle ground between a term and its *negative* (hot and not-hot). Wherever you draw the boundary line between hot and not-hot, there is no middle ground between them—the law, true to its name, excludes any such middle ground: any temperature that isn't hot is not-hot, but of course the not-hot includes *both* lukewarm and cold.

2. "According to the Law of Excluded Middle, Jones must be either at home or not at home. But what if Jones is dead? Then he's neither at home nor not at home; so the Law of Excluded Middle doesn't hold true in this case."

But this is a double-barreled proposition. According to the statement quoted, (1) there is a man named Jones; and (2) he is either at home or not at home. The second statement presupposes the truth of the first. If the first is false, there is no person for the second statement to apply to. Let us take each one separately. Either there is a live man Jones or there is not (true). And if there is, he is either at home or not at home (also true). The trouble comes if we confuse the two parts.

We are often confronted with double-barreled questions: have you stopped beating your wife? Have you shed your horns? Have you stopped using your roommate's toothpaste? We are supposed to answer these questions with a "yes" or a "no." You have stopped? Then you did do it! You haven't stopped? Then you are still doing it! Many people fall into this trap. The trap is the failure to separate the double-barreled question into its components. Ask first: *did* you ever use your roommate's toothpaste? And only if the answer is yes, does the second question arise: Are you still doing it?

3. "You either believe that the Abominable Snowman exists or you disbelieve it." "Not so. Skeptics *neither* believe nor disbelieve it—they suspend both belief and disbelief. They don't say yes, they don't say no; they may not think there is reason to believe either one."

But of course the Law of Excluded Middle doesn't say that you either believe or disbelieve it; it doesn't even say that you exist. It says only "Either it is true that you believe it or it is not true that you believe it." Not believing it would include both disbelieving it and not knowing (or not caring, etc.) about it one way or the other—just as not-hot includes both cold and lukewarm.

The limits of proof. How would you prove to someone that A is A or that a thing can't be both A and not-A at the same time? Don't we just *know* that it's true?

All discourse, all argument, presupposes it: if A isn't A, then an argument isn't an argument, a proof isn't a proof, and so on. Without assuming that A is A, no argument can get off the ground.

How would you prove that if no A's are B's, then no B's are A's? You can draw two circles, one labeled "A" and the other "B." The circles don't overlap; nothing inside the one is inside the other. You label the first "dogs" and the second "cats." Now, if no dogs are cats, no cats can be dogs—the two completely exclude one another. But what if the person you are talking to claims that she "just doesn't see it"? She admits that no dogs are cats, but questions whether some cats are dogs. You might question her intelligence, and say that your statement is a necessary truth whether she admits it or not. That it's true is one thing; that she fails to see it is something else. "Too bad for you, lunkhead!" you might say; but of course that doesn't convince her either.

If the goal is to convince her, you may never succeed. Propositions as basic as these are not capable of proof. Proof requires bringing in *other* propositions from which these are deduced. And in the case of such basic ones as Aristotle's laws of thought, no others can be brought in which are more clearly true than they are. You can't prove that "A is A" by means of other propositions; in fact every attempted deduction would *presuppose* the truth of "A is A" (the proposition "P is P" would be just another case of "A is A").

You can't prove "A is A" by means of itself; that would be arguing in a circle (assuming the very thing you're trying to prove). And you can't prove it by means of something else, because everything else rests on it. Even if we could deduce "A is A" or some other basic necessary truth from other propositions, we would then be faced with the problem of proving those other propositions. And if we deduced these from still others, we would then be asked to prove those.

Even if it could be done, it would not help us. Suppose we could deduce principles of logic, L, from a body of other statements, K. Then how would we prove K? By something else, J? And how prove J? The question here is infinitely self-repeating. We are caught in an *infinite regress*. We cannot establish the principles by means of themselves; we cannot establish them by means other than themselves; therefore, we cannot establish them at all. (Even in saying this we are using a principle of logic, although a slightly more complex one: "If P, then Q or R; not Q; not R; therefore not P.")

If proof is not to go on infinitely, it must stop somewhere. But we are so accustomed to being barraged with the request "Prove it" that we tend to think that this is required also of the very bases of proof themselves: "if you can't prove it, you can't know it." But proof is always by means of something *else*, which in turn demands proof by something else, and so on ad infinitum. What we *can* do is exhibit the consequences of denying them.

Still, the uneasiness may persist. We want every statement to rest on another one. We are in the position of the woman and the rock. She asks what the earth rests on and is told: the earth rests on an elephant. What does the elephant rest on? A rock. What does the rock rest on? Another rock. What does that rock rest on? Another rock . . . , and so on, ad infinitum. The woman in the audience keeps asking this question over and over again; finally, in exasperation, the speaker says to her, "Lady, it's rock *all the way down!*"

All the way down–to what? The speaker can stop her endlessly repeated question only by teaching her a little astronomy and curing her of naïve notions of up and down—although perhaps she will never quite overcome a feeling of dissatisfaction with the explanation. You too may remain dissatisfied with our conclusions about proof unless you get over the idea that the ultimate principles of proof must themselves be proved. What we can do is attempt to *justify our acceptance* of these statements. For example, in the case of "A is A," we could justify it by saying that all argumentation and discourse would be impossible without it.

Experience

Let us now consider the other principal source of knowledge, experience. The word "experience" is somewhat vague, and it is not clear what all it is supposed to include. So let's break it down into more manageable parts. Not every alleged source of knowledge that is claimed under this heading is equally acceptable, for reasons we shall consider.

Sense-perception. "How do you know there's a table in front of you?" "Through my senses; I see it, I touch it; I can take pictures of it if you like, and other people can see and touch it also. What more do you want?"

This is such a plain and obvious claim to knowledge that we generally take it for granted and don't think much about it. We believe that there is a physical world and that we can perceive it through our senses. But perceptual knowledge, as we shall see, is an unexpectedly complex and arduous subject, and we shall devote the entire next chapter to it. Meanwhile, it will be enough to mention here some stumbling blocks to such a claim:

1   Sometimes our senses mislead us; we perceive things as having qualities they don't have, or even perceive things that aren't there at all.
2   Perhaps our senses mislead us totally; maybe we're dreaming all the time, and there is no physical reality to perceive.
3   Frequently we claim to perceive more than we actually perceive. A person says that she saw a spaceship traveling through the air last night, although a more accurate description would be that she saw a light in the night sky (that's all she really saw) and that she *interpreted* what she saw as a spaceship, although the evidence doesn't yet warrant this conclusion.

Meanwhile, we may assume, for a few pages more, that we do have knowledge through our senses of a physical world. If we didn't believe this, the other sources of knowledge we shall now list couldn't get off the ground, for they all assume that we do sometimes have reliable information through our senses.

Introspection. We also have knowledge of our own thoughts and feelings. I know what I am thinking about right now. I know that I do (or do not) have a toothache at the present moment. I know that I feel a bit drowsy. And so on. Can't I be just as sure of this as that I am now sitting at a desk or reading a book?

Still, it's easy, when we make such statements, to confuse a report of what we feel or think, with some *interpretation* of what we feel or think. If someone says, "I feel anger rising in me like a huge tide," is that a report of how she feels, or is she adding something to it? What about "I feel as if the whole world has deserted me"? What about "I feel . . . I feel . . . I don't know what I feel, but oh, how I feel it!"?

A patient in therapy, asked to report his feelings, will often give an introspective report that is interlaced with bits of theory he has learned from the therapist. Asked to report his feelings, he says, "I feel that my Oedipal feelings have subsided somewhat and that some of my aggressiveness has given way to passivity." The therapist says, "Don't give me any psychological theory, just tell me what you are feeling at this moment. As Jack Webb used to say on *Dragnet,* 'Just the facts, ma'am.' Tell me what you are feeling; don't mix it up with speculations about what may have caused it; leave that part to me."

Thus warned, the patient may say, "I have a feeling of dread, as if something terrible is about to happen." Or, "I have no energy today. I just want to curl up on the beach and sleep all afternoon." And once we are clear about not getting the feeling mixed up with the interpretation, don't we know the truth of many such statements as surely as we know anything? These are direct reports of our conscious states, and how could they be mistaken? Other people may infer from my behavior how I feel, but only I know how I feel—I am the final authority on that. No one else has this first-person knowledge!

Still, it's often difficult to know whether you are in a certain psychological state. If someone asked you at this moment, "Are you happy?" what would you say? You know whether you have a headache right now, but you may not know whether you're happy. But this may be because happiness, unlike pain, is not just a momentary state. Happiness is a long-term business; you may not know till the end of your vacation whether it was happy. You're not happy at 12:00 noon and unhappy at 12:01, although you might well have a stab of pain at 12:00 noon and none at 12:01. "Call no man happy until he is dead," King Darius of Persia said—which doesn't mean that he's happy when he is dead, but that you can't be sure till the end of your life whether you had a happy life.

Moreover, some conditions, like being happy or being in love, involve not only momentary feelings but tendencies to *behave* in certain ways—what are called "dispositional states." If you are in love you will miss the person when she is away, and will be concerned when she is sick or in pain; if these things do not occur, others can rightly say, "He's not in love; he's only infatuated." People are not very careful in describing how they feel. They may say they feel angry when they only feel frustrated; they may say they're in love even though it's only a passing fancy. Others who watch how you behave can often give a more accurate account than you can, not because they are having your feeling but because they are better observers of your behavior than you are.

Psychologists tell us that we are often "not in touch with our own feelings" and that we not only misdescribe our feelings but may actually think we feel one thing when we feel another. A woman claims sincerely that she doesn't feel depressed, but after some months of therapy she says, "I see now that I was depressed all the time, but I didn't know what it was like to be happy. Now that I am finally happy, I see that I was in a continuous state of depression." Some would say, "She wasn't really depressed, because she didn't feel depressed"; others would say, "She was depressed all the time but didn't know it, because she had never experienced anything (happiness) to contrast it with."

A man says that he felt real grief at his father's death. He even shed tears at the funeral. But he went out carousing that night, and he showed none of the concern that his sisters did, fondly recalling incidents in their father's life. Did he feel grief or didn't he? Some would say, "He felt it, but for only a few minutes during the funeral." Others would say, "What he felt wasn't grief at all—not that he was lying when he said it, but he was just kidding himself. He wanted to feel it, and even shed a tear to prove it, but what he felt wasn't grief. He showed none of the manifestations of grief." Consider this conversation:

A: He's trying hard to locate his family in Germany. But no attempts to get in contact with them have succeeded.

B: I believe he really doesn't *want* to locate them.

A: But he is really sincere; he's not lying about this.

B: I don't claim that he's lying; he's just taken in by his own rationalizations. He really thinks he wants to locate them, and he might well do OK on a lie-detector test on it.

A: Why should he not want to get in touch with them, as he says he does?

B: Because they saw him off to the United States with high hopes that he would be successful. And he wasn't. He was sometimes unemployed and sometimes employed at minimum wage at a low-level job. He was ashamed of this and didn't want to face them. But he keeps this fact even from himself.

Whether he's mislabeling what he felt or misinterpreting it, the person is not being accused of lying—or saying what he knows is not true. Just the same, what he says is inaccurate. Often there is a kind of "protective veil" of self-deception between what we feel and what we believe we feel. In reporting one's own feelings, "There's many a slip between cup and lip."

"Feeling that." "I feel X" is misleading enough, but even more likely to mislead are statements of a different kind that are often confused with it, namely, "I feel *that* X," where X is not a state of mind but a proposition.

1. "I feel that the defendant is guilty." "I feel that the witness is going to come clean when the trial resumes." Suppose that the person who says this has no "inside knowledge" of the trial or the persons involved. What does "I feel . . ." mean? Usually "I feel that this is going to happen" means nothing other than "I *believe* that this is going to happen." In daily life "I feel that . . ." is often synonymous with "I believe that . . ." (sometimes not very strongly). For example, "I feel that he's going to leave her again." What decides the matter, of course, is not what she feels, but whether the man in question does leave her again. The fact that she "feels" that he will only tells us what she believes is going to happen, not what *is* going to happen.

2. "It's going to rain tomorrow. I can feel it in my bones," says a person with arthritis whose pain comes back every time rain is on the way. Here the fact that he *feels a certain sensation* may well be evidence that the belief ("It's going to rain tomorrow") is true. In such a case, inner feelings may well be evidence for a belief that is not *about* one's inner feelings (but about the rain that has yet to come), much as a falling barometer may be evidence that a storm is on the way. This is so only in a limited class of cases in which there is some cause-and-effect relation between one's feelings and the event that is predicted.

In most cases, however, there is no such relation between what the person "feels" (believes) is going to happen and what in fact will happen. If I "feel" that I'm going to win the lottery, and a million other people think that *they* are going to win the same lottery, and only one person can win it, how can the fact that each of us "feels" (believes) that we are going to win be any evidence at all that we all *are* going to win?

Memory. "How do you know that you met this person before?" "I remember it." "How do you know that you and your parents took a trip to Lake Mead when you were a child?" "I remember it as vividly as if it were yesterday." We constantly use memory as a claim to knowledge. Isn't remembering an event just as good as seeing it happen right now?

Not quite. People often misremember. You may "remember" that you went to Denny's for dinner last Tuesday, and then you suddenly remember that it was Wednesday—on Tuesday you were out of town. Or, you relate to guests how, when you were a small child, you were bounced up and down on your mother's lap. But this may not be true at all: your parents have repeated that story so often that you're sure it happened; you even have a memory-image of being bounced on your mother's lap, even though it's only a product of your mother's imagination. Nevertheless if you were asked, "Do you remember it?" you'd say, "Of course I do."

Memory often plays tricks on us. Under pressure by a therapist, a girl may "remember" being sexually assaulted by her father, although no such thing ever occurred. But the therapist has convinced her that this is a genuine memory that she has repressed. The father may even be convicted and go to prison for the misremembered offense.

It is comparatively easy to develop "false memories":

A professor of psychology at the University of Washington has shown how easy it is to create a false memory. She asked older siblings or other relatives of 24 people to make up a story about the young person being lost in the mall between the ages of 4 and 5. While 18 participants insisted that the incident had never happened, six of them not only believed the story but also developed their own memories of the fictitious event.[3]

---

[3] *Time*, April 17, 1994, p. 55.

Such passages may make us so skeptical about memory that we may conclude that we should never trust it. But let us not jump from "*Some* memories are mistaken" (or are apparent memories only) to "*All* memories are mistaken." On what basis could we know that all memories are mistaken? Doesn't that rely on memory too?

Without relying on memory, how could we complete a single sentence? When I utter the last word in a sentence, I have to remember the first words in the same sentence, else I wouldn't even know what I was asserting. Surely you remember what you saw two seconds ago just as clearly as you perceive whatever you are perceiving at this moment? It is possible, of course, that you may sometimes misremember what you saw two seconds ago, but is that possibility really greater than the possibility that you "incorrectly perceive" what you are perceiving right now?

In fact, how can I know that a past memory was mistaken, unless I know that this act of remembering really did occur in the past, and that there was a previous state of affairs of which it was a memory? And how do I know *that*? If I know that my memory has deceived me in the past, I have to know some facts about the past—and how do I know these, except through memory?

Suppose I remember that I spent last week in Chicago, and suppose some argument convinces me that this memory-judgment was mistaken. How might I become convinced of this? I run into someone today who describes a conversation he had with me (or says he had) last week in Los Angeles; and then still another person, unknown to the first one, also tells me that she had lunch with me last week in Los Angeles. I have never known either of these people to lie; perhaps they were just mistaken—but on the other hand, perhaps it was I who was mistaken. They are as convinced that they remember seeing me in Los Angeles as I am

that I was in Chicago. Suppose that I keep a daily diary and look up what appears in it for last Wednesday's date, and the record indicates that I was in Chicago that day. Doesn't that prove my case? Not quite. Sometimes people write only what they *think* has happened, not really happened.

But could I have deceived myself on so important a point? I may say to myself, "What I write in my diary, since it's written the same day, is usually true"—but in concluding this, am I not again relying on memory? Not only that, I am assuming other things that are in turn based on memory—for example, that the ink marks on the page of my diary have not changed their shape and that the words written in it have not somehow turned into very different words, which I now read. If the shape of the words changed overnight, what I read in the diary now wouldn't be evidence for what really happened last Wednesday.

And what makes me so sure that ink marks don't change their shape in this way? Again, the fact that thus far they never have. But how do I know *this*? This belief too is based on memory. I *remember* that in all my experience ink marks never change their shape in this way. And so I am propping up my memory-judgment by reference to the diary, but that judgment in turn has to be propped up by all manner of assumptions, such as "Ink marks don't change their shape," which are also based on memory of how ink marks have behaved in the past.

Thus we have no good reason to say that some memory-judgments are false, unless the truth of *some* memory-judgments is assumed. Unless we grant that some memory-judgments are true, our judgment that some memory-judgments are false can't even get off the ground, for there could be no evidence to support them. All such evidence comes from the past and is itself derived from memory.

Testimony. Most of us would probably claim to know—at least in the weak sense of "know"—that George Washington was the first president of the United States, that Abraham Lincoln was assassinated, that the earth existed for many years before we were born, that we are so-and-so many years old, that Brutus killed Caesar, and that dinosaurs roamed the earth many millions of years ago. But we ourselves have never seen any of these things for ourselves, nor do we remember them—we weren't there and many of them occurred before we were born. We don't even remember our own birth; although we were there, we were not then in a position to remember anything.

Suppose you deny that Lincoln was assassinated. Others will show you the accounts in history books as well as pictures of Lincoln in his last days. But couldn't all these tales be false, invented by others in order to mislead or misinform us?

A: Well, I suppose this *could* happen; some events related in history books may not have happened at all, like George Washington and the cherry tree. But historians have combed through this material pretty thoroughly, and they have no doubt that Lincoln was assassinated, but do doubt the story of Washington and the cherry tree. Doesn't that convince you?

B: No, they could have made that up also. How do I know that they haven't?

A: If any historian, who is competing with others for fame or even just for that promotion to a professorship, had any scrap of evidence that Lincoln wasn't assassinated, he would be famous overnight. So we are quite justified in accepting Lincoln's assassination as fact—even though there is no way that you or I could have observed this for ourselves.

The longer the chain of testimony, the more chances of mistake there can be. We tend, as a result, to accept the claim unless it conflicts with something else we know. Most of what Herodotus tells us in his history can be checked against other sources, but we don't believe him when he says that in Egypt cats jump into the fire, because this claim conflicts with everything we know about cats. If someone walks into the room right now and says that the house next-door is still there, we believe his testimony without further question because we know nothing to the contrary: it's the normal way things go (houses remain standing unless they are destroyed), and anyway we can check it for ourselves if we so choose. But if the same person walks in and says that there is a unicorn in the garden, we won't believe it without checking it ourselves (and taking a camera along) because we've never seen a unicorn and don't know of anyone who has.

What about the dinosaurs who lived more than 65 million years ago? No person was there to testify to their existence. But we do use the testimony of paleontologists and others who have investigated these matters; there is a wealth of evidence from surviving bones, together with evidence from dating techniques and countless other pieces of evidence that scientists have arrived at painstakingly and with constant challenge from others. Belief in dinosaurs is a complex inference in which many lines of testimony converge—as we shall see in Chapter 4.

In the case of Lincoln, we believe that the chain of testimony will lead back to what some people *did* perceive. In the case of dinosaurs, nobody did perceive them, but we believe that *if* we had been there, we *would* have seen them for ourselves. This process is involved in most claims based on testimony: we weren't at that place or at that time, but we believe that if we had been there, we could have observed for ourselves what we now believe on testimony.

Demanding firsthand verification of everything is a rather wasteful procedure. Would you want to verify for yourself every statement you read? It would take forever, and you couldn't do anything else. The motto "I'll believe it unless I have some reason not to" pays off better than "I won't believe anything until I can see it for myself."

"Nothing ventured, nothing gained," is preferable to "Safety first." If I'm in a strange town and ask where the post office is, I'll believe it unless I have reason not to, and if it turns out that the person I asked has not told the truth, I'll disbelieve her testimony in the future (but not necessarily the testimony of others). We all depend on the testimony of others for almost everything we know. Try to imagine a society in which nobody accepts anyone else's word for anything until he has satisfied himself that the statement is true. If I don't believe there are groceries in any store in the city until I've checked the stores myself, I'll never be able to do much except check—and probably do without the groceries.

Faith. "How do you know that your statement is true?" "I have faith that it's true." A second person is asked, "How do you know that the same statement is *not* true?" "By faith." What do we do now? Is that the end of the argument and the beginning of the fight?

The problem with faith is that *by itself* it doesn't justify any belief. Two people can both "play the faith game," and faith alone won't tell you which view, if any, is right. If you say that you know by faith that everything in the Bible is true, another person can say with equal sincerity that everything in the Koran is true, yet at many points the texts contradict one another. At the points where they contradict each other, they can't both be true.

People who claim to know one thing "by faith" often are unwilling to grant the same appeal to their opponents. "Faith is all right" as a justification of their own beliefs, but they won't grant it as a justification of their opponents' beliefs. Yet the same criteria that would justify their own beliefs would also justify their opponents'. The problem with faith is that it is a double-edged knife. Often people use it when it suits them and deny it when others also claim it.

Sometimes we have a *reason* for "having faith," and that reason does not lie in faith itself. If you are a trusted friend and I say, "I have faith in you," my trusting you is not just "a matter of faith." I have *reason* to trust you because you have always been truthful, reliable, and forthright with me. If I have *evidence* of your trustworthiness, as I do, I don't trust you just "by faith"; I trust you because, based on your behavior as long as I have known you, you deserve that trust. It wouldn't be giving credit to you to refer to my trust in you merely as "faith." It's not as if I were meeting you for the first time and you said, "Trust me."

"But we have to use faith every day of our lives; otherwise we couldn't continue living. When I drive my car onto the highway, I have faith that the cars coming toward me from the opposite direction aren't going to hit me. If I didn't have that faith, I wouldn't dare to drive."

Is this true? One might respond, "I don't have *faith* in the other drivers—I don't even know them. I just go by the evidence—most drivers don't hit other cars. I realize there's a danger, but the risk is worth taking. I surely don't have blind trust. I only have a tentative kind of confidence, not very secure, but not so tentative that I won't risk driving. After all, I have to get to my job. I weigh the advantages and disadvantages both ways—and this is hardly "blind faith."

Intuition. Instead of saying, "I feel that so-and-so is the case," people sometimes say, "I know by intuition that so-and-so is the case." People often appeal to intuition to support their claims to knowledge. "My intuition tells me that you're lying." When travelers are lost in the desert, one of them may say, "*That's the way out.*" "How do you know?" "I know it by intuition." What is one to make of such claims, especially when they are correct?

Sometimes people speak of "intuition" when there is *no* claim to knowledge. How does a composer create new compositions? She has intuitions. What are these? Well, she can't explain exactly; an idea comes to her, apparently from nowhere, and she starts working feverishly on her new score. She doesn't know how the inspiration came to her, and, it seems, she uses the word "intuition" for lack of any other way to describe how she is able to compose what she does. Neither she nor anyone else knows much about the process of artistic creativity, and the word "intuition" has a certain flavor of mystery, although it tells us nothing about *how* the composer came by her ideas.

In the case of the composer, there is no claim to *knowledge* by intuition. But when there is, what are we to say about the claim? We don't see how the person was able to know the way out of the desert. She claims to know by intuition. Did she know? We are inclined to say that it's merely a lucky guess. This often happens: a person guesses the answer to a question and happens to get it right; someone else asks, "How did you know?" and he answers, "By intuition." The problem is that often when people claim to know something by intuition, they turn out to be mistaken. The same intuition that leads to the right answer in some cases leads to the wrong answer in other cases. Intuition, whatever it is, is highly fallible. How, then, does it sustain a claim to truth? It's easy to say, after one has guessed right, "I knew by intuition," but what does the same person say when she gets it wrong?

But, as with "feeling," there are times when "I know by intuition" is more than a lucky guess. In the childhood game "hide the thimble," some participants are able to locate the thimble more often or more quickly than the others. "How did you know where it was?" "I knew by intuition." But what they call "intuition" was actually careful observation: they noticed what psychologists call *minimal cues*—they noticed subtle "body language" that others didn't notice, they observed the person who had hidden the thimble to see where he studiously refrained from looking, and so on. What enabled them to be confident was their prior *careful observation* of small details of behavior and body language that most people fail to notice. "Women's intuition" seems to be largely an ability to notice such details that never catch the attention of others.

What shall we say, however, when there are no such minimal cues to go by and the person still turns out to be right time after time? What is it that enables her to be repeatedly correct? We can say, "It's good luck," but can we plausibly continue to say this when she continues to be correct every time?

"No," one may say, "she has *extrasensory perception* (*ESP*). Most of us need to see, touch, and hear things in order to have knowledge of them. But people with ESP have a special ability to acquire knowledge without the use of their senses."

ESP has been hotly defended and widely attacked; those who "get it right" are said to be cheating or to have special access to informants, secret mirrors, hidden cameras, disguised radio beams, and so on—all said to eliminate the possibility of the existence of ESP in favor of the kinds of knowledge that we admittedly already have. Champions of ESP, however, allege that many cases cannot be accounted for by the use of the senses.

The question before us now, however, is not whether ESP exists—that is an empirical question for psychologists to investigate—but what it is *if* it exists. Of what does it consist? If the person "knows" what a certain stranger in Afghanistan, whom she never heard of until someone mentioned his name and age on the telephone just now, is doing at this moment, *how* did she come by this knowledge? What is the process? Is it just "having a vision" or seeing a sentence "in her mind's eye" and writing it down? Lots of people do that, but the difference is (let's assume) that this person is always right; how do we account for that?

One thing seems clear: it won't do merely to use the *words* "it's ESP" or "it's intuition." For no one has given an account of what these alleged abilities consist. Suppose we grant that the person knows because she is always right; but that doesn't answer the question "How—by what means—is she able to be regularly right?" Mouthing the word "intuition" or the phrase "ESP" will not provide an answer to this question, any more than the label "Terrors" that Columbus's mapmakers wrote on certain parts of the map when they didn't know what the territories contained told explorers what those lands were like. The word "intuition" tells us nothing of what the process is supposed to be. We know what perceiving through the senses is; what is lacking is an account of what perceiving without the senses could be.

What should we say if a young girl who hasn't yet gone to high school presented us a list of all the earthquakes in California, great and small, during the next twenty years, including the locations of their epicenters? Suppose that during the next twenty years this youngster turns out to be always exactly right. "You must know a lot more about fault lines and tectonic plates than the rest of us do," we may say. But she has no such knowledge; she barely knows what geology is about. As far as we know this has not happened, but what should we say if it did?

Surely, we would be inclined to say, she knew—there is no better evidence of genuine knowledge than being always right. (Being right once could be a fluke or a stroke of luck, but being right five thousand times with no misses?) What would be worrisome in this case is the question, *How* did she know? By what process was this infallible record achieved? And if we don't know this, skeptics will be inclined to say that the youngster did not really know at all. If we can't say how she knew, we will demand a greater run of successes before admitting that she did know. Still, it is important to keep the questions distinct: one, did she know? and two, *how* did she know? We may sometimes be justified in asserting the first without being able to provide an answer to the second.

EXERCISES

1. Consider "knowing" in animals:
a. Does the dog know who its master is?
b. Does the dog know that it can't climb trees? Does it try and fail? Does the cat know all along that it can, or does it learn by trial and error?
c. Does the cat know where its food is?
d. Does the dog know how to swim? Does it know that it does?
e. Does the rabbit, which eats vegetables but not meat, know that vegetables and not meat are good for it?
f. Does the snake know that it is poisonous, enabling it to be more aggressive with other animals as potential prey? Does the nonpoisonous snake that resembles poisonous ones know that it possesses the same threat value as the poisonous one? (If it doesn't, why does it act as if it does?)
g. Hyenas and other African carnivores attack the does but not the bucks among antelopes. Is this because they know that the bucks have

sharp horns with which they can kill the attacker?

2. Evaluate these knowledge claims:
  a. "You can say what you like. You weren't there. I know what I saw, and what I saw was a spaceship manned by extra-terrestrials."
  b. A skeptic says he doesn't know he has a hand in front of him. But does he know, in spite of what he says?

3. A person who has recently studied geometry is asked, "What is the expansion of *pi* to four decimal places?" He says, "I don't know." A minute later he remembers, and says, "Yes, I do know; it's 3.1416."[4] Did he know the first time, even when he said he didn't? Comment on the following responses:
  a. "If he knows P, he believes that he knows P. And he didn't believe the latter. So he didn't know P at the time of his initial report."
  b. "He knew the correct answer, although he didn't know that the answer was correct."
  c. "He knew it because he had memorized it."

4. A woman is asked on a television quiz program, "In what year did George Washington die?" She says, "1799," the correct answer, and wins a new car. "She knew the answer," we say.
  a. Did she know it if she just happened to guess it right?
  b. Did she know it because she remembered reading it in a history book?
  c. Suppose she had read it in a history book, but wasn't sure she remembered it correctly at the time she gave the answer; did she know it?

5. Can you ever say truly:
  a. "I am dreaming."
  b. "I am asleep."
  c. "I am not breathing."
  d. "I am dead."

6. Do you require anything other than your

present experience, plus knowledge of what the words mean, to know that the following propositions are true?
  a. I have a toothache.
  b. I ate breakfast this morning.
  c. I exist.
  d. I hope it rains tomorrow.
  e. I think it will rain tomorrow.
  f. It will rain tomorrow.

7. Do you consider the following to be occurrent states, dispositional, or both?
  a. He is angry.
  b. She is quick-tempered.
  c. He is religious.
  d. She is boiling over with rage.
  e. He is fat.
  f. She is restless.
  g. The fruit is rotten.
  h. Her face is ashen.
  i. The coffers are empty.
  j. His tastes are expensive.

8. Analyze the meaning of the word "true" or "truth" in each of the following:
  a. She is a true friend.
  b. He is true to his wife.
  c. This character (in a novel) is true to the way people of that kind behave in actual life.
  d. The equator is not a true physical place.
  e. The true way of solving this problem is. . . .
  f. This line is not a true plumb.
  g. The true meaning of "democracy" is. . . .
  h. It's the truth that hurts.
  i. This is certainly a true portrait of her.
  j. You can't draw a true circle.

9. In which of the following cases does the "feeling" guarantee the truth of the statement about what is felt? Give your reasons.
  a. I feel anxious.
  b. I feel sick.
  c. I feel as if I'm about to be sick.
  d. I feel that I am about to be sick.
  e. I feel able to do anything.
  f. I feel as if I have a frog in my throat.
  g. I feel that she has been unjustly treated.
  h. I feel that God exists.

[4]This example is used in Keith Lehrer, *Knowledge* (Oxford: Clarendon Press, 1974), p. 60.

10. Is it true now that the sun will rise tomorrow?

11. In each of the following examples, do you *know* (not merely believe, or even have some reason to believe) that the proposition is true? Defend your answers.
   a. The road continues on the other side of the hill.
   b. If I let go of this piece of chalk, it will fall.
   c. The first floor of this building is not now submerged in water.
   d. The table has a back side and an inside, even though I'm not now perceiving them.
   e. This crow before me is black.
   f. All crows are black.
   g. You have an optic nerve.
   h. You are not now a multimillionaire.
   i. Julius Caesar once lived.
   j. You had breakfast this morning.
   k. The sun will rise tomorrow.
   l. I have blood and bones and vital organs and am not made of straw.
   m. This table won't turn into an elevator and carry us all downstairs.
   n. A dog will never give birth to kittens.
   o. You will not some day be father (or mother) to an orange.
   p. You are not now asleep (or dead).
   q. You did not eat mothballs for dinner yesterday.
   r. This table is the same one that was in this room yesterday.
   s. You were born (not hatched or spontaneously generated).
   t. All human beings are mortal.
   u. The earth is (approximately) spherical.
   v. The earth did not come into existence five minutes ago.
   w. You are not dreaming at this moment.
   x. You are now seeing several colors.
   y. You are younger than your parents.
   z. You are not a nightingale.

12. Which of the above propositions would you claim to know in the strong sense, and why?

13. Evaluate this assertion: "Some propositions must be certain, for if none were certain, none could be probable. Probability is a concept derived from that of certainty. If we didn't know what it was for something to be certain, we would have no standard of reference for estimating probability. We wouldn't even be able to know what the word 'probable' would mean."

14.
   a. In D. H. Lawrence's story "The Rocking Horse Winner," a little boy, every time he rocks frantically on his rocking horse in the evening, is able to predict which horse will win a race the following afternoon. His uncle is skeptical about this until it turns out time after time that the little boy's predictions are always right. Would you say that the little boy *knew* which horse would win the next day's race?
   b. At the beginning of the same story, we are told about the boy's mother, "When her children were present, she always felt the center of her heart go hard. This troubled her, and in her manner she was all the more gentle and anxious for her children, as if she loved them very much. Only she herself knew that at the center of her heart was a hard little place that could not feel love, no, not for anybody. Everybody said of her: 'she is such a good mother. She adores her children.' Only she herself, and her children themselves, knew it was not so. They read it in each other's eyes." Did she *know* this of herself? Did others know it of her?

15. Suppose that a self-proclaimed psychic is able to predict unerringly (with no exceptions) international events that nobody else can, such as the day that a major war breaks out, the day that a new outbreak of Ebola virus occurs in Zaire, the date and hour of every earthquake of 8.0 strength or higher, and the date and strength of hurricanes that even meteorologists are unable to predict. Would you say that she knew that these things were going to happen? Would you say she had an uncanny ability to *guess* right? If so, why would the guess not be knowledge? Would you say, "I don't know how she knew, but she knew"?

SELECTED READINGS

ARMSTRONG, D. M. *Belief, Faith, and Knowledge.* New York: Cambridge University Press, 1973.

AYER, ALFRED J. *Philosophical Papers.* New York: Macmillan, 1963.

AYER, ALFRED J. *The Problem of Knowledge.* New York: Macmillan, 1956.

BLANSHARD, BRAND. *Reason and Analysis.* LaSalle, IL: Open Court, 1963.

COHEN, JONATHAN. *An Essay on Belief and Acceptance.* New York: Oxford, 1992.

FLEW, ANTONY, ed. *Essays in Conceptual Analysis.* London: Macmillan, 1956.

FLEW, ANTONY, ed. *Logic and Language.* 1st and 2nd ser. Oxford: Blackwell, 1950 and 1953.

FOGELIN, ROBERT. *Evidence and Meaning.* London: Routledge, 1967.

HAACK, SUSAN. *Evidence and Enquiry.* Oxford: Blackwell, 1983.

HARTLAND-SWANN, JOHN. *An Analysis of Knowing.* London: Allen & Unwin, 1958.

HUME, DAVID. *An Enquiry Concerning Human Understanding.* 1751. Many editions.

LEHRER, KEITH. *Knowledge.* Oxford: Clarendon Press, 1974.

LOCKE, JOHN. *An Essay Concerning Human Understanding.* Books 2 and 4. 1689. Many editions.

MALCOLM, NORMAN. *Knowledge and Certainty.* Englewood Cliffs, NJ: Prentice Hall, 1963.

MOORE, GEORGE E. *Philosophical Papers.* London: Allen & Unwin, 1959.

MOORE, GEORGE E. *Philosophical Studies.* London: Routledge & Kegan Paul, 1922.

MOORE, GEORGE E. *Some Main Problems of Philosophy.* London: Allen & Unwin, 1952.

PITCHER, GEORGE. *Truth.* Englewood Cliffs, NJ: Prentice Hall, 1964.

PLANTINGA, ALVIN. *Warrant.* New York: Oxford University Press, 1992.

POPPER, KARL. *Objective Knowledge.* New York: Oxford University Press, 1972.

PRICE, H. H. *Thinking and Experience.* London: Hutchinson, 1953.

RUSSELL, BERTRAND. *Human Knowledge: Its Scope and Limits.* New York: Simon & Schuster, 1946.

RUSSELL, BERTRAND. *The Problems of Philosophy.* New York: Oxford University Press, 1912.

UNGER, PETER. *Ignorance.* New York: Oxford University Press, 1979.

WILLIAMS, C.J.F. *Being, Identity, and Truth.* New York: Oxford University Press, 1992.

3 *What Is the World Like?*

PERCEIVING THE WORLD

1. COMMON-SENSE REALISM

If anything seems certain, it is that we acquire knowledge through our senses: sight, hearing, touch, taste, smell. How could anyone deny that we have such knowledge? Even in asking one another about it, don't we assume that we do?

Nevertheless, there are people who have doubted it. They are *skeptics* about knowledge of a world revealed to us by our senses. A person may, of course, be skeptical about many things: a person may be a skeptic about religion, or about ethics, or about unobservable entities such as quarks, but there are not many skeptics about sense-perception. I see the chair, I walk close to it, now I sit on it. How could anyone deny this?

"But I don't know that these things exist. I know that it *seems* to me now as if they do. But perhaps I am mistaken in thinking this. Maybe none of those things I think I see really exist."

René Descartes (1596–1650), who is often seen as the founder of modern philosophy, recorded such a thought in his *Meditations* in 1641: "I have convinced myself," he wrote, "that nothing in the world exists—no sky, no earth, no minds, no bodies." And he added, "So am I not likewise nonexistent?"[1]

Doubts and Deceptions

No, said Descartes. If I doubt any of these things, then at least I, the doubter, must exist. How could there be a doubt without someone to do the doubting? Doubt doesn't just float around somewhere waiting for someone to do it. Thus, if I doubt, at least I, the doubter, exist, at least while I am doubting. I am conscious that I doubt; therefore

> there is consciousness; of this and this only I cannot be deprived. *I* am. *I* exist; that is certain. For how long? For as long as I am experiencing. . . . I know for certain that I am, and that at the same time it is possible that all these images, and in general everything of the nature of body, are mere dreams. . . . What then am I? A conscious being. What is that? A being that doubts, understands, asserts, denies, is willing, is unwilling. . . . Even if I am all the while asleep; even if my creator does all he can to deceive me; how can any of these things be less of a fact than my existence?[2]

So I exist. But I can still doubt that I see, hear, etc., a real world. There is a leap from my existence to the existence of a world outside my mind. In fact, I can suppose that what I take to be real is just an enormous deception. Descartes supposes

---

[1]René Descartes, *Meditation I*, in Descartes, *Selections*, Modern Students Library edition (New York: Scribners, 1927), pp. 94–95.

[2]René Descartes, "On the Passions of the Soul," in Descartes, *Selections*, Modern Students Library edition, pp. 95, 99.

that there is an evil spirit, who is supremely powerful and intelligent, and does his utmost to deceive me. I will suppose that sky, earth, colours, shapes, sounds and all external objects are mere delusive dreams, by means of which he lays snares for my credulity. I will consider myself as having no hands, no eyes, no flesh, no blood, no senses, but just having a false belief that I have all these things.[3]

The demon, let's suppose, has as his sole purpose to deceive me. He plants illusions in my mind to make me think that I am seeing trees, houses, and so on—but actually there aren't any. The demon might even deceive me into thinking I have a body, when I don't. He can't deceive me into believing I exist when I don't, for there must be a "me" to be deceived. But perhaps he deceives me about everything else.

A: It's ridiculous to believe there is such a demon. I believe only what there is some *evidence* for, and there's not the slightest evidence that such a demon exists.

B: But how do you *know* that there isn't one?

A: I can't prove that there isn't—just as I can't prove that Zeus, Poseidon, and the other ancient Greek gods don't exist. But that doesn't give me the slightest reason to believe that they do.

B: In the case of the Greek gods, we know what it would be like for them to exist. Wouldn't we be surprised if they showed up one day at the top of Mount Olympus? But that isn't like the deceiver case. I submit that we don't even know what it would be like for the deceiver to exist; there is nothing we could experience that would count as showing that there is such a deceiver.

A: Granted, we can't see him. But we might have evidence of him through his deceptions.

B: Try to imagine such a deception. The deceiver deceives me into thinking there's a table over there. I approach, I bump into it, and then I sit on it. There really *is* a table there. It was no deception. I know what the conditions are for the table's existence, and those conditions are fulfilled.

A: But don't you see the deceiver is *deceiving* you into believing there's a table there. He planted the sense-impressions in your mind so cleverly that you can't tell the difference.

B: That's just the point: there *is* no difference. What we all *call* seeing and touching a table, Descartes *calls* being deceived into believing there's a table. These are two verbal expressions for the same thing—two labels for the same bottle. There's a difference in the description, but no difference in what is being described. There's no difference in fact, only in words.

A: There's no difference in *discernible* fact, but a difference just the same. The deceiver is so clever that *we* can't discern the difference.

B: And I say there's no difference to discern. When someone says to me, "Maybe there's no table over there," I go there, I see it, I touch it, I sit on it, I photograph it. In everyday discourse we would say that this is the proof that there *is* a table there. And it is. What better proof could there be? A moment later I might see something else, but at that moment I do see and touch a table. I have *not* been deceived into thinking there's a table. There it is—there's no deception.

A: But for all you know the demon hypothesis may be true. You don't *know* that it isn't true.

B: But I do. If something fulfills all the criteria for being an X, then it's an X. If it looks like a duck, walks like a duck, and

---

[3]Ibid., p. 95.

quacks like a duck, it is a duck; that's what we *mean* when we say there's a duck. Give me the slightest bit of contrary evidence—about magic tricks or optical illusions—and I'll have my doubts. But if all the tests for being an X come out positive—*all* the tests, not just the ones we happen to have conducted thus far—well, then, by definition it *is* an X.

A: *As far as we can tell* it's an X. But Descartes's demon may be deceiving us.

B: No. If there is a deception, there must be some way to know whether one has been deceived. Otherwise the word "deception" doesn't distinguish anything from anything else. I am wandering through the desert and see what looks like water; but when I get closer it disappears, and I see it's only a mirage. I have *found out* that I've been deceived. This is an honest-to-goodness garden variety deception, and I unmasked it for what it was. What you are doing is taking *everything*—seeing and touching the table *and* seeing the mirage in the desert—and calling them all a deception. That's as if we took all animals together and called them all dogs.

A: But Descartes's deceiver is deceiving him through all his senses at once. He is so clever that his deception can't be detected. His deception always comes off without a hitch. Suppose the deceiver writes in his diary: "Today I deceived Descartes into believing that he is seeing and touching real physical things." And the next day he writes the same thing: "Still managed to fool Descartes." Every day his deception is perfect. Descartes is always fooled into thinking that he sees physical things, and every day the deceiver is triumphant.

B: A chair that you see and touch and sit on is a real chair. That's how we use the phrase "a real chair" and distinguish it from "only apparent" chairs.

A: As the deceiver got better at deceiving, he found that he could deceive so cleverly that nobody ever discovered what he was up to. And that's what he actually achieved.

B: The demon wanted to fool me. But he didn't succeed. I may have been deceived about the oasis, but not about the table. If I see and touch and sit on the table, it's not a delusion. The deceiver has outfoxed himself. Do you really think the demon could deceive me into only *thinking* that I'm eating food when all the while I'm not? Could he deceive me about that *all the time*? But if I never really eat food, how could I stay alive?

A: The demon deceived you into thinking you have a body. Even believing that you have a body is a deception.

B: I don't have a body? Here are my hands, here is my torso, which I see as I sit here. Can I doubt that?

A: Of course. As long as the deceiver is deceiving you, he can make you believe falsely that you have a body. As Descartes said, the one thing you can't doubt is that you, a conscious being, exist, else there would be no one to be deceived. In fact, the demon may have achieved still more: maybe the whole series of your experiences is a *dream*.

Dreams

A: In fact, maybe there isn't a physical world out there at all. You're dreaming the whole thing. You think you are awake, yet you're dreaming it all.

B: No. The word "dream" has meaning only when it is *contrasted* with something else, namely the experiences of waking life. We make the distinction constantly in our daily lives. "I only dreamt that." We have no trouble making this distinction.

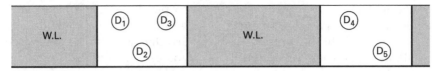

W.L. = waking-life experiences.
D_1, D_2, etc. = dream experiences.

There are moments when I may not know whether I dreamt something, especially when the dream has been vivid. I dreamt that my sister had died, but I awaken and there she is, walking about the house.

A: Perhaps *that* is what you dreamt.

B: For a moment I might consider that; but I look again and there she is, and I talk with her, and it's the same house, the same furniture, everything that is *coherent* with the experiences I had before I went to sleep. By contrast, the dream experience is fleeting, insubstantial, even though it was very vivid. I find myself in bed, the same bed I went to sleep in earlier, the same furniture and windows I've seen a thousand times, and I remember going to bed, getting drowsy, turning off the light. And so I conclude that my experience of witnessing my sister's death was a dream.

A: But how can you be sure that it was the sister's death that was a dream? Maybe that was the reality and your present experience is the dream; perhaps you were dreaming that you were in your bedroom just awakening. How can you tell which is which?

B: It isn't any lack of vividness that tells me; dreams, especially nightmares, can be vivid and powerful. But they don't last. The dream experiences are the *islands of experience* that *don't fit in* with the rest of my experiences. I eat lunch, go to class, return home, read, watch television, and go to bed. Then I have numerous strange experiences, which we call dreams, in which I am living far away or long ago, in which the law of gravity doesn't operate, and so on. I may have several of these dream experiences during the night, and they don't cohere with *each other* any more than they cohere with the experiences of waking life. Yes, dreams are experiences, but they are *anchorless*. They are vivid but fleeting and insubstantial. They lack the massiveness and the tremendous degree of internal coherence that waking-life experiences possess. That's why we call them waking-life experiences rather than dreams. The dream experiences are the ones that *don't fit in* with the rest. (See figure.)

A: I know how we make the distinction between waking experiences and dream experiences. I am just suggesting to you the possibility that *both* of these types of experiences are really dreams. The whole thing—everything. Maybe it's all *one big dream* that we're in all the time. How do you know that this isn't so?

B: Your suggestion sounds very profound, but you're being taken in by a simple verbal maneuver. Suppose someone were to tell me that there's only one color, blue. Then what about red, green, yellow, and so on? "Oh," she says, "these are all shades of blue; there's red-blue, green-blue, and then there's blue-blue. All are shades of blue." Now what have you achieved by this change of verbal usage? Nothing, except confusion. The colors are just what they were before, only you've labeled them differently. Nothing has changed except the words.

Well, that's what you've done in the dream case. We use the term "waking experiences" to refer to the vast mass of internally coherent experiences we have most of the time; then we use the term "dream" to refer to those islands of experience that don't fit in with the main mass. You want to use the word "dream" to label them all. Surely that isn't because they're all alike, because they aren't!

A: But they're all experiences.

B: Yes, and you use the word "dream experiences" to label *all* experiences. That's just verbal contrariness. It achieves nothing, it changes nothing. Look: if the word "dream" is so precious to you, I'll give you the word. Let's say then that *all* experiences are dreams. But in that one big dream that we're in all the time, there is still a distinction to be made: between what we ordinarily *call* dreams (the islands of experience) and the huge mass of experiences we call those of waking life, in which laws of nature operate and the world doesn't shift about chaotically from moment to moment like an ever-changing phantasm.

Besides, we can *explain* the dreams we have by means of waking-life experiences we've had, often dating back into childhood. But the dreams do not explain why we have the waking-life experiences we do, such as washing the dishes and going to class. Dreams exist only in the dreamer's mind, and other people don't have your dreams—they have *their own* dreams. It is the waking-life experiences that are fundamental. We can do without the dream experiences if we have to, but it is the waking-life experiences that re-

veal to us the existence and nature of the world around us.

Illusions and Hallucinations

There is no evil demon. And not every experience is a dream. But we are not yet finished with "errors of the senses." Don't we often make mistakes of perception, seeing things that aren't there, or seeing things that are there but as having qualities that they don't really have? And how can we know we are not constantly making these mistakes?

Ordinarily we perceive, or believe we perceive, material things (physical objects). They are part of the physical world. The physical world is a public world, one that can be perceived by anyone who has functioning eyes, ears, and so on. I can touch the table, and so can you; it's not private to you or me, like our dreams. There are items in the physical world other than material things: items such as electric charges, magnetic and electrical fields, and gravitational fields. But for the moment let's consider material things, or what is called "matter." What is a material thing? What is it we perceive, or believe we perceive, when we perceive a material thing?

1. We believe that material things exist even when they are not perceived. The tree doesn't cease to exist when you turn away from it or blink your eyes or go to sleep. It exists *independently of perception.*

2. Material things are accessible to more than one of the senses. You can see the tree, but you can also touch it. Some objects can also be smelled and tasted and heard: I can hear the bell as well as see and touch it. In some cases it is impossible in practice to touch the thing—such as the moon and the rocks a mile below where you are standing; but we believe that *if* we were in close proximity to touch it, we could do so.

3. Material things also have certain *causal powers*. The boulder that rolls down the hill causes objects in its path to move. The sun cannot be touched (we would burn to death before we got close enough), but it emits heat and light and has gravitational effects on the surrounding bodies.

These beliefs are universal among humankind: people live and die but the earth continues to exist, whether or not any organism is around to perceive it. This belief is called *perceptual realism.*

But we also believe that we sometimes don't perceive them as they really are. We sometimes make mistaken judgments about their qualities (illusions), and we sometimes have perceptions when there is no material thing there at all (hallucinations).

Illusions. An illusion occurs when we believe an object has certain qualities when it doesn't, or believe it doesn't when it does. The green trees on the faraway mountainside look grayish blue in the haze of distance. The dark blue dress looks black under artificial (yellowish) light. This building appears to be taller than that one, but that's only because it isn't as far away. The round coin looks elliptical from a 45-degree angle and flat from a 90-degree angle. When we enter the hallway of a restaurant, we "see" lots of people there, but it's only a mirror image: there are people only on this side of the glass.

Usually we are not taken in by these appearances; we have learned about the laws of optics, and we correct for them. We don't really believe that the taller-appearing building really is taller, because we take into consideration that it's closer to us. The appearance is *illusory,* but as long as we don't conclude that it really is taller, we are under no *delusion* about it. A delusion is simply a false belief. If we knew nothing about the different ways things look because of distance and the an-

gle of vision and so on, the illusory appearance might lead to a delusion.

Sometimes it does: we think we see a person in the distance when it is only a cleverly painted statue. It is not the senses themselves that delude us: the senses just *present* to us these various appearances. If we are taken in (deluded) by them, that is a mistake of *judgment* on our part. We draw a check on reality, which reality fails to honor. The straight stick looks bent in water, and if I say that it *is* bent, I am being deluded by the appearance.

Sometimes the illusion doesn't depend on external conditions of perception but on our own internal condition. A person takes LSD and the colors of objects seem different: they have a changing variety of colors and often appear phosphorescent at the edges, but when the drug wears off, the colors return to normal. Other drugs make everything look yellow for a while. If you put on green glasses, the white wall looks green (although this could be called an external condition, because the glasses aren't inside you).

Hallucinations. If you are hit on the head you may see red spots before your eyes, although there are no red spots out there. A person may feel pain in a limb that has been amputated. A man recovering from alcoholism sees pink rats going up and down the wall. Macbeth, intent upon murder, hallucinates, saying, "Is this a dagger which I see before me?" If you are expecting someone to knock at the door, you may "hear" knocks on the door throughout the evening, although no one is there—the false belief is induced by your expectation. If you are hypnotized into believing that there is a vase on the table, you may see one there even though the table top is quite empty.

Sometimes what we call the perception (hallucination or illusion) depends on how we choose to classify it. In the twilight in the forest you think you see a man, but it is only a tree stump that presents a peculiar appearance amidst the bending branches and the shifting shadows. You could call this a hallucination, because you think you see a man and no man is there; or you could say it's an illusion, because you see the tree as having qualities that it doesn't have. Or you light a candle in the darkness, and when you press your finger against your eye, you see two candles. Of course there aren't two candles. Is this a hallucination, because one of the two candles isn't there? Or is it an illusion, because you're seeing one candle as having a quality (being two) that it doesn't have? Can twoness be a quality of *one* candle?

Why do we say that certain perceptions are illusory or hallucinatory and that others are correct, or as we say, *veridical*? Why not say that the stick in water is really bent and only appears straight when it is out of water? Why do we say that the dress is blue although it looks black in artificial light, rather than that it's black all the time and only looks blue in sunlight?

Is it because we usually or normally see the stick as straight and the dress as blue? No; if the stick were immersed in water most of the time, we would still say it's straight, and if we usually see the dress as black (as people do whose waking hours are usually spent at night), we would still say it was really blue. There are certain *standard conditions* that we use to describe a thing's qualities, and we say it has those qualities that it appears to have under these standard conditions.

These standard conditions are not always the same. The straight stick *feels* straight to the touch even when it is immersed in water; and its bent appearance is an example of certain laws of optics. The coin that looks elliptical from most angles still feels round to the touch, and again the elliptical appearances illustrate well-known laws of optics. If we can't see the invisible glass used in some de-partment stores and try to touch the diamonds on the other side of it, we find that we can't because we bump against the glass even though we can't see it.

The round appearance of the coin is the center of a *distortion series* from which the other appearances deviate: the further we get from a perpendicular, the more elongated the shape appears to be.

In the case of color, we use sunlight as the standard condition because with it we can make more *color discriminations* than we can in artificial light. We can distinguish many shades in sunlight that we cannot distinguish in other lights—just as color-blind people can't distinguish certain colors (typically they can't distinguish red from green) that the rest of us see. In general, we take as standard those conditions that afford the *maximum predictability* of future experiences.

Microscopes and Telescopes

To our unaided vision, a piece of cloth looks smooth and uniform in color, but under a microscope it shows many details that the unaided eye does not. Since we can distinguish more such qualities under a microscope, we say, "If you want to see what it's really like, look through the microscope."

Ordinarily we say that blood is red, because it looks red in standard conditions of vision. But when we look at a drop of blood through a microscope, what we see is mostly transparent with a few flecks of red in it. Shall we say then that blood isn't really red and only looks red to our unaided vision? This would surely be more accurate than saying it's all red. We can distinguish many more colors and textures under a microscope than we can without it. At the same time, ordinary eyesight is the standard people have used for thousands of years, and we continue to think and talk in that way. We might say, "To ordinary vision it *is* red—and we would expect it to *look* red under those conditions; but a microscope will reveal more of its real qualities." The chair I am sitting on seems to be quite smooth, and we would not mislead people if we said it is smooth, since that's the way it feels to people who touch it. Yet a microscope reveals a considerable degree of roughness that is not apparent to our sense of touch. We can say, then, "It is actually quite rough, but if you touch it, you won't feel that roughness."

Microscopes reveal properties of objects that are too small to be perceived without them. Similarly, telescopes reveal properties of objects that are too distant to be seen in any detail without them. Is there a problem here?

A: When I look at the North Star (Polaris), I see only a tiny speck of light in the night sky.

B: That's right.

A: But actually what I see is a huge star many times larger than the sun, hundreds of thousands of miles in diameter, a huge ball of incandescent gas.

B: Yes. So?

A: But how can what I see be *both* a point of light *and* a huge incandescent ball of hot gas?

B: No problem. If I were asked to describe what I see, I would say it's just a point of light. But that point of light I see is not what the star is really like: it really has very different properties from what it appears to have. In fact, the star—which we see only as a point of light—may have ceased to exist many years ago. The light you see tonight started on its way from the star about 450 years ago, traveling at 186,000 miles per second. The star might have exploded 450 years ago, and yet the light emanating from it is still traveling toward us. We see the star as it *was then.*

In all vision, as well as hearing, there is a time lapse. Even when you look just at the tree outside your window, it took some time for the light to reach you— only a tiny fraction of a second. The case of the star is no different; it just took longer because of its enormous distance.

A: But surely what I see must be something that exists *now*. The point of light that I see in the sky exists at this moment, not 450 years ago.

B: The light exists now, although its original source may no longer exist. This is a startling fact to most people, but there's no more puzzle in it than the fact that the distant thunderclap may no longer exist at the moment you hear it. It's still the real star that you see; it's not like "seeing stars through a coat sleeve" in the old parlor game, or seeing stars after you've been hit on the head. It's still the star you see, no matter how different it may look from this enormous distance or how long it took the light to reach you. We have every evidence—not only through telescopes but spectroscopes and observation of its gravitational effects—that the star is real and has the properties that astronomers say it has. It is a familiar fact that things don't always appear to be the way they are.

Atoms and Electrons

If we discover more of "how it really is" by looking through microscopes and telescopes, what about things that are too minute for microscopes and telescopes to discover? The table, we believe, is composed of molecules, which are in turn composed of atoms and electrons, and beyond these, quarks and leptons and who knows what else—and these we shall never observe through instruments. These particles, if this is what they are, belong to scientific *theory:* these entities are the result of *inference,* not of observation. Reality at this level of minuteness is hidden from us by the limitations of our senses.

An early Greek philosopher, Democritus (c. 460–370 B.C.) set forth a primitive but remarkably prescient theory about the ultimate constituents of matter. His follower Lucretius (95–55 B.C.) made his view famous in his long poem *De rerum natura (On the Nature of Things).* The universe, said these ancient atomists, consists of very minute particles moving in empty space. These particles Democritus called atoms (from the Greek *atomoi,* or "unsplittable"). Atoms have different masses, sizes, and shapes, but they do not have color or smell or taste: these qualities enter the scene only when there are perceivers with eyes, noses, and palates.

A similar view, set in the context of modern science, was advanced by John Locke (1632–1704). Material things, said Locke, have *primary* qualities, which exist even if there are no perceivers. But there are also *secondary* qualities, which have no existence without perceivers. Vinegar has a certain chemical composition that doesn't depend on perceivers, but its pungent smell exists only when there are perceivers.

Are secondary qualities then "subjective," like dreams? No, said Locke, they exist as *powers.* The color of an object is the power to produce a certain kind of sensation in perceivers. This power resides in what Locke called the "insensible parts of objects" (that is, the parts too small to be perceived). It is these powers, residing in the atomic structure of things, that cause objects to have the appearances they do. The power is in the object, but the red and the blue we see exist only as sense-impressions.

Take a grain of wheat, divide it into two parts, each part has still solidity, extension, figure, and mobility; divide it again, and it retains still the same qualities, and so divide it on, till the parts become insensible; they must retain still each of them all those qualities. For division (which is all that a mill, or pestle, or any other body, does upon another, in reducing it to insensible parts) can never take away either solidity, extension, figure, or mobility from any body, but only makes two or more distinct separate masses of matter, of what which was but one before; all which distinct masses, reckoned as so many distinct bodies, after division, make a certain number. These I call *original* or *primary qualities* of body, which I think we may observe to produce simple ideas in us, viz. solidity, extension, figure, motion or rest, and number.

Secondly, such qualities which in truth are nothing in the object themselves but powers to produce various sensations in us by their primary qualities, i.e. by the bulk, figure, texture, and motion of their insensible parts, as colors, sounds, tastes, etc. . . . These I call *secondary* qualities.[4]

What then of secondary qualities—do they exist only in the mind? If we all agree that the tree is green, isn't the greenness a property of the tree, like its height and weight? No, says Locke, the greenness is not in the tree, but the physical *basis* of the greenness is. Locke advanced the corpuscular theory of light; today we would talk about light waves, whose varying lengths cause us to see the various colors. One wavelength causes us to see red, another orange, and so on. It is no accident, then, that we all agree that the tree is green, for the tree has certain properties that cause us to see it as green.

The particular bulk, number, figure, and motion of the parts of fire or snow are really in them—whether anyone's senses perceive them or not; and therefore they may be called *real*

---

[4]John Locke, An *Essay Concerning Human Understanding* (1689), Sections 9 and 10.

qualities, because they really exist in those bodies. But light, heat, whiteness, or coldness, are no more real in them than sickness or pain is in manna. Take away the sensation of them; let not the eyes see light or colours, nor the ears hear sounds; let the palate not taste, nor the nose smell, and all colours, tastes, odours, and sounds, as they are such particular ideas, vanish and cease, and are reduced to their causes, i.e. bulk, figure, and motion of parts.[5]

But now a problem emerges, which Bishop George Berkeley (1685–1753) used to attack Locke. What we can know in sense-experience, said Berkeley, is merely the contents of our own sensations. The mind, according to Berkeley, has knowledge only of its own contents, or ideas. (We use the word "idea" more narrowly today, as when we say, "I've just had a bright idea." Locke and Berkeley, however, used the word in a broader sense, to include any content of consciousness, such as sensations, images, and thoughts.) If our knowledge is only of our sensations (visual, auditory, tactile, and so on), then how can we know that there even *exists* a physical world outside us that produces in us these sensations? How did Locke know that the primary qualities belong to things apart from our senses, whereas secondary qualities do not? Can we compare our sensations with the objects out there to discover whether the sensations resemble, or in some way correspond to, the objects?

2. BERKELEY'S IDEALISM

No objects independent of the mind exist, said Berkeley, and we could not know them even if they did. There is no independently existing matter; what exists is *minds* and their *ideas* (sensations, feelings, thoughts, etc.). These are all we know, and these are all

that exists. (The word "idealist," used to describe Berkeley's view, does not come from the word "ideal" but the word "idea," in the eighteenth-century sense just described; all reality is mental, and consists of minds and their ideas.) "That's all there is; there ain't no more." There are not trees *and* tree-impressions; there are only tree-impressions, impressions in our mind that we call trees.

The first response Berkeley's view creates is simply that of indignant disbelief: "What! No trees and mountains out there? He must be mad!" Samuel Johnson (1709–1784), when asked how he would refute Berkeley's view, kicked his foot against a stone and said, "I refute it thus!"

But Johnson's refutation was no refutation at all. Berkeley didn't believe all our experiences were hallucinations. He didn't deny that a certain visual experience is followed by a certain touch experience (which is all that Johnson had when he kicked the stone). He didn't deny that there was a stone, or a tree, or a chair. He only denied the existence of anything outside the realm of our sense-impressions.

Berkeley did indeed believe that there are chairs, but *not* that our chair experiences "represent" anything existing outside us and independently of us. He believed, rather, that "chair" and all other physical-object words are names for *recurring patterns,* or complexes, *of sense-experiences,* and nothing else. Berkeley would say, "If by 'physical objects' you mean anything *other* than our sense-experiences, I insist that they do not exist, nor could we know that they existed even if they did. But if by 'physical objects' you mean groups or complexes of sense-experiences, then they undoubtedly *do* exist—indeed, we are aware of them every waking moment of our lives, since we are constantly having sense-experiences that fall into ordered patterns or groups."

---

[5]Ibid., Section 15–17.

What exactly is meant by saying that a chair, or any other physical object, is a pattern, or complex, of sense-experiences? This is somewhat difficult to convey in a few words; let us first take an example. Consider a table, which we believe to have a rectangular top. Now as I look at this table top (ordinarily speaking), I find that my experience has the following characteristics:

1. The appearance of the tabletop varies in systematic ways. If I move away from it, it appears to get smaller, and when I approach it it appears to become larger again. When I view it from above, it looks rectangular, but if I look at it from any other angle, it looks more like a trapezoid with the acute angles on the nearer side. The apparent shape and size vary systematically with the angle of vision.

2. As I stand still, it continues to look the same; but when I move, the apparent shape changes, and when I get back to my former position, it looks as it did before. After I have had a little experience of the way the apparent shape changes, I can predict how it will look after my next change of position: the whole series of sense-experiences is systematic and predictable.

3. As I move, the visual sense-experiences from moment to moment resemble one another: shape A shades into shape B, B into C, C into D, etc., although A may not greatly resemble D. Apparent shape 1 may not resemble apparent shape 50, but the two are connected by a series of apparent shapes, each of which closely resembles the one on each side of it. Again, the change is gradual and regular.

4. There is no discontinuity in the series. As I look, or walk while looking, there is no moment at which I do not have the sense-experience (unless I turn my head or blink). The shape does not jump out of my field of vision and then pop back into it again somewhere else.

5. The series of apparent shapes has a center from which the others deviate in a progressive *distortion series*. (Referring back to our earlier example: the round apparent shape of the penny is the center around which all the elliptical ones congregate.)

6. My visual experiences act as *signs* of my tactual ones: if I go up to what I believe (on the basis of my visual sense-experiences) to be the table, I have tactual sense-experiences. My visual experiences are lightly correlated with tactual ones. Occasionally they are not, to be sure: if I don't know I am looking in a mirror I may approach what I believe to be the table, only to bump into the mirror—there will be no tactual sense-experience corresponding to the visual one. The tactual experience will be of the mirror, not of the table; there is no table beyond the mirror.

In short, the table-top sense-experiences form an *orderly series*. The entire series of shapes constitutes, as it were, a *family*: they all "belong together" in a different way from the way the series of shapes we see looking at a coin do—these constitute another, and very different, family. A physical object is nothing more or less than a *family of sense-experiences*. When we have hallucinations, on the other hand, we have sense-experiences that don't belong to a family: they are "*wild*" (unattached). The pink rats the man sees in a state of intoxication are "wild," for they belong to no family.

It is a fortunate fact about the universe that the vast majority of our sense-experiences belong to families, thus making them, on Berkeley's analysis, real things—what we would call 'physical objects." We could easily imagine a state-of-affairs in which this would not be so. Imagine for a moment that all our sense-experiences occurred hit-or-miss, with visual sense-data hopping all about our visual field, changing shapes and sizes in chaotic and unpredictable ways, each visual sense-experience discontinuous with the next one, coming and going and changing character every moment, visual sense-experiences not being followed by tactual ones, and tactual ones occurring unpredictably without visual ones having occurred to warn us. You could easily imagine most or even all of your sense-data being "wild," and in this case there would be no such things as trees and tables since there would be no such things as families of sense-experiences. One might say that there would be at least one family present, your own body. But that could also be otherwise: you might have the chaotic series of sense-experiences without even having any of the sense-experiences you now attribute to your own body. But fortunately, our experiences are not like this. Most of our sense-experiences belong to families.

The criterion we actually use in determining whether something is a hallucination, says Berkeley, is to observe whether the sense-experience in question belongs to a family. In doing this, we relate our sense-experiences *to one another*. We do not do what Lockean realism would seem to require: relate our sense-experiences to a reality outside our sense-experience to see whether they correspond. According to Locke, if we have a table experience and there's no table, it's a hallucination; and if there is a table, it's not a hallucination (it is then *veridical*—a "true" perception). But we could never *apply* such a correspondence test, for we could never get outside our sense-experiences to discover whether there is something outside them to correspond to them. We never in fact even attempt to apply such a test. We compare our sense-experiences with one another, not with something else that isn't sense-experience.

It is true, of course, that in hallucination "there is no table there"; but this means, according to Berkeley, only that in hallucination there is no family of table experiences. It takes only a little time to discover whether or not the experience we are having is wild. The distinction between veridical perception and hallucination is always to be found in the relation of sense-experiences *to one another*—specifically, in whether they belong to a family. Those that don't belong to a family we call hallucinations.

Much misinterpretation of Berkeley has occurred on this point. Some have alleged that according to Berkeley everything is imaginary. But there is plenty of difference between a real table and an imaginary table. I can't sit on an imaginary table, or place books on it, nor will it hold my weight if I try to step on it; the sense-experiences don't cohere as a family. Samuel Johnson refuted nothing when he kicked a stone and exclaimed, "I refute it thus!" because Berkeley, of course, did not deny the existence of the stone. He would have said merely that a stone is a family of sense-experiences (not at all a hallucination), and that kicking the stone only confirmed his point: Visual stone experiences are followed by tactual stone experiences, just as they could be expected to do in any well-ordered family of sense-experiences.

And as for dream experiences, they are also "wild" in relation to the well-ordered series of sense-experiences that constitute what we call waking life. These are also "outside the family." All these perceptual distinctions that we make—illusions, hallucinations, dreams— are made by relating and comparing sense-experiences *to one another*, not by comparing sense-experiences with some unknown something to which our sense-experiences "correspond." The test for veridicality is *coherence* among sense-experiences, not correspondence with something that is *not* sense-experience.

Esse Est Percipi

We must now consider another aspect of idealism. According to idealism, physical objects are families of sense-experiences. But obviously experiences do not exist unexperienced. Physical objects, then, do not exist unexperienced either.

This last assertion certainly conflicts sharply with our common-sense beliefs. We believe that physical objects continue to exist whether they are experienced or not. Idealism is committed to denying this. According to idealism, for all physical objects, *esse est percipi* (to be is to be perceived). Idealism says about physical objects the same thing that common sense says about experiences of all kinds: that they do not and cannot exist unexperienced; and if they cannot do so singly, combinations of them (by which idealism defines physical objects) cannot do so either. Pains and pleasures do not exist unexperienced: for them to exist *is* for them to be experienced. The same applies to trees and tables. There can be no reality apart from experience, says idealism. Tables, trees, and other physical objects are families of experiences.

But, you might say, surely the table doesn't cease to exist when I go out of the room! No, not if someone else stays in the room and continues to perceive it. It exists as that person's experiences. But suppose everyone leaves the room; does the table then cease to exist? Yes, if no one is having table experiences. If we think no one is in the room, and we leave for fifteen minutes and then go back, we may find our friend Jones saying, "It existed all the time; I was looking through a peephole in the wall, and I can assure you that I had table experiences while you were gone exactly as I did when you were here." No idealist would deny this.

But suppose that *no* one is in the room—no person, no organism of any kind that could have table experiences. Does the table exist during that period? No; *esse est percipi*, and there is no *esse* because there is no *percipi*.

"Well, what difference does it make?" one might ask. "As long as the table is always

there when we get back, what do we care? The question whether it exists during intervals between perceptions can make no difference whatever to our actual experiences." The idealist, of course, would not deny this. Still, whether it is a practical question or not, it would be interesting to know what the answer is, and how it can be known to be true.

"Physical objects do exist during interperceptual intervals, and I can easily prove it," one might suggest. "Bring a motion-picture camera into the room, set it going, and then have everyone leave. Come back a few minutes later, develop the film, and project it on the screen. We will then all witness the exciting drama of table-continuing-to-exist-during-our-absence."

The idealist would not be convinced by any such experiment. The motion-picture camera is itself a physical object, and is also, according to idealism, a family of sense-experiences that also ceases to exist when not experienced. The camera, the table, and indeed the room itself and the building it is a part of are all in the same boat; *esse est percipi* applies equally to all of them.

Moreover, our account of the entire series of events is all given in terms of experiences: we have table experiences, then table-and-camera experiences, then other-room experiences, then table-and-camera experiences again, and later table-projected-on-a-screen experiences. No one, certainly not the idealist, doubts that we have this sequence of experiences. And that is *all there is*—just this sequence of experiences. Nothing apart from the series of experiences exists, and we wouldn't know it even if it did.

Our frustration at this point may be similar to that of the boy who was told by his brother that the street light went out whenever his eyes were shut. He watched the street light intently, studiously shut his eyes, then furtively opened them again for a moment; the street lamp was shining as usual. The little boy said: "But you told me it went out!" "Yes," said his brother, "when your eyes are shut; but when you peeked, they were open." How could the boy ever prove otherwise? Is idealism, as one eighteenth-century critic remarked, "utterly absurd, and utterly irrefutable"?

Let's try this argument: "We have to believe that physical objects exist unperceived in order to account for what we see when we perceive them again." You light a fire in the fireplace, watch it burn for a time, then leave the room for half an hour. When you return, nothing is left in the fireplace but a pile of glowing embers. Surely the fire must have burned down even though no one was perceiving it; how else can you explain the fact that there were burning logs on the fire when you left and only embers when you returned? The wood must have burned while you were gone, and in order to burn, it must have existed while you were gone.

Or, many times you have seen a house and also its shadow; this time you see the shadow but are not yet in a position to see the house. But surely the house must be existing at this moment even though neither you nor anyone else is perceiving it, else what would be casting the shadow?

In these examples we are appealing to well-established laws of nature about the behavior of fire and shadows. But, the idealist reminds us, we have known these laws to hold true only for cases we could observe; we have no justification for extending them to unobserved cases. For example, one might say: "Every time I have observed X I have observed Y; therefore it is probable that this time when I observe X, I shall observe Y." But this says nothing whatever about what happens when I do *not* observe X. No observation can possibly tell me what exists when nobody observes it. Even if physical objects continue to exist when no one perceives them, how can we have any reason to believe that they do, since no one can observe them existing unobserved?

Weak versus Strong Idealism

It is misleading, however, to say that "even if physical objects do continue to exist unobserved," for this assumes something that Berkeley would never grant, namely that it is possible, or even conceivable, for physical objects to exist unobserved. According to Berkeley, it's not that physical objects *might* exist unobserved but that we can't know it even if they did (weak idealism). Rather, to speak of physical objects existing unobserved is a *contradiction in terms* (strong idealism)— or as Berkeley called it, a "manifest repugnancy," like a square circle. Remember that physical objects are *nothing but* families of sense-experience. We don't believe that sense-experiences can exist unexperienced— we all admit that that's a contradiction in terms—and since physical objects are only complexes of sense-experiences, the physical objects too can't exist unobserved. The reasoning goes like this:

1 We do have knowledge of physical objects (trees, mountains, buildings, etc.).
2 Our knowledge is limited to our experiences. Therefore,
3 Physical objects are experiences (families of experiences).
4 But experiences can't exist unexperienced, so physical objects can't exist unexperienced either.

The idealist says that if we find this conclusion surprising it's because we have really never digested the initial premise, that physical objects *are* families of sense-experiences. We are surprised by the conclusion only because we still have lurking in the back of our minds the idea of tables and trees as inhabiting a world of things that are independent of minds—that is, of tables and trees as *not* being families of sense-experiences. Once we really grasp this, we shall no longer bring up any question of their existing unperceived, any more than we do now in the case of pains or pleasures, thoughts or ideas.

Causation of Sense-Experiences

But don't our sense-experiences have a *cause?* Ordinarily we say that our experience of the tree is caused by the tree itself, existing independently of our perception. This avenue is not open to Berkeley, who said that the tree simply *is* the complex of sense-experiences. But what then causes us to have the sense-experiences that we do?

Berkeley *might* have said, "Since physical objects are families of sense-experiences, when we say that A causes B, we are saying that A is regularly followed by B *in our experience.* We cannot use the idea of cause, so useful *in* our experience, to go *beyond* experience, where in any case we would have no knowledge of it." (We shall discuss the nature of cause in Chapter 5.)

But, good bishop that he was, Berkeley did not say this. He said that all our sense-experiences are caused directly by God. The reason the sense-experiences occur in an orderly way—barring hallucinations and so on—is that God gives us our sense-experiences, and he does so in an orderly way so that we can make predictions on the basis of them and thus guide our actions accordingly. God *could* have made our experiences so chaotic that there were no families-of-sense experiences at all, and hence no regularities of experience that we could call physical objects. But God, being good, has chosen instead to give us orderly sets of sense-experiences. He plants these in our minds directly: he does not need the intermediary of the realist's physical objects. (Since we could not know the existence of these physical objects anyway, they wouldn't do us any good even if they did exist.)

Reality thus consists of *minds* and *their experiences.* God is an infinite mind, and you and I finite minds. There are minds (God's and ours) and their experiences (God's and ours). Experiences are events in the history of minds. That is all there is—there is no more. God causes us to have our experiences in the order that we have them. There is no need for anything else.

Why is it that when we both look in the same direction we have similar sense-experiences? Because God feeds us similar sense-experiences in similar contexts, so that we may communicate with one another. If you saw a tree where I saw an elephant, and the next moment you saw in that place a sofa and I a bushel of apples, we would not be able to communicate. But by correlating the series of your experiences with mine, God makes prediction and communication possible. God works in an orderly manner—so orderly, indeed, that God not only enables different minds to communicate but also regulates the course of various persons' sense-experiences, so that we can notice regularities within the total series. Thus is science made possible. The laws of nature are the will of God manifested in the orderly series of sense-experiences that we have.

Berkeley's theory has been aptly commented on in the following limerick:

> There was a young man who said "God
> Must think it exceedingly odd
> If he finds that this tree
> Continues to be
> When there's no one about in the Quad."

Reply

> Dear Sir: Your astonishment's odd.
> *I* am always about in the Quad.
> And that's why the tree
> Will continue to be
> Since observed by
>
> Yours faithfully,
> God.[6]

---

[6]By an Oxford scholar, Ronald Knox, a critic of Berkeley.

Criticisms

1. Many readers who have followed Berkeley up to this point may throw up their hands at his introduction of God into the scene. First, Berkeley began by saying that the mind is acquainted only with its own ideas [experiences]. If this is true, how can we know that there is a God who causes the experiences, since God is not himself one of the experiences? If we do know this, then we know something other than sense-experiences after all. And if we *can* know something other than sense-experiences, namely God, why can't we just as well bring in a world of independently existing physical objects as the causes of our experiences? Hasn't Berkeley, in bringing in God as cause-of-experience, betrayed his own basic premise, that we can have knowledge only of our own experiences?

2. Berkeley said that we can have knowledge only of our minds and their ideas; but what of *other people's minds?* I can have knowledge of my own experiences; one family of experiences is the desk, another the tree out there, still another your body and clothing. I cannot have your experiences; I can only observe your body, its movements, facial expressions, and so on. My knowledge of you is limited to these sense-experiences of mine. Similarly, your knowledge of me is limited to those sense-experiences of yours that constitute my body.

This is surely a very strange situation. To you, I can be nothing more than certain sense-experiences of yours; and to me, you can be nothing more than certain sense-experiences of mine. But *I* know that I am more than certain sense-experiences of yours, and presumably you know that you are more than certain sense-experiences of mine. Aren't we *both* minds who have sense-experiences? But how can either of us know this? If all I can know is that I (a mind) exist, together with the experiences of that mind, then, since my knowledge is limited to my experiences, shouldn't I believe that my mind and its experiences are *all that exist?* In other words, shouldn't I be a *solipsist?* Solipsism (myself-alone-ism) is the belief that all that exists is my mind and its experiences. I have no knowledge of, and therefore no reason for believing in, the existence of minds other than my own. So I assert that mine is the only one.

Almost no one in the history of thought has been a solipsist. We all believe that there are other persons, with minds like ours, who think and feel and have sense-experiences as we do. A person would be in a curious position who said, "I am so convinced of solipsism that I believe everyone ought to be a solipsist!" If a solipsist writes books to advance her views, to whom is she addressing them, since she believes there are no minds other than her own to read and understand them? Besides all this, solipsism breaks down into as many views as there are persons: if Jones is a solipsist, he believes that only Jones exists; but if Smith is a solipsist, she believes that only Smith exists—which is a very different view, and in fact conflicts with the first one. It can't be true both that Jones is the only person existing *and* that Smith is the only person existing.

Berkeley was not a solipsist; but how did he avoid being one? Isn't solipsism the view that his own premises would drive him to? No, Berkeley said, "*esse est percipi*" applies only to physical objects, not to minds. For minds the motto is *esse est percipere* (to be is to perceive, rather than to *be* perceived). But how could Berkeley know this? If human minds have no windows to observe anything but the course of their own sense-experiences, it would appear that Berkeley's mind must have had at least a door, else how could he know, on his own premises, that other minds than his exist?

3. According to Berkeley, the statement that physical objects exist unexperienced is

self-contradictory, because physical objects are families of sense-experiences and sense-experiences can't exist unexperienced. One's first reaction to this definition—"Physical objects just *are* (families of) sense-experiences"—is that such a definition is absurd. "You can define terms as you wish," we may say; "I can define 'circle' as an eighteen-sided polygon," and thus the statement "Circles have no corners" will be self-contradictory by that definition. But why in the world should one accept such a definition?

Berkeley, of course, argued that there *is* a good reason for accepting that definition: that if you do not, you are left with complete skepticism about the existence of physical objects. Try, he says, to imagine something as existing apart from a mind:

> But, say you, surely there is nothing easier than to imagine trees, for instance, in a park, or books existing in a closet, and nobody by to perceive them. I answer you may so, there is no difficulty in it; but what is all this, I beseech you, more than framing in your mind certain ideas which you call books and trees, and at the same time omitting to frame the idea of anyone that may perceive them? But do not you yourself perceive or think of them all the while? This therefore is nothing to the purpose; it only shows you have the power of imagining or forming ideas in your mind; but it does not show that you can conceive it possible the objects of your thought may exist without the mind. To make out this, it is necessary that you conceive them existing unconceived or unthought of, which is a manifest repugnancy.[7]

The statement "Physical objects cannot be thought of as existing apart from a thinking mind" is ambiguous, however. If you mean "Physical objects cannot be thought-of-as-existing apart from a thinking mind," this is doubtless true. You cannot think of them or

anything else as existing without first having a mind to think with. But this should not be confused with a very different statement containing the same words, "Physical objects cannot be thought of as existing-apart-from-a-thinking-mind," which is not trivial at all, and in fact is false; we do think of them in this way all the time. I cannot think without a mind, but I can think of something as *existing* without a mind. Thought cannot exist without minds, but this doesn't prove that tables and trees cannot exist without minds. Whether they do exist or not—and perhaps we can't know whether they do or not—at least we *think* of them as existing without minds. Doesn't the realist think of them thus—even if, as Berkeley said, the realist is wrong?

And the same with perception as with thought: you can't perceive without a mind any more than think without a mind, but it doesn't follow that *what* you perceive can't exist without a mind. Maybe it doesn't, of course, but at least we can't prove that it doesn't by Berkeley's argument. *Perceiving* can't occur without a mind, but *that which you perceive* can—at least it is logically possible. Whether there is some positive way of defining "physical object" other than as a family of sense-experiences remains to be seen. But if the logical barrier is removed, we may go further.

4. If we think—correctly or incorrectly—of physical objects existing apart from a mind, then perhaps we should take another look at weak idealism, which says that perhaps objects may exist apart from minds, but that we have no reason to believe that they do because we can't observe them existing unobserved. But now let us ask whether even this is true. In daily life we do not hesitate to believe that physical objects exist unobserved. If I leave the tub running in the bathroom and come back later and find that it is full of water, I assume that water flowed into the tub during my absence—how else, I be-

---

[7]George Berkeley, *Principles of Human Knowledge* (1710), Paragraph 23.

lieve, could I explain how the water got there? And so on. The idealist (weaker version) argued, however, that there is no way of proving this: I cannot perceive it unperceived, and no argument will enable me to conclude anything about the unobserved when all the data we have to go on are about the observed. Thus the view that physical objects exist unobserved, even if not self-contradictory, is one for which there is absolutely no evidence.

But is this true? *Is* there no evidence? If I am alone in the room, and I shut my eyes for a moment, must I say that there was no table during the moment I shut my eyes? If the table is covered completely by a cloth, so that I see the cloth but not the table, must I say that the cloth exists but not the table?

According to Berkeley, the series of my sense-experiences are just what they would be *if* the tub and the water had existed during my absence, but of course they didn't, because there were no tub experiences during that time (except for God's—God held the fort and kept the tub existing by perceiving it even if no other perceiver was there). But why go this circuitous route if we can say the tub and water and table *did* actually exist during my absence?

Well, we can *say* it, but what *evidence* can we adduce? We can't perceive it existing unperceived, and we can't deduce its existence when it is unperceived from its existence when it is perceived.

In ordinary life we claim knowledge, not only from *observation* but from *inference*. We see bear-tracks in the mud, and we infer that a bear was there even though we didn't see one. We wake up and find the yard is wet, and we infer that it rained during the night while we were asleep. Why can't we say, similarly, that the existence of physical objects unobserved is an inference? We didn't *see* the bathtub fill up during those few minutes we were gone, but we *infer* that it did, and isn't

our inference justified? Saying that the tub did exist during those minutes, and that water continued to enter it during that time, is the *best explanation* we have of why the tub was full when we returned. How else would we account for it?

The same with the existence of other minds. I ask you, "What would it take for me to persuade you to go to Mazatlan for four days during the next fortnight?" and you think for a moment (or furrow your brows and at least give the appearance of thinking) and then answer, "Since I have other important plans for next week, I wouldn't do it for less than ten thousand dollars." Surely the best explanation of the fact that you respond thus to my question is that you are (or have) a mind and that you think, deliberate, choose, and give reasons for your choices, just as I do. How else would I explain the occurrence of the sentences I hear in the English language coming from your lips?

It seems that Berkeley will accept only *direct* evidence: seeing or touching a tree is direct evidence, the evidence of our senses. But what's wrong with *indirect* evidence, one may ask, such as seeing only a tree's shadow? We don't observe the table under the cloth (although we could if we lifted the cloth), but we infer that it is still there; how else would the cloth stay up there? If we see the cat sleeping under the table, but our view of the cat is partially obscured by the table leg, aren't we entitled to say that the whole cat is there, not just the part we are seeing? We *infer* from the part that we see that the whole cat is there, and isn't that a justified inference too? We use indirect evidence every day, almost every moment, of our waking lives. What is so bad about it, that we can't accept it?

Berkeley said that what's wrong with indirect evidence is that our knowledge is limited to our own sense-experiences, and we have no sense-experiences of part of the cat. And that is after all Berkeley's fundamental premise: our knowledge is limited to our experiences. That fundamental premise is something we have yet to come to grips with. The views we have yet to consider have different ways of handling such a premise. We shall now consider such a view: the theory called *phenomenalism.*

3. PHENOMENALISM

Of all the features of idealism, the one that is most likely to elicit scorn and disbelief is *esse est percipi*—"to be is to be perceived." That the physical world exists unperceived is not only one of our most deeply held beliefs, it is one that we feel completely justified in believing—not because we perceive it existing unperceived, which would be a contradiction in terms, but because it shows absolutely no signs of depending for its existence on anyone's perceiving it. The bathtub fills with water whether we are there or not; the house is still there even if we have left it for years; people die and the stars and the earth continue as before, and we have every reason to believe that they will continue when you and I are no longer here.

At the same time, it seems plausible to say—as Locke and Berkeley both held—that we are acquainted only with our own ideas. Whatever exists out there, we can know only through our experiences; and isn't the content of these experiences all we can really know?

The theory called *phenomenalism* attempts to incorporate both of these elements. It doesn't say "to be is to be perceived," but only "to be is to be perceiv*able*." The table exists when I see it, but it also exists when I don't see it—it's in the next room—because when I do go to the next room, there it is.

The sense-experiences of the table are *available* to me any time I want to place myself in the right perceptual circumstances (looking around the corner or going to the next room). If the tree has been cut down and burned, then it no longer exists and I can no longer perceive it; but if it is still out there, and I'm just at the other side of the building, if I doubt that the tree still exists I can walk to the other side of the building and see it for myself. Matter, said John Stuart Mill, is the *permanent possibility of sensation.*

But if I say that a physical object exists, I must be able to *put this assertion to the test:* if it is not being perceived, I must be able to specify the conditions under which it *would* be perceived. If I say there's a watch in my desk drawer, and I open the desk drawer and it's empty, then I have to admit that my statement was false. Not all perceptual claims, of course, are as easy to check as this one, in which I only have to open the desk drawer. If I say there are certain flora and fauna at the bottom of the sea, I must be able to produce evidence, such as from underwater photographs. One can also talk about what went on during the long geologic ages before there were any human or other perceivers; here it is *not* possible for us to go back to that time and perceive it, but we must rely on *indirect* evidence, for example, the fossil record; we must have reason to say, "If I had been there at the time (which I wasn't), I *would* have perceived . . . ," and back it up with reasons. Isn't this what geologists do all the time? They look in the present for traces of the past, which they were not here to see; but they provide reasons for believing that the past was as they describe—that is, what they *would* have perceived *if* they had been there at the time. The statement "Dinosaurs lived on the earth 70 million years ago" doesn't mean that perceivers saw them, but that they *would* have perceived them if they had been there at the right place and time. It is the *possibility* of perceiving them, not the actual occurrence of it, which phenomenalists assert when they say that such-and-such really happened at a remote time in the past.

Sense-Data

Much of the controversy in perception theory during the past century has to do with exactly *what* it is that we see, hear, and so on. You might say, "We see trees, tables, and so on." Very well, but what exactly is it that we are aware *of* in perception—what is it that we are *immediately* (nonmediately) aware of, without any element of inference? Locke and Berkeley said "ideas," used in a very broad sense of the word; Hume said "impressions"; Mill said "sensations." But all these terms are confusing. Even the word "sensation" does not tell us whether it is *what we sense* or *our sensing of it* that is meant. You might say that you have a sensation but not that you *see* a sensation. What then is it that you see? You *have* certain visual sensations, but *what* you see is not these sensations but a certain pattern of colors and shapes (which you may then *take* to be a tree). Even if you are having a hallucination you are still experiencing a pattern of colors and shapes. What you see, regardless of whether you are hallucinating or perceiving veridically, has been called *sense-data* by many twentieth-century philosophers.

The contemporary philosopher G. E. Moore (1873–1958) wrote, in a famous passage:

I hold up this envelope: I look at it, and I hope you all will look at it. And now I put it down again. Now what has happened? We should certainly say (if you have looked at it) that we all *saw* that envelope, that we all saw *it, the same* envelope: I saw it, and you all saw it. We all saw *the same* object. And by the *it,* which we all saw,

we mean an object, which, at any one of the moments when we were looking at it, occupied just *one* of the many places that constitute the whole of space. . . .

But now, what happened to each of us, when we saw that envelope? I will begin by describing *part* of what happened to me. I saw a patch of a particular whitish color, having a certain size, and a certain shape, a shape with rather sharp angles or corners and bounded by fairly straight lines. These things: this patch of a whitish color, and its size and shape I did actually see. And I propose to call these things, the color and size and shape, *sense-data,* things *given* or presented by the senses—given, in this case, by my sense of sight. Many philosophers have called these things which I call sense-data, *sensations.* They would say, for instance, that that particular patch of color was a sensation. But it seems to me that the term "sensation" is liable to be misleading. We should certainly say that I *had* a sensation, when I saw that color. But when we say that I *had* a sensation, what we mean is, I think, that I had the experience which consisted in my *seeing* the color. That is to say, what we mean by a "sensation" in this phrase, is my *seeing* of the color, not the color which I say: this color does not seem to be what I mean to say that I *had,* when I say I *had* a sensation of color. It is very unnatural to say that I *had* the color, that I *had* that particular whitish grey or that I *had* the patch which was of that color. What I certainly did *have* is the experience which consisted in my seeing the color and the patch. And when, therefore, we talk of *having* sensations, I think what we mean by "sensations" is the experiences which consist in apprehending certain sense-data, *not* these sense-data themselves. I think, then, that the term "sensation" is liable to be misleading, because it may be used in two different senses, which it is very important to distinguish from one another. It may be used either for the color which I saw or for the experience which consisted in my seeing it. . . .

Part, at least, of what happened to me, I can now express by saying that I saw certain sense-data: I saw a whitish patch of color, of a particular size and shape. And I have no doubt whatever that this is part, at least, of what happened to all of you. You also saw certain sense-data; and I expect also that the sense-data which you saw were more or less similar to those which I saw. You also saw a patch of color which might be described as whitish, of a size not very different from the size of the patch which I saw, and of a shape similar at least in this, that it had rather sharp corners and was bounded by fairly straight lines. But now, what I want to emphasize is this. Though we all did (as we should say) see *the same* envelope, no two of us, in all probability, saw exactly the *same sense-data*. Each of us, in all probability, saw, to begin with, a slightly different shade of color. All these colors may have been whitish; but each was probably at least slightly different from the rest, according to the way in which the light fell upon the paper, relatively to the different positions you are sitting in; and again according to differences in the strength of your eye-sight, or your distance from the paper. And so too, with regard to the size of the patch of color which you saw: differences in the strength of your eyes and in your distance from the envelope probably made slight differences in the size of the patch of color, which you saw. And so again with regard to the shape. Those of you on that side of the room will have seen a rhomboidal figure, while those in front of me will have seen a figure more nearly rectangular. . . .

Now all this seems to me to show very clearly, that, *if* we *did* all see the same envelope, the envelope which we saw was not *identical with* the sense-data which we saw: the envelope cannot be exactly the same thing as each of the sets of sense-data, which we each of us saw; for these were in all probability each of them slightly different from all the rest, and they cannot, therefore, *all* be exactly the same thing as the envelope.[8]

You and I are both seeing an envelope; but what appears in our vision is somewhat different. You are looking at the envelope from a slightly different angle, or I am further away from it than you so what I see is somewhat smaller; so although we are both seeing the same envelope, we are experiencing somewhat different sense-data. If I change my position, or angle, or the light

changes, I myself see sense-data somewhat different from those I sensed a moment ago. I can't *describe* them in words other than saying that I see the envelope rather differently than I did before; nevertheless, *what* I see—the sense-data, not the envelope—is somewhat different from what it was a moment ago.

That I am sensing certain sense-data, phenomenalists would say, I cannot doubt; these are indubitable. But that I am perceiving a real physical object, that I *can* doubt. For example, I can sense reddish, roundish sense-data without there being a tomato in front of me:

> When I see a tomato there is much that I can doubt. I can doubt whether it is a tomato that I am seeing, and not a cleverly painted piece of wax. I can doubt whether there is any material thing there at all. Perhaps what I took for a tomato was really a reflection; perhaps I am even the victim of some hallucination. One thing however I cannot doubt: that there exists a red patch of a round and somewhat bulgy shape, standing out from a background of other color-patches, and having a certain visual depth, and that this whole field of color is directly present to my consciousness. What the red patch is, whether a substance, or a state of a substance, or an event, whether it is physical or psychical or neither, are questions that we may doubt about. Whether the something persists even for a moment before and after it is present to my consciousness, whether other minds can be conscious of it as well as I, may be doubted. But that it now *exists*, and that *I* am conscious of it—by me at least who am conscious of it this cannot possibly be doubted. And when I say that it is "directly" present to my consciousness, I mean that my consciousness of it is not reached by inference, nor by any other intellectual process.[9]

Physical objects, by contrast, are reached by inference—inference from sense-data.

---

[8]George E. Moore, *Some Main Problems of Philosophy* (London: Allen & Unwin, 1952), pp. 30–33.

[9]H. H. Price, *Perception* (London: Methuen, 1933), p. 3.

Why in the world, we might object, should our knowledge of material things be called inferences? Am I not as directly and noninferentially aware of the tomato as I am of anything? We don't say to ourselves, "I am directly aware of such-and-such sense-data, therefore I infer that there's a tomato there." Psychologically it is not an inference, but logically it is: it is on the basis of experiencing certain sense-data that we are entitled to make claims about physical objects. The basis is certain, the inference is not; that we are having certain experiences we cannot doubt, but that there's a physical object there we surely can.

If you sense the reddish, roundish bulge you cannot be mistaken: your report is one of direct (unfiltered, unmediated) experience. Even if the experience abruptly ceases, you are simply reporting your sensory experience of that moment. But when we say there is a real table over there, we are making an implicit *prediction*—it won't suddenly disappear from sight unless we turn our heads or close our eyes; it won't suddenly change into a cabbage or an elephant. Further sense-experiences may make us change our minds about whether it's a real table over there (was it a clever optical illusion?), but not about whether we had the sense-experiences at that moment that we (perhaps falsely) attributed to a physical thing.

Sense-data, according to phenomenalism, constitute the very foundations of empirical knowledge. If someone asks you, "What evidence have you that you are seeing a tree?," you might say, "Because I am having sense-experiences of such-and-such a description." But if you were asked, "What evidence have you that you are now having such-and-such sense-experiences?," what could you say, except possibly, "I just have them, that's all"? Haven't we here reached the bottom of the epistemological ladder? Doesn't everything

above it on the ladder of knowledge depend on this one?

4. THE ATTACK ON FOUNDATIONS

Many philosophers, however, have questioned that sense-data can be a foundation for empirical knowledge, and even that there is anything at all that should be called a "foundation."

1. *Noticing.* Material things often do not have the qualities they appear to have. But the language of sense-data was designed to tell us how things appear, not how they are. Whatever qualities things appear to have, those are the qualities the sense-data do have: it wouldn't even make sense to ask whether sense-data have qualities they don't appear to have. If the green forest looks bluish-gray in the distance, the sense-data we experience when we see the forest from a distance *are* bluish-gray.

Suppose now that you pass through a rose garden and don't notice the color of most of the roses. You didn't pay particular attention to any of them, and all you remember seeing is some bright splotches of color. Well, if sense-data are what we are aware of, and you weren't aware of any particular colors, don't we have to say that the sense-data *had* no determinate color? But how can this be? You *could* have examined the color of each one, but you just didn't notice. "Didn't you notice that black rose?" "No, I just noticed that it was dark." How would you now describe your sense-data—dark but not dark blue, dark red, or any particular dark? Can this be?

We run into a similar problem with numbers. The hen has a certain number of speckles on its feathers, but you didn't notice how many—you didn't stop to count them. How many speckles did it *appear* to have? Well, lots of them, an indeterminate number; I can't say how many. But can there be many apparent speckles without there being a definite number of them? Can there be "numerosity without number"? Not of material things. Perhaps of sense-data?

Let's say you are listening to Leoš Janáček's music for the first time. How does it sound to you? At first, it sounds like one huge, cacophonous confusion. After a few hearings you notice (and remember) some tones and fragments of melody, and after a while those same sounds (let's assume it's the same recording each time) take on a whole new structure; what you now hear is a revelation to you, and you can't imagine its ever having seemed a mass of auditory confusion. The sounds that reached your ears were the same—but what characteristics did the auditory sense-data have? Can we describe them?

You are having your eyes examined by an optometrist. Some of the letters on the chart look blurred to you. "Is this an E or an F?" you are asked. The optometrist knows very well what the letter *is*—it's been on his wall for years. He wants to know how it *appears* to you. And you don't know: does it look to you more a blurry E or a blurry F? You can't say. In this case you do try to notice very carefully, but you still can't be sure, not of what the letter *is,* but of how it *appears* to you.

You might say, "I know how it appears, but I don't know how to *describe* how it appears." But this raises a fundamental philosophical issue about experiences in relation to the language we use to describe them.

2. *Sense-experiences and certainty.* "Statements about the physical world are subject to error; things may not be as they appear. But statements about your own sense-experiences are certain." It is the search for certainty that chiefly motivates phenomenalism. But perhaps such certainty can't be achieved. Perhaps we were chasing the rainbow all along.

Can your report of your immediate experiences be mistaken? Of course it can: (1)

you may be lying to others about what you experience; or (2) you may mean one thing and say another—you may "get the wrong words out." Most importantly, however, (3) you may *misdescribe* what you experience. And you may misdescribe anything, even the immediate experiences of which you are so certain.

If you look steadily at a green square on the white wall and then close your eyes, you may have a reddish afterimage in the shape of a square. Suppose someone says to you afterward, "Are you sure it was red? Couldn't it possibly have been magenta?" You may pause, think a moment, and say, "You're right; the afterimage was magenta." Here of course there's no question of being mistaken about the color of a physical object, for there was no object. But sense-data can be misdescribed as well as anything else.

"But that may be an error of memory; you don't remember now quite what it looked like then." Perhaps. But what if it's an experience occurring now? You are dizzy and see red spots before your eyes. Can't you misdescribe them by calling them red? Since you're seeing them now, there's no error of memory—but still, can't there be an error of misdescription? (Don't say, "The spots *look* red to me, but perhaps they aren't really." The difference between being and appearing applies to physical things, not to the way they appear. *Appearances* can't appear to be one way and yet *be* another.)

When you call the spot "red," even if you are describing only your present momentary experience and not red objects, you are *going beyond* the experience of the moment when you describe it. The word "red" doesn't describe only this present experience of yours but countless others as well—your experiences and those of others. Using this word connects what you are experiencing now with what you *have* experienced in the past. In calling it red you are saying that this experience is *similar to* other experiences you have had before, similar enough for the same word ("red") to be applicable to it. And in saying this, *may* you not be mistaken?

Descriptive terms are not proper names. Proper names don't describe, they *refer to* one individual (person or thing) only: "That's Franklin Roosevelt." But descriptive terms are used for many things, each connected by a relation of similarity. To *describe* it is to say *what it is like,* and what this color experience is like is numerous other color experiences. And in saying this—in the very use of a descriptive term—you are always *going beyond* the data of the moment. Sure, you sense what you sense—this is a tautology; but that what you sense is correctly described as red, this is "putting yourself out on a limb"— it's lumping this experience together with other ones and saying that this is *enough like those* to merit the same label. And in saying that, *might* you not, at least sometimes, be mistaken?

Any report of immediate experience, then, involves the possibility of being mistaken, just as reports of the features of a physical object may be mistaken—less of a possibility in the case of sense-data because you're not going as far out on the limb, but you're on the limb just the same, by the very fact of using general words to describe a specific experience.

Indeed, there may be no one class of statements (as sense-data statements are supposed by phenomenalists to be) that constitute the foundation of empirical knowledge. We say things like this: "I noticed that my cat was sitting on the porch, but I didn't notice her color. However, my cat is black, and I assume that she *looked* black to me, because I would have noticed it if she had looked to be any other color." In this case it is the statement about how things *look* that is inferred from a statement about how things are. If you were driving along a turnpike but don't

remember what color the vegetation appeared to be, I may say, "It must have looked grayish, because they always plant ice plant along the turnpike, and ice plant is grayish whereas the other vegetation isn't." *All* statements, even about how something appears to us, at a given moment, is subject to correction in the light of subsequent experience.

The Given

What is directly present (or "presented") to our senses, prior to any interpretation or classification, has been called "the given." We can change what we see by turning our heads or closing our eyes, but once our eyes are open we cannot, in general, help what we see. But in order to report in words what we see, we have to *classify* it under some heading—red, round, sweet, etc. And once we do this, we bring in all the possibilities of misinterpretation that we have just discussed.

Moreover, we classify the data before us in different ways, depending on our cultural background and our interests. A primitive tribesman seeing Western artifacts for the first time would not classify this curious-looking object as an automobile; he would not even have such a concept. It's not that he is color-blind or that his senses are different from ours, but that he would interpret the data of his senses in a different way. Similarly, a baby would not conceive of this object in my pocket as a pen, something to write with, but perhaps as something smooth and shiny and good to bite. Even something as seemingly clear and obvious as the color spectrum has been "carved up" in different ways in different cultures. Clarence I. Lewis wrote:

> There are in our cognitive experience, two elements, the immediate data such as those of sense, which are presented or given to the mind, and a form, construction, or interpretation, which represents the activity of thought. . . . If

there be no datum given to the mind, then knowledge must be altogether contentless and arbitrary; there would be nothing which it must be true to. And if there is no interpretation which the mind imposes, then thought is rendered superfluous, and the possibility of error becomes inexplicable.[10]

Isn't the given then certain, indubitable? Prior to interpretation and classification, isn't it certain? One might be tempted to say yes, here at last we have certainty—until we remember that what is certain or uncertain is assertions, statements, *propositions*. Propositions involve concepts, and concepts involve classification, and these in turn involve the possibility of error. Just "staring at the given," if we could do so without interpreting it at all, is not knowledge: it is only *acquaintance*. We can call it "knowledge by acquaintance" if we prefer, but it doesn't provide us with knowledge *that* anything is or is not true. A claim to know something always involves the possibility that the claim is mistaken.

The Attack on Sense-Data

Here is a sheet of white paper. You put on green glasses, and I put on red glasses, and what you see is green, and what I see is red.

But no: what we see *is* white and only *looks* green or red. There is just one *existent* in the affair, and that is a piece of white paper; the rest is only the way the piece of white paper *looks* to you or me. There is no red or green existent involved. So says the "theory of appearing."

The coin is round, but from various angles it looks elliptical. Sense-data theorists say that what I am immediately aware of is an elliptical sense-datum. But why not just say that we all see a round coin that presents an elliptical appearance from some angles? Isn't that what common sense says?

> *Objects themselves* appear to us in sense-perception. . . . When I see a circular penny as elliptical I am seeing the circular surface of the penny, not some elliptical substitute. This circular surface, it is true, appears elliptical to me, but that fact has no tendency to show that I am not directly aware of the circular surface.[11]

This is a theory of *direct realism:* I am aware of physical objects directly, and require no intermediary such as sense-data "between" me and the object. The object and myself— that is enough. To be sure, the way we perceive objects depends on the *conditions of observation:* things look smaller as we move away from them, the coin looks elliptical from an angle, the sheet of paper looks green when seen through green glasses. But it is still the physical thing that we see. How things appear to us depends also on the *nature of the organism*. Objects don't appear colored (only black and white) to most animals. Blind people don't see at all, and deaf people can't hear. Everything looks yellow when you take certain drugs. And so on. But it is still the physical things themselves that we see, however different they may look to you or me.

Consider this argument:

1 I see the coin.
2 The coin is round.
3 The coin appears elliptical to me. Therefore,
4 I see an elliptical sense-datum.

A: That argument is fallacious. The coin appears elliptical; that's no reason to say that there's something there that *is* elliptical. There's nothing in the situation

---

[10]Clarence I. Lewis, *Mind and the World Order* (New York: Scribners, 1929), p. 38.

[11]Winston H. F. Barnes, "The Myth of Sense-Data," *Proceedings of the Aristotelian Society*, vol. 45 (1944–1945), p. 112.

that is elliptical; there's only a round coin that appears elliptical to me from this angle.

B: But there *is* something elliptical in my visual field; here it is; I am aware of it. How could I see something elliptical unless there were an elliptical something to be seen?

A: No, there are only physical things and their *ways of appearing.* A way of appearing is not itself an existent. Ways of appearing vary, of course; would you expect something to look just as large when it's twice as far away? Would you expect the tree to look vivid green even in twilight or in the dark? When I see a red balloon, I won't see the red if there's a fog, but it's still a red balloon that I see, even if I don't even know that it's a balloon I'm seeing—just as the animal I'm watching in the zoo is a gnu even though I don't know what a gnu is or how to recognize one.

B: If I see double, am I seeing two candles? Isn't there one candle and two sense-data? Which of the apparent two candles is the real one?

A: There's just one candle that looks like two.

B: What about hallucinations? What happens when there is no coin at all but you still see one? What is it that appears now?

A: Strictly speaking, there are no such things as appearances. If Mr. X put in an appearance, was there something over and above Mr. X that he was kind enough to put in?

B: No, there's nothing over and above Mr. X, but there is something over and above a single coin, namely a double appearance; and when there is no coin at all there is an appearance but no coin; there is nothing there to do the appearing. Yet we do see something, and that's why we introduce sense-data.

A: Perhaps we can settle for this: In the *metaphysical* order, the order of *being* (of how reality is), the physical universe exists quite independently of us: it was there before we were, and will doubtless continue long after we are gone. We human beings are only an incidental episode in the vast drama of ongoing reality, which might well have arisen and continued to exist without us.

B: I would then remind you that in the *epistemological* order, the order of *knowing* (which is what we epistemologists study), it is we, the observers of (and participants in) this drama, who come first. It is only the existence of living beings with sensory and cognitive powers that makes the conception and knowledge of this vast drama, as you call it, possible. And it is only because our sense-experiences conform to certain patterns that we have the idea of a physical order that exists independently of these experiences. David Hume called this orderliness in our experiences "constancy" and "coherence".

First, *constancy.* When I look at the table, unless I move, my sense-experiences of it are pretty much the same from moment to moment, and things in motion move in regular and fairly predictable ways. The sense-data don't jump about erratically, changing shape and color from moment to moment or darting from here to there.

Second, *coherence.* My experiences of sight are usually "backed up" by those of touch. Your experiences are also correlated with mine and those of other perceivers: you can see what I see. If I say, "There's a table over there," you don't say, "There's nothing there" or "There's a crocodile there." If these features of constancy and coherence did not occur, and sense-experiences followed one another in total chaos in a constantly shifting phantasmagoria, we wouldn't even have the *concept* of an enduring physical order.

A: Very well. Sense-experiences provide *access* to physical things; but they are not the things *to which* we have access. The concept of a physical order is that of a vast interlocking network of objects that on the whole behave in a fairly uniform way, which we describe as laws of nature.

A vast array of books on perceiving have been published in recent decades. It would require many pages even to summarize their contents. It has already taken us many pages just to get the show on the road. Instead, we turn now from problems about perceiving the world to a different set of problems about the world that is perceived.

EXERCISES

1. If I look at the tree, I see a tree. If I see it through a mirror, am I seeing the *tree* or an *image* of it? If that's an image, how about seeing it through a pane of glass? What about seeing a part of it through an electron microscope, or through a telescope when it is five miles away, or in an x-ray, or on a computer screen?

2. Is it possible that I might be, not an illusion produced by a Cartesian evil demon, but a brain in a vat? Is it possible that I might look out of any window and see *nothing*—no shapes, no colors, no black or white, just nothing?

3. Consider hallucination and illusion:

a. We look at a motion picture. What's on the screen appears to be moving, but in fact it's a series of still pictures, succeeding each other so rapidly that we have the illusion of motion when we look at them. Shall we call this an illusion, because there are still pictures that we misperceive, or a hallucination, because we see motion when there isn't any?

b. How would you classify the following experiences (under LSD)? "The wall began to be covered with an incredibly beautiful series of patterns—embossed, drawn, painted, but *continuously changing*. More color. Indescribable color. And all the colors, all the patterns, were *in the wall* in any case—only we don't usually see them, for we haven't eyes to.... Looking at my bright blue pyjamas on the bed eight feet away, I saw that the blue was *edged with flame:* a narrow flickering, shifting nimbus, incredibly beautiful, which filled me with delight to watch. Clear flame: golden scarlet. Then I understood that this flame was *music*, that I was *seeing sound*."[12] "The faces of people around me were slightly distorted as if drawn by a cartoonist, often with the emphasis on some small, humorous, but nevertheless rather characteristic feature."[13]

4. Assess Berkeley's view that "the real object is the touch-object." Can you think of any exceptions to this? (Note: Humans have not yet touched any of the planets besides the earth. Why, nevertheless, do we consider them to be real physical objects? What about flashes of lightning, or rainbows, or stars?)

5. If we had no visual or tactual sense-experiences but only experiences of hearing and smell, would we have been able to form the concept of a physical object? If you had never seen or touched a bell but only heard the ringing, would you be able to say, "The sound comes from a bell" or even "The sound comes from a physical object"?

6. What are the criteria in making the following distinctions?

[12]R. H. Ward, "A Drug-Taker's Notes," quoted in Sir Russell Brain, *The Nature of Experience* (Oxford: Oxford University Press, 1959), pp. 12–13.
[13]W. Mayer-Gross, "Experimental Psychoses and Other Mental Abnormalities Produced by Drugs," *British Medical Journal*, vol. 2 (1951), p. 317.

a. We say that the trees on the distant mountain-top are really green, although they look purplish-gray in the distance.
b. We say that a certain area in a pointillist painting looks green but really is dots of blue and yellow side by side.
c. We say that the curtains are blue, although they don't look blue when seen through red spectacles.[14]
d. We say that the whistle of the railway engine has a constant pitch, although if you are moving away from the engine the pitch appears to be falling and if you are approaching it the pitch appears to be rising.[15]
e. We say the orange really has a certain taste quality, although we have one kind of taste experience if we eat it without anything preceding, another if we eat it after eating a lemon, and still another if we eat it after eating a lump of sugar.[16]
f. Could the afterimage I had have really been red, although it appeared yellow to me at the time?

7. We approach an object that appeared to have one uniform color, say green, and on closer approach find that it consists of small blue and yellow squares. This closer view is more differentiated—has more specific detail—and so we consider it the preferable view. But what if I see double? I see two things and you see only one. Is that not more differentiated? Or when I "look through uneven glass, is not my view more differentiated than usual? . . . I see a kinked object of complex shape when you see only a homogeneous straight-sided one. Then ought not my view to be called the better one of the two? But of course everyone holds that it is the worse."[17] Explain why this is.

8. State as precisely as you can:
a. How we know whether a certain sense-experience is hallucinatory.

b. How we know when a certain sense-experience is illusory.
c. How we know when we are dreaming (or have been dreaming).
d. How we know that all of our experience isn't one big long dream.

9. I am the only perceiver about, and I see only the top half of a building. But the bottom half must be there even if I don't see it: How could it continue to stand there without the bottom half existing to support it? Would Berkeley have a reply?

10. What would you say to someone who declared that she was a solipsist? Do you think that solipsism can be disproved?

11. Set forth arguments either defending or attacking each of the following views:
a. "Weak" idealism: Even if physical objects do exist when no one is observing them, we can have no reason to believe that they do, for no one can observe them existing unobserved.
b. "Strong" idealism: The proposition that physical objects exist unobserved is not only without supporting evidence; there *could* be no evidence for (or for that matter against) it, for it is *self-contradictory*.

12. Would the following help in determining which is dream and which is waking life?
a. Just before experiencing the series T_2 I remember going to bed, becoming drowsy, and trying to sleep; so T_2 must have been a dream.
b. As Freud has shown, a person's dream experiences are a good basis for inferring what his waking-life experiences (especially conflicts) are; but his waking-life experiences provide no basis for inference about his dreams. So we can tell which is which by discovering from which group inference is the more successful.
c. All the people in a given locality have very similar waking-life experiences (seeing the same buildings, etc.), but the dreams of each person will be wildly discrepant with those of every other person. I can distinguish the wak-

---

[14]Price, *Perception,* pp. 210–213.
[15]Ibid., p. 214.
[16]Ibid., pp. 214–215.
[17]Ibid., p. 224. Price suggests an answer on pp. 224–225.

ing-life experiences from the dream-experiences by checking with other people to see if they had experiences similar to mine.

13. "Nobody knows what physical objects are like really; we only know how they *appear* to us, not how they really *are*, what qualities they really have." Comment.

14. "Provided one is not making a verbal error or lying, sense-data statements are certain." "But no pure sense-data statements can be made." Evaluate both of these assertions. Do they have any bearing on the acceptability of phenomenalism?

15. Explain the meaning of the assertion that every physical-object proposition is an implicit prediction. Prediction of what? Is the series of predictions involved in "That's a table over there" infinite or finite? Justify your answer.

16. Is belief in Berkeley's God just as satisfactory an explanation of the order of our sense-experience as is the belief in enduring physical objects? Defend your opinion.

17. Here are six suggested ways of distinguishing primary from secondary qualities. Try each of them in turn. Is there a distinction in each case, and when there is, does shape become primary and color secondary (that is, does the distinction into "primary" and "secondary" yield the Lockean position)?

a. Primary qualities are present in the world even when they are not being perceived; secondary qualities are not.
b. Primary qualities are perceived by more than one sense; secondary are not.
c. Primary qualities have not the variability of secondary qualities: for example, color may change, while shape remains constant.
d. Primary qualities are those left in the object after we break it down physically. (Descartes said that if we melt wax it loses its solidity and shape—both of which Locke called primary qualities—but never loses its extension, and accordingly he considered extension the only "primary" quality of matter. But does the wax lose shape or only a particular shape?)
e. Primary qualities are those left after we remove as many properties from things by abstraction as we can and still have objects. (Something without color or smell would still be an object, but not without shape or size.)
f. Primary qualities are qualities of the "insensible parts" of objects. They are the qualities the individual molecules have.

18. Can you ever have experiences you don't think you're having?[18]

a. Someone is blindfolded and told that he will be branded with a red-hot poker. A piece of ice is pushed into his bare stomach, and he screams. Did he mistake the sensation of cold for one of warmth?
b. I have been suffering from a severe toothache. I get a tingling in my cheek, and for a moment I think it is the toothache again. Can I think I have it when I don't?
c. Is it possible to think that you feel a pain when you feel nothing at all, but only see blood on your knee?

19. State, in the light of your knowledge of physical science,

a. Whether a molecule should be called a physical thing
b. Whether it is solid
c. Whether it is impenetrable
d. Whether it can be called hard or smooth
e. Whether atoms or electrons have any of these properties

---

[18]Examples a–c are from Don Locke, *Perception and Our Knowledge of the External World* (London: Allen & Unwin, 1967), pp. 86–87.

SELECTED READINGS

AUNE, BRUCE. *Knowledge, Mind, and Nature.* New York: Random House, 1970.

AUSTIN, JOHN L. *Sense and Sensibilia.* London: Oxford University Press, 1962.

AYER, ALFRED J. *Foundations of Empirical Knowledge.* New York: Macmillan, 1945.

BENNETT, JONATHAN. *Locke, Berkeley, and Hume.* New York: Oxford University Press, 1971.

BERKELEY, GEORGE. *Principles of Human Knowledge.* 1710. Many editions.

BERKELEY, GEORGE. *Three Dialogues between Hylas and Philonous.* 1713. Many editions.

BOUWSMA, O. K. *Philosophical Papers.* Lincoln: University of Nebraska Press, 1963.

CLARK, J. AUSTEN. *Sensory Qualities.* New York: Oxford University Press, 1993.

DANCY, JONATHAN. *Berkeley.* Oxford: Blackwell, 1993.

DANCY, JONATHAN. *Perceptual Knowledge.* New York: Oxford University Press, 1988.

DESCARTES, RENÉ. *Meditations on First Philosophy.* 1641. Many editions.

EWING, ALFRED C. *Idealism: A Critical Survey.* London: Methuen, 1936.

HANKINSON, R. J. *The Sceptics.* London: Routledge, 1995.

KELLEY, DAVID. *The Evidence of the Senses.* Baton Rouge: Louisiana State University Press, 1986.

LEWIS, CLARENCE I. *Analysis of Knowledge and Valuation.* LaSalle, IL: Open Court, 1946.

LOCKE, DON. *Perception and Our Knowledge of the External World.* London: Allen & Unwin, 1967.

LOCKE, JOHN. *An Essay Concerning Human Understanding.* Book 2. 1689. Many editions.

MCGINN, COLIN. *The Subjective View.* New York: Oxford University Press, 1983.

MALCOLM, NORMAN. *Dreaming.* London: Routledge, 1959.

MALCOLM, NORMAN. *Thought and Knowledge.* Ithaca: Cornell University Press, 1977.

MATHAL, RIMAL KRISHNA. *Perception.* New York: Oxford University Press, 1992.

MILL, JOHN STUART. *An Examination of Sir William Hamilton's Philosophy.* London: Longmans Green, 1865.

MOORE, GEORGE E. "A Defense of Common Sense." In Moore, *Philosophical Papers.* London: Allen & Unwin, 1959.

MOORE, GEORGE E. *Some Main Problems of Philosophy.* London: Allen & Unwin, 1952.

MUNDLE, C.W.K. *Perception: Facts and Theories.* New York: Oxford University Press, 1971.

PRICE, H. H. *Perception.* London: Methuen, 1933.

PRICE, H. H. *Hume's Theory of the External World.* London: Oxford University Press, 1940.

ROBINSON, J. HOWARD. *Perception.* London: Routledge, 1994.

ROSS, J. J. *The Appeal to the Given.* London: Allen & Unwin, 1970.

SLOTE, MICHAEL. *Reason and Skepticism.* London: Allen & Unwin, 1970.

STACE, WALTER T. *Theory of Knowledge and Existence.* Oxford: Clarendon Press, 1932.

STROUD, BARRY. *The Significance of Philosophic Skepticism.* London: Oxford University Press, 1984.

SWARTZ, R. J., ed. *Perceiving and Knowing.* New York: Anchor Books, 1965.

WESTPHAL, JONATHAN. *Color: A Philosophical Introduction.* Oxford: Blackwell, 1991.

WILLIAMS, MICHAEL. *Groundless Belief.* New Haven: Yale University Press, 1977.

WILLIAMS, MICHAEL. *Unnatural Doubt: Epistemological Realism and the Roots of Skepticism.* Oxford: Blackwell, 1991.

WINKLER, KENNETH. *Berkeley.* London: Oxford University Press, 1989.

YOLTON, JOHN. *John Locke and the Way of Ideas.* London: Oxford University Press, 1956.

4 *The Way the World Works*

SCIENTIFIC KNOWLEDGE

As we observe the world, we notice certain *regularities* in the course of events. Many things occur in the same way over and over. The sun rises in the east, not in the west. Iron rusts, but gold does not. Chickens lay eggs, but dogs don't. We attempt to chart these regularities, tracing what George Santayana (1863–1952) called "the thin red vein of order in the flux of experience."

If we were as interested in discovering irregularities as we are in regularities, the task would be easier. Some trees yield lots of fruit, some none. Some seasons are rainy, some dry. Some dogs are friendly, some hostile. If all experiences were as irregular as these, we wouldn't know what to expect next. Past experience would provide no guide to the future.

But fortunately for us, some regularities do occur. Most of them, however, are not *invariable.* You may keep your son Billy away from the neighbor's son Johnny because Johnny has a cold, but Billy may get a cold anyway, and he may not get it even if he does play with Johnny. Yet it is more likely that he will get a cold if he plays with someone who has one. We then look for genuine invariants in nature, conditions under which a certain type of event occurs without exception. The scientific enterprise could be described as the search for genuine invariants in nature.

Sometimes we think we have found a genuine invariant when further investigation shows that we have not. We may have been sure that water always boils at 212°F, But when we go to a mountaintop, we find that the boiling point of water is somewhat less than that. By repeated observations we discover that the boiling point depends not on the temperature, not on the moisture in the air, not on the time of day, but on the pressure of the surrounding air. We can then formulate a statement of invariance about the boiling point of water.

Why are we interested in discovering these regularities? Because we are interested in *predicting* future events. If we can predict them, we can act in accordance with the prediction: if we see the sun low in the west, we can predict that the sky will soon be dark and that we won't be able to conduct activities that require more light. If experience indicates that certain snakes are poisonous, and we see one of them, we can get out of the way. Science is the systematic search for *uniformities* in the way things behave. These are called laws of nature.

1. LAWS OF NATURE

Usually, when people speak of a law, they mean an edict that has been issued by a head of state or enacted by a legislative body (and been enforced, at least sometimes). Laws in this sense are *prescriptive:* they prescribe how the people within its jurisdiction are supposed to behave or not behave. They are imperatives: "Do this," "Don't do that."

But laws of nature are not like this: they are not prescriptions, but *descriptions* of how nature works. The laws of planetary motion set forth by Johannes Kepler (1571–1630) did not prescribe to the planets that they should move in such-and-such orbits, with penalties invoked if they should fail; rather, they describe how planets actually *do* move. Only conscious beings can prescribe, since only they are capable of giving orders; but the uniformities of nature would still occur even if there were no human beings to describe them.

Several confusions can now be avoided:

(1) "Laws should be obeyed." Whether or not you should obey all the laws of the land is a problem in ethics. But a law of nature is not the sort of thing you can obey or disobey, since it is not an order or command anyone has given. What could you do if someone said to you, "Obey the law of gravitation"? Your motions, along with those of stones and every particle of matter in the universe, are *instances* of this law; but since the law only tells us how matter *does* behave, and doesn't prescribe how things *should* behave, you cannot be said either to obey or disobey it. A prescriptive law, moreover, could still be said to exist even if it were universally disobeyed.

(2) "Where there's a law, there's a lawmaker." Again this applies clearly to prescriptive law: If a course of action is prescribed, someone must have prescribed it. But laws of nature are not prescriptions; they only describe how nature works. (The workings of nature may have been designed by God, but this is another issue, to be discussed in Chapter 7.)

(3) "Laws are discovered, not made." This applies, again, only to descriptive laws. We *discover* how nature works, we do not make it

work that way. But the *formulation* of these uniformities is the work of human beings.

Laws of nature constitute a smaller class of propositions than empirical statements in general. Any statement whose truth can be confirmed by observation of the world is an empirical statement. "Some chickens lay eggs," "World War I lasted from 1914 to 1918," "She fell ill with pneumonia yesterday," and "New York City contains approximately 8 million residents" are all empirical statements. Indeed, most of the statements we utter in daily life are empirical statements. But none of these is a law of nature: Laws of nature are a special class of empirical statements. Since laws of nature are at the very core of the empirical sciences—physics, chemistry, astronomy, geology, biology, psychology, sociology, economics—it is important that we try to be clear about what they are.

When can a statement be considered a law of nature? Several features are usually counted as defining of laws of nature, but not everyone agrees that *all* of them are defining.

1. A law of nature is a *universal* statement, of the form "All A's are B's" or "If something is an A, then it is (or has) B." Simple examples would be, "All lead melts at 327.5°C," "All iron rusts when exposed to oxygen," and "All copper conducts electricity."

If not all A is B, but only 95 percent of A's are B's, we have what is called a statistical law; for example, that 95 percent of the people infected with a particular virus recover from it is a statistical law. A statistical law is preferable to no law at all, but of course the next question is, why should 95 percent of A's be B's but not the other 5 percent. Sometimes we find a reason for the difference, but sometimes not—in which case we are left with a statistical law.

But being universal isn't enough. "All the dogs in this kennel are black" would not qualify as a law of nature. It is limited to a definite area in space and time—this kennel, today. Even if you widen its scope to read "All the dogs I've ever had are black," it still would not say anything about all dogs or even all dogs of a certain breed. So we come to a second condition:

2. A law of nature must be *open-ended*—it must have an unlimited range in time and space. Whenever and wherever there is an A, it will be or have B. Wherever there is iron, it is magnetic. Wherever there is lead, it melts at 327.5°C.

Some statements were once thought to be laws, but were found to be either not universal or not open-ended. Consider "Water boils at 212°F." If we go to a mountaintop we observe that it boils at a lower temperature. We then discover that the temperature at which water boils varies with the pressure of the atmosphere: the greater the pressure, the higher the boiling point. Once this is discovered, a law can be formulated expressing the relation between the pressure and the boiling point.

3. Natural laws must be expressible as *hypothetical* statements. Even if all the crows we have ever seen have been black, we would be unlikely to count this as a law of nature, because it's still possible that we might discover an albino crow. (Of course, if being black is considered *defining* of crows, then we have the blackness right there in the definition, and the statement becomes, "All black creatures of a certain kind are black"—true, but providing no information about the world.) If we can see no connection between being a crow and being black, we will not stake our reputation on the truth of "All crows are black." Usually color is a variable within a species, and we see no reason why that should not also be true of crows. So we wouldn't commit ourselves to saying, "If there *were* a crow (anytime, anywhere), it *would* be black."

We might, however, respond differently to "If this were a stone, it *would* fall" (if we let go of it). We would have to put in a few qualifiers, such as that the stone must be within the gravitational field of some star or planet such as the earth, and not out in the midst of space somewhere (in that case, where would it fall *to*?), and that the atmosphere must not be of greater specific gravity than the stone (in that case it would float, as balloons do in our atmosphere). But we are confident not only that stones do fall, but that if we were to release a stone (specifying the conditions first), then it *would* fall.

Galileo (1564–1642) was confident that all bodies fall at the same rate in a vacuum and that only the atmosphere keeps them from falling at the same rate now. The nearer we get to a vacuum, the more nearly the proposed law holds true. Apparently Galileo was right: if we *were* in a total vacuum, every object would fall at the same rate.

4. The greater the *generality* of a statement, the more likely it is to be accorded the status of a law of nature. Laws about the melting point of various metals are sometimes called merely "low-level generalizations." If the melting point of lead were different from what it is, this wouldn't affect much else in the universe. If some birds had three legs, this wouldn't affect much besides birds. But "If there is friction, then (always) there is heat" seems to be more fundamental: friction generates molecular motion, and heat (in the physical sense of the term) is molecular motion.

Even wider in scope is Sir Isaac Newton's (1642–1727) Law of Universal Gravitation: that every particle of matter in the universe attracts every other particle with a force varying inversely as the square of the distance between them and directly as the product of the masses. This is a claim about every bit of matter in the universe; it covers motions from the fall of apples from a tree (which inspired Newton to formulate the law) to the motions of planets in their orbits, as well as many others, such as the motions of double stars and the shapes of galaxies, which were unknown in Newton's time. Here is a universal statement of the widest possible scope. (Sometimes it is called a theory and not a law; the boundary between them is not sharp, as we shall see.)

Since laws are universal in scope, they include the future as well as the past and present. If all A's are B's, then all *future* A's will also be B's. Knowledge of laws, to the extent that we have it, enables us to predict future occurrences.

Newton had already formulated his laws of motion when William Hoerschel first observed the planet Uranus through a telescope in 1721. Its motions were carefully studied and its orbit charted. But the motions observed through the telescope were not what one would have expected on the basis of Newton's law. Had Newton been mistaken or inaccurate? Or was there something else in the picture that had not been taken into consideration? Then two astronomers, acting independently of each other, suggested that the deviation in Uranus's motion could be accounted for if one assumed that there was another planet beyond Uranus. They calculated the position of the undiscovered planet, and using maximum telescopic power (for that time), they saw the hitherto unseen planet. Since it looked like just another dim star, its slow motion among them was carefully tracked for many months (to make sure that it was indeed a planet). This discovery gave an enormous boost to Newton's laws, because a prediction based on them had been fulfilled with such precision—a prediction that could not have been without the laws.

But what seems to be a law isn't always a law; often it requires correction or qualification. Newton's laws remained secure until well into the twentieth century, when Albert Einstein (1875–1955) hypothesized that light is gravitationally attracted by heavy bodies, and that light from a body near the sun would be deflected by the gravitational pull of the sun. Ordinarily the light of the sun makes it impossible for us to see stars in the daytime, but during a total eclipse of the sun in 1919, the predicted difference in position (of the planet Mercury) was observed. Similar observations have since been made repeatedly, and Einstein's theory is now secure—again, pending future discoveries.

2. EXPLANATION

Scientific knowledge enables us to *explain* why many things occur as they do.

We don't need much scientific knowledge to explain lots of particular events. Why is the door open? I opened it because it's a hot day. Why wasn't she at the meeting last night? Because she had a conflicting engagement. Why do I hear that strange barking sound? Because there's a coyote out there in the hills. Why is that little swinging door there? Because I want to let the dog go in and out without having to open the big door every time. And so on for thousands of cases. Someone doesn't know why something occurs as it does or is as it is, and we explain it.

Explanations are not always answers to the question "why"; sometimes they are merely a request for clarification: "explain that passage in the poem—I don't understand what it means". Or, "Explain what you are doing." "I'm building a birdhouse." Sometimes when we give an explanation, we merely tell the inquirer *how* we do something or how a device works: you press that button, and all the dominoes fall down.

The sciences are most concerned with explaining the *why* of events. We may ask why a particular event occurred: why did the water pipes in the basement burst last night? Because it froze last night. More often we ask why this or that *kind* of event regularly happens: why do the water pipes burst in cold weather? Because they're full of water, and water expands when it freezes.

We can't get far in explaining without introducing *theories*. Why does water, unlike most liquids, expand when it freezes? Now the chemist explains to us the crystalline structure of the water molecule. But this is theory—theory not merely in the ordinary sense of a hypothesis ("It's my theory that he came back during the night") but in the more specialized sense that the entities invoked in the explanation *could not be observed* by our senses. The water molecule is theory: it can't be seen, not even through the most powerful microscopes. We can't see it, but we *infer* its existence from what we do see. The origin of planets is something we can't observe either, but for a different reason—it happened before there were any human observers—so this too is generally counted as theory.

3. THEORIES

Unlike the conclusion of a sound deductive argument, a theory is never proved (conclusively established). It is always subject to revision in the light of further investigation. If we were to say,

> If it rains, the street will be wet.
> The streets are wet.
>   Therefore,
> It rained,

we would probably see the logical fallacy at once: it is called "affirming the consequent." A street sprinkler might have made the streets wet. But scientific theory does the same thing:

> If the theory is true, certain observable
>   consequences will occur.
> Certain observable consequences do occur.
>   Therefore,
> The theory is true.

This is also an example of affirming the consequent.

Is science, then, based on a logical fallacy? Only if you claim that science provides logical certainty. But of course it doesn't. The observable facts never prove the theory: at most they only *confirm it* to some degree or other. You can never deduce the theory from a description of the observed facts; the theory can, however, provide an explanation of the observed facts.

But many explanations are *false* explanations. One may say that the storm at sea is brought about by the wrath of Zeus. And if Zeus did exist, his wrath might be a plausible explanation of the storm. Many other things have been explained as witchcraft or sorcery, although we believe that these are false explanations: "there are no witches." There is no evidence, we say, by means of which we could *confirm* such theories, that is, render them even slightly probable.

To confirm a statement is to render it probable to some degree. I can confirm that there are thousands of trees in the city where I live. One might also say that I can *verify* it, that is, confirm it "all the way"—that is, render it certain, so that I can truly say I know it, not just have evidence for it, but know it. (We might know it in the "weak" sense but not in the "strong" sense; see Chapter 2.) In this sense at least I can verify that I am now sitting at a desk, but I cannot verify even a simple generalization about nature, such as, "All swans are white." Every time I see a white swan I can truly say that I confirmed the statement just a bit more than before, but since I can't see all the swans there are (or have been, or will be), I can never verify the statement. (Even if I had seen them all, how could I know this?)

But if I come across a swan that is not white—if it's really a swan and not of another species, and if I'm not hallucinating or dreaming and so on—then I have definitely disproved (falsified) the statement "All swans are white." It would take an infinite set of observations to verify the statement, but it would take only one example to render it false. One exception to the law disproves the law.

Nevertheless, a single observation is not usually taken as sufficient to disprove a scientific theory. Scientists will hold on to a theory for some time, particularly if it is already well confirmed. If Saturn were to deviate from its orbit, the deviation would be ascribed to the gravitational attraction of another cometary or planetary object, not to a defect in the law of gravitation. Even if no such object were ever found, astronomers would be more likely to trust the law than their ability to detect hitherto unseen gravitating bodies.

But empirical laws can't be true "no matter what": there must be something that would disconfirm them. What kind of occurrence might be taken as refuting, or at least placing in serious question, something as highly confirmed as Newton's law?

Suppose that another star, larger than the sun, made a close approach to the sun but exerted no discernible gravitational effect on it; suppose that the planets nearest the sun, such as Mercury and Venus, which one would expect to be pulled quite out of their orbits by the gravitational impact of the star, appeared to be totally indifferent to its presence. If such a thing were to occur, it would surprise (shock?) the scientific community, and some explanation would be sought. Perhaps the star is large but of small mass—but that possibility could be tested. What if on the other side of the sun, so as to cancel out its effects, is a dark star (massive gravitation but no light)—but this can be checked as well (although by using gravitational effects on other bodies in doing so).

Laws and theories are often assumed to contain a *ceteris paribus* (other things being equal) clause; if something turns up that's "not equal," such as the intrusion of a dark star, this may refute the current prediction but leaves the theory untouched.

Scientific theories require a lot of empirical observation to build them up and even more to tear them down. They *can* be preserved in the face of seemingly powerful evidence against them, because scientific claims do not occur (as a rule) in isolation: they form an interlocking, highly coherent set of claims, and if we find something wrong with one claim, we can place the blame on another one somewhere in the system.

> Individual scientific claims do not, and cannot, confront the evidence one by one. Rather . . . "Hypotheses are tested in bundles." . . . We can only test relatively large bundles of claims. What this means is that when our experiments go awry we are not logically compelled to select any particular claim as the culprit. We can always save a cherished hypothesis from refutation by rejecting (however implausibly) one of the other members of the bundle.[1]

The Law of Conservation of Matter—that the total amount of matter in the universe remains always the same—has long been abandoned because of the discovery of the transformation of matter into energy. But the Law of Conservation of Energy—that the total amount of energy in the universe remains always the same—still holds sway. But (or so it has been charged) this may be partly because there are numerous "kinds" of energy—chemical energy, kinetic energy, potential energy, and so on—and various types and amounts of energy can be postulated in order to make the principle come out right in the end.

---

[1]Philip Kitcher, "Believing Where We Cannot Prove," in his *Abusing Science* (Cambridge: MIT Press, 1982), p. 44.

Why is this "cookery" tolerated? A law or theory becomes accepted in the scientific community because of the large amount of confirming evidence it already has, and once the theory has become a trusted friend, we prefer to pursue our attack in another direction and to require massive amounts of disconfirmation before we will abandon it.

Nevertheless, this may occur. The theory of the ether—that there is something permeating all space that conveys radiation through it (for example, from sun to earth), just as the air conveys sound waves—was finally abandoned, after numerous attempts to discover it had totally negative results. No scientific theory is forever impervious to disconfirmation; it's just that it takes much disconfirming evidence before we will abandon it—just as it takes more evidence of criminal actions to make us distrust a longtime friend than it would in the case of a stranger whose credentials are unknown.

A Theory in Astronomy

When you look up at the sky at night, you see the moon, planets, and stars moving steadily across the sky from east to west, setting, and then rising again some hours later (although you can't see them when the sun is above the horizon). They all go round the earth—isn't that what we see? What could be more evident to the senses? This has seemed such an obvious fact to most people throughout human history that anyone who thought differently was considered quite mad. The earth, or the place you're standing on, is (or seems to be) the center of the universe, and the celestial bodies revolve around it.

The ancient Greeks and Arabs noted that the sun, moon, and planets (the latter is the Greek word for "wanderer") moved about among the stars, whereas the stars, although they moved across the sky, never showed any apparent change of position in relation to one another: the pattern of the constellations remained the same. How could this be explained? The sun and moon and each of the five visible planets, it was thought, were each infixed on the interior surface of a hollow crystalline sphere, and each planet had a sphere of its own, since each of their relative motions was different. The stars were all fixed on the interior of the outermost sphere. The theory of the crystalline spheres seemed only a slight remove from obvious observed fact.

The Egyptian astronomer Ptolemy (active A.D. 127–151) noticed some peculiarities in the motion of the planets; for example, Jupiter would move slightly eastward among the stars for some time, then temporarily turn back and move westward (retrograde motion). Why should they do this? Ptolemy believed that the circle was the only perfect curve and that all the celestial bodies moved in circles; but if you imagined them traveling in little circles around the big circles (the little circles were called "epicycles"), then you could account for the apparently erratic retrograde motions of the planets. Every time more careful observation showed another slight variation in a planetary motion, the new motion could be explained by introducing another epicycle (a small circular orbit around a larger one, which in turn circled around a still larger one). There was no general theory that could *predict* that the planets would move in epicycles, but once the theory was accepted, it was possible to use it to track the path of the planets through the years and even (since the variations over a period of years was regular) to predict their future location. Even eclipses were predicted by this theory.

Yet today no one believes the theory. Copernicus (1573–1543) held that the earth, along with the other planets, goes around the sun; if you assumed this, you could account for all the motions, including the retrograde motion, very simply. The earth, being closer to the sun than Jupiter, moves

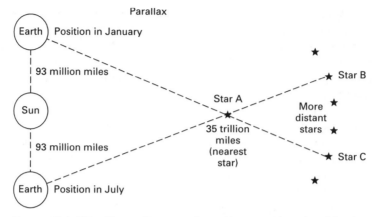

The earth is 93 million miles away from the sun. Since it orbits the sun, its position in January will be 186 million miles distant from its position 6 months later. Hence, the nearer star A will be seen in January against the background of more distant star C, but in July it will be seen against the background of more distant star B.

more rapidly in its orbit, and when it is rounding a bend in its orbit, the more distant planet will appear for a time to be going in the opposite direction, just as to the driver of the fast car on the race track the slower driver on the outer track appears for a time to be going in the opposite direction. Here then was a simple and plausible explanation for the observed motions of the stars and planets through the sky. Observably, however, there was no difference between them: both theories explained the same observed data, only the Ptolemaic was more cumbersome, having to hypothesize a new epicycle whenever the motion did not go as predicted.

There was, however, one observable consequence of the Copernican theory that would not occur under the Ptolemaic: if the earth were going round the sun in an orbit, in June it would be 186 million miles distant from its position in December; therefore, there should be a slight difference in the apparent position of the nearer stars in relation to more distant ones (parallax)—just as if

you look at a nearby tree from one window, then from another window, the tree will seem to be in a different position in relation to the distant hills in the background. But in spite of careful telescopic observations, no such parallax was observed, and this was taken as evidence against Copernicus's view. Copernicus did not abandon his view, and held that the stars must be so distant that no parallax could be detected, but in this he had no observational evidence to support him. It turned out that he was right, but Copernicus died in 1543, and the first parallax was not discovered until 1838. No one had suspected that even the nearest star was trillions of miles away. Thus, as far as the empirical evidence was concerned in Copernicus's own day, he had no more confirmation for his view than Ptolemy had had for his, although his account had no need for the burdensome epicycles that had to be introduced ad hoc into the Ptolemaic theory.

If the two theories both explain the same set of observed facts, the theory that is simpler, in the sense of requiring fewer general principles, is the one likely to be accepted. If the evidence indicates that one man robbed the house, no one is likely to take seriously the theory that a dozen men did it. Of course, the simplest theory may not account for all the facts. If several different people's fingerprints are found, the solo-robbery theory cannot account for it. And the simple theory, although it may explain all the observed facts at the time, may turn out to be inadequate in explaining facts discovered later—and then the simple theory must be scrapped. (The simplest theories of atomic structure have long been abandoned.) But if a simple theory will indeed explain all that is required, it is (other things being equal) the simple theory that wins the day—as Copernicus's did long before the confirming evidence of parallax. Simple theories are neat, tidy, elegant, and aesthetically pleasing—and it has long been a goal of science to explain as much as possible by means of as little as possible. Accept the simplest theory that explains all the known facts: that is the precept known as Ockham's razor—"Entities are not to be multiplied without necessity"—which was first set forth in medieval times by William of Ockham (1285–1349).

Even with powerful telescopes, we cannot see the planets revolving around the sun, as we do in a diagram or an orrery. What we see is Uranus and other planets at various successive places in the sky; we only *infer* from the observed motions that it is going around the sun. Perhaps if we could travel to a distance of a billion miles, we might see the planets revolving. But since we are not in a position to do this, the revolution of planets around the sun is not observed fact but theory. Still, it is highly confirmed theory. We have sent *Voyagers* and space probes to Uranus and beyond, based on complex calculations that would not have been possible without the heliocentric theory—the theory that the sun is the center of the solar system and that the planets revolve around it.

A Theory in Geology

We turn now to another theory, which includes data from astronomy and biology, with one science reinforcing the observational data of other sciences to form a coherent, unified theory.

The fossilized remains of many large reptiles, including dinosaurs, have been dug up for more than a century in various places on the earth. According to various methods of determining the age of rocks, these reptiles flourished for more than 100 million years until, about 65 million years ago, they disappeared from the earth quite suddenly. Why did they so quickly disappear? Biologists and paleontologists have long sought an explanation of this strange event.[2]

As frequently happens in science, a clue was found that seemed to have nothing to do with the problem. A thin layer of clay was discovered in a deep gorge in Italy, in strata of rock at the boundary between the Cretaceous period and the Tertiary period—laid down during the period in which the dinosaurs became extinct.

"So what?" one might ask. But in this layer large quantities of iridium were found—a metal rarely encountered on the earth's surface, but 10,000 times the normal amount was found in this layer. Iridium is heavy and would tend to go downward while the earth was still molten; perhaps it was spewed out through volcanic activity. Or perhaps it fell to earth in a collision with an asteroid or a comet. Here were two theories, each of which would explain the presence of the iridium. But which theory was correct?

[2]For a detailed account of the cometary theory, see Jonathan Weiner, *Planet Earth* (New York: Bantam Books, 1986).

Other deposits of iridium from the same period were discovered, and on sifting through the clay geologists found grains of quartz that looked cracked and strained. No such thing had been seen before except near meteorite craters, at nuclear bomb test sites, and on the moon (collected during the Apollo mission). Geologists could figure out only one way in which quartz with these features could be formed, namely when subjected to enormous heat and pressure from a powerful explosion.

Meanwhile biologists had been busy compiling lists of animals that had become extinct during the last half-billion years. Tremendous amounts of data were fed into computers, and to the scientists' surprise, the extinctions showed a recurring pattern—continuous long periods of evolution, then a brief period when they disappeared. There was a definite periodicity to these extinctions—recurring cycles of about 26 million years.

And how was *that* in turn to be explained? Ice ages were much too short. Astronomers now got into the act. Perhaps the explanation was extraterrestrial—solar flares or supernovae. But each of these theories was tentatively rejected for lack of evidence. Then it was pointed out that most stars are double stars, not visible through telescopes or photographs but detectible by their gravitational effect on other stars. Let's assume, they said, that the sun too is a double star with an invisible companion star; and let's assume that, like comets, it has a highly elliptical orbit. During the thousands of years that it's far away it has little effect on the solar system, but when it nears the sun it moves much faster, as comets do when they approach the sun.

One could still say, "So what? What has that to do with dinosaurs?" But now a fairly recent astronomical discovery becomes relevant. Outside the boundaries of the solar system—beyond the orbit of Pluto, the furthest planet from the sun—is a vast array of comets, called the Oort Cloud (after its discoverer). When the sun's invisible companion, astronomers hypothesized, intersects the Oort Cloud, about every 26 million years, it carries with it, through gravitational attraction, many of these comets, some of which are drawn into the earth's orbit. The dust from these impacts obscures the light of the sun, causing plants and the creatures that feed on them to die.

The 26-million-year cycle has now been repeatedly confirmed. The missing link in the puzzle is still the sun's dark companion, which has never been detected. Millions of such stars exist in our galaxy, and to locate one of them, through its gravitational effects alone, would be a task of tremendous difficulty. If it were achieved, however, the principal missing piece in the puzzle would be supplied, and the cometary theory would be much more highly confirmed. At the moment, no one can be sure.

This account illustrates, first of all, how empirical science is a vast, interconnected network of facts, laws, and theories. The system must be *coherent:* if any inconsistency is found within it, it must be removed. Perhaps what was thought to be an observed fact was an observational error; perhaps a fact was misinterpreted; if neither of these things has happened, and an inconsistency remains, something will have to give way—some fact reinterpreted, some theory abandoned or revised.

Second, the testing procedures are *interdependent.* When we try to determine the temperature of an object, we assume that there is a correlation between a rise in temperature and the rise of mercury in a tube. This of course is not a mere assumption and has been confirmed countless times for several centuries. In trying to determine the age of rocks, the correctness of certain testing procedures—such as the carbon-14 test, based on the rate of disintegration of uranium into lead—is assumed, but this in turn has also been confirmed (for each time span). If evidence turned up that the methods of dating were inaccurate, doubt would be cast on the figure of 26 million years. Any doubt cast upon one statement reverberates through many other statements in the system.

Third, let us notice what assumptions we are willing to make if they are coherent with an already confirmed theory. When perturbations in the orbit of Uranus were noticed, a choice had to be made: was Newtonian mechanics inaccurate, or was there a hitherto unobserved planet exerting a gravitational effect on Uranus? The latter was chosen, because Newtonian mechanics was already highly confirmed. A tried and tested friend may betray you, but the more you know her, the more evidence of betrayal you will require. The astronomers opted for Newtonian mechanics. When the planet was observed, the choice turned out to be correct. In the far less confirmed cometary theory, an assumption is also made, that the sun has a dark companion star. If such a star exists, it may never be discovered. Even with current computer technology, astronomers have estimated that there is about one chance in three of ever finding it.

If it is never found, will that count against the cometary theory? It would surely be a gap in the total explanation, which would leave an enduring question mark around the theory. If years pass and no dark companion to the sun is discovered, some will say, "It must be there; the entire explanation—including iridium and extraterrestrial objects and Oort Clouds—fits together so well as an explanation of what we have observed, that we should continue to accept the hypothesis rather than discount it just because we haven't found one link in the chain, a link that in any case would be extraordinarily dif-

ficult to discover." But others will say, "Don't let your passion for closing gaps run away with you. The fact is that one important link in the chain is missing. There is no independent evidence of the existence of a companion star to the sun—we simply *postulate* it in order to make it fit in with the rest of the account."

This controversy involves many hypotheses—educated guesses as to what happened way back when, with lines of inductive evidence going one way or another. But they do not involve theory in the strict sense: they deal with macroscopic objects available to our senses, not with unobservable entities that aren't available even to microscopes and telescopes. Iridium, rocks, craters in the earth, and meteorites crashing into the earth are all the kind of thing that we can observe. They may be called theory only in the sense that we can't observe them *now*: they happened many millions of years ago. We are making inferences from our *present* observation of gashes in the earth and so on to *past* events such as huge meteorites hitting the earth, killing the plants, and killing off the dinosaurs along with many other living species. Since we cannot witness these past events *now*, we could say that what went on then is theory. We might say that statements about dinosaurs are theory because what they are about is too remote in time to be observed, and that statements about electrons are theory because what they are about is too small to be detected through our senses.

A Theory in Physics

Physics is the principal stamping ground of scientific theory. Physicists deal constantly with not only atoms and electrons, but even more minute entities such as quarks and leptons, for which there is no claim that anyone could possibly see them even with greatly enhanced microscopic power. Why, if there is no direct evidence for them, do physicists believe that they exist? What *is* the evidence for them?

When scientists cannot explain the things they observe by means of other things they observe, they attempt to explain the observed by means of the unobserved, and sometimes the unobservable. This is what happens in dealing with the issue that is called "the ultimate constituents of matter."

We have already considered some of the views of the ancient Greek philosopher Democritus (see Chapter 3). His follower Lucretius, in his long poem *On the Nature of Things,* set forth the following observations and his theory to explain them:

Stone steps, Lucretius noted, wear away bit by bit, year after year. One can't notice the difference in a year or perhaps even five years, yet the slow wear-and-tear becomes visible in time. The stone steps must be composed of very small particles, invisible to the eye, that are stripped away one by one. Or, put a drop of berry juice into a vessel of water, and in a few moments the entire liquid will become red. The tiny particles of juice move so rapidly in the water that they color all the water in the vessel. Similarly, the sugar we dissolve in water almost instantly makes the entire liquid taste sweet. The best (and only) explanation for this, said Lucretius, is that material things are composed of these tiny particles.

I can cut a piece of chalk in half and rub it against my fingers, coloring them white. The small flakes of chalk are in turn composed of smaller ones, and these in turn of still smaller ones. But at the end of the process there are particles that cannot be split any further; these are atoms. They cannot be seen or touched, but if we posit that they exist, we can explain an enormous number of things that we do observe. So argued Lucretius.

This ancient atomic theory was primitive, but it differs only in details from modern theories. More refined atomic theories, involving protons and electrons, have been devised to explain countless facts of chemistry: why element A combines with elements B and C but not with elements D and E, and why some elements (the inert gases) combine with nothing at all; why certain elements and compounds have the properties they do, and why they evaporate or ignite at the temperatures they do and freeze when they do. A multitude of unobservable entities—particles, waves, energy, fields of force—have ushered in a new conception of physical reality undreamed of less than a century ago.

> Behind the world of appearances, the everyday world of common sense and ordinary human observation and experience, there is a reality of a different order which sustains that world and presents it to our senses. Now it is precisely such a reality that science reveals—a world of unobservable entities and invisible forces, waves, cells, particles, all interlockingly organized and structured down to a deeper level than anything we have been able to penetrate.[3]

Since these "ultimate constituents of matter" are not observable by the senses or through instruments, one can allege that they do not exist: one can "be a phenomenalist about matter" and say that these theories are nothing more than fancy ways of talking about the observed phenomena themselves. Most physicists, however, have no truck with such suggestions: they are concerned, they say, with what material things *really are* composed of, down to their ultimate constituents; electrons are inferences, but they do exist.

---

[3]Bryan Magee, *Philosophy and the Real World* (LaSalle, IL: Open Court, 1985), pp. 34–35.

Not everything can be explained, however. A is explained in terms of B, and B in terms of C, and so on. But this process always leaves the last item in the series unexplained. However far the process goes on, it cannot explain why everything is as it is or does as it does. There remains what is called *"brute fact"*—"that's the way reality is and we can't say why it is that way." To explain something is to put it into the wider context of something else (law or theory), and that something else is either explained in turn or remains unexplained. Whatever the ultimate constituents of matter are, and we have probably not reached them, they are a certain way: the ultimate laws of the universe remain unexplained, although we may have explained countless other things by means of them. It was once thought that Newton's laws provided the ultimate explanation of motion in the universe, but Einstein alleged that gravitation is a special case of a more general "unified field theory." Einstein hoped that gravitation, electricity, and magnetism could all be subsumed under such a general theory covering all of physics, although no such general theory has yet found widespread acceptance. If it does, then *that* will be "brute fact"—unless it is explained in its turn.

Emergence and Reducibility

A: I think that there are different levels of reality in the universe.

B: What do you mean by that?

A: For the most part, the universe is composed of inorganic matter. But here on earth—and perhaps elsewhere, although we still don't know this—are living things, which grow, reproduce, and die. Nothing in inorganic nature does this. And then, when living things achieve a certain level of complexity, something else happens: they become *conscious*—they are aware of their environment, they perceive things and act on the basis of that perception, and they feel pain and pleasure, desire and frustration, and so on.

B: Let's save consciousness for later (Chapter 6). But why do you consider life a "different level"? I grant that living things do what nonliving things don't. But electrically charged things like batteries also do things that stones don't. What's the big deal?

A: There are qualities of things that are said to be *emergent*. You couldn't have predicted them from even a complete knowledge of what went before. They "emerge" at a higher level than anything that preceded.

B: Water is composed of hydrogen and oxygen. Hydrogen is gaseous at ordinary temperatures and is highly combustible; oxygen is also gaseous at ordinary temperatures and is not combustible—it's a necessary condition for combustion. The two together form water, which is not gaseous but liquid at ordinary temperatures, and is neither combustible nor necessary for combustion—quite the contrary, it is used to *extinguish* combustion. Isn't it strange that two elements should combine to form something so different?

Chemistry is full of examples. Sodium is highly corrosive when exposed to air or water, and chlorine is a poisonous greenish gas—but when they combine they form ordinary table salt.

A: OK—and if we had never had any experience of water or salt, would we have been able to predict what properties they would have, when we knew only the properties their elements had in isolation, before they combined? If we would not be able to predict the nature of the combination, then we say that the properties they exhibit in combination are emergent. We would not be able to predict what properties they would have in combination just from observing what properties they had prior to the combination. Even a complete knowledge of hydrogen and oxygen alone would not enable us to predict the properties of water.

B: I don't know what you mean by "complete knowledge." Wouldn't we say that our knowledge was incomplete until it *did* enable us to predict the properties of water? Then the claim becomes tautological: "a complete knowledge (including a knowledge that would enable us to predict X) would enable us to predict X."

A: I am saying that a complete knowledge of their behavior in isolation would not enable us to predict what qualities they would have when combined as water.

B: I think a person with an advanced degree in chemistry would have a pretty good idea of what these two elements would combine to form, even without having yet observed it. For example, if you've seen several elements of the "halogen" family, chlorine and bromine, you'd have a pretty good idea of how a newly discovered element, fluorine, would behave. I don't know what chemists would say about the water example, but I don't see anything here to get excited about.

A: It's living organisms that I'm interested in. From a complete knowledge of the chemical ingredients of an organism, I say we would never be able to predict that when combined they would form a living thing that grows, reproduces, and is aware of its environment. And we would never be able to infer that it would behave purposively, as organisms

do. Consider the intricately complex behavior of wasps and bees, such as scouting around through a neighborhood to familiarize themselves with the terrain before settling down there. This is surely a different level of reality from anything we can observe in inorganic matter.

B: I don't understand what you mean by the term "level of reality." It is surely a different kind of behavior from anything we find in inorganic nature. Are you saying that the organic could never have grown out of the inorganic? The majority of biologists would surely contest you on that. Richard Dawkins's book *The Blind Watchmaker* gives an extremely coherent account of how this may have occurred.[4]

A: What I mean is really *reducibility;* from any number of propositions about inorganic matter, you could never logically deduce any proposition about living things. There is a "gap" in reality between the inorganic and the organic.

B: Let's take a simpler case first. Physicists agree that one branch of physics, thermodynamics, has been reduced to another branch, mechanics. And what does it mean to say this? The term "heat" is central in thermodynamics, not in mechanics. But every proposition about heat can be translated without loss of meaning into other propositions about molecular motion, *if* you assume (which physicists grant is true) the kinetic theory of heat, that is, that heat is molecular motion (not the feeling of heat, but the physical phenomenon of heat). Granted that assumption, thermodynamics is reducible to (deducible from) mechanics. Is that the sort of thing you want to say?

---

[4]Richard Dawkins, *The Blind Watchmaker* (New York: Norton, 1987).

A: I am saying that that is just what *can't* be done in biology.

B: Let's try one more case first. There are good grounds for saying today that all of chemistry—let's say inorganic chemistry, so as not to prejudice the issue—is reducible to physics. Everything we can say about the weight, color, melting point, and other chemical properties of elements and compounds can be deduced from the theory of molecular structure. If you grant what physicists say about molecules, atoms, and electrons, all of chemistry follows. Chemistry has been reduced to physics.

A: That may be. But even from a complete chemical knowledge of chlorine, you wouldn't be able to say that it would have a pungent smell when it was in contact with the human nose.

B: No, you'd first have to have some knowledge of human noses.

A: And human consciousness. You'd never be able to predict how it would smell until you actually smelled it.

B: Again, let's leave consciousness for later. What you are saying, I take it, is that a person could know everything that there is to be known about physics and inorganic chemistry, and still not have any idea that these physical substances would combine to form living things?

A: Yes, that's what I'm saying.

B: You may be right. But I don't see how you can be so sure that you're right. We know a lot more than we used to about complex chemical compounds and also about the conditions that existed on earth a few billion years ago, when life began on this planet. How can you be *sure* that if you know exactly what these conditions were, as well as the properties of the various chemical compounds, you would not be able to predict the occurrence of living, self-replicating beings?

A: One thing makes me sure: in biology we have recourse to teleological explanations, explanations in terms of function or purpose. In physics and astronomy we never have to resort to these.

Explanation in Biology

Unlike inorganic matter, living things are born or hatched; they grow, they reproduce others of their kind, and they die. Neither atoms nor stars do these things. In biology, it seems, we use explanations of a kind that is quite different from what we use in physics, astronomy, and inorganic chemistry. Specifically, we constantly use the idea of *purpose* in dealing with living organisms. Consider such assertions as these:

1 The bird flies about in order to gather materials for building its nest.
2 This species of bird preys at night in order to escape daytime enemies.
3 Arctic mammals are often white, which provides them with protective coloration against the background of snow.
4 These flowers are composed of a sticky substance in order to catch flies.
5 When the body is endangered, millions of red blood cells go to the part of the body where they are needed in order to keep the organism alive.

We certainly *talk* as if we believed that these living things are imbued with purposes and that they do what they do in order to achieve this purpose. If a biologist is puzzled by some organ in an organism, she may ask, "What is its purpose?" and will remain puzzled until she can discern what purpose it serves. We may ask, "What's the purpose of the appendix?" until we are told that in primitive humans it was useful in storing certain materials like pebbles that could not be digested. But we never ask such questions in physics; we are not told that the planets move in their orbits with the speed they do in order to keep them from falling into the sun. Primitive humans tried to explain storms and earthquakes as manifestations of the wrath of the gods, but science no longer accepts such statements as explanations of natural phenomena.

Explanations in terms of purpose are no longer accepted in biology when there is an evolutionary explanation, such as the Darwinian struggle for existence and the "survival of the fittest." The Arctic fox is not white *in order* to stay alive; it can't help what color it is. But in the Arctic, being white serves as protective coloration; white animals are difficult to detect against the snowy background, so they are less likely to be preyed upon, and thus they survive to pass their genes on to their offspring. Animals born with one eye or three legs are less likely to survive and reproduce.

Still, it often seems that the individual creature *is* imbued with a purpose and does certain things in order to achieve that purpose. The squirrel stores nuts for the winter, the bird builds nests, the deer runs fast to escape the preying carnivore. What can we say of these purposive (or teleological, from the Greek *telos*, "end" or "goal") explanations? To answer this question we must first distinguish several ways in which the word "purpose" is used.

1. We explain why a person does what she does by saying what her purpose is in so doing. "Why did you go downtown this morning?" "To go to the dentist" is a plausible answer; she did what she did in order to achieve a purpose that she had in mind. A plausible, and universally accepted, explanation of why people do what they do is that they wish thereby to carry out some purpose they have in mind.

We often extend this kind of explanation to animals. Why does the dog scratch at the screen door? Because he wants to get in. Why does the cow stand beside the empty water trough? Because she's thirsty. We may not be sure how far down the "ladder of life" to extend these purposive explanations: does the lobster wriggle about in the hot water because it wants to escape being boiled to death? We hope that it doesn't feel pain and thus tries to escape the pain-inducing situation, as *we* would if we were in that situation, but we may feel sufficiently uncomfortable about it not to boil the lobster.

2. We also use the term "purpose" in another sense. What's the purpose of the hammer? To pound nails and so on. What's the purpose of an air conditioner? To cool the room. Of course, the hammer and the air conditioner are not living beings imbued with purposes. But they have purposes in the sense that they *reflect* the purposes of their human makers. The hammer itself has no purpose, but *human beings* do have a purpose in making hammers, and that is what we are speaking of when we talk about the purpose of a hammer, or a car, or a computer, or a temple.

3. Finally, there is a more puzzling case. "What's the purpose of the heart?" someone asks. "To pump blood through the body," another answers. But the heart, although part of an organism, is not itself a conscious being that has a purpose, so we can't explain its action in our first sense of "purpose." Nor is the heart a manufactured object that human beings have made, so we can't use the second sense of "purpose" either: it doesn't reflect the purposes of its human makers, because in this case there were no human makers. Perhaps then we are asking what purpose God had in mind in making human beings with hearts. A theologian might be asking just that. But a biologist or physician who asks such a question is not asking a theological question: he may or may not believe that God made human beings and their hearts,

but the question he is asking is not about divine purposes—that, he would say, is a different question.

What then is he asking? He is asking what the *function* of the heart is, what part it plays in keeping the body alive and working. What part does it play in the whole bodily economy? What does it *do*? And that is not a question about purpose at all—or, if you want to call it "purpose," it is purpose simply as function, not as any conscious motivation.

This, however, does not put an end to questions. What explains why organisms—and the various organs of organisms—function in the ways that they do? We know why carburetors function as they do because we human beings have built them. But what explains why the heart, the liver, the lungs, the blood vessels, and so on function in the ways that they do?

Here evolutionary biology steps in to provide explanations. If an animal was born without one of these features essential to life, it would die and not reproduce, and the strain would die out. A creature without a heart wouldn't last long. Similarly, somewhere along the evolutionary line squirrels came to gather nuts; they didn't have any conscious purpose in doing so, they were just "genetically programmed" to do it. Those that didn't gather nuts starved during the winter and didn't carry on their genes. And mountain goats have hard, rough-surfaced feet because those that didn't have them fell down the slippery slopes and died, and the ones that survived and reproduced were the ones that had feet with better traction.

Once living organisms are on the scene, one may explain a vast array of their characteristics and behavior by invoking "evolutionary survival" as a principle of explanation. But that, of course, assumes that the organisms are already here. The next question is, how did they get here? Did organisms arise from inorganic matter, and if so, exactly how? At this point there is an ongoing controversy between those who say that divine creation is the only explanation for the existence of life, and those who say that evolution from inorganic substances is a sufficient explanation. We are not yet ready to embark on the philosophy of religion, but this is one point at which biological explanation (evolutionism) competes with a religious explanation (creationism) of the existence of living things.

Creation versus Evolution

CREATIONIST: Life, you say, arose from inorganic matter. Do you know what the probability is of such a thing happening? Almost zero.

EVOLUTIONIST: Lots of events of very low probability happen every day—like the probability that you would happen to be on that street at the very moment when some drunken driver came crashing into you. What would the odds against that be, if you had had to take bets on it a few years ago?

C: The odds would be greatly against that particular thing happening, I suppose—although not against this *kind* of thing happening to some members of a community during a lifetime. But the odds against living things originating from nonliving things if far greater than that. For example: one constituent of all living things is protein, and the simplest protein molecule contains about two thousand atoms of five different kinds, organized in a very specific way. The probability of this occurring as a result of any combination of inorganic molecules has been calculated as 2.02×10 to the 221st power—a number of 12 followed by six lines of zeros. Pierre Lecomte duNouy, in his famous book *Human Destiny,* wrote:

The volume of substance necessary for such a probability to take place is beyond all imagination. It would be that of a sphere with a radius so great that light would take 10 to the 82nd power years to cover this distance. The volume is incomparably greater than that of the whole universe including the farthest galaxies, whose light takes only two million years to reach us. In brief, we would have to imagine a volume more than one sextillion-sextillion-sextillion times greater than the Einsteinian universe. [And]the probability for a single molecule of high dissymmetry to be formed by the action of chance and normal thermic agitation remains practically nil. . . . The time needed to form, on an average, one such molecule . . . in a material volume equal to that of our terrestrial globe is about 10 to the 243rd power billions of years.

But we must not forget that the earth has only existed for two billion years and that life appeared about one billion years ago, as soon as the earth had cooled.[5]

E: Those lines were written in 1946. Since then the age of the earth has been revised to five-plus billion years, and life is believed to have begun less than a billion years after that. The occurrence of life in the universe *is* vastly improbable. Among all the planets in our solar system, and among all the millions of stars we know of, there is not one known instance of life. The combination of conditions that lead to the evolution of living things may well be very rare. But I don't think we know enough to be sure about this. In the last fifty years we have gained much more knowledge of biochemistry and of the conditions that existed in the early centuries of the earth's existence, when life began. There are many steps in the process:

One takes some lime (calcium oxide) and heats it with carbon to produce calcium carbide, which then reacts with water to yield acetylene. This can be oxidized to produce acetaldehyde, and further oxidation of the latter compound yields acetic acid. But every step in the process consists in bringing certain ingredients together at certain pressures and temperatures, whereupon the desired reaction occurs spontaneously.[6]

If you follow the process *step by step,* instead of starting with step 1 and then looking at step 100 and being surprised at the result, the outcome at each successive stage doesn't seem improbable at all. If you study each step in the process carefully, the final result will come to seem not only probable but inevitable. Given conditions A, B will result, then given conditions C, D will result, and so on. Take it step by step, and it won't seem improbable at all. A child seeing the foundations of a house, and then returning three months later and seeing a completed house, might be surprised in the same way.

C: We all can see how a house could result from the building process; we have seen it many times—there is no mystery about it. It is not the same with life.

E: That's because we are only beginning to understand the multiple steps in the process. Anyway, if you say that the existence of life is so vastly improbable (at least on the basis of DeNouy's data of fifty years ago), how can you assign *any* probability to the theory that God created them all out of his own mind? How could one assign any numerical probability to such a unique event? What basis would you have to form any *estimate* of probability for such a one-time unique event?

[5]Pierre Lecomte duNouy, *Human Destiny* (New York: Harper & Row, 1946), p.34.

[6]Wallace I. Matson, *The Existence of God* (Ithaca: Cornell University Press, 1963), p. 106.

C: I don't pretend to assign such a unique act as divine creation any probability. But the chances of life arising from non-life is so small that I don't think you have much room to lecture me about improbability.

E: At least evolution provides some *coherent explanation* of how living things evolve— a billion years of only micro-organisms, then gradually microscopic aquatic life, then fishes, then reptiles, and finally mammals. The account that lay concealed in the rocks and has now begun to take shape through our discoveries of fossils in those rocks is pretty coherent. It still has gaps, but at least we know roughly *how* it happened. Your account doesn't give me anything to latch on to: how would one set about investigating whether God created all living things and planted the evidence in the rocks? I can't think of a single definite step one could take to discover whether the creationist theory is true, or even how one would amass *evidence* for it. It's a scientific dead end.

C: It's not my fault if God's ways are mysterious and not open to verification by scientific method.

E: And if I am right, you don't need to appeal to "God's ways" to account for it.

C: However living things came to be, it is clear that they exist. And their existence has to be explained in some way or other. You believe that human beings' existence, with all their knowledge and sense of beauty, can be accounted for by a theory that places their origins in primeval slime. I do not. I find it much more plausible to say that God created all living things, and that the same being also created the universe and all that it contains. My view of the origin of life is part of a far wider theory about the existence of God. But that general theory will have to wait for another day (see the section on the argument from design in Chapter 7).

E: Life arose under conditions that can't be exactly duplicated today. But biologists have a pretty detailed idea of what they were. The sequence has been fairly well confirmed. (Just look at any book on evolutionary biology.)

C: Even if I grant evolution, I can still hold that God initiated the entire evolutionary process. Evolution and creation don't exclude each other.

E: It's just that when the evolutionary theory has done its work, we don't *need* anything else.

C: Scientists don't even entertain creationism as a possibility to be reckoned with.

E: We don't discuss it in the sciences because it is not subject to scientific testing. There is no way to confirm it. Theological beliefs lie outside the realm of science. How would a biologist confirm that God was behind the whole evolutionary process? What observations could she make that would confirm that?

C: We could confirm the existence of the Flood at the time of Noah.

E: That would confirm the Flood, not divine creation. And the evidence for a flood such as that depicted in Genesis is totally lacking. I see nothing in the creation story that I could get a handle on as a scientist. I can dig up the remains of Lucy or some million-year-old example of early man, and show its place in the saga of human evolution. What can you as a creationist show me?

C: I can't show you specific bones or other remains. I can show you the whole drama of life on this planet, but that won't convince you of God.

E: Surely not, since what you call the drama of life is millions of years of struggle for existence, with organisms surviving by killing and eating each other. It's kill or be killed, with no mercy to the vanquished. Which of these organisms would you care to be? (See the discussion of the problem of evil in Chapter 7.)

4. POSSIBILITY

"I know that there were no footprints. If he had tried to erase them, there would have been some trace of it. I just don't know how he got in the house. Perhaps he was dropped from a helicopter and came down the chimney like Santa Claus."

"Well, anything's possible."

But not everything *is* possible. Let's see how we actually use the word "possible" in our day-to-day interactions. "Your Aunt Bess is coming to visit you, and it's possible that she may arrive tomorrow." This doesn't mean that it is certain or even that it's very probable, but at least that its probability is greater than zero—we don't exactly know how probable it is, but at least, we say, it's possible. "It's possible, but very unlikely, that she had learned calculus by the age of four." "It's impossible for the car to run without a distributor."

Sometimes when we say that something is impossible, we mean that it is *empirically* impossible, that is, not in accordance with laws of nature. "The car couldn't have got in that condition unless it had been hit by another vehicle." "The pages of the book had to be put together and bound. They didn't just get there by themselves, without people to do the printing and the binding."

Sometimes, of course, we are mistaken in our judgments of empirical possibility and impossibility. It was once thought that heavier-than-air objects could not fly through the air. When railway trains were first devised, it was thought that if they went over 50 miles per hour, all the passengers would die from suffocation because they couldn't breathe in enough air at that speed. These judgments of course were mistaken. But scientists still believe, apparently with excellent evidence, that nothing can travel faster than light and that it requires the impact of one solid object to put a dent in another solid object. But as our knowledge of laws of nature expands, many things that were thought to be empirically impossible have turned out to be possible. (They can't be impossible if they actually happen.)

Sometimes we use the word "possible" to mean *technically* possible. No law of nature prevents people from traveling to the planet Pluto, but it is not at this time technically possible: we can't build the spaceships that can do it. What is technically possible, of course, changes as our ability to apply laws of nature expands. Aircraft that exceed the speed of sound were not technically possible in 1940, but now they are everyday occurrences. Technical possibility depends on human ability to apply laws of nature in inventing new things. As far as we know, laws of nature don't change (only our knowledge of them changes), but our use of them is constantly changing.

Something is said to be *logically* possible if the statement of it contains no contradiction. It is logically possible to travel faster than light (there is no contradiction in stating that something goes 200,000 miles per second). But there is a contradiction in saying that a square can contain curved lines: a figure that had curves would, by definition, not be a square. All points of a circle are by definition equidistant from the center, but the far corners of a square are further from the center than the midpoint of its lines. It is logically impossible for a tower to be 100 feet high and 150 feet high at the same time (if it's 100, it can't be 150). It is logically impossible for something to have a feature that contradicts its own definition. But of course if we have two different definitions of the same word, something might be logically possible in one sense of the word but not in another: "Can you remember something that never happened?" The answer is "no" in one sense (if remembering it implies that it really happened) and "yes" in another sense (if seeming to remember, or a feeling of remembering, counts as remembering).

Time Travel

Can we witness the past? Of course; we do that every time we see a photo album or a documentary movie. That is, we are seeing now things that have happened in the past.

Light has a finite velocity of 186,330 miles per second. If we could find some way to travel faster than light, might we not witness past events on earth by catching up with the light waves, perhaps as they passed Neptune, and see for ourselves what happened? But this, we are told, is impossible: according to Einstein, and no one has refuted him on this point, the velocity of light, along with other forms of radiation, is the maximum possible speed of anything. If this is true, we could never catch up with the light waves. Indeed it is conceivable that the Egyptians had a photographic device, like motion pictures, which, if it were discovered, would show us the Egyptians building the pyramids.

But couldn't we *travel into the past* and witness for ourselves the Egyptians building pyramids? We wouldn't be seeing in 1997 events that occurred in 1200 B.C.; we would ourselves *be* in 1200 B.C. and witness the building of the pyramids *in the present.* Isn't this logically possible? Anything is logically possible that doesn't contain a contradiction, and where's the contradiction here?

A: How could we go "backward" in time? If today is Tuesday, January 22, isn't tomorrow January 23? There may not be a to-morrow, but if there is, and today is January 22, doesn't tomorrow have to be January 23?

B: No, that's the point of time travel: we don't go from today to tomorrow, we go from today to *yesterday* and the other days before. We really do go backward in time. We speak of going backward in space, such as when we put the car into reverse; we are now talking about going backward in time.

A: How could you be in 1200 B.C. and also in A.D. 1997 at the same time?

B: But this isn't so in time travel; we aren't in two times at the same time. We *are* no longer in A.D. 1997, we are in 1200 B.C. As in H. G. Wells's time machine, you press a few levers, and you are back thousands of years in the past. You don't just seem to be—but you *are.*

There is a problem, however. Those centuries have passed; the events have happened; they're over. And they all happened *without you*—you weren't even born until the twentieth century. The ancient civilizations came and went, and you weren't anywhere in that picture. How then can you say that you could now *go back* there and *be* among the people then living? It all happened without you, and now you want to say you could go back and participate in it, that is, that it did *not* happen without you. It did happen without you and it didn't—surely that's a contradiction.

The past is what has happened; not even God could make what has happened *not have happened.* Let's say the pyramids were built by 100,000 laborers. Now if you "go into the past" and join these laborers, there would be 100,001 laborers. If it was 100,000, it wasn't 100,001; there's a contradiction in saying it was both.

There are many logical possibilities: some-day we may be able to fly about in space in ways not now technically possible, but we cannot make the past happen differently than it did—the past is "in the bag," and nothing can change it. We may punish people for crimes committed in the past, but we cannot make the murders *not have happened,* nor can we make their pain and suffering not have occurred.

It's no better if we propel our time machine into the future. A young man of today "goes into" the future and stops at, let's say, the year 3000. He steps out of the spaceship, meets a girl, marries her, has a child, and then they "go back" to the year 2000. Can someone who wasn't born before the year 3000 "go back" to the year 2000 and influence the course of events then? What if he invented something that blew up the world in 2100, thus putting an end to all human existence after that? But how then could he be born in 3000, since there would no longer be human beings at that time?

> There was a young lady named Bright,
> Who could travel much faster than light.
>   She eloped one day
>   In a relative way
> And returned on the previous night.

But what if on the "previous night" she decided, because of an unpleasant nuptial experience, not to elope at all? (But she already had!) Can any amount of talk about time "going backward" or "turning back on itself" change one jot or tittle of the childhood you have *already* had? Can you harvest today the seeds you will plant next month? And what if you then decide not to plant them after all?

5. THE PROBLEM OF INDUCTION

"If all dogs are mammals, and all mammals are living creatures, then all dogs are living creatures." This is a *deductive* argument: we can log-ically deduce the conclusion from the premises. If the premises are true, the conclusion (logically) *must* be true. And if all those aboard the ship were drowned, and Mabel was aboard that ship, then Mabel was drowned. That doesn't prove that Mabel was drowned; she might not have been aboard, and perhaps not everyone aboard was drowned. We know only that *if* all aboard were drowned and she was aboard, then she was drowned.

Inductive reasoning is not like this. Inductive arguments are not deductively valid, and the conclusion doesn't logically follow from the premises. The premises only provide *evidence* for the conclusion; they make the conclusion more probable but not certain. If every time you let go of a stone it has fallen, you consider it *probable* that it will also fall the next time.

You may say that it is *certain*. But at any rate it is not *logically* certain: "It fell a thousand times, therefore it will fall the next time," is not a logically valid argument. But if some kind of event in nature, such as stones falling, has occurred thousands of times in the past, with no exceptions, we are more confident that it will happen the same way the next time. We consider the fact that it's happened this way thousands of times in the past as *evidence* that it will continue to do so in the future.

Often, however, the fact that something has occurred repeatedly in the past is *not* taken as evidence that it will continue to occur in the future.

1. You have played on the school playground several times a week for the past five years. Yet even at age twelve you don't consider it probable that you will continue to do so for the next five years. Why not? You see that most kids don't do that past a certain age, and that you yourself are beginning to amuse yourself in other ways. What you do consider probable is that children will continue to play on playgrounds for a few years

and then gradually turn to something else; for this you do have some inductive evidence.

2. In past centuries people got from one place to another on the backs of animals. If you had lived a hundred years ago, would you have said it was probable that this would continue to be the main source of transportation? Perhaps, if you saw no alternative—horseback riding is easier than walking and will probably continue to be so; but if you had noticed a few new inventions, such as the bicycle and the automobile, you would say, "The new inventions are faster and more efficient. I think it's probable that these will largely replace horses and camels." It's more likely that people will continue to do what's easiest for them than that they will stick to one practice indefinitely.

3. If every president of the United States elected in a year ending in zero died in office, would you take that as evidence that the next president to take office in a year ending in zero would also die in office? No. Why not? You see no connection between the event (dying in office) and the numbers attached to the years. You may say, "It's coincidence—it may happen again, but it's not very likely." If it does happen next time, you'd be surprised.

4. A person of twenty says that he has come out of his sleep alive for 20×365 nights, and that therefore it is highly probable that he will awaken tomorrow morning after his sleep tonight. But then a person age ninety says that he has even more evidence that *he* will be alive tomorrow: he has the evidence of 90×365 nights! Yet we are much more confident that the twenty-year-old will be alive tomorrow than that the ninety-year-old will be. But surely there is a much greater accumulation of evidence for the ninety-year-old?

Why are we more confident in the case of the twenty-year-old? We believe in induction, but not in "induction by simple enumera-

tion." The greater number of years doesn't by itself provide the needed evidence. In fact the inductive evidence is all the other way: many more people die at ninety than at twenty. Moreover, we know something about cellular deterioration and the incidence of diseases, and all this evidence favors the twenty-year-old; we would bet on him rather than on the ninety-year-old. What biological laws we have favor the young and vigorous.

When it's a law of nature, we expect it to continue to operate in the future—unlike historical phenomena like transportation via animals. But *why* should we expect it to continue in the future?

"A law of nature is *defined* so as to be open-ended: if it stopped in the year 2,000, it wouldn't *be* a law of nature." Doubtless that's true—that is part of how we conceive of a law of nature. But that doesn't prove that there *are* any uniformities that extend into the future. You can't define anything into existence, and you can't say that a law will continue to operate in the future because that's how we define "law." We can define words however we will, but there may be nothing in reality that corresponds to our definition; maybe there *are* no laws of nature in the sense we require. David Hume raised this point dramatically in a famous passage:

The bread which I formerly ate nourished me; that is, a body of such sensible qualities was, at that time, endued with such secret powers. But does it follow that other bread must also nourish me at another time, and that like sensible qualities must always be attended with like secret powers? The consequence seems nowise necessary. At least, it must be acknowledged that there is here a consequence drawn by the mind that there is a certain step taken, a process of thought, and an inference which wants to be explained. I *have found that such an object has always been attended with such an effect*, and *I forsee that other objects which are in appearance similar will be attended with similar effects*. I shall allow, if you please, that the one proposition may justly be inferred from the other; I know, in fact, that it always is inferred. But if you insist that the inference is made by a chain of reasoning, I desire you to produce that reasoning. The connection between these propositions is not intuitive. There is required a medium which may enable the mind to draw such an inference, if indeed it be drawn by reasoning and argument. What that medium is I must confess passes my comprehension. . . .

That there are no demonstrative arguments in the case seems evident, since it implies no contradiction that the course of nature may change and that an object, seemingly like those which we have experienced, may be attended with different or contrary effects. May I not clearly and distinctly conceive that a body, falling from the clouds and which and in all other respects resembles snow, has yet the taste of salt or feeling of fire? Is there any more intelligible proposition than to affirm that all the trees will flourish in December and January, and will decay in May and June? Now, whatever is intelligible and can be distinctly conceived implies no contradiction and can never be proved false by any demonstrative argument or abstract reasoning a priori.[7]

One may say, "True, we can't validly deduce propositions about the future from propositions about the past; that's deduction, and we don't have that in this case. But the evidence here is *inductive:* Induction gives us probability, not certainty, but it does tell us that if stones have always fallen there is a probability, not certainty, that they will fall tomorrow." But this, of course, is just what Hume is questioning: the acceptability of inductive argument. To say that there is inductive evidence that induction will continue to be reliable is to beg the very question at issue:

You say that the one proposition [about the future] is an inference from the other [about the past]; but you must confess that the inference

in not intuitive, neither is it demonstrative. Of what nature is it then? To say that it is experimental is begging the question. For all inferences from experience suppose, as their foundation, that the future will resemble the past. . . . It is impossible, therefore, that any arguments from experience can prove this resemblance of the past to the future, since all these arguments are founded on the supposition of that resemblance. Let the course of things be allowed hitherto ever so regular, that alone, without some new argument or inference, proves not that for the future it will continue so.[8]

And thus Hume lays down the challenge: how do we get out of this impasse?

We might try to get out of it by laying down a general principle, sometimes called the Principle of Uniformity of Nature: "As the laws of nature have been in the past, so they will be in the future." We are referring not to particular events or series of events, like the coin always turning up heads, that could change utterly without a change in the laws; rather, we are referring to the laws themselves; and one should perhaps say "presumed laws," since a genuine law of nature by definition does operate in the future as well as in the past and present. Armed with this principle, one can argue, "Law X has held in the past; therefore law X will hold in the future." The argument is valid:

Certain kinds of events (instances of laws of nature) that have occurred regularly in the past will continue to occur regularly in the future.
This kind of event has occurred regularly in the past.
Therefore,
This kind of event will occur regularly in the future.

But of course this won't do: the major premise, the Principle of Uniformity of Nature, is the very thing we are trying to estab-

[7]David Hume, "Skeptical Doubts Concerning the Operations of the Understanding," *Treatise of Human Nature* (1736), Part 2.

[8]Ibid., Part 2.

lish. To assume it in the process of trying to prove it is the logical fallacy called "begging the question." You can't lift yourself by your own bootstraps.

Hume attempts to explain *why* we expect uniformities we have observed in the past to continue in the future in terms of *custom* and *habit*. When someone has been friendly or hostile to us in the past, we expect her to act in that same way again. A dog who has been mistreated by its master in the past will tend to act suspiciously toward him now, but if it has been well treated, it will wag its tail and expect the friendly treatment to continue. But this only gives an explanation of *why* we behave in this way: we are by nature inductive creatures. It doesn't provide what we are asking for: a *justification* of our inductive expectations. (It won't do to say, "The justification is that our expectations have been fulfilled in the past," because again this begs the question of how this fact entitles us to make any claim for the future.)

Solving the Problem of Induction

Is there any way out of these difficulties? Let's consider a few suggestions:
   1. One possibility is the *linguistic solution*.

SKEPTIC: There is no evidence that as the uniformities of nature have been in the past, they will be in the future.

COMMON-SENSE PHILOSOPHER: *No evidence?* A thousand times in the past I let go of my pencil, and a thousand times it has fallen; never once has it flown into the air or turned into powder. This, and all the things I have learned about the behavior of solid objects, lead me to be confident about the behavior of these objects, and make me confident that the pencil will fall next time as well. Is this *no* evidence at all? If not, then what *would* you count as evidence? Surely we have

here the very paradigm of good evidence; if the repeated fall of the pencil isn't evidence, what could be?

When you say that in the case of the pencil falling there is no good evidence that it will fall the next time, what would you count as being good evidence if this isn't? What is it that we *lack*? What are you waiting to have supplied, which, if supplied, would satisfy you? And the answer of course is, "Nothing;" there is nothing you would count as evidence, nothing that is now missing that, if supplied, would be evidence, other than the occurrence of the future event itself—and when that happens, it is no longer future.

When you say there is no evidence for the future, it's not as if you were awaiting some new or surprising event, some magic rabbit to be pulled out of a hat, some momentous empirical discovery that, if we only had it, would remove your skepticism. There is *nothing* that would allay it, for the simple reason that anything we can show you now is *now* and not future, and you refuse to consider anything that happens now as evidence for the future.

S: I still don't see that you have answered my question. What evidence have you today that stones will fall tomorrow?

C: The only evidence you will admit is the future event actually happening—in which case it's no longer future. Nothing in the present would do the trick for you. What we all adduce as evidence, you refuse to consider evidence. For you, no present event would count. No matter what I say, you simply reiterate that what I present isn't evidence.

You don't count it as evidence. As what? As evidence? And what's that? There is no evidence, you say; no what? What is it you mean by the term? You repeatedly tell me that there are no X's, but refuse to tell me what you would count as being an X.

Change the terminology, and you still have the same problem. "There is no *reason to believe* the pencil will drop next time," you say. And what, pray tell, if it occurred, would count as a reason? If there is nothing that would so count, it's because you refuse to attach any meaning to the word "reason" in this context. You say there is no reason. No what? Reason. And what does it mean to say so, since nothing would be admitted by you as a reason? You have not told us what "reason" means as you use the term. I say that the fact that pencil has fallen every time we dropped it is the very *paradigm* of a good reason for thinking it will continue to do so. If this isn't a good reason, what is?

S: The fact that the pencil has always fallen provides no good reason to believe that in the future it will continue to do so. We simply have no reason to believe one way or the other, until it happens. You may, of course, use the *word* "evidence" in such a way that you will count the past as evidence for the future. But I ask how you know that the past *does* constitute evidence. What has it, after all, to do with the future? What makes you so confident that future uniformities will resemble past ones? And all you can say in reply is that this is what has occurred *in the past*. I agree that what you call evidence *is* commonly *called* evidence; but that proves nothing—it just tells us how a word is generally used. But it never occurs to you to question whether data from the past *should* count as evidence for the future.

2. Let's try another defense for induction. We can't *deduce* any statement about the fu-

ture from any statements about the past. And we can't *inductively* show it, since induction is the very thing in question; we can't assume it without begging the question (assuming the point at issue). But we can do something else; we can give a *pragmatic justification* of it—not of the principle itself, but of our *adoption* of it. We can interpret it as a kind of *rule* of the scientific enterprise. We justify the adoption of a rule of baseball only if the rule makes the game more interesting or challenging. We justify the adoption of the uniformity of nature principle in terms of the goals that would be realized by such adoption, the understanding of nature's workings, and the ability to use that understanding to predict future events and sometimes even to control them.

We don't know, of course, that there exists an order of nature that extends into the future. But *if* there is, then what we call the scientific method—observing the data, noting apparent uniformities, discovering possible exceptions to them, varying the conditions, devising explanatory hypotheses—is our *best bet* for making future discoveries. Guessing, armchair philosophizing, crystal gazing, or having intuitions or mystical seizures won't do it: only painstaking observation and experiment will enable us to succeed. We are rather in the position of a patient who is told by her physician, "I don't know whether an operation will save you, but if you don't have an operation, you will die." So she submits to the operation as a "best bet," although she does not know whether she will survive even after having it.[9]

Still, we may wonder: *in the past* the painstaking method of observation, experiment, and devising theories has yielded

---

[9]This view was first set forth by Hans Reichenbach, *Experience and Prediction* (Chicago: University of Chicago Press, 1953), p. 349.

tremendously impressive scientific results. Crystal gazing and transcendental meditation have not. But is there any assurance that this situation will remain so in the future? What if, starting tomorrow, more of nature's secrets were unlocked by one of the "unscientific" methods now considered unfruitful—by doing auguries, gazing into crystals, chanting incantations, or going into a trance? If the course of nature were to change abruptly, how do you know that what we *now* call "scientific method" would be a better basis for prediction than these other procedures that we now discount? If the course of nature changes, our "scientific method" might be entirely useless as a predictor of the future. How could one tell *which* method of prediction, if any, would work in such an altered state of affairs?

3. Still others have taken the position that we make the unreasonable demand of induction that it follow the pattern of deduction. True, we can't validly deduce conclusions about the future from premises that don't mention the future; so what else is new? Induction isn't an inferior form of deduction; it isn't deduction at all—it is something quite different. There is no point in blaming a dog for not being a cat.

It has been argued, accordingly, that there can be no such thing as *general* justification of induction; the whole quest for it is a mistake. What we can do is to justify certain *particular procedures* that are instances of induction to discover which ones yield reliable results. We can ask, "Is random sampling reliable?" But we neither can nor need to justify induction in general:

It is generally proper to inquire *of a particular belief,* whether its adoption is justified; and, in asking this, we are asking whether there is good, bad, or any evidence for it. In applying or withholding the epithets "justified," "well

founded," etc., in the case of specific beliefs, we are appealing to, and applying, inductive standards. But to what standards are we appealing when we ask whether the application of inductive standards is justified or well grounded? If we cannot answer, then no sense has been given to the question.

Compare it with the question: Is the law legal? It makes perfectly good sense to inquire of a particular action, of an administrative regulation, or even, in the case of some states, a particular enactment of the legislature, whether or not it is legal. The question is answered by an appeal to a legal system, by the application of a set of legal (or constitutional) rules and standards. But it makes no sense to inquire in general whether the law of the land, the legal system as a whole, is or is not legal. For to what legal standards are we appealing? The only way in which a sense might be given to the question, whether induction is in general a justified or justifiable procedure, is a trivial one. . . . We might interpret it to mean "Are all conclusions, arrived at inductively, justified?" i.e., "Do people always have adequate evidence for the conclusions they draw?" The answer to this question is easy, but uninteresting; it is that sometimes people have adequate evidence, and sometimes they do not.[10]

This is doubtless a position that will appeal to our "common sense." Yet the controversy aroused by Hume's question has not died down. Has Hume really been answered? Has anyone presented any evidence that in ten minutes the course of nature will not radically change? And then all bets are off—it's "deuces are wild." And *if* this should happen, wouldn't we have been mistaken in believing that "what is commonly viewed as evidence" really *is* evidence? Scientists may go on believing that nature will continue to work as it has in the past, but *is* this any more than a "scientific faith"? Scientists continue their activities, never giving thought to this question;

[10]P. F. Strawson, *Introduction to Logical Theory* (London: Methuen, 1952), p. 257.

but the question has continued to fascinate (and plague) philosophers.

EXERCISES

1. What do you agree with and what do you disagree with in this dialogue?

A: One thing I am sure of, nature is *one*.
B: I don't understand what you mean by that. What if I said that nature is composed of a vast array of things?
A: I mean, it's one *system*. Everything in nature is interconnected with everything else.
B: I don't quite see how. How is the occurrence of a storm on Jupiter connected with the fact that I'm about to turn on this light? I can't see that the one has any effect on the other.
A: I can't prove that the storm on Jupiter affects this particular act, although it does affect many things on the earth. But events on Jupiter and events on the earth are both governed by the same *laws*.
B: You don't mean laws in the usual sense of rules of behavior passed by a legislature prescribing punishments if people don't obey them, do you?
A: No, I mean the ways in which nature works. The stone on earth and the stone on Jupiter are both subject to the same Law of Universal Gravitation.
B: I agree that they are. But that doesn't cover most things, such as why organisms reproduce and die.
A: That is in turn covered by other laws. Everything that happens in the universe is covered by some law or laws.
B: And how do you know this? What law is there about what your response will be to the question I'm asking? If you know of one, tell me what it is.
A: At the moment I can't: psychology is not

yet far enough along as a science to do this. Still, I'm sure that every occurrence is an instance of some law.

Evaluate what A and B are saying.

2. Keeping in mind the distinction between descriptive laws and prescriptive laws, evaluate the following comments:
a. We shouldn't disobey laws of nature.
b. Laws of nature have preordained what I shall do tomorrow.
c. When there's a law, there must be a lawgiver.
d. We don't make laws, we find them.
e. Laws of nature control the universe.
f. Our behavior must conform to psychological laws.

3. Which of the following propositions would you consider to be laws of nature? Why?
a. Iron rusts when exposed to oxygen.
b. Gold is malleable.
c. All human beings are mortal. (They die at some time or other.)
d. All white tomcats with blue eyes are deaf.
e. When organisms reproduce, the offspring is always of the same species.

4. Evaluate the following as explanations. In the case of unsatisfactory explanations, show what makes them unsatisfactory.
a. Why do birds build nests? Because they want to have a place to lay their eggs and bring up their young.
b. Why do birds build nests? Because it's their instinct to do so.
c. Why do most creatures lay more eggs than can possibly develop into full-grown offspring? Because they want to protect the species from extermination by competing organisms, cold, storms, and other destructive agencies.
d. Why does this substance become lighter (per unit of volume) as it becomes hotter? Because it contains an invisible substance, phlogiston, and the more of this it contains, the hotter it becomes; phlogiston is so light than an object is heavier for losing it.

e. Why did he arrive last night? Because God willed it so, and whatever God wills happens.

5. "Why did she stab him?" Answer 1: "Because she hated him intensely and wanted more than anything else to see him dead." Answer 2: "Because, as a result of the motion of certain particles of matter in her brain, electrochemical impulses were discharged along certain neuronic pathways, stimulating certain efferent nerves, activating the muscles in her hand and arm, causing them to move in a certain way." Do these two explanations conflict with each other? Does purposive explanation necessarily conflict with such "mechanical" explanations as given in Answer 2? How do you conceive the relation between them? Are they both parts of the whole explanation?

6. Examine the following dialogue, noting what you consider to be its good points as well as its bad points.

A: Did Newton discover any hitherto undiscovered empirical facts?

B: Yes, he discovered gravitation.

A: But we didn't need Newton to tell us that apples fall.

B: He explained *why* apples fall. They fall because of gravitation.

A: But gravitation isn't an explanation of *why* they fall. It is simply a fancy word stating a familiar fact, namely that things *do* fall. It is not an explanation, but simply a redescription in more general terms of the familiar fact that they do fall. (Compare the physician's statement that you are in this physical condition because you are run down.) What *is* gravitation but the fall of apples and the like?

B: Ah, you have admitted my point: gravitation is, indeed, much more than the fall of apples—it is the fall of apples *and the like*. Newton connected apples in or-

chards with stars in heaven. He brought seemingly disconnected events together under a general law, and to do this is to have explained them. Of course, if you think animistically of gravitation as a pull exerted as if by some supergiant, you are mistaken. Gravitation is not a pull; the word is simply a name for the fact that matter behaves in a certain definite and specifiable way. But the law that it does behave in this way is a genuine explanation, and it explains a vast number of phenomena, including the revolution of planets and the fall of apples.

7. What is theory and what is observed fact in the account of the cometary theory? How much of what is called "observation" or "observed fact" presupposes theories in its very formulation?

8. "Laws of science are *discovered,* but theories of science are *devised.*" Does this distinction hold up? Was the law of gravitation discovered or devised?

9. Would you consider the following to be *scientific* theories? Why or why not?

a. Everything has expanded to double its former size during the night—including all our measuring instruments. Could we ever know the difference? What if anything would it mean to say that everything had expanded?

b. "Imagine a community of men living on a cell in the blood stream of one of us, but so small that we have no evidence, direct or indirect, of their existence. Imagine further that they themselves are provided with scientific instruments of the type we use and possess a method of science and a body of scientific knowledge comparable to ours. One of the bolder of these thinkers proposes that the universe they inhabit is a Great Man. Is this hypothesis admissible on scientific grounds or is it to be laughed down on the grounds that it is "metaphysical"? Why at our own level can a similar hypothesis not be raised: namely, that *we* are parts of a Great Man, the whole of our known universe being perhaps but a portion of the Great Blood Stream?"

10. Induction is similar to deduction in that there are unprovable basic principles in both. We can't prove the law of identity or the law of noncontradiction, yet we accept them. Why can't we do the same with the principle of uniformity of nature?

11. Are the following logically possible? Justify your answers.

a. To jump 10,000 feet into the air.
b. To see a sound.
c. To have an unconscious desire.
d. To see something that doesn't exist.
e. To read tomorrow's newspaper today.
f. To cross a river and be on the same side you started from.
g. To see without eyes.
h. To be knocked into the middle of next week.
i. For a solid iron bar to float on water.
j. For a sound to exist that no creature in the world can hear.
k. For a table to eat the book that's on it.
l. For a box to be pure red and pure green all over its surface at the same time.
m. For Thursday to follow Tuesday without Wednesday in between. (Assume that you remain in the same spot, not crossing the International Date Line.)
n. For no world to exist at all.
o. For a part of space to move to some other part of space.
p. For a thought to occur without someone to think it.
q. For a straight line not to be the shortest distance between two points.
r. For someone to have experiences after she no longer has a physical body. (For more on this, see Chapter 6.)

12. Is it logically possible for there to be a bird that

a. lays its eggs upward through a hole in the bottom of the nest?
b. flies about in smaller and smaller concentric circles until, with a wild scream, it disappears up its own anus?

SELECTED READINGS

BLACKBURN, SIMON. *Essays in Quasi-Realism.* London: Oxford University Press, 1993.

BURTT, E. A. *Metaphysical Foundations of Modern Science.* New York: Harcourt Brace, 1932.

CHARLES, DAVID, and KATHLEEN LENNON, eds. *Reduction, Explanation, and Realism.* New York: Oxford University Press, 1992.

COHEN, JONATHAN. *Introduction to the Philosophy of Induction and Probability.* New York: Oxford University Press, 1989.

ELIAS, NORBERT. *Time.* Oxford: Blackwell, 1992.

FRAASSEN, BAS VAN. *Laws and Symmetry.* Oxford: Clarendon, 1992.

GOODMAN, NELSON. *Fact, Fiction, and Forecast.* Indianapolis: Bobbs Merrill, 1955.

HANSON, NORWOOD. *Patterns of Discovery.* Cambridge: Cambridge University Press, 1958.

HEMPEL, CARL. *Aspects of Scientific Explanation.* New York: Free Press, 1966.

HEMPEL, CARL. *Philosophy of Natural Science.* Englewood Cliffs, NJ: Prentice Hall, 1966.

KATZ, JERROLD. *The Problem of Induction and Its Solution.* Chicago: University of Chicago Press, 1962.

KITCHER, PHILIP. *Abusing Science.* Cambridge: MIT Press, 1982.

KUHN, THOMAS. *The Structure of Scientific Revolutions.* Chicago: University of Chicago Press, 1970.

MOSER, PAUL. *Philosophy after Objectivity.* New York: Oxford University Press, 1993.

NAGEL, ERNEST. *The Structure of Science.* New York: Harcourt Brace, 1961.

PUTNAM, HILARY. *Mind, Language, and Reality.* 2 vols. Cambridge: Cambridge University Press, 1975.

PUTNAM, HILARY. *The Many Faces of Realism.* LaSalle, IL: Open Court, 1991.

RAY, CHRISTOPHER. *Time, Space, and Philosophy.* London: Routledge, 1991.

REICHENBACH, HANS. *Experience and Prediction.* Chicago: University of Chicago Press, 1953.

RUBEN, DAVID HILLEL. *Explanation.* London: Oxford University Press, 1993.

SALMON, WESLEY. "An Encounter with David Hume." In Joel Feinberg, ed., *Reason and Responsibility.* Belmont, CA: Wadsworth, 1981.

SALMON, WESLEY. *Foundations of Scientific Inference.* Pittsburgh: University of Pittsburgh Press, 1968.

SALMON, WESLEY. *Limitations of Deductivism.* Berkeley: University of California Press, 1988.

SELLARS, WILFRID. *Science and Metaphysics.* London: Routledge, 1968.

SELLARS, WILFRID. *Science, Perception, & Reality.* London: Routledge and Kegan Paul, 1963.

SKLAR, LAWRENCE. *Philosophy of Physics.* Boulder, CO: Westview Press, 1992.

SKYRMS, BRIAN. *Choice and Chance.* Belmont, CA: Dickensen, 1964.

SMART, J.J.C. *Between Science and Philosophy.* New York: Random House, 1968.

SMART, J.J.C. *Problems of Space and Time.* New York: Macmillan, 1964.

SOBER, ELLIOTT. *Philosophy of Biology.* Boulder, CO: Westview Press, 1993.

WILL, FREDERICK L. *Induction and Justification.* Ithaca: Cornell University Press, 1974.

WOODFORD, ANDREW. *Teleology.* Cambridge: Cambridge University Press, 1976.

What Is and What Must Be

FREEDOM
AND NECESSITY

In the empirical sciences, the ultimate test of a law or theory is empirical observation. What the theory says may seem far removed from sense-experience, and there may be ever so many steps between the theory and our experience. We can redefine or rework theories in such a way that they seem immune to refutation by giving up one theory or one aspect of a theory in order to preserve others. But in the end, science must not be *immune to disconfirmation* by experience. It cannot be true "no matter what."

1. MATHEMATICS

But there are other statements that don't seem to be subject to empirical disconfirmation at all, and yet we speak of them as being true. Isn't it *true* that 2 + 2 = 4? We may not know what occurs on some distant planet and have no idea of what kind of life (if any) exists there, but don't we know that if there are two things and two more things, then there are four things? Isn't that true in *any possible world,* not just on ours?

We have laboratories for discovering truths about nature, but we don't have mathematics laboratories, and we don't need them, do we? We don't need test tubes and Bunsen burners to discover that 3 × 12 = 36; we have ways of figuring it out, deductively, as we do in logic. What we don't have to do is "go out into the world and look." Mathematics is a matter of "pure reason," not of experience.

Or so it seems. Let's run through a few considerations that may clarify the issue:

How do you know that 2 + 2 always makes 4? We look at these two trees and those two trees, and they always add up to four trees. And the same is true with four dogs, four books, four boxes, and so on. Is "2 + 2 = 4" a *generalization* from experience, to which no exceptions have yet been discovered? Shall we say merely that we've never found any two things and two more things that didn't add up to four things? Is "2 + 2 = 4" like a law of chemistry, such as the one about the boiling point of water? Water boils at a lower temperature as the pressure decreases; could 2 + 2 add up to less than 4 if there were different pressure, or a different pull of gravitation, or a different temperature?

Might 2 and 2 *not* equal 4 on Mars or somewhere else in the universe? We may not know much about what takes place on Mars, what species of life (if any) exists there, whether it has volcanic rock, and so on, but can't we say we *know* that if there are two things and then two more things, then there are four things—on earth, on Mars, and everywhere else? Could two things and two things add up to anything but four things, no matter where or when?

If not, statements of arithmetic like "2 + 2 = 4" are quite unlike statements in the sciences, which are always subject to amendment in the light of subsequent experience. It's true of course that we *learn* that 2 + 2 =4 in our early school years (we weren't born knowing it); but *what* we learned was not a law of nature like the Law of Gravitation, but an "eternal truth" like "Not both A and not-A" (Law of Noncontradiction) and "If *p* implies *q* and *q* implies *r*, then *q* implies *r*" (Principle of Logic). Indeed, there is almost no one today who would say that statements of arithmetic are like laws of nature. Mathematics, like logic, consists of *necessary truths*.

Suppose, however, that someone argued, "The propositions of arithmetic *aren't always true*. Two and two doesn't always make four. For example, if you add two quarts of water to two quarts of alcohol, you ought to get four quarts—but you don't; you get a little less, owing to the interpenetration of molecules of the two substances. If you put together two lions and two lambs, and turn your back for a moment, you will not have four things, but only two—two lions. When two amoebas subdivide, they become four—what was two is now four! How can arithmetical propositions be necessary at all if they aren't even true in all cases—when observation often shows them to be false?"

But there is a misunderstanding. When we say that 2 + 2 = 4, we do not deny for a moment that what *was* two can *become* four (the amoebas), or that you can have four things at one time and have only two things at a later time (the lions having eaten the lambs). It says only that *if* you have two and two, then *at that moment* you have four. Arithmetic does not tell you anything about natural processes—how two things can become four things, or how what was four can become two things. Arithmetic doesn't even tell you that there are four of anything in the world at all, or even that there *is* a world in which such distinctions can be made. It says only that *if* there are two and then two more, *then* there must be four: that to say there are two plus

two and to say that there are four is to say the same thing. When there are two lions and two lambs, then there are four things; when there are only two lions, then there are only two—that is, one plus one—things. If two things give rise to a million things, this would not violate "2 + 2 = 4" or any other proposition of arithmetic. Two rabbits soon become a million rabbits; and if two things exploded into a million things, or into nothing at all, this occurrence would not refute any law of arithmetic. What turns into what, what becomes what, how one thing changes into another—all of these have to do with what happens in the world. The laws of arithmetic are not concerned with what happens in the physical world—whether two things placed in the presence of two other things sit quietly side by side, or melt, or explode, or tear the room apart. What if two things *fuse into one*—can we say then that 1 = 2? No, we can say that what *was* two has *become* one—just as an A can become a B without disturbing the Law of Identity (which we discussed in Chapter 2). 2 + 2 = 4 because "4" is another way of saying "2 + 2," and "2 + 2" is another way of saying "1 + 1 + 1 + 1."

But suppose that every time you counted trees, two over here and two more over there, another tree mysteriously popped into existence and so you had five. Wouldn't "2 + 2" then (at least sometimes) equal "5"? No, "2 + 2 = 4" would hold true no matter what happened during the counting process. Maybe you were systematically miscounting, or maybe as a result of the counting another tree came into existence. In that case, you wouldn't have two and two, but two and two and one, that is, five!

It is easy to confuse statements of pure arithmetic (statements about numbers, not things) with statements about what happens to things in the world if you mix or combine them. "2 + 2 = 4" is a truth of arithmetic, but "If you add two apples to two apples, you'll get four apples" is not. Just as you don't *add* water to alcohol, you don't add apples to apples; you put them together and see what happens. In the cases of apples, they sit side by side until someone moves them—that's a fact of nature, not of arithmetic. The correct statement would be not "If you add two apples to two apples, you get four apples," but rather "If you place two apples next to two other apples, you will end up with four apples" (rather than an explosion or a meltdown)—making it clear that the second statement is about nature, not about numbers.

How do we distinguish the two kinds of statements? By asking, "When we say 'two apples,' *does it matter* whether it's apples or elephants or grains of sand or thoughts about Thursday that we're talking about?" If it does, it's not a statement of arithmetic; in the case of water and sodium, there might be an explosion and not four of anything. But if it *doesn't* matter whether it's apples or anything else; if it's only about numbers, then it's a statement in arithmetic and not about any natural processes. Elementary arithmetic textbooks often get this mixed up by trying to "make things concrete": instead of saying, "If you add 2 and 2," they say, "If you add 2 spoonsful of alcohol . . . ," as if they were talking about alcohol instead of about numbers, whereas the statement isn't about alcohol or any other substance.

Suppose you are counting trees: two trees to your left, two trees to your right, but every time you tried to count them all together, you got five as your result instead of four. What would we say if this kept on happening? Would textbooks of arithmetic have to be revised, saying "Sometimes 2 and 2 makes 5"? Not at all; "2 and 2 makes 4" would remain true *no matter what happened in the counting process.* If you kept on getting five trees as a result, you might decide that you were sys-

tematically miscounting, or that in the very act of counting, another tree was created or just popped into existence. But the one thing you would *not* say is that 2 and 2 sometimes makes 5. If you found an additional tree every time you tried to count them all together, you would say that two trees plus two trees, plus one tree that seems to pop into existence when you count, together make five trees. Arithmetic would remain untouched.

Other necessary truths. But there are other statements that nothing could falsify (or so it seems). Philosophers have different ways of stating this: the statements couldn't possibly be false; they are necessarily true; they would be true in all possible worlds. Let's consider a few suggested examples.

1. *Nothing can be red all over and green all over at the same time.*

A: We can mix red and green paints, and thus end up with both colors all over the object's surface at the same time.

B: But then it isn't all red and all green. It's a mixture of both.

A: It can be striped red and green, or mottled.

B: Of course. That still isn't being all red and all green all over.

A: What's red is red, and what's green is green. Of course it can't be both.

B: But a marble can be both red and hard at the same time. Why can't it be both red and green at the same time?

A: Because being red excludes being green, but being red doesn't exclude being hard.

B: But why is the green excluded from being red and the hard is not?

A: That's by definition. Color terms are defined in such a way as to exclude each other.

B: Why do you suppose they're defined in that way? As I said, redness doesn't exclude hardness. Why not?

A: I don't know why terms are defined as they are; but as now defined, they exclude each other.

B: The problem is that you can't verbally define "red" and "green" at all. That's what makes this example different from "The vase can't be both 12 inches high and 18 inches high at the same time." If it's 18 inches high, it can't also be *not* 18 inches high (such as 12 inches); that would be a contradiction.

A: Why wouldn't it also be a contradiction to say that it's both red and hard? Hard is not-red, and green is not-red; what's the difference?

B: Being hard is merely *other than* being red—just as being large, being loud, being fragrant, etc., are all other than being red. But being green is not merely *other* than being red; it is also *incompatible* with being red.

A: Yes, in reality the two qualities are incompatible. You can call this "natural necessity" if you like. If it's the one, it can't be the other. But in the case of red and hard, if it's the one it *can* be the other—and sometimes is. It's just a "necessity of nature" that we can say "red, therefore not green," but not "red, therefore not hard."

B: This illustrates what philosophers call the Principle of Determinables. Red, green, blue, etc., are all determinates under the general heading of color, and square, circular, elliptical, etc., are all determinates under the determinate of shape. The Principle of Determinables says that you can't have more than one determinate at the same time under the same determinable. Thus, you can't have red (all red, that is) at the same time and

the same place as green, but the red thing can be all hard or all square, because shape and hardness are different determinables.

A: Very neat. And where do you get this Principle of Determinables? Where does it come from? What proof is there of it? I say that it's a metaphysical necessity. It's not like a scientific generalization to which an exception might turn up tomorrow. It's something to which there *can't* be any exceptions. What is red all over is forever excluded from also being (at the same time) blue all over. That's the way reality is. Necessarily.

2. *Two things can't be at the same place at the same time, and one thing can't be in two different places at the same time.*

Suppose I see you enter at the door, and at the same time I see you come in at the other door. Impossible, isn't it? Because if you're at the one place, you can't be at the other. There might be an optical trick or a mirror image, but *you* can't be both at the one door and at the other door at the same time. That would be two people, not one. One person can't be at two places simultaneously.

And the same holds for two things in one place. You can't have two books that are both at that one corner of the desk at the same moment. What you see there is one book; if there were two books, they would have to be at two different places.

A: You could have two candles and melt them into one; wouldn't that be two things at the same place? Or if two cars collide, wouldn't that be two cars in the same place at the same time?

B: You might say they were both trying to be in the same place. But what happened was only that a part of the one car now occupies the portion of space that was previously occupied by a part of the other car.

A: But consider just that one spot: two things can't both occupy it.

B: I don't know how big the "spot" is that you have in mind. Couldn't two amoebas occupy it? two specks of dust? What people mean by the phrase "the same place" is quite vague. Two bicycles can be in the same place, if you mean the same automobile stall; they're both in stall 15-C.

A: If you mix a clear liquid with a green liquid, don't you have the two liquids at the same place at the same time?

B: In ordinary usage we'd probably say, "Yes, there are molecules of both in the same area, say the same hundredth of a cubic inch."

A: Yes, but each of the molecules is still at a different place. Can two molecules both be in the same place?

B: In the same millionth of an inch area? I'm still not sure what you mean by "same place."

A: I doubt that there is a clear definition of "same place." I am sure only that if there are two things in a certain area, we would say that they were in two different places—we'd *call* it two different places; and that if there is only one thing, whether it's one marble, one fleck of dust, or one molecule, we'd say it's not in two different places. It's the phrase, not our thoughts about it, that's vague.

B: It's a matter of *how far* we are prepared to go in *calling* it the same place.

A: Let's recapitulate. "2 + 2 = 4" is a necessary truth, because to deny it is self-contradictory—it would be saying that "1 + 1 + 1 + 1" does not equal "1 + 1 + 1 + 1." In that respect it's like "A is A" and "If all A is B and all B is C, then all A is C." These are necessary truths, truths of logic. Their denial is unintelligible because a

person who asserted them would be saying that 1 + 1 etc. is *not* 1 + 1 etc. or that A is not A, and these are self-contradictory.

B: "A thing can't be red and green all over" is also a necessary truth, but I don't see how its denial involves any contradiction. There's no contradiction in saying, "It's red and hard"; why not the same with "red and green"? "Red and not-red" is self-contradictory, but "red and green" isn't. Can you show me that it is? Is it then a fact of nature, like the number of trees in the park, which might have been different from what it is? Yet "2 + 2 = 4" is a logical truth, which could not be other than it is.

A: What is it then—a fact of nature, like the number of trees in the park, which might have been different from what it is?

B: No, the problem is that "2 + 2 = 4" is a logical truth, but that "It's both red and green" is a necessary truth (try to imagine a world in which it was not so) but not a logical truth. I see no more contradiction in denying it than in denying "It's both red and hard," which is often true! Shall we say that at last we have a genuine example of a synthetic necessary truth?

2. KANT AND THE SYNTHETIC A PRIORI

Do you want to be certain that nature works in certain uniform ways? that causality operates throughout the universe? that the laws of nature endure through all space and time? that 7 + 5 always equals 12? There is a way, said Immanuel Kant (1724–1804). But it comes at a price.

All judgments, said Kant, can be divided into two kinds, which he called *analytic* and *synthetic.* In analytic judgments the predicate repeats all or part of what was already in the subject; in synthetic judgments the predicate says something over and above what was in the subject. Analytic judgments are of the form "All A is A"; synthetic judgments are of the form "All A is B." "All bachelors are bachelors" is analytic; so is "All bachelors are unmarried," when you substitute the definition of "bachelor," an unmarried man, for the word and get "All unmarried men are unmarried men," which is analytic. On the other hand, "All bachelors are tall" is not analytic but synthetic (and this one is false).

Analytic propositions can also take the form "All AB is A": only a defining characteristic, not the whole definition, appears in the predicate. Thus, "All triangles are three-sided" and "All fathers are male" are both analytic, although the predicate term contains only a part of the definition. The statement is still true entirely by virtue of the meanings of the words in it: all fathers are male, because anyone who was not a male would not be called a father (as we use the word "father").

Kant then introduces another pair of terms, "*a priori*" and "*a posteriori.*" These terms have to do not with the propositions themselves (as "analytic" and "synthetic" do) but with our *knowledge* of them. An a priori truth is one that can be known "independently of experience"—which isn't to say that we didn't have to learn it at some time or that we didn't need to have experience of learning the *words,* but only that we don't have to discover it inductively, by amassing instances, as we do with laws of nature. All analytic statements are knowable a priori: we need only to know the meanings of the terms in order to know whether they're true; we don't have to look to nature. By contrast, "All crows are black" is knowable only a posteriori—that is, after (posterior to) people have

had experience of crows. And the same, of course, is true for laws about the temperature at which water freezes, lead melts, and so on—all have to be established in a case-by-case basis through sense-experience. Laws of nature are all a posteriori: only experience can confirm them, and experience can also refute them if experience does not bear them out.

There is no controversy about whether analytic propositions are knowable a priori: clearly they are. We don't need to examine any bachelors to discover whether they are unmarried; the definition of "bachelor" tells us that they are. Nor are there any controversies about whether statements knowable only a posteriori are synthetic: we have to wait for experience to tell us whether all crows are black and whether all white tomcats with blue eyes are deaf. These statements, which we can know only a posteriori, are synthetic—what occurs in the predicate (black) goes beyond what is mentioned in the subject (crows).

But there is a third category, said Kant; statements that are both synthetic *and* knowable a priori. "How can this be?" we may wonder. How can a statement be true independently of experience—we can know it to be true for all cases even before examining these cases—and yet, unlike analytic statements, give us knowledge, not knowledge of what a word means (like "All bachelors are unmarried") but knowledge of the world outside language? How can a statement be true of the world and yet not be subject to refutation by any possible experience of the world? It would be nice if we could acquire knowledge of what the world is like without having to do the work of going through countless examples to discover whether "All A's are B's" is true. But isn't this just trying to have the best of both worlds? If someone says that all swans are white, and the statement isn't analytic—that is, being white is not part of the definition of "swan"—then how could one possibly know it to be true a priori, that is, without examining all swans to discover whether the statement is true? Synthetic a priori truths have seemed to many philosophers to be a hopeless will-o'-the-wisp—like trying to have your cake and eat it at the same time.

Many philosophers before Kant held that human beings can have a priori knowledge of reality. These are philosophers in the tradition of *rationalism,* as opposed to *empiricism,* the view that knowledge of reality is always a posteriori. The rationalism we discussed in Chapter 1 was "concept rationalism," the view that there are some innate ideas; the rationalism we are concerned with now is about propositional knowledge. But rationalists have often disagreed with one another about which propositions have this privileged status. No one has denied that analytic statements such as "Fathers are male" are knowable a priori: the word "father" means male parent, so the statement becomes merely "A male parent is a male parent." But what empiricists have denied is that there is a priori knowledge of reality. (Aristotle's laws of thought may be, as Aristotle contended, laws about reality, and in this sense Aristotle was a rationalist. But whatever the status of the Laws of Thought, they are not synthetic propositions: to deny "A is A" is to say "A is not A," which is self-contradictory—and our question at the moment is whether there is *synthetic* a priori knowledge.)

Which propositions are synthetic a priori, and what justifies us in saying this, have always been worrisome points for rationalists. But Kant had a different and original way of meeting these challenges. The question he put to himself was not "Is there synthetic a priori knowledge?"—the answer he gave was Yes—but rather "*How* is synthetic a priori knowledge possible?" Most of his famous *Cri-*

tique of Pure Reason was devoted to an attempt to answer this question.

We ordinarily believe that our knowledge must "conform to the way things are". Indeed it must, said Kant, but it is also true that "objects must conform to our knowledge." But how can this be? we may ask. Do our own mental faculties determine the way the world is? Does the world accommodate itself to our wishes and demands? No, said Kant, but the world as we perceive it through our senses and understand it through our reason must be adapted to our mode of perception and cognition. To take a crude example, if we always looked at the world through green glasses that we could never remove (and didn't even know we had on), everything would look green to us—not that everything would *be* green, but that it would appear so to us because of the nature of the lenses through which we looked at it.

It is not the world "as it is in itself" that we perceive, but the world as it is filtered through our senses and our understanding. The world as it is, and the world as it appears to us, are utterly different:

Surely, one may think at first sight, it is quite fantastic to assert that "objects must conform to our knowledge"; for how could it possibly be that the nature of our faculties should determine, or even influence in any way, what is the case in the world? Surely we are simply obliged to take the world as we find it; it would be a gross absurdity to suppose that it must somehow accommodate itself to our needs or our demands. Now, Kant feels the full force of this objection and to meet it he draws and insists upon a vital distinction between the world as it is *in itself* and as it *appears to us.* What exists, exists; its nature simply is what it is; with that, we ourselves can have nothing to do. It is, however, equally certain that what exists *appears* to human beings in a particular way, and is by them classified, interpreted, categorized, and described in a particular manner. If our sense-organs had been radically different from what they are, certainly the world would have appeared to us as being radically different; if our languages and modes of thought had been utterly different, the descriptions of the world that we should have been given would also have been different from those that we now give. Thus, though our faculties and capacities make no difference at all to the nature of what exists in itself, they do partly determine the character of the world as it appears; they determine the general *form* that it has; for whatever the world may be in itself, it appears to us in the way that it does because we are what we are. It is, then, with the world as appearance that Kant is concerned; it is objects as *phenomena* that must "conform to our knowledge."[1]

We must distinguish, said Kant, between what we *find* in the world and what we *bring* to the world. We find, for example, that swans are white and that most animals are four-legged; we can easily imagine it to be otherwise. But can we imagine space to have (for example) twelve dimensions? Do we "just find" that there is only one space? that the nature of temporal sequence is the same in undiscovered parts of the universe as we have found it to be thus far?

Kant concluded that we do not treat assertions about space and time as ordinary assertions of fact that have possible alternatives. We *come to* the universe with the postulate that whatever it contains, its contents shall be in three-dimensional space, and that whatever events occur, they shall take their place in a single time series. We do not know what reality in itself is like; but the world of appearances, the phenomenal world, can appear only in a way we are capable of perceiving. Our sensibility is such that we are able to perceive only what has a spatial and temporal character; the world as it appears to us (the phenomenal world) *must* then have this spatial and temporal character. That the

phenomenal world will have these features is both synthetic and a priori.

Kant called the world of ordinary sense-perception and of science the *phenomenal* world. The phenomenal world is *spatial*—one thing is bigger than another, one thing is at a certain distance removed from another; the phenomenal world is also *temporal*—one event occurs before another, one occurs after another, one occurs simultaneously with another. But space and time—filters through which we are aware of anything and everything—are simply the "forms of our intuition," the way that reality inescapably appears to us. Space and time belong to the phenomenal world only. They are the molds into which our experiences are cast. We cannot even think of any object that does not occupy time or space. But this fact reflects the nature of the human mind, not the nature of reality. Phenomenal space has three dimensions (length, breadth, height); could it just as well have had twenty-seven dimensions? We never doubt that there is only *one* space; nor can we imagine anything different. But our imaginations are limited to what is "filtered" to us—to the phenomenal world. We also assume that time is everywhere the same, and that if A precedes B and B precedes C, A will precede C; and this *is* a necessary truth about the phenomenal world; that is the way time presents itself to us in the phenomenal world.

There are also the *categories* by which our minds synthesize the data of experience (we shall not attempt a complete list). One of these is *substance:* We perceive the phenomenal world in terms of things (such as iron) and their properties (such as heavy, magnetic). Another is *causality:* we speak of events causing one another, being bound by a relation of cause and effect. Another is *number:* We say there are a certain number of things, and we count them—but this cate-

---

[1] G. J. Warnock, "Kant," in D. J. O'Connor, ed., *A Critical History of Western Philosophy* (New York: Free Press, 1964), p. 300.

gory (number) exists only in the phenomenal world.

If we caught fish in nets, and the reticulations in the net were 2 inches square, we would catch no fish less than two inches long, for they would slip through the net; but if the nets were underwater and we couldn't see the small fish slipping through, we might report that there are no fish in the sea less than 2 inches long. But this would not really report the contents of the sea—it would only reflect the nature of the nets. We might think that we were making a true statement about the fish in the sea, but we would not. So it is, according to Kant, with our knowledge of the phenomenal world, which we mistakenly believe to be knowledge of the real (noumenal) world. Of the noumenal world we can make no statements at all, having no access to it.

The noumenal world is neither spatial nor temporal. "That's absurd!" we may say. "Do you mean to tell me that in reality Aristotle didn't come before Descartes, and that an elephant isn't larger than a mouse? Is New York not really north of Miami? And if there is no before and after, are you saying that the crops aren't planted before they're harvested, and that dinosaurs didn't live on the earth before people did? Wasn't I born *after* my parents were born? Moreover, if time isn't real, how did we ever *learn* the meanings of temporal words? Isn't this Parmenides' problem all over again—"Motion is unreal," said Parmenides, and then he walked away—and indeed a problem for anyone who denies the reality of time? We distinguish between phenomenal time (apparent time: "the lecture lasted thirty minutes but it seemed like hours") and clock time, but we don't throw time out entirely."

There have been other objections to Kant's view besides their alleged absurdity. For example, Kant held that arithmetical propositions like "7 + 5 = 12" are synthetic, whereas many others would say they are analytic: that "2" just *means* 1 = 1, and "1 + 1 = 1 + 1" is analytic. Kant also held that the propositions of Euclidean geometry (the only geometry known in his time) are synthetic and a priori, whereas most geometers today would say that they are not a priori, but very general empirical statements about the world, true only insofar as Euclidean geometry reflects the nature of actual space.

There are more general criticisms as well. For example, if reality is "filtered" by the mind, how do we know that the nature of the mind won't change? Also, that there is a noumenal world is not an observation but an *inference,* and if the curtain of reality closes on the noumenal, how was Kant justified in saying anything about it? (He offered a lengthy explanation for this, attempting to prove that we would run into contradictions if we failed to posit the noumenal.)

Copernicus originated a revolution in astronomy, from the sun going round the earth to the earth going round the sun. Kant believed himself to have originated a Copernican revolution in philosophy: instead of our minds reflecting the nature of reality, what we have viewed as reality reflects the nature of our minds. It was an exciting and imaginative creative endeavor. But, to put it mildly, not everyone has been convinced of its truth.

3. CAUSALITY

What Is a Cause?

We haven't yet finished with necessity. The word "necessary" is used constantly in our everyday conversations, although we don't always mean the same thing by it. "For combustion to occur, it is necessary that there be oxygen." "To lose weight, it's necessary to stay on a healthful diet." When A is required in order for B to occur, we won't get result B unless the prior condition, A, is fulfilled.

What is necessary as a means toward one end may not be for another. "To stay in good condition, it's necessary that you have regular exercise." Exercise may be necessary as a means toward *that* end, but maybe we don't care about achieving that end. "To gain the respect of the gang, it's necessary for you to commit at least one murder." The end (goal) may not be achieved without this, but one could dispute the value of the end itself. "If you want to compete in the Olympics, it's necessary to . . ." "But I don't want to compete in the Olympics!"

All these are *empirically* necessary conditions; the world being as it is, you won't get B without A. But they are not *logically* necessary conditions: there's no contradiction in saying that a person can lose weight without a certain diet. But being three-sided *is* a logically necessary condition for being a triangle, because something wouldn't *be* a triangle unless it had three sides; "X is a triangle but doesn't have three sides" would be a self-contradictory statement.

Are there necessities in nature? It's not very clear what the question is supposed to mean. Does it mean "Are there events in nature that *must* occur as they do?" Why do people say not only that stones *do* fall, but that they *must* fall?

1. The "home base" or "home turf" of the word "must" is in the context of *command*. A child is told that she must do her homework tonight; otherwise a certain punishment will follow. But when we say that wood must burn or water must flow downhill, are we saying that wood and water are being commanded?

It is easy to confuse laws of nature, which *describe* how nature works, with *prescriptive* laws, such as those enacted by a legislature, saying in effect, "If you don't do so-and-so, you are subject to such-and-such punishment."

Historically, the two senses of the word "law" were not distinguished. The uniformities of nature were conceived as the expression of the will of God, or of the gods. God *commands* the forces of nature to act in certain ways; by His will He *compels* events to occur as they do. Since God is far more powerful than any government, God's laws are inviolable. They are the expression of a divine order that God imposed upon the universe. Effects follow causes much as punishment follows sin. Saying that events "must" occur as they do may contain a residue of this theistic conception of the world. However, "The question which must be put to those who speak as if there were necessity in nature is whether they really mean to imply that the laws of nature are normative rules, enforced by a divine will. If they do not mean to imply this, then talk of necessity is at best an unfortunate metaphor."[2]

Constant conjunction. The most influential philosopher to have discussed causality was David Hume. What is usually meant by saying, "A causes B"? Three things, said Hume, of which the third is by far the most important:

1. *Temporal precedence.* The cause precedes the effect. The crops are planted before they are harvested, not the other way round. You prepare your speech before you deliver it to an audience, not vice versa.

We sometimes say that your future goal (to pass the course) is what caused you to study today. But it is not the future goal that does it (the future doesn't yet exist), but your present commitment to your future goal that is causally operative now.

---

[2]Alfred J. Ayer, *Foundations of Empirical Knowledge* (London: Macmillan, 1945), p. 198.

2. *Contiguity in space and time.* When you light the fuse and the gunpowder explodes some yards away, the explosion would not occur unless in between there is a fuse. The electricity goes along the wire: if the electric wire between the lights and the source of power were cut, there would be no light. There is no "action at a distance."

Hume was somewhat hesitant about this condition, and with good reason. When light and heat from the sun cause the earth's atmosphere to warm, what is there between the sun and the earth except empty space? According to the ether hypothesis of the nineteenth century, there is an undetectable and weightless medium, the ether, that transmits the radiation. But no evidence for this was found, and the theory was abandoned more than a century ago. Neither does gravitation require any proximity between bodies.

3. *Necessary connection.* A part of the common concept of causality is that the cause and the effect are necessarily connected—that if the cause occurs, the effect *must* occur; it *cannot but* occur.

But in this, said Hume, the common view (perhaps the common view only among philosophers) is mistaken. We never observe any necessary connection or "must" or "has to" among events:

> When we look about us towards external objects, and consider the operation of causes, we are never able, in a single instance, to discover any power or necessary connexion; any quality, which binds the effect to the cause, and renders the one an infallible consequence of the other. We only find, that the one does actually, in fact, follow the other. The impulse of one billiard ball is attended with motion in the second. This is the whole that appears to the *outward* senses. The mind feels no sentiment or *inward* impression from this succession of objects. Consequently, there is not, in any single, particular instance of cause and effect, anything which can suggest the idea of power or necessary connexion.

> From the first appearance of an object, we never can conjecture what effect will result from it. But were the power or energy of any cause discoverable by the mind, we could foresee the effect, even without experience; and might, at first, pronounce with certainty concerning it, by mere dint of thought and reasoning.[3]

Those who attribute necessary connections to nature, or say that effects necessarily follow their causes, are going beyond anything that anyone can observe. We never observe that one event *must* follow another but only that it *does* in fact follow another. We can attribute necessity to the *relations among propositions* ("If all A's are B's, then all B's must be A's") but not to the *sequences of events in nature*. "There are no objects," wrote Hume, "which by the mere survey, without consulting experience, we can determine to be the cause of any other, and no objects, which we can certainly determine in the same manner not to be the causes." In every case we have to wait and see what happens; we cannot say a priori (in advance of experience) what will happen.

If we see two trains rapidly approaching one another on the same track, can't we say that there *must* be a collision? No, said Hume. Prior to any experience of how solid objects behave and move, we would have no idea of what would happen when they approach each other. Without prior experience, we would be no more entitled to say they will collide than that they will turn to mush or disappear into thin air. Only *with* a background of experience, which we have, are we able to predict that they will collide. Certain regular sequences have been observed through thousands of cases; it is this experience of regularity that entitles us to

---

[3]David Hume, *An Enquiry Concerning Human Understanding*, Selby-Bigge ed. (Oxford University Press, 1951), Section 7.

make claims about what causes what. As Hume put it, only when A and B are *constantly conjoined* in our experience, can we say with any confidence that A causes B. As one contemporary Humean puts it,

> To say that the electric current causes a deflection of the magnetic needle means that whenever there is an electric current there is always a deflection of the magnetic needle. The addition in terms of *always* distinguishes the causal law from a chance occurrence. It once happened that while the screen of a motion picture theater showed the blasting of lumber, a slight earthquake shook the theater. The spectators had a momentary feeling that the explosion on the screen caused the shaking of the theater. . . .
> Since repetition is all that distinguishes the causal law from a mere coincidence, the meaning of causal relation consists in the statement of an exceptionless repetition. . . . The idea that a cause is connected with its effect by a sort of hidden string, that the effect is forced to follow the cause, is anthropomorphic in its origin and is dispensable; *if-then-always* is all that is meant by a causal relation. If the theater would always shake when an explosion is visible on the screen, then there would be a causal relationship.[4]

Necessary connection has dropped out, and what remains, said Hume, is *constant conjunction* among events. But don't we want to know *why* certain A's are conjoined with certain B's—why ingesting arsenic causes death, for example? Sometimes we can break the sequence down further: we can observe what happens in the organism, such as loss of blood when the arsenic eats away at the stomach walls, and so on. But, said Hume, this is nothing but more constant conjunctions: the original constant conjunction (ingestion of poison, death) has been broken down into more detailed constant conjunctions, which

may help to explain why the original constant conjunction occurred.

Person-to-person causality. But it's different when people are the causes of their own inner states. People have an inner experience of *power.* Don't we know without observing any constant conjunctions that we have the power to move our limbs? and that if we conclude that a loved one is guilty of unfaithfulness, we will feel distressed? Don't we know without constant trial and error what we can cause?

No, said Hume, we don't. I may have an inner *sense* of power, but I have to try and see what *actual* powers I have. If I decide to raise my arm, it goes up; but if I decide to move my heart or sternum, I can't. I may, as a child, feel that I can fly through the air like a bird; but if I get on a ladder and try, I have a nasty fall. "I can do anything," a child may feel, but only experience will reveal what she can do and what she can't. From our earliest years we have experienced *so often* that distress follows disappointment, and that we can bend our knees backward but not forward, that we have forgotten how we first learned this and may conclude that we "always knew it." Suppose that I try to move my legs to walk as usual and then find that I can't: I have just had a paralytic stroke. But when I tried to move my legs, I was just as confident of a power to do this as I was in the former cases when my legs did "obey the command of my will." "Neither in the one case nor in the other," wrote Hume, "are we ever conscious of any . . . necessary connexion. We learn the influence of our will from experience alone. And experience only teaches us, how one event constantly follows another."[5]

Hume's negative thesis about causality—that nature presents us with no necessary

---

[4]Hans Reichenbach, *The Rise of Scientific Philosophy* (Berkeley, CA: University of California Press, 1951), pp. 157–158.

[5]Hume, *An Enquiry Concerning Human Understanding,* Part 7.

connections (whatever they are)—has been widely accepted, but his positive thesis—that what we have left are constant conjunctions—has been criticized as being either mistaken or unfinished in detail. Thus:

1. There would appear to be many examples of constant conjunction that aren't examples of causality. Night regularly follows day and day follows night, but they don't cause each other. The growth of hair in babies is regularly followed by the growth of teeth, yet the first doesn't cause the second.

How constant, one wonders, must the conjunction be? If we have observed A to be followed by B a hundred times, is that enough? a thousand times? And what if there are one or two exceptions—should we say then that A doesn't cause B, or does so only sometimes?

2. There would appear to be many examples of causality that aren't examples of constant conjunction. Heart attacks are often the cause of death, yet many heart attacks don't lead to death, and many deaths do not result from heart attacks. We say that scratching the match caused it to light, but scratched matches often fail to light. Being depressed and irritable, we say, caused him to lash out against his wife, and may this not be true although it happened only once?

In daily life, when there is a fairly constant conjunction between two events, we may *suspect* that there is a causal relation "lurking somewhere in the neighborhood." The more regular the correlation, the more we suspect the existence of a causal relation. There is some correlation between smoking cigarettes and getting lung cancer, although some people who don't smoke get lung cancer, and many people who do smoke never get it. Apparently there are lots of other variables. There is no one factor A that we know to be constantly conjoined with an effect B, but a variety of factors that occur with some degree of regularity.

Necessary and sufficient conditions. John Stuart Mill endeavored to flesh out Hume's account. There are many examples of regularity that aren't causal. But we have first to be clear on what kind of regularity we have in mind.

1. *Necessary condition.* When we say that C is a necessary condition for E, we mean only that if C had not occurred, E would not have occurred. Oxygen is a necessary condition for fire—that is, fires don't start in the absence of oxygen. The presence of oxygen isn't enough—fires depend on other conditions as well—but it is necessary not in the sense of "necessary connection" but merely in the sense that in the absence of C, E would not have occurred.

We do not ordinarily speak of a necessary condition as the cause. The cause of the street being wet is that rain has just fallen, yet rain is not a necessary condition for the street being wet; a water sprinkler will also make the street wet. For you to be ill, it is necessary that you first be alive, but one would not speak of being alive as the cause of your illness.

At this point, however, we should make an important distinction. Thus far we have spoken loosely of C as causing E, as if C and E were particular events. But particular events are not repeatable. The fall of a stone is a particular event, and if we drop this stone again this will be *another* event—an event of the same class or type, but not the *same* particular event. A more accurate formulation, then, would be: "In the absence of an event or condition of type C (presence of oxygen), an event of *type E* (combustion) does not occur." The examples of causation presented thus far have been of this kind.

But we may also say, "In the absence of this *particular* event or condition C, this particular event E would not have occurred." For example, if the speeding driver had not struck her car, she would not have died at this time (or at least not from this accident). We do not mean that having one's car struck by a speeding driver is a necessary condition for deaths in general. Death can occur from many causes, and car accidents are in no way necessary conditions for death. All people will die, but most of them will not die from car accidents. Still, it may be true that, *but for* being struck by this car, she would not have died at this time: if this particular event (collision) had not occurred, this particular outcome (her death) would not have occurred.

The legal profession often employs this "but for" test: *but for* the fact that she stepped into the road, she would not have been hit by the passing car; *but for* his being in the air terminal at the moment that the terrorist's bomb went off, he would not have been killed in the blast. Here we do not mean to imply that events or conditions of type 1 (bomb blasts) are always necessary for events of type 2 (death), but only that in the absence of *this* occurrence (bomb blast), the person's death would not have occurred as it did. The bomb blast is called the cause of the death.

The law, however, does not use the "but for" test in all cases: "But for the fact that my father conceived me and my mother gave birth to me, I would not have committed this crime; therefore my parents are the cause of my committing this crime." Having parents is a necessary condition for your existence and thus for your being here to do anything; yet it would be considered ridiculous to say that just because having parents is a necessary condition for your committing the crime, therefore they are the cause of it.

When we do say that C is the cause of E because "but for this particular event, that particular event would not have occurred," how do we know this? What entitles us to say it? Such statements, it seems, are grounded in our general background knowledge of how nature operates. Bomb blasts do injure peo-

ple, often destroying vital organs or producing enough blood loss to cause death. Bomb blasts aren't necessary conditions for deaths in general (people die from other causes); still but for this bomb blast, the death would not have occurred when and as it did, and we call the blast the cause of the death.

2. *Sufficient condition.* For every event there is a set of conditions that were sufficient to produce it, otherwise it would not have occurred. But when Mill used sufficient condition to define causality, he meant more than this: "The cause, philosophically speaking," wrote Mill, "is the sum total of the conditions, positive and negative taken together, the whole of the contingencies of every description, which being realized, the consequent *invariably* follows."[6] To state what is the cause of an occurrence is to enumerate this whole set of conditions.

What is the cause of combustion, for example? First, there must be a combustible material. Second, the substance must be heated to this temperature (which varies for different substances). Third, there must be oxygen. When all these conditions are present, the substance burns—the conditions are sufficient.

Let's see how this applies to some of the cases discussed earlier as "constant conjunction but not cause." Isn't there a constant conjunction between day and night? But, as Mill said, day is not the cause of night, nor night the cause of day. If the earth's period of rotation on its axis were the same as its period of revolution around the sun, like Mercury's, one side would always have day and the other side night. And if the sun's light were to be extinguished, there would be constant night all over the earth. The alternation of day and night depends on these factors: (1) the presence of sunlight; (2) the

---

[6]John Stuart Mill, *A System of Logic* (1842), Book 3, Chapter 5.

earth's rotation on its axis; and (3) the absence of opaque material between earth and sun that would obscure the sun's light. The cause of the day-night sequence is these three conditions together.

Most examples of causality are more complex than this. What set of conditions is sufficient for a car to run properly? The number of conditions runs into the thousands. And the number of conditions sufficient for an organism to breathe is surely even greater. The conditions that are sufficient by themselves are those for "negative events"—the *failure* of something to occur. For your electric radio not to work, it is sufficient to pull the plug. Any of a number of things you could do to it would be sufficient for it to stop working.

It is not usually a single *event* that causes something to happen; the cause of the effect is a whole set of conditions of which some are events (such as lighting the fuse), while others are states of a substance (such as the powder being dry) and still others are states of the environment (such as oxygen being in the air). Mill was careful to include in the list factors that most of us take for granted but that are just as important for the effect to occur as are the more apparent ones, such as the presence of oxygen in the air and the influence of gravitation.

Out of the vast array of conditions that are together sufficient, said Mill, we speak of *the* cause (quite inaccurately) as either: (1) the condition the hearer doesn't already know about (we say his fall was caused by a slippery ladder, not by the pull of gravity, although that was equally important for the effect); (2) the last event to take place before the effect does—the "proximate cause" (we say that lighting the fuse caused the gunpowder to explode, although many conditions prior to that also had to be fulfilled); or (3) the condition whose role is superficially the most conspicuous (we say that firing the gun caused it to go off, rather than the fact that the gun was loaded).

Many conditions may be relevant to a certain outcome, but different people will select different ones, depending on their interests or their interpretation of the event. If a car skids off the highway on a mountain road, one person may say that it's because the driver was trying to round the corner too fast; another will say that it's because the car had no traction, or the tires were bald; still another will say that the curve was banked the wrong way, or that the car was of inferior design.[7] And all of them may be right—they may all have something to do with the outcome.

3. *Plurality of causes.* Several conditions together make up a sufficient condition, but is each of these always a necessary condition? Perhaps conditions 1, 2, and 3 are together sufficient to produce E; but perhaps conditions 4, 5, and 6 are also together sufficient to produce E, even when 1, 2, and 3 do not occur. Then we have *two* sufficient conditions for E. Or perhaps there is an overlapping: 1, 2, and 3 may be sufficient for E, and 1, 2, and 4 are also sufficient for E. In that case, conditions 1 and 2 are necessary, for E does not occur without them, but conditions 3 and 4 are not, since sometimes E does occur without them.

It certainly seems as if the same effect may occur from a different set of conditions. If we want to remove a stain from a garment, we can do so by using gasoline, carbon tetrachloride, or any of a number of other chemical reagents. We can produce certain organic compounds either by inducing chemical reactions in living organisms or by synthesizing them out of their elements or simpler compounds. You can get expelled from school by writing inflammatory material in the college

---

[7]See for example H.L.A. Hart and A. M. Honore, *Causation in the Law* (Oxford: Clarendon Press, 1964), Chapter 4.

newspaper, by planting a bomb under the president's desk, and so on.

On the other hand, it often happens that the plurality of causes is only apparent. Sometimes *too much* is included in the statement of the sufficient condition. If pulling the plug is sufficient for the radio not to work, then pulling the plug *plus* the moon being full is also sufficient; every time you pull the plug and the moon is full, the radio stops working. But we do not consider the moon a causal factor because the radio stops playing when you pull the plug whether the moon is full or not.

In this example the irrelevance of the moon is easy to see, but other examples are not quite so obvious. Thus we may say that billiard ball B is caused to move in a certain direction not merely by being struck by billiard ball A but also by being struck with your elbow, or by jiggling the table, or by a slight earth tremor. But this can hardly be considered a genuine case of plurality of causes. What is necessary and sufficient for the movement of the ball in this direction is that a certain degree of force be applied upon it in that direction; it does not matter who or what wields the force, and therefore no mention of these particulars need be made in a list of the conditions on which the event depends. Thus, in the numbered conditions we considered three paragraphs above, to include 3 and 4 as conditions may be including too much; what really does the causing is a component, C, that 3 and 4 have in common. If this is so, plurality has been eliminated, because the total set of conditions is in both cases 1, 2, and C.

Sometimes the same *general type* of effect can be brought about by different means: a house may burn down as a result of lightning, an overheated furnace, arson, and so on. If "a house burning down" is the effect, then it can certainly be brought about by different sets of conditions. But the insurance inspector who examines the ruins after the fire can often detect the difference between fire from lightning and fire from overheated furnace through a careful examination of the ruins. The effect *is* somewhat different in the two cases, and "destruction by fire" is a blanket term that covers many different specific effects. Perhaps if we broke down the effects as carefully as we do the causes, we would end up with no plurality of causes at all.

The Causal Principle

Does everything that happens have a cause?

We know only a tiny fragment of what is occurring in the world, an even smaller fragment of the past, and have yet to witness the future. Isn't the only possible answer to our question, then, an emphatic *no*? If this bag contains a million marbles and you've examined only six of them, all black, and you are asked, "Are all of them black?," wouldn't you have to say no for the same reason?

Yet many people, if asked this question, would answer with a confident yes. We may not know what most of the causes are, they would say, but we do know that they exist. To believe that everything that happens in the universe has a cause is to believe in the Causal Principle, or, as it is often called, *determinism*.

Determinism doesn't say what kind of causes there are: they could be anything. Theological determinism says that everything is caused, directly or indirectly, by God. Scientific determinism says that everything that happens is the result of prior causes in the natural world (as opposed to supernatural causes). Mechanistic determinism says that everything that happens is caused by events and conditions in the physical world—thus denying mental causation. (More of this is discussed in Chapter 6.)

Many philosophers since ancient times have believed *that* everything is caused. What is different in our own time is that we have so much more knowledge of *what* the causes are: causes of diseases, causes of economic inflation, causes of psychological states such as depression and narcissism.

Many would say that the Causal Principle is obviously true. Suppose a medical researcher who had been trying for years to find the cause of a certain kind of cancer said, "I don't think it has a cause." Wouldn't he be laughed out of his field, and rightly so?

Still, is there anything that entitles him to be so certain? Why should the Causal Principle seem to him more plainly true than an empirical generalization about the melting point of lead? The claim about the Causal Principle is a much wider and more inclusive claim than any claim about lead: the melting point of lead concerns only a tiny number of items in the vast universe, but causation is supposed to cover all events of whatever kind everywhere. How can we be so certain of such a massive claim?

Here is something of unknown cause. Suppose we find its cause—then of course we know it has one. But suppose we don't find it; then we can say, "It has a cause, but the cause hasn't yet been found." Even if we didn't find a cause after a thousand attempts, we could still say the same thing. Finding a cause provides one more confirmation of the Causal Principle, but failing to find a cause doesn't seem to disconfirm it. What kind of empirical law is this, which nothing disconfirms?

"Well, if we don't find the cause, that only shows that we haven't looked hard enough." We try many times again and still fail. "You still haven't looked hard enough." How hard is "hard enough"? "Until you find it!" But this reduces the principle to a tautology: if you look till you find it, you'll find it! Surely *that* can't be what this vaunted principle comes to, can it?

Scientists know what it's like to find the cause of something: they consider a set of factors they consider sufficient to produce an event E, and they try to reproduce those conditions and see if E happens again, and if it does, over and over, while trying to vary the conditions to be sure that these and no others are the causally relevant ones, they conclude that they've found the cause of E (that is, of events of type E). But now, what would it be to *discover that it had no cause*? Close your eyes and try to imagine *that* discovery. Aren't we inclined to conclude, "We can never discover that it has *no* cause. The most we can say is that no cause has yet been found."

But wouldn't we eventually give up and conclude that there *is* no cause? We believe, for example, that there are conditions for a light bulb going on and off, and we believe we know what they are. We press the button and the light goes on; we press it the other way and the light goes off. But this isn't the sole causal condition, of course; sometimes we press the button and the light doesn't go on. But we investigate and find that the bulb has burned out, and when we replace the bulb, the light goes on. Another time we press the button, the light doesn't go on, and the bulb isn't defective (it works on something else); then we conclude that there's something defective in the wiring, or that there's a short somewhere, or (if all the electricity goes off at once) that the cable has snapped or that there's a strike at the power plant. But there is a finite set of conditions on which, we believe, the functioning of the light depends. If the bulb goes out and we check all these conditions and as far as we can see nothing is wrong, we are puzzled. Do we now say the Causal Principle is mistaken or has exceptions? No, probably we shall insist that there is a condition we don't yet know about, but that if we did know it, the light would go on; so the Causal Principle is still intact.

Now suppose, however, that starting immediately the light goes on and off with no apparent regard for these conditions. Sometimes the bulb lights up and then just as unpredictably goes off again. Sometimes it suddenly shines even when the wires are disconnected. This is contrary to everything we know—but suppose it happened. Well, maybe it depends on the time of day, or the moisture in the air, or the condition of the ozone, or the temperature of the room. We vary these factors, but nothing works: a group of assembled scientists can make no sense of it. "It's got to depend on something!" we say, but we can't think of anything more, and meanwhile the bulb goes on and off in its own unpredictable way. What now? Does there come a point at which we just give up and say, "This event *has no cause*—the Causal Principle is mistaken"? And if so, haven't we described a situation in which the Causal Principle has been proven wrong?

The problem is, we could *say* that this event has no cause, but wouldn't we still be troubled about it, and with good reason? We could say it had no cause, but how could we know that it was true? And what if, after all this, the real cause did turn up? Then weren't we premature in saying, even after all this expenditure of effort and energy, that it had no cause?

1. *Is the principle immune to refutation?* Suppose you set up an experiment in a laboratory to obtain a certain result, and the compound formed a precipitate that you hadn't expected. You want to check with your chemistry teacher but she's gone for the day, so you set it up again the next morning, prepared to surprise her. But this time the precipitate doesn't form. Frustrated, you say, "There must have been some difference in the setup this time, to account for the difference in the outcome." If the effect is different, wasn't at least one of the causal factors

different this time? Didn't at least one of them, as we say, "have to be different"?

If there are two clocks, which as far as you can tell are identical in every detail, next to each other in the same room, with the same temperature and atmospheric conditions, but you discover after a time that one of them is running just a bit fast although the other still keeps perfect time, wouldn't you conclude that there was (had to be?) a difference in one or more of the conditions, to account for the difference in keeping time? How would you respond to the suggestion that maybe there was *no* difference in the conditions? Wouldn't you take the very fact of difference in the effects as evidence of difference in the causes—even if you never found any difference? Don't you believe that if you could throw the ball against the wall in exactly the same way as you did before— same speed, same direction, same starting point, same environmental conditions—it would bounce right back into your hand, just as it did the last time? And that if this didn't happen, it was because of some difference in the conditions?

How far might we go rather than admit that there was a difference in the effect without any difference in the cause? We would look outside the set of factors we had considered relevant before: maybe it has to do with the electric wires a mile away, or with the phases of the moon, or with the fact that there are onlookers this time. There is always *some* difference, isn't there? Reaching out further and further, you might even say that in order to prove that the causes were the same (when the effects were different), you would have to show that the prior state of the whole universe was exactly the same in the two cases—and only *then* would you have proved that different effects can result from identical causes. But of course you could never show this. Innumerable conditions are different the next time. And if they weren't, *you* (at least your psychological state) would be different the second time. So you could never come up with a clear case of "different effects, but no difference in the causes."

But if nothing could count against it, isn't it strange that some observations count *for* it? Wasn't it repeated observations of the world that led scientists to formulate the Causal Principle in the first place? Suppose that starting tomorrow morning things began to happen very chaotically: sometimes stones fall and sometimes they stay in the air, sometimes cats bark and dogs meow, sometimes tables turn into frogs and wasps into pillowcases, with no apparent rhyme or reason. Wouldn't we now have to abandon the principle? Couldn't we still say, "No, the principle still holds, but events are a lot more complicated than they used to be, and causes are much harder to find these days"?

2. *A rule, not a proposition?* Perhaps nothing would falsify the principle, but events such as those just described might lead us to *abandon* it. It has been suggested that the Causal Principle—and perhaps others in science as well—is not a statement about the world at all, and therefore is neither true nor false. Perhaps it is not something we learn from the world, but something we bring *to* the world—something that we may adopt if we choose and abandon if we choose.

Adopting and abandoning are things we *do*. We can adopt a rule of behavior, a practice, a method of doing things. An accepted rule of baseball is "The batter may not have more than three strikes." Presumably it was adopted because it made baseball a more interesting or challenging game. The rule could be changed for various reasons, but the rule itself is neither true nor false. It is adopted because doing so achieves certain ends or goals, and it is abandoned if it fails to

do this. Why not consider the Causal Principle a kind of rule of the scientific game, a rule whose adoption makes the game more fruitful or yields some other desired result? If we adopt the rule we may be more encouraged to find causes.

We might adopt it for its value in encouraging us to keep finding causes, or in offering *hope* that more conditions will be found on which events depend, or even in serving as a bit of wishful thinking (whistling to keep your courage up when things get tough). And we could also *abandon* it—which doesn't mean we suspect it of being false (a rule is neither true nor false), or of not being a description of the universe (it doesn't describe the universe at all, but only prescribes what we want to find in it). We would abandon it as we might abandon a mine, not because there is no more gold in it, but because it is no longer worth the mining—if, for example, the gold is so minute in amount, so thinly scattered, or so hard to reach that we say, simply, "Let's give it up."

3. *Back to the empirical interpretation.* But would we ever give it up? Does the Causal Principle actually operate as a rule of procedure? Perhaps so, in some of the sciences. In medicine, if the cause of a disease hasn't yet been found, it is universally assumed that a cause exists but hasn't yet been detected. In psychology, if a patient reacts in some unexpected way to a stimulus, we ask, "What's the cause of this behavior?" and never speculate on whether such a cause exists—even if we never discover it. When meteorologists try to predict the weather more than a week or so in advance, the predictions are so unreliable that even an avid supporter of the Causal Principle might give up in despair. But no, we say, that's because the causes are too complicated to be tracked, and there's no way we could discover them all.

But is this assumption true?

The basis idea of Western science is that you don't have to take into account the falling of a leaf on some planet in another galaxy when you're trying to account for the motion of a billiard ball on a pool table on earth. Very small influences can be neglected. There's a convergence in the way things work, and arbitrarily small influences don't blow up to have arbitrarily large effects.[8]

Weather prediction is subject to what is called the "butterfly effect":

> For small pieces of weather—and to a global forecaster, small can mean thunderstorms and blizzards—any prediction deteriorates rapidly. Errors and uncertainties multiply, cascading upward through a chain of turbulent features, from dust devils and squalls up to continent-size eddies that only satellites can see.[9]

A butterfly that happens to be flying at a certain place at a certain time may affect the course of a rainstorm. Is this genuine chaos or tremendous causal complexity? In our own century, a large crack has appeared in the original heartland of determinism, namely physics. The details are so technical, the equations so complex, that even students of physics do not usually understand them. But the upshot is that certain atomic and subatomic events appear to occur without being determined by any set of prior conditions. Certain atoms, for example, when shot between the poles of a magnet, will be deflected either up or down, but there is no way of predicting which way a particular atom will go.

"But that," we might say, "is only because we don't yet know the cause—surely there is one." This, however, is exactly what modern physics (Heisenberg's Principle of Indeterminacy) denies; it is nature that is indeter-

---

[8]James Gleick, *Chaos* (New York: Penguin Books, 1987), p. 15.
[9]Ibid., p. 20.

ministic on the subatomic level; it is not merely our knowledge of it that is incomplete. Some physicists have resisted this conclusion—Einstein, among them, said that God does not play dice with the universe—and the matter is still in dispute. But the mere fact that the possibility of a noncausal "particle physics" is admitted, or even considered, indicates that physicists today do not consider the Principle of Universal Causation a necessary truth, nor even a rule of the game to be adopted or abandoned.

It has been suggested that particle physics is stuck with statistical laws: 40 percent of the time the particle goes this way, 60 percent that way. Scientists have tended to assume that if 40 percent of A is B and 60 percent of A is C, this difference itself must have a cause. This is what is taken for granted in the other sciences: if a medication or a vaccine works with some people but not with others, we assume that there must be a cause for the difference. But in particle physics this is no longer assumed. We need no longer attribute the difference to our ignorance. We believe it is nature itself that is indeterministic.

4. DETERMINISM AND FREEDOM

Many people are worried about determinism, not because they feel any concern with whether the laws of physics are statistical, but because they believe that determinism is incompatible with freedom. I act as I choose, but my choices are themselves caused—caused by my previous choices, my temperamental characteristics, my early environment, my genetic features over which I have control. Even when we trace our voluntary choices back to their sources, we soon reach items over which we have no choice. Bertrand Russell (1872–1970) once said that we can act as we please, but we can't please as we please.

But what has all this to do with the indeterministic cast of modern physics? How does the fact that the course of an electron is undetermined (if that is the case) affect our freedom to act and choose? Perhaps subatomic particles are "governed" by statistical laws, but when there are billions and billions of such particles, how is one particle supposed to make a difference? We may not know which individuals, of all the people in the nation, will kill someone else during the current year, but we can be pretty sure (within limits) how many will be killed. But surely this does not affect the freedom of the individual killer to choose what she will do.

Let's consider, first of all, what is meant by the word "freedom." When people declare that they are free, what exactly is it that they are asserting?

Freedom

Almost everyone believes that as human beings we are free, at least in some ways and in relation to some conditions. Nobody, we are inclined to say, is 100 percent free, but we all have freedom in various degrees and in various respects.

A person would be totally free, with respect to a course of action, if there is *no obstacle whatever* to doing or pursuing that action. All you have to do is will it, and it happens. God said, "Let there be light," and there was light. But no human being is that free. Our freedom is limited. In what ways?

We are not free to fly in the air like birds; we weren't born with wings. We are not free to be born male or female; we have no control over that. Men are not free to bear children. We are also "slaves to our genes"— there are hereditary conditions and tendencies, including inherited diseases, over which we have no control whatever.

Some philosophers have said that none of these things are limitations on our freedom. But this seems like a verbal quibble. If as a child you wanted desperately to fly but were unable to do so, you would surely have considered this inability as a limitation on your freedom. And if you were born paralyzed, surely the inability to walk was a limitation on your freedom.

At any rate, we are free *to* perform those actions that we can perform by choosing to do them. I am free to read a book or walk to the kitchen; I am not free to fly over the moon or turn into a vampire.

But I am also free *from* many things. I am free from the whims of a dictator, who (if I lived in his country) would have me put in prison or shot. But I may not be free from regulations that inhibit my freedom to cross the border or to conduct a business. These restrictions on my freedom are the result of the actions of others. I am free to the extent that I am free *from* domination by others and free to make my own decisions without forcible interference from others. "Freedom-from" is called negative freedom.

We are not free from the dictates of others if we are *coerced* by others. More controversially, our freedom-from is restricted if we have inner *compulsions* over which we have no control.

If someone forces you to do something, you do not do it freely. A robber holds you up at gunpoint and demands your money; you give up your money rather than your life (or rather than your money *and* your life). It's not that you had no choice—you could have refused the robber's demands and surrendered your money (and maybe your life as well). Although you had a choice, it wasn't a free choice because the alternatives were forced upon you—the alternative you wanted (not to give up anything) was not open to you. In that respect, your freedom was limited: you were not free from his coercion.

There are degrees of coercion: someone stronger than I am places my fingers around the trigger. "Do as I say or I'll kill you." "Do as I say or I'll burn the place down." "Do as I say or I'll leave you forever." "Do as I say or I'll walk out of your house." "Do as I say or I'll sneeze." All these are threats, but of decreasing severity. "Go ahead, sneeze," we would probably say, and as for our mother-in-law walking out, we might say, "Is that a threat or a promise?" You are not coerced unless you believe that the threat is genuine (that the person will carry it out if you don't succumb), that she has the power and the will to carry it out, *and* that the threatened loss is serious enough to make you do as ordered.

If you do whatever the hypnotist commands, is that coercion? Is a woman coerced if a man with a powerful personality turns her to jelly when he speaks and "she just can't say no" to his commands? Are you coercing someone if you know her so thoroughly that you know just "what buttons to push" to get her to do your bidding?

We usually speak of coercion as an external constraint, constraint by others. But people also have powerful internal *compulsions,* which they are unable to control and in whose clutches they are helpless. From early boyhood the young man hated his tyrannical father, and later, when he became an electrician, he still "told off the boss" (as if he were telling off his father), even though doing so regularly cost him his job. Even years of psychotherapy, with constant reminders of what he was doing to himself, failed to break this unconscious identification. He is not master in his own house.

Another man has a "thing" about promptness. He was always hours late for appointments. He drove his family crazy by making them wait endlessly, by not showing up for a family dinner until his children had gone to sleep dinnerless. His behavior ruined his marriage and his family life, terminated his jobs, angered his hosts. It seemed to everyone as if he were in the clutches of a force so powerful that even when he was about to be on time, he would desperately invent last-minute crises that again made him late. The "inner Hitler" in his life destroyed him as effectively as if the historical Hitler had threatened him with death or torture. He did not acknowledge so much as the existence of such a driving force within him, but everyone around him suffered in its shadow.

Not having legs is an impediment to freedom of movement, and this fact is obvious to everyone; but deep-seated psychological disorders such as those just described (psychologists call them character disorders) are not generally recognized as impediments to freedom, even though they may be as debilitating as being quadriplegic. Many people are sunk in deep depression for years and are as unable to make it lift as they would be to lift a railroad car, yet people say to them, "If you're depressed, find something to do; don't just sit there feeling sorry for yourself"—as if it were within the person's power to snap his fingers and make it go away. Sometimes the condition does go away (it disappears one day, and no one knows why), or sometimes it is relieved through extended psychotherapy, but while it is ongoing, one is as helpless to alter it as if one were being dashed into the sea by a hurricane.

There is much popular misunderstanding about freedom: people untrained in psychology have little conception of the extent to which inner compulsions occur. They have no personal acquaintance with schizophrenia or endogenous depression or any of the other psychological conditions that can be as crippling as having no hands or feet. Still, no one believes that *all* human behavior results from such conditions: our freedom is limited, we say, more limited than we had thought, but we do have it to some extent.

But there is another problem about freedom—the "free will" problem—that doesn't confront us in our daily lives and is largely the creation of philosophers. In discussing this problem some philosophers have concluded that freedom is an illusion, and that in fact *no one* is ever free. All our actions are determined by prior conditions (causes), and if this is true, how can we be free? But there are various strands of thought here that need to be disentangled.

Fatalism

One such strand is *fatalism,* which is sometimes confused with determinism. According to fatalism, whatever happens is "fated" to happen. Nothing that happens could have had a different outcome from what it did: it was all fated to happen.

However, it is far from clear what all this means. Does it mean that no matter what you try to do, your attempt won't succeed? (And what if it does succeed? Was it then not your attempt but "fate" that made your attempt succeed?)

One might well ask, "Isn't fatalism simply *silly*?" (In philosophy a view is said to be silly when one could not act on it or live by it.) There is no empirical statement (one might suggest) that is more certain than that some human actions do make a difference. You work hard to pass a difficult exam and you succeed. Isn't it insulting to your efforts to be told that you were "fated" to succeed?

A student says, "If I'm fated to pass this exam, I'll pass it whether I study or not; and if I'm fated to fail it, I'll fail it even if I try to pass it." So she does nothing, and fails. Is this supposed to show that she was "fated" to fail and that her failure to study had nothing to do with it?

What if you said, "If I'm fated to have dinner today, the dinner will come to me regardless of what I do"? If you did nothing to obtain your dinner, isn't it quite clear that you would soon starve?

People are seldom fatalists with regard to the immediate future, such as whether they will eat dinner tonight; they know well enough that some action on their part is required. But they are more likely to be fatalistic about long-term outcomes over which they have no control, such as what will happen to American civilization some hundreds of years from now. There are of course countless events, such as solar eclipses, over which no one has any control. We can say if we like that "we may as well be fatalistic about them," but surely this means only that we can't change them, not that they are in some way "fated to happen."

Some have claimed that everything that happens is divinely predestined to happen: whatever happens was caused to happen by God. But this is not fatalism but *predestination:* instead of being caused by "fate" (whatever that is), it was brought about through God's will. But here God is conceived as a conscious being who has unlimited powers to bring about events in the universe; God is like a human being, only bigger and better—not an impersonal "fate."

The early Greeks sometimes referred to "the Fates." In Homer's *Iliad* and *Odyssey,* and in some Greek tragedies, there are some things humans would never succeed in doing: if they tried to do them, "the Fates" would stop them. It was far from clear what these "Fates" were and how they operated. But they were not the same as the gods, who were conscious beings intent on fulfilling their varied purposes.

Determinism, by contrast, says nothing about fate or being fated. It alleges merely that whatever happens has some cause or other. But human beings too are causes of events in the world. I decide to walk to the next room, and I do; my decision was the cause (or one causal factor) of my action. I decide to do something, and I do it: that is my freedom. And if that isn't freedom, what is? I am free because *I* can be the cause of my actions.

We constantly assume the truth of determinism in our dealings with other people. When you attempt to change your child's behavior, you hope that the corrective measures you take will cause a change in that behavior. If the child's action had no cause, what would be the point of trying to alter it? We presuppose causality every time we try to change anyone or anything. In fact, doesn't "to change" mean "to cause a change"?

Indeterminism

According to indeterminism, not all events have causes. Most of them do, but in human affairs, specifically the decisions that human beings make, what we do is not entirely the result of prior conditions. What *happens* to you may be the result of prior conditions, but what you *do* is not. What you do may be *influenced* by prior conditions, but it is not *determined* by them. *I* initiate my actions, and the actions I initiate are not the inevitable result of previously existing conditions. What I do is *up to me.* I may sometimes choose to do something that is entirely "out of kilter" with what happened in my past. A person who had complete knowledge of my past would not be able to predict what I was about to do. Human actions transcend causality.

The determinist will find this view quite ridiculous. "You have no evidence for such a view," he will say, "you only introduce it because you think you need it in order to rescue free will. And you don't." Everything that happens is a result of what happened in the past, and this includes "acting out of character" (such as Saul being suddenly converted on the road to Damascus—this too had its roots in the past).

Suppose you have a friend whom you have known and trusted for years. And suppose that this friend were to do something that had no cause—no roots in her character or past dispositions. You would no longer have any reason to trust her; she might behave like a fiend—after all, her action isn't caused, so anything might happen. Wouldn't whatever she did be like a bolt from the blue—except that bolts from the blue do have causes? If such a thing occurred, would it be *her* act? Wouldn't it rather be something that *happened* to her? A reliable and trustworthy friend, with such an attack of free will, might suddenly become a murderer. After all, her act has no foundation in her formed habits and past dispositions. If it just sprang into existence from nowhere, could you even call it *her* act? No, says the determinist: indeterminism, which was devised for the sole purpose of rescuing freedom, is actually the greatest enemy of freedom. An uncaused act did not issue from you, had no basis in you, and was something for which you could bear no responsibility. Freedom presupposes determinism and is inconceivable without it.

Are all our actions caused? Of course, says determinism, and we may be grateful that they are, else we would be stuck with the indeterminist's causeless actions. Our actions, says determinism, are caused *by us.* Freedom says, "I cause my actions" (active voice); determinism says, "My actions are caused by me" (passive voice)—both say the same thing. Without causality, how can we even speak of human *action*?

Predictability

Eclipses of the sun and moon can be predicted, for we know all the relevant causal factors; the occurrence of eclipses is entirely determined by previous events (in accord with laws of nature). But human actions are not entirely predictable, and never will be, says the indeterminist, because some human events are not entirely caused by past events or conditions. The lack of predictability is inherent in the situation, and not only a result of our lack of knowledge of the causes.

Determinism, on the other hand, says that all events, including human action, have their causal roots in the past. If I predict that you will do X and you do Y instead, this shows only that there were causal factors of which I was ignorant. In eclipses we know the causal factors; in human action we don't. There lies the difference—not in lack of causality, but in lack of knowledge.

Suppose I have known you well for years and you have always been totally honest with me. And suppose I am told that you were offered money to do something that would ruin someone's good reputation. I predict that you will not accept the money. Let's say I know you won't accept it. The point is, says the determinist, that my knowledge of you in no way interferes with *your* freedom; you are still free to do X or not to do X—it's still your choice; it's up to you. I am only predicting what choice you will freely make. You make it freely, since no one coerced you; you may have been pressured, but you are capable of resisting pressure, as I have often observed in your past behavior.

But there is something, the indeterminist insists, which is different in human beings—much more, but at least this: people can act purposely to flout other people's predictions. If I predict an eclipse, the sun and moon will not be affected by my prediction. But if I predict that you will leave the room during the next five minutes, you may stay in the room just to refute my prediction. This places a limitation on my ability to predict what you will do.

The determinist need not be fazed: "Among the causes of your staying in the room, in spite of your desire to leave, is the fact that I predicted that you wouldn't. Knowledge of my prediction was a causal factor that influenced your subsequent behavior. In fact, if I knew you better than I do, I might have been able to predict that you would act as you did, just to refute my prediction."

Consider human creativity. How could any detailed predictions *ever* be made about it? What would it take to predict that Beethoven would be born, that he would become a composer, and that he would create the specific compositions that he did? The requirements are practically endless. To predict that he would be born at all would require the predictor to foresee that his parents would meet and that they would have sexual relations at a certain time. Who could have predicted all that? If you saw that he had musical ability, you might venture a guess (and that's all it would be, a guess) that he would become a composer. But how could you predict what compositions he would write and what each note was going to be in each of those compositions? Wouldn't you have to create those compositions before Beethoven himself ever thought of them? How could anyone predict just those manifestations of creative endeavor that characterize every artist? One couldn't begin to do this even on the basis of

> a thorough analysis of its circumstances and the qualities of the materials—that if one takes into account features of the piano, the history of music at the end of the classical era, an appreciation of the romantic movement, and the characteristics of the sonata form, one could foresee Beethoven's piano sonatas.[10]

But that knowledge of course wouldn't be enough. It wouldn't enable you to predict what compositions he would write and what

---

[10]Stephen A. Mitchell, *Relational Concepts in Psychoanalysis* (Cambridge: Harvard University Press, 1988), p. 257.

each note was going to be in every one of those compositions. To predict that, wouldn't you have to know exactly what was going on in every cell in Beethoven's brain? And wouldn't that be tantamount to creating the compositions *before* Beethoven himself thought of them?

The same applies to scientific creation. For a person to predict the achievements of an Einstein, she would have to know not only that Einstein would be born (a monumental task, as we have seen), but also the details of Einstein's Theory of Relativity before Einstein ever conceived of it himself.

Chance

We all speak of events occasionally happening by chance. Don't chance events imply indeterminism? The determinist replies that chance events imply no such thing. However, the word "chance" is ambiguous.

1. *Coincidence.* It was a coincidence that two fires occurred in the same neighborhood on the same afternoon—that is, there was no causal relation between them, and one fire would have occurred even if the other had not. Nevertheless, each of the separate fires had a cause. Similarly, you and I met at a certain supermarket yesterday by chance—that is, neither of us had gone there with the intention of meeting the other. But this in no way shows that there wasn't a cause for your going or for my going.

2. *Ignorance of causes.* When biologists say that mutations occur by chance, this does not imply that mutations have no causes, only that their occurrence cannot be predicted because the causes are not known. When we say that it's a matter of chance which way the football game will turn out, again we do not mean that the outcome of the game will be causeless, but only that we

are ignorant of at least some of the many thousands of factors on which its outcome depends.

3. *Mathematical probability.* If there are 52 cards in the deck, the chances of your drawing the ace of spades is one in 52. Since there are only two faces to a coin, heads and tails, the chance of the next throw being heads is 1 in 2, or 50 percent. We say this even if we are quite ignorant of the actual past behavior of such throws. In mathematical probability we enumerate the possibilities (52, 2) and use that figure as the denominator of a fraction of which the numerator is 1 (assuming that there's just one drawing or one throw). When we say that the outcome of the toss of a coin is a matter of chance, we are not implying that there's no cause for its turning up heads or tails, but that we are ignorant of the relevant factors: the direction of the throw, the energy in the upthrust, how many times the coin will turn over before it hits the table, and so on. But ignorance of causes is not causelessness.

4. *Statistical probability.* Statistical probability is based upon past frequencies. If 50.2 percent of past human births have been male, the chances of the next child being male is 50.2 percent. If the coin has turned up heads 50 percent of the time, we say that the chances of its turning up heads the next time is 50 percent. This, however, is not the same as mathematical probability, for if the frequency had been different our estimate of the chances would be different. If the coin has always turned up heads in thousands of throws, we would strongly suspect that the coin was "loaded" and use statistical probability to place our next bet—not mathematical probability, which we can estimate even in total ignorance of the qualities of this coin.

5. *No cause.* Does "chance" ever mean no cause at all? In ordinary life the answer is un-

doubtedly no. If someone were to tell us that the outcome of the football game or of the next toss of the coin had no cause at all, most people would regard such an assertion with disbelief and ridicule.

Determinism as Incompatible with Freedom

INDETERMINIST: The parole officer says to the ex-prisoner, "You're out of prison now. No one in your new job will know that you came from prison. No one will treat you as if you have. The future is *what you make it.* You will be the determiner of your own future." Do you disagree with that?

DETERMINIST: Of course not. What you do will cause what will happen in your job and in your future. This is a perfectly familiar—and true—example of a statement about human causation. Freedom exists only to the extent that determinism is true.

I: And if everything is caused, then every human action is also caused.

D: Of course.

I: But suppose that you goof off on the job—that too has causes, according to you, doesn't it? Perhaps you had a tyrannical father and just can't stand kowtowing to the boss; perhaps it just isn't in you to make the adjustment to a demanding nine-to-five job. Perhaps the temptation to make more money by dealing dope is just too difficult to resist, since you are financially so strapped and your wife is pregnant again. Those things might all cause you to fail, might they not? And so your future will be ruined—by you, by your actions, but also *through* you. The stream of causality runs from these difficulties to your goofing off on the job to your being fired. You are just a chip on the causal current, ac-

cording to determinism. I, as an indeterminist, say that causes incline without necessitating. You can, often with great effort, surmount many of the bad influences of your early background.

D: Yes, provided that other things in your background—the habits you have developed, the amount of self-discipline you have achieved—are as they should be. Otherwise, it won't work. In each case there is causation, but which way the cause leads to the effect depends on countless complex factors in the cause itself.

I: So some people have the ability to exercise their will power because they've developed it in the past and now have that inner reserve to call upon when they need it. But it all depends on what happened before, and *that,* according to determinism, depends on what happened before that, and so on back. If your desires determine your choices, and your choices determine your ensuing actions, how are they free with regard to their actions if they aren't free with respect to their desires? And in general people aren't: once again, we can act as we please, but we can't please as we please. What you call freedom is just "going through the motions," isn't it? People *feel* that they are free in acting as they do, but that doesn't count for much: most people have very little idea of what John Locke called "the inner springs of action." They feel that they are originating their actions, but actually (if determinism is true) they are no more free than the hand of a clock is able to move freely over the face of the clock. Their acts are the inevitable product of prior conditions, which in turn are the inevitable product of still prior conditions, and so on. Very soon in this chain of events we reach conditions over which they had no control whatever. If determinism is true, you are the product of the conditions that brought you into being and in which you developed into maturity.

D: I might say that people born on the other side of the tracks are made into criminals because of their early environment on the streets, if there weren't so many college presidents who were also born on the other side of the tracks.

I: But you know the answer to that. Those who succeeded had *other* causal factors in their history that the losers didn't: trust and good upbringing by their parents, or instillation of hope in spite of dire poverty.

I am just following your view to its logical conclusion: you are not free because you are, in the most inclusive sense, the product of the total influences working on you throughout your own life (including the determination not to live the way your parents did). Whichever way it comes out, it's because of those past factors—according to you. So I don't see how you can escape the conclusion drawn by Edward Fitzgerald (1809–1883) in his *Rubaiyat of Omar Khayyam:*

With earth's first clay they did the last man knead
And there of the last harvest sowed the seed;
And the last morning of creation wrote
What the last dawn of reckoning shall read.
  (stanza 73)

D: Such words often create a powerful mental picture that tends to dominate one's mind when one thinks of determinism. But it's a confusion. Who is supposed to ensure the final reckoning—God? Fate? Who or what was it that kneaded the clay? And assuming that this was done, how do we know that the final event was "inevitable"?

Here is another error. In daily life when we say someone is free we never

mean "free from causation"—we always assume that events have causes, and nobody in practical life is an indeterminist unless she has been corrupted by bad philosophy. When we say that a person's act is free, we mean only that these acts are caused *in a certain way,* for example, not coerced. If I'm able to walk to the door, I'm free to do so, but if I'm paralyzed, I'm not. We distinguish between free and unfree actions constantly, and everybody makes the distinction even though they may not be able to articulate it. I fear that you blur this important distinction entirely.

Similarly, you say that events are an "inevitable product" and so on. But "inevitable" means *unavoidable.* Death is inevitable, because we cannot avoid dying at some time. But death by a certain disease is avoidable if we don't get exposed to that disease. And by taking care of our health we can usually avoid dying prematurely. Some things can be avoided, some cannot. You lump them all in the same category by calling them all "inevitable." By these semantic maneuvers you caricature my position.

I: I am still right. According to determinism, if E is the effect of D, and D is the effect of C, and you weren't free with respect of C (some fundamental desire), you aren't free with respect to E either.

D: Not so, E is the effect of D *and* lots of other causal factors; D is the effect of C *and* lots of other causal factors. That's why in one person a strong desire to commit a crime still doesn't result in that crime being committed, whereas in another person the same strong desire does result in the crime. Will power, for example, is a factor, and this is something that can be developed with practice and self-discipline. Lots of kids from the slums turn to a life of crime, but some of them also become college presidents and famous writers. You are deluded by this mental picture of a causal chain, with C connected with D and D with E, so there's no escape from E once you have C. But it's not like that at all. It's not like a string of dominoes, where, by pushing the first domino, you knock over all the other ones. Human causation is a much more complex affair than that. There is multiple causation at every step. Encouragement, praise and blame, advice, and attempted influences offered by one person can often be causally effective in changing what the other person does—what the other person chooses, and even what the other person desires; but sometimes not—it depends on a huge concatenation of causal factors.

I: But if determinism is true, don't you have to admit that if a certain complex of causal factors C-1, C-2, and C-3 occur, then E, the effect of these factors, will inevitably (and I do mean unavoidably) occur?

D: Not at all. My desire *not* to have E occur may well be a causal factor in E's not occurring. I may not feel like studying, but I wish to avoid failure (E), and so I study anyway. My desires, my strength of will, and countless other things that are, to varying extents, under my control can *change* the outcome. *My will is a causal factor too.* So the outcome is *not* inevitable.

I: But isn't your strength of will at a given moment also determined by various causal factors that aren't under your control? And even if some are in your control, aren't they the effect of prior factors that are *not* under your control? And so, either way, your actions are the effect of a complex of factors that, in the final

analysis, you couldn't help. You are what you are because of the causal factors playing on you during your entire preceding life. If determinism is true, your every action, every choice, every desire, is the effect of a host of those prior conditions on which they depend. *Given* those conditions, you *couldn't* have done anything *other* than what you did. What you did, you (causally speaking) *had* to do; there was no alternative, if determinism is true.

D: You are misusing words again. First, I didn't *have* to sit down just now; I chose to, and I did so freely, that is, without coercion. If I had really been compelled to do so (for example, by someone pushing me into the chair), then I would admit that my sitting down wasn't done freely. Being coerced is one form of causation, one way of being caused; all coerced acts are caused, but not all caused acts are coerced. I was not coerced just now, my act was free.

Second, neither is it true that I *couldn't* have done other than I did. I stayed in my chair, but I could have gone to the kitchen to get a drink instead; I almost did, then decided not to. Is there any doubt that I *could* have done it? I couldn't if I were suddenly paralyzed, but since I wasn't, I could have gone. I could at this moment discontinue my conversation with you, but I probably won't. There are lots of things that I *could* do even though I don't do them. Don't say that according to determinism I could never have done anything other than what I did. That is simply not so. To say I *can* do X is to say I have the *ability* to do X; I can walk to the kitchen but not fly to the moon. I do have the ability to walk to the kitchen—want to try me out and see? Do you want to take bets on it?

I: I am merely saying that, if determinism is true, you couldn't have done anything other than what you did in fact do. The past being what it was, you had no choice in the matter; you couldn't have done anything else.

D: Not even if I wanted to? Nonsense. If I'd wanted to open the window, I would have done so. If I'd wanted to stop talking with you, I would have done that. Ordinarily when we say, "I could have done that," we mean that "I *would* have done that *if* I had chosen to do so." The fact that I didn't choose to doesn't show that I couldn't have done it, if I had chosen to.

I: You could have done it if you had chosen to, I admit. But whether you were going to choose to was already determined, if your theory is correct.

D: Determined? Determined in spite of me? (That's the misleading overtone that "determined" often carries.) No, determined *through* and *by* me. *I* am a causal factor too! I am not free to have different parents or a different childhood environment (if I could, I might select different ones). But I am free with regard to my *choices*. I chose to do X, and my choice doubtless had causes; but I chose X and as a result I did X. What else would you want? Do you want me to choose X and find myself doing Y instead? Is *that* your idea of freedom? If so, I'm glad I don't have it. I'm glad that choosing X leads to X, and choosing Y leads to Y—and that *my choosing makes a difference* in whether it is X or Y that occurs. What more freedom do you want than that?

I: You keep on evading the consequences of your position. Being just what you are at the moment, with just the factors operating on you that are operating (whatever they are), your deliberations as to what to do could have no other outcome than the one they did (that is, if determinism is true). You only think the outcome could have been different, but that is a delusion.

D: But it could have had a different outcome, if I had wanted it to. That is my freedom.

I: No. You don't see the implications of your own view. Given just *this* set of conditions, you could have done only *this* particular act. If the set of conditions had been somewhat different (for example, if you had desired Y rather than X), then you would of course have done some *other* act. Either way, if determinism is true, you could have done only what you *did* do.

D: You are once again being confused by a misuse of words. You want me to say that I *could not* have done anything other than X, the next time, if *all the conditions* leading up to X the second time had been exactly the same. But you forget that *one* of those conditions is that I chose; so I still say, if I had chosen X I would have done X, and if I had chosen Y I would have done Y. I *could have* done either one. What I decide makes the difference. What you want me to admit is something self-contradictory. You want me to say that I couldn't have acted differently if *all* the conditions had been the same; but you forget that if I had made a different choice, that would have changed the conditions so that they would *not* all be the same the second time. If I had chosen differently, then one of the conditions of action, the choice, would have been different, and so not all the conditions *would* have been the same.

I: I say you might have acted differently even if all the conditions had been the same. A golfer misses a short putt and kicks himself because, with things being exactly as they were, he *could have* holed it. John Austin writes:

> It is not that I would have holed it if conditions had been different. That might of course be so. But I am talking about conditions as they precisely were, and asserting that I could have holed it. There's the rub.
>
> Nor does "I can hole it this time" mean that I shall hole it this time if I try, or if anything else; for I may try and miss, and yet not be convinced that I couldn't have done it. Indeed, further experiments may confirm my belief that I could have done it that time although I didn't.[11]

D: It sounds appealing, but it just isn't so. Under *just those exact circumstances* I couldn't have succeeded, even though I may think I could have. *Something*, either some external condition (it was beginning to drizzle) or some internal condition (I didn't get much sleep the night before, and I hesitated because I wasn't quite confident enough) made the difference. If I succeeded one time and failed another time, there was something that caused that difference. It just isn't true that you could have succeeded (even though you didn't) if *every* condition, both external and internal, had been the same.

I: You are confident in saying this, but I don't see how you can claim to know it. You certainly haven't shown that I couldn't have done something other than what I did even if all the conditions had been exactly the same. I say, with common sense, that you could have: not that I could have acted differently if some condition had been other than it was (for instance, if it hadn't started to drizzle), but that I could have done it even if everything else had been the same.

D: Why then the difference between the case of success and the case of failure? Was it magic?

I: No, it was free will. That's what you need in order to admit responsibility for your actions. "Moral responsibility requires that a man should be able to choose alternative actions, everything in the universe prior to the act, including his self, being the same."[12] We hold others responsible for actions they could have avoided.

D: We can ascribe responsibility as a pragmatic device. When the baby-sitter neglects the children we say to him, "I hold you responsible"—that is, he did it and he wasn't forced by others to do it. But he was not responsible in *your* sense (which nobody uses anyway) that he could have acted differently even if *all* the conditions had been the same.

I: Why not say (this is called the "theory of agency") that for an act to be free, it must have been caused by the agent who performs it, but that no antecedent conditions were sufficient for the person to perform it?

The Theory of Agency

Here is yet another attempt to reconcile determinism with freedom:

> In the case of an action that is free, it must be such that it is caused by the agent who performed it, but such that no antecedent conditions were sufficient for his performing just that action. . . .
>
> Now this conception is what men take themselves to be, namely, beings who act or who are agents, rather than things that are merely acted upon, and whose behavior is simply the

---

[11]John Austin, *Philosophical Papers* (London: Oxford University Press, 1961), pp. 119–120.

[12]J. D. Mabbott, in H. D. Lewis, ed., *Contemporary British Philosophy*, 3rd ser. (New York: Humanities Press, 1952), pp. 301–302.

causal consequence of conditions which they have not wrought. When I believe that I have done something, I do believe that it was I who caused it to be done, I who made something happen, and not merely something within me, such as one of my own subjective states, which is not identical with myself.[13]

I believe that I am a *self-moving* being, a genuine originator of actions. These acts, although caused by me, are not the inevitable product of antecedent conditions: if they were, I would not be the agent (actor) but only the vehicle or instrumentality through which the causal chain proceeded. I am a genuine originator, a *first cause* of my actions.

If this "theory of agency" is true, it enables us to escape both indeterminism, in which an act is not really caused by me, and determinism, in which every action, desire, impulse, and thought is the consequence of antecedent conditions.

But is it true? That our acts are caused by our decisions is plausible enough. But can it be true that our decisions are *self-originating,* not the causal product of what went before? (Close your eyes and try to imagine this situation, in fact, not merely in words.) What does "self-causing" mean? Can anything be the cause of itself? And if so, what is its relation to preceding conditions?

Without further clarification, it would seem that this view is palatable but unintelligible, whereas the previous ones are intelligible but unpalatable. Not an appetizing choice!

I: Let me suggest to you that in daily life we use the word "cause" in a double sense. When we talk about causation of purely physical events, we use the word "cause" in the sense of causal *necessity* (not logical necessity, of course). The cause of

the eclipse was that the moon came between the earth and the sun, and, given the laws of nature and the initial conditions, any other outcome was empirically impossible. But we don't use the word "cause" in that strict sense when we talk about human actions. If I throw a party for you because I want to celebrate your birthday, there is a cause of throwing the party (there are many factors, but the main one is that I want to celebrate your birthday), but we don't speak here of the party being causally *necessary* or of any other outcome being *impossible.*

D: I grant that we don't. And you have instructed us on the use of language: in this case, the different senses of "cause" in ordinary discourse. But what does your example prove, except that we don't always use the word "cause" in quite the same way? It doesn't show anything about reality. It doesn't show that there isn't a set of conditions that are together sufficient for the party being held (and that, if exactly repeated, would result in the same event, or an event identical to it, being repeated). The conditions are so numerous and complex that we have no idea what they all are, but that doesn't show that there is no such set of conditions.

Isn't this Austin's example all over again? He says he could have made that short putt not only if conditions, including his own mental set and other internal conditions, had been different, but if they had been exactly what they were at the time. And I deny this. If all the conditions had been the same, the outcome would have been the same. But of course they never are quite the same.

I: I believe that often people, especially if they are in a moral quandary, say, "I had no choice." A man has to choose between going to jail and turning in an in-

---

[13]Richard Taylor, *Metaphysics,* 3rd ed. (Englewood Cliffs, NJ: Prentice Hall, 1983), p. 50.

nocent person; he chooses to go to jail, and says, "I had no choice"—but he *did* have a choice; it's just that one of the choices was morally unacceptable to him. That's what Martin Luther said when he nailed his Ninety-Five Theses on the church door at Wittenberg: "Here I stand, I can do no other." He felt morally obligated to do what he did. But he did have a choice—to do it or not to do it. If we believed that he had no choice, we wouldn't praise him (as Protestants do) or blame him (as Catholics do). If he had been suddenly afflicted with paralysis and just couldn't get the papers off the door, we wouldn't say he had a choice, and we wouldn't give his action our moral endorsement or condemnation. It's because he did have a choice that we praise or blame him for his action. In fact, if you believe that every act is causally necessitated by the events and conditions that preceded it, then he couldn't have helped doing it—thus moral responsibility for his actions goes out the window, and we wouldn't praise him. We are all *agents;* an agent is someone who *originates* acts, someone who is not just a chip on the causal current. I'm afraid that the determinism you espouse is logically committed to saying that you are just a chip.

D: Here we go again. Of course I originate acts: a composer has an idea for a symphony, and she writes it down. She is the creator—she has originated something that never existed before anywhere. She brought something new and different into existence. I don't deny any of this. I only say that there is a whole series of complex causes that led her to create this symphony. We don't know most of them, and *she* doesn't know most of them. She has no idea where her ideas came from, but I am sure that they all

had causes. One originates, one creates, but what one originates or creates has a massive congeries of causal factors. They didn't come from nowhere, and they won't come again if later conditions are different.

I: I say again that causes incline without necessitating. That you have a certain background and training and talent makes it more likely that you will be a Mozart, but doesn't necessitate it.

D: Of course not, because you haven't listed enough factors. There is such a multitude of factors that made this particular man, Mozart, write these particular notes at this particular time, that we shall never know them all. But that doesn't mean there aren't any. Surely there was a vast set of conditions whose combination at this place and time made Mozart.

I: And I don't know how you can be so confident that this is true. We have pretty good evidence for it in some of the sciences; we are confident that there was a set of conditions that causally necessitated the eclipse of the sun, and without which the eclipse would not have occurred. I see no evidence that there is any set of conditions, even far more numerous and complex than those that produced the eclipse, that would produce a Mozart or for that matter any voluntary action. You are taken in by the seventeenth-century model of Newtonian mechanics and the philosophical speculation of Pierre Laplace (1749–1827) that, if he knew the laws and the initial conditions, he could predict every future event. This may be true in astronomy, but you are extending it *without warrant* to the realm of human action. You are still being taken in by the Laplacean mental picture. You have no evidence that it can be extended to human action, or even to biology or anthropology. It's a promissory note with nothing to back it up. But it seems to me that determinism is stuck with it. Baron Paul d'Holbach (1729–1789) wrote in his *System of Nature:*

Man's life is a line that nature commands him to describe upon the surface of the earth, without his ever being able to swerve from it, even for an instant. He is born without his own consent; his organization does in no wise depend upon himself; his ideas come to him involuntarily; his habits are in the power of those who cause him to contract them; he is unceasingly modified by causes, whether visible or concealed, over which he has no control, which necessarily regulate his mode of existence, give the hue to his way of thinking, and determine his manner of acting. He is good or bad, happy or miserable, wise or foolish, reasonable or irrational, without his will being for anything in these various states. Nevertheless, in spite of the shackles by which he is bound, it is pretended that he is a free agent, or that independently of the causes by which he is moved, he determines his own will, and regulates his own condition.

This, I think, is the logical conclusion that you as a determinist must come to. I as an indeterminist reject it.

However much we try to get around it, there is an enormous tension between these two views of human action. When we view human beings "from the inside," as acting beings in the drama of life, we conceive ourselves not as the product of outside forces, not as chips on the current, but as the genuine *originators* of actions. We think, we deliberate, we provide reasons, and we act in accordance with those reasons (good or bad). Viewed in this way, there is no doubt that we are free to do this or not to do it; it's up to us. Yet on the other hand, the more we discover about the inner springs of human action, the more we view our actions "objectively," from the outside, the more we see how even our apparently freest actions are the results of impulses and inner defenses such as every psychiatrist can point out to us again and again. In this mode, we are not really originators of actions, although we may believe we are; we are actually flotsam on a causal stream that passes through us and around us, and in which we are but one incident in the progression of events in which we are involved. How to reconcile these two views or two perspectives from which we can view human action is a matter that even after centuries of dispute remains today as much as ever a field of controversy and paradox.

EXERCISES

1. Are any of the following synthetic a priori truths? Explain.
a. Everything that has shape has size.
b. Everything that has volume has shape.
c. Everything that has shape has color.
d. All sounds have pitch, volume, and timbre.
e. All colors have hue, brightness, and saturation.
f. Everything that has shape has extension.
g. Everything that has extension has shape.
h. $40,694 + 27,593 = 68,287$.
i. A straight line is the shortest distance between two points.
j. Given any line L and any point P not on that line, only one line can be drawn through P that is parallel to L.
k. If P is true, P is not also false.
l. Either P is true or P is false.
m. If A is north of B and B is north of C, then A is north of C.
n. If A is east of B and B is east of C, then A is east of C.
o. If San Francisco is east of Tokyo and Tokyo is east of London, then San Francisco is east of London.
p. A person cannot be born three months after the death of his mother.
q. A person cannot be born three months after the death of his father.
r. All cubes have twelve edges.
s. If A occurs before B and B occurs before C, then A occurs before C.
t. If A hires B and B hires C, then A hires C.

u. Every even number is the sum of two prime numbers. (Goldbach's theorem.)
v. If A is indistinguishable from B and B from C, A is indistinguishable from C.

2. In each of the following examples, is the proposition a necessary (a priori) truth? Is it a truth at all? Justify your answers.
a. "Everything that has color has shape." But what about the sky?
b. "Everything that has shape has color." But what about an ice cube?
c. "Everything that has shape has size." What about a rainbow or the round spots in front of your eyes?
d. "Everything that has shape has volume." What about a triangle? (Is the statement true if three-dimensional shape is meant?)
e. "Everything that has volume has shape." What about the water in a glass or gases released into a chamber?
f. "All matter is either solid, liquid, or gaseous." What about a single molecule?
g. Events in nature can't contradict one another; only propositions can.
h. True propositions cannot contradict one another.

3. How is the word "must" being used in the following examples?
a. You must do as you're told or you'll be punished.
b. It simply must be nice weather tomorrow or our picnic will be ruined.
c. If I had $10 yesterday and haven't lost or spent any or received any since, I must still have $10.
d. In order to catch a walrus, there must first be a walrus.
e. If we want to understand topic B, we must first discuss topic A.
f. If you want this cake to turn out well, you must have three large, well greased cake pans.
g. Why must you say such things?
h. He must have been pretty thoroughly intoxicated or he never would have done it.
i. You must be a mind reader.
j. You must have your yard looking quite beautiful by this time.
k. Everything is disarranged—there must have been someone in the house while we were gone.

4. In each of these examples the relation of A to B is that of necessary condition. State whether it is a *causally* necessary condition, such as we have been examining in this chapter, or a *logically* necessary condition, such as we discussed in Chapter 4.

	A	B
a.	Presence of oxygen	Occurrence of combustion
b.	Having three angles	Being a triangle
c.	Having extension	Having shape
d.	Existence of sodium	Existence of salt
e.	Presence of moisture	Growth of crops
f.	Presence of nonopaque object	Looking through that object
g.	Presence of heat	Occurrence of flame

5. In the following examples, is the relation of A to B that of necessary condition, sufficient condition, both, or neither?

	A	B
a.	Overeating	Illness
b.	Deciding to raise your hand	Raising your hand
c.	Writing an essay	Reading that essay
d.	Running	Feeling fatigue
e.	Plug pulled out of socket	Radio not working
f.	Plug inserted in socket	Radio working
g.	Rock hitting window	Window breaking
h.	Occurrence of friction	Occurrence of heat
i.	Rain falling on the street	Street being wet

6. In what way is *too much* being included in the statement of the cause in these examples? In what way is *too little*? (Assume the correctness of Mill's account.)
a. Scratching the match caused it to light.
b. Eating the poison caused her to die.
c. Throwing the lighted match into the pile of paper caused it to ignite.
d. The cause of the dart hitting its target was its being wielded by a man in a blue suit.

e. The flood in the river was caused by heavy rainfall upstream.

7. Do you think there is genuine plurality of causes in the following cases?
  a. Headaches can be caused by many things: eyestrain, emotional tension, etc.
  b. The same message can be communicated by telephone, telegram, letter, etc.
  c. The stone can be moved by your lifting it, by my lifting it, by a pulley, etc.
  d. A woman can bear a child by sexual contact or by artificial insemination.
  e. There are many causes of death: heart disease, cancer, pneumonia, automobile accident, drowning, poisoning, stabbing, etc.
  f. Many different chemicals will take a stain out of a garment.
  g. There are various possible causes of erosion: wind, rapid drainage of water, failure to adopt contour plowing, etc.

8. Analyze critically the following expressions; if you find them faulty, indicate how they could be amended.
  a. The first billiard ball *compelled* the second billiard ball to move.
  b. When the first ball hits the second, the second one *can't help* moving.
  c. The motion of the second ball is *inevitable* when the first one hits it.
  d. The first ball hitting the second *made* the second one move.
  e. The first ball hitting the second *produced* the motion of the second one.

9. According to the regularity ("constant conjunction") view of cause (for example, that of Hume, Reichenbach, Schlick), "there would be no more special connection between the striking of a match and the flame which followed it than between the striking of a match and an earthquake which might also occur just afterwards. It would merely be that the striking of a match is usually followed by a flame and not usually followed by earthquakes, and that would be all. We could not say that the striking *made* the flame fol-

low. . . . On this view to give a cause . . . does not in the least help to explain why the effect happened, it only tells us that it preceded the effect."[14] Evaluate this passage sentence by sentence. (For example: Does the regularity interpretation of "C caused E" render it impossible to explain why C caused E?)

10. What would you say is the cause in these cases?
  a. The fire would not have spread to the neighboring house without a normal breeze, yet we say that lightning and not the breeze was the cause of the disaster. Would it be different if someone deliberately fanned the embers, or if just as the fire was dying out, a leaking gasoline can fell from the back of a jeep?
  b. We say that the flowers died because the gardener neglected to water them. But couldn't we just as well say that they died because you or I or the president of the United States neglected to water them?
  c. A pushes B off a skyscraper; during his fall, C shoots him from a window halfway down. What is the cause of B's death?
  d. A ship engaged in convoy duty in wartime is insured against marine perils other than war. Under orders, the ship pursues a zigzag course and dims her lights, meets unexpected high waves, and is driven off course and onto rocks in a fog. Should insurance be collectible?

11. "Suppose someone claimed to have discovered the cause of cancer, but added that his discovery though genuine would not in practice be of any use because the cause he had discovered was not a thing that could be produced or prevented at will. . . . No one would admit that he had done what he claimed to do. It would be pointed out that he did not know what the word 'cause' (in the context of medicine) meant. For in such a context a proposition of the form 'x causes y' implies the proposition 'x is something that can be produced or prevented at will' as

---

[14]Alfred C. Ewing, *The Fundamental Questions of Philosophy* (New York: Macmillan, 1951), p. 160.

part of the definition of 'cause.' "[15] Do you agree or disagree? Give your reasons.

12. "I do not need to examine more than one case to know that C caused E. If someone bribes me into doing something, I know from this one case alone that the bribe caused my action; I do not need any further examples, nor is any prediction implied that I would ever respond to a bribe again. If you persuade me to attend a concert, I know that your persuading has caused me to go to the concert; I may never respond to your persuasions again, but from this one instance alone I know that your persuasion caused me to go to the concert this time. I know that it was the unannounced arrival of my sister from India (whom I hadn't seen in 30 years) that caused me to be surprised—although if she were to appear again, I wouldn't be surprised at all." Assess this view.

13. Do you agree or disagree with the following reasoning: "The cause and the effect must be simultaneous, for the effect occurs at the very moment that the last condition (of a sufficient condition) is fulfilled. If there is even the slightest waiting period between it and the effect, there must be something *else* that has yet to occur before the effect can occur; otherwise, why wouldn't the effect occur immediately?"

14. "I said that because it's true." Can the truth of a statement be the cause (or a causal factor) of your uttering it? What change of formulation would make the statement more accurate?

15. "What significance is there in my mental struggle tonight whether I shall or shall not give up smoking, if the laws which govern the matter of the physical universe already pre-ordain for the morrow a configuration of matter consisting of pipe, tobacco, and smoke connected with my lips?" (Arthur S. Eddington). Evaluate.

16. Evaluate the following statements.
a. Determinism can't be true, because I *feel* that I'm free; I know this by introspection. This is a much better proof than any arguments.
b. Freedom is incompatible with determinism.
c. Freedom is incompatible with fatalism.
d. Freedom is incompatible with indeterminism.
e. Laws of nature make everything happen the way it does.
f. My background compels me to behave as I do.
g. If I had been under different influences, I would have acted differently; and if the set of influences acting upon me on two occasions had been exactly the same, I would have acted the same way the second time as the first—I couldn't help doing it. So I'm not free.
h. I couldn't have acted differently from the way I did act. No matter what the act was which I contemplated doing, there was only *one* road open to me (although I didn't know it at the time), only *one* thing that under those peculiar circumstances I *could* have done: namely, the one I did do.
i. It is true—at any rate, more obviously true than any theory about determinism—that human beings *deliberate*. Now, deliberation involves a genuine choice among alternatives, with the outcome in doubt at the time of the deliberation. But if the outcome is already "in the cards," it's not a case of genuine deliberation. Since there is deliberation, determinism must be false.
j. "According to determinism," it is said, "every desire, every impulse, every thought, is the inevitable consequence of antecedent conditions." But the word "inevitable" here is misused. "Inevitable" is synonymous with "unavoidable"; and it is not true that everything is unavoidable. Some things can be avoided. The fallacy here is the usual one of taking a word that is applicable to some things and extending its meaning so that it becomes applicable to everything.
k. Heisenberg's Principle of Indeterminacy is now fairly well accepted in physics. If indeter-

---

[15]Collingwood, "On the So-Called Idea of Causation," in *Proceedings of the Aristotelian Society*, 1938, p. 87.

minism is operative in the realm of inorganic nature, why not in humans also? In that case, we have freedom after all.

SELECTED READINGS

Necessity

BENACERAF, PAUL, and HILARY PUTNAM, eds. *Philosophy of Mathematics*. Englewood Cliffs, NJ: Prentice Hall, 1964.

BENCIVENGA, ERNANNO. *Kant's Copernican Revolution*. London: Oxford University Press, 1987.

BLANSHARD, BRAND. *The Nature of Thought*. 2 vols. London: Allen & Unwin, 1939.

FREGE, GOTTLOB. *The Foundations of Arithmetic*. Oxford: Blackwell, 1953.

KANT, IMMANUEL. *Critique of Pure Reason*. Translated by Norman Kemp Smith. London: Macmillan, 1929. Originally published 1781.

KRIPKE, SAUL. *Naming and Necessity*. Cambridge: Cambridge University Press, 1979.

NAGEL, ERNEST. *Logic without Metaphysics*. New York: Free Press, 1956.

PLANTINGA, ALVIN. *The Nature of Necessity*. Oxford: Clarendon Press, 1974.

QUINE, WILLARD V. *From a Logical Point of View*. Cambridge: Harvard University Press, 1953.

RAMSEY, F. P. *Foundations of Mathematics*. London: Routledge, 1931.

WITTGENSTEIN, LUDWIG. *Remarks on the Foundations of Mathematics*. Oxford: Blackwell, 1958.

Causation, Determinism, and Freedom

AYER, ALFRED J. "Freedom and Necessity." In Ayer, *Philosophical Papers*. London: Macmillan, 1963.

BEARDSLEY, ELIZABETH. "Determinism and Moral Perspectives." In Joel Feinberg, ed., *Reason and Responsibility*. Belmont, CA: Dickensen, 1981.

BEROFSKY, BERNARD, ed. *Free Will and Determinism*. New York: Harper, 1966.

CAMPBELL, C. A. *In Defense of Free Will*. Glasgow: Jackson & Co., 1938.

DOUBLE, RICHARD. *The Non-Reality of Free Will*. New York: Oxford University Press, 1990.

DUCASSE, CURET J. *Truth, Knowledge, and Causation*. London: Routledge, 1968.

ENTEMAN, WILLIAM, ed. *The Problem of Free Will*. New York: Scribners, 1967.

FRENCH, PETER, and CURTIS BROWN, eds. "Backward Causation." In *Puzzles, Paradoxes, and Problems*. New York: St. Martin's Press, 1987.

HEIL, JOHN, and ALFRED MELE. *Mental Causation*. London: Oxford University Press, 1003.

HOBART, R. E. "Free-Will as Involving Determinism and Inconceivable without It." *Mind,* vol. 43 (1934), pp. 1–27. Widely reprinted.

HOLBACH, BARON PAUL D'. *The System of Nature*. 1795. Vol. 1, Chapters 11 and 12.

HONDERICH, TED. *A Theory of Determinism. Mind and Brain* (Vol. 1) and *The Consequences of Determinism* (Vol. 2). London: Oxford University Press, 1990.

HOOK, SIDNEY, ed. *Determinism and Freedom in the Age of Modern Science*. New York: New York University Press, 1957.

HOSPERS, JOHN. "Free-Will and Psychoanalysis." In Joel Feinberg, ed., *Reason and Responsibility*. Belmont, CA: Dickensen, 1981.

HUME, DAVID. "On the Idea of Necessary Connection." In Hume, *An Enquiry Concerning Human Understanding*. 1751. Many editions.

INWAGEN, PETER VAN. *An Essay on Free Will*. London: Oxford University Press, 1983.

INWAGEN, PETER VAN. *Metaphysics*. Boulder, CO: Westview Press, 1993.

JAMES, WILLIAM. "The Dilemma of Determinism." In James, *The Will to Believe*. New York: Longmans Green, 1897.

KIM, JAEGWON, and ERNEST SOSA, eds. *A Companion to Metaphysics*. New York: Oxford University Press, 1993.

LEHRER, KEITH, ed. *Freedom and Determinism*. New York: Random House, 1966.

LUCAS, J. R. *Responsibility*. London: Oxford University Press, 1993.

MACKIE, J. L. *The Cement of the Universe*. Oxford: Clarendon Press, 1974.

MILL, JOHN STUART. "Are Human Actions Subject to the Law of Causality?" In Mill, *A System of Logic*. 1842. Book 3, Chapter 3, and Book 9, Chapter 2.

MORGENBERSSER, SIDNEY, and JAMES WALSH, eds. *Free Will*. Englewood Cliffs, NJ: Prentice Hall, 1962.

OPPENHEIM, FELIX. *Dimensions of Freedom*. New York: St. Martin's Press, 1961.

PEARS, DAVID. *Freedom of the Will*. London: Macmillan, 1965.

RASHDALL, HASTINGS. *Theory of Good and Evil*. 2

vols. London: Oxford University Press, 1924. Book 1, Chapter 3.

RYLE, GILBERT. "It Was to Be." In Ryle, *Dilemmas*. Cambridge: Cambridge University Press, 1954.

SALMON, WESLEY. "Determinism and Indeterminism in Modern Science." In Joel Feinberg, ed., *Reason and Responsibility*. Belmont, CA: Dickensen, 1981.

SUPPES, PATRICK. *Determinism, Computation, and Free Will*. Oxford: Blackwell, 1993.

TAYLOR, RICHARD. *Metaphysics*. 3rd ed. Englewood Cliffs, NJ: Prentice Hall, 1983.

WATSON, GARY. *Free Will*. London: Oxford University Press, 1982.

WOLF, SUSAN. *Freedom without Reason*. London: Oxford University Press, 1990.

6 *What Am I?*

MIND AND BODY

You have a head, two hands, and two feet, and all these are parts of what is called your body. But, surely, you also have a mind. This may be less obvious because you can't see it. Still, you think, you deliberate, you make decisions, and how could you do these things without a mind?

You can't think without a brain, of course, but this means only that having a brain is a necessary condition for thinking, something without which you can't think. But (we are inclined to say) it isn't the brain itself that does the thinking—it's the wherewithal for thinking, but not what *does* the thinking.

What then does the thinking? Why, the mind—isn't that the proper answer? René Descartes said, "I am a mind which thinks." The brain is the vehicle, the mind is the you. Is the mind what you are or something you have?

Sometimes when I talk about myself, I do mean my body. When I say I am 6 feet tall, I mean that my body is 6 feet tall; when I say I weigh 170 pounds, I mean that my body weighs 170 pounds. Yet I am not my body; aren't we correct in saying, "I *have* a body," not "I *am* a body"?

Often when I use the pronoun "I," I don't seem to be talking about my body at all. "I am thinking about Paris" doesn't mean "My body is thinking about Paris" or even "My brain is thinking about Paris." My brain isn't what thinks, although I can't think without it. When I think, wonder, dream, hope, be-

lieve, it doesn't seem to be my body or any part of it that does any of these things.

Could it be that I am a mind that happens to have a body associated (connected?) with it, but that it would still be me if I had no body? Saint Augustine (354–430) believed that I am a soul that is "chained" to a body until death unchains me from it. It isn't very clear what a soul is—is it the same as a mind except that perhaps the soul is immortal? Can I admit that I have a mind but deny or question whether I have a soul?

What *is* the mind? Is it a kind of container that holds your thoughts and feelings? This seems to be just a figure of speech, a way of speaking. Descartes held that the mind is a mental *substance,* just as physical elements and compounds are physical substances. But what could such a substance be? Try to imagine it. Does it have parts? ingredients? constituents? In what sense is it a thing at all?

The word "mind" occurs in the subject of a sentence, as in "I've changed my mind." But that alone doesn't imply that there is a thing corresponding to the word. Don't assume that for every substantive (noun) there is a substance. ("Something happened to me today," we say, but is there a thing or substance that did the happening?) "My mind isn't very alert today," I may say. But must I conclude from this that there is a thing, my mind, of which alertness is a present quality?

Sometimes when we use the word "mind" we can substitute other terms to say the same thing. "I am not going to change my mind" means that I am determined to retain my present opinion. "It's all in your mind" means that you are only imagining it. "She has a mind of her own" means that she is independent, perhaps even stubborn. "She has a creative mind" means that she develops new and original ideas. "She is of sound mind" means that she is sane.

But is mind eliminated by this terminology? If she is of an independent mind, she *thinks* for herself, she doesn't accept beliefs on mere authority. But isn't thinking a mental activity, something that minds do? "I've changed my mind" means that I no longer think what I thought before. "What do you have in mind?" is a request for what you're thinking about. If a person says there is no such thing as a mind, would we conclude that she is mindless?

Still, some philosophers have held that there are only bodies (including brains), and that minds do not exist as any independent entity. *Materialism* is the view that there is matter but no mind; all that exists, as Democritus said, is particles of matter in motion. Of course there is also energy and gravitation and electrical and magnetic fields, but these are all in the realm of the physical; materialism says that there is no other "realm."

Does this imply that there are no thoughts, feelings, sensations? No; "I think that there are no thoughts" is a self-refuting statement. If there were no thoughts, you couldn't think that there were none. Materialism says only that even thoughts, feelings, and sensations are physical, part of the physical world studied by physics and chemistry and biology.

Democritus believed that the universe consists only of "matter and the void" (empty space). Everything is composed of atoms. The body is composed of atoms. The mind is also composed of very tiny atoms. What then

is it that *perceives* the world that is composed of these atoms? *Other* atoms, which he called mind atoms, do the perceiving. What perceives the atoms in the outside world is mind atoms.

But this view has not seemed very plausible. The world is composed of atoms, but doesn't it require something that isn't matter to *perceive* the world? How can matter itself be *conscious*? Are there consciousness atoms? Isn't consciousness something different, something that has to be distinguished from the atoms *of which* we are conscious?

1. THE PHYSICAL AND THE MENTAL

Whatever we say about mind and body, it seems that there are physical events and processes going on in space and time, and also mental events, conscious experiences. It is the mental part that has been subjected to the most challenges. What we shall describe here is "the traditional account" of the issue, and not everyone would agree with this way of describing it. But regardless of agreement or disagreement, it is important to be acquainted with this approach to setting up the issue.

What happens when you hear a noise? There are sound waves—alternating condensations or rarefactions of the air—that cause air particles to strike repeatedly on your eardrum so that it vibrates. The eardrum is connected by three small bones to a membrane that covers one end of a spiral tube in the inner ear. The vibration of your eardrum is transmitted through this chain of three bones to the membrane at the end of the tube. The tube is filled with a liquid, perilymph, and the vibration in the membrane attached to these bones causes a corresponding vibration to pass through this liquid. Inside the first tube is another one, filled with a liquid called endolymph; vibrations in the perilymph cause vibrations in the membranous wall of the inner tube and waves in the endolymph. Small hairs that stick out from the membranous walls into the endolymph are made to vibrate by the vibrations in the endolymph. The auditory nerve is joined to the roots of these hairs. The vibration of the hairs causes impulses to pass up the auditory nerve to a part of the brain called the auditory center.

The whole process takes only a small fraction of a second. But now, when the auditory nerve has carried the stimulus to the appropriate portion of the brain, something else happens; *you hear a sound* (sense an auditory sense datum). This is "something new under the sun"—a *conscious event*. We could give similar accounts of the process leading to experiences of sight, smell, taste, and touch. What is there about these experience-events that is different from anything we could say about physical events?

1. We can always locate physical things, events, and processes somewhere in space. They take place some*where*. The sensory and neural processes take place inside the person's head. But what about the sensory experience itself? If you hear a bell ringing, where does your auditory experience occur? The sound*waves* are in the space adjacent to your body, between the bell and your ears. Still less is it in the bell, which is a physical object at a certain place in space. But what of the experience—is it inside your head somewhere? Would a surgeon opening your head ever find it? If your skull were transparent and a surgeon with proper equipment could see what was going on inside it, she might witness the stimulation of your auditory nerve, but would she also be witness to your sound *experiences*?

Suppose the experience is not caused by anything outside your body. Suppose you are "seeing red spots before your eyes." Where are the spots? A few inches in front of your eyes? They don't seem to be in physical space at all. (We sometimes say that they are in *phenomenal* space, or experienced space.)

"But they aren't real; they don't exist at all." But don't they? They aren't physical spots like the spots on a leopard, but you do have the experience of seeing spots, and a complete story of your life would include the fact that you saw them. If we say they aren't real, doesn't that mean only that they aren't a part of the public physical world, the world that others can see as well as you, the world that can be photographed and so on? But they are real in the sense that they really do occur in your experience. Yet they aren't inside your head, nor apparently outside it either, near the bookcase you are looking at. They aren't in physical space at all.

The spots do appear to be *extended* in space—some appear bigger than others. How big then are they? two inches wide? The Empire State Building has a certain height; a statue of the Empire State Building also has a certain height; but what is the height of your *image* of the Empire State Building? onetenth of the height of the statue, perhaps? How could you tell? Would there be an image of a certain height in the occipital lobe of your brain? And if there were, would *that* be what you are seeing? (Can you see things inside your own head?)

2. Physical objects, processes, and events are all publicly observable. Some of them are hard to get at, like those taking place inside your head. Still, neurologists can and do observe them with various instruments. They can consult with other specialists who also see them. But who other than you can have your experiences?

Can anyone but you feel your pain? You may strongly *empathize* with someone who is in pain, so strongly that it's as if you felt the pain yourself. But if you do, is it *her* pain that you are feeling, or your own (in empathy with hers)? Doesn't she feel her pain and you yours? And aren't there then two pains and not one?

Even if neurological laws were different from what they now are, and you felt pain when someone else's body was injured, you could then say, "I feel pain in your body," but could you say, "I feel your pain and not mine"? Doesn't the fact that you feel it make it your pain and not hers? Isn't the experience *private to you* and never experienceable by anyone else?

"But at least I feel pain *in a certain location*—in my head if I have a headache, in my tooth if I have a toothache." Pains are experienced as being some*where* in your body; they can even occur in a limb that has already been amputated. No one else can feel your pain, but isn't your pain at a definite place? Indeed, it is *experienced* as being in a definite place. It is in your phenomenal space (apparent space or experienced space). You might feel it in another location from where the trouble is: people with stomach ulcers often experience the pain in the small of their back. But is the pain in physical space? Could anyone else experience it there? No, it is still private to you. A physician tapping various places on your body and asking, "Where's the pain?" would see only your body; she wouldn't feel your pain; she would have to *infer* that you had a pain, based on her examination of you and your verbal pain reports. Your pain is as private to you as the red spots you see from being hit on the head.

Other Minds

When my finger is cut and bleeding, I know that I have a pain in the most direct way possible: I feel it. I do not *infer* from my behavior or anything else that I feel pain, I am *directly* *aware* of it—what philosophers sometimes call "immediate acquaintance." But when *your* finger is cut and bleeding, I do not know in the same way that you are feeling pain. I *infer* it from the fact that I see the blood and hear you saying that it hurts, and so on, but I do not feel your pain. (I may feel great empathy toward you and feel distressed at the thought that you are in pain, but that still isn't feeling your pain in the way I feel my own pain when my finger is cut.) It seems to be impossible for me to feel your pain or for you to feel mine. We are each aware of our own experiences and no one else's.

This is not to say that I cannot *know that* you are in pain. Probably I do know it, at least in the weak sense of "know." I have strong evidence that you are in pain and no evidence against it; on the whole I have good reason to believe you are in pain, just as I am when my finger is cut. Thus, I may know both propositions to be true: "I am in pain" (in the strong sense of "know") and "You are in pain" (in the weak sense of "know"). But even if I know *that* you are feeling pain, I do not know it by *feeling it myself*. That direct means of access is available only to me. I may look at your face and say, "I'll bet you're feeling worried today," and you may confirm what I say. But in my own case I don't need to look in the mirror and say, "My face looks tense and worried today, so I must be feeling worried." In my own case, I don't have to make such an inference: I know right off whether I am worried or not. (The only doubt would be whether the *word* "worried" correctly describes what I feel; perhaps the word "tense" would describe it better. I feel what I feel, but it may not be easy to describe in words what I feel.)

Thus, even if it is granted that I can know you're in pain, I still can't *feel* your pain, or think your thoughts, or experience your worry. If you tell me what you're worried about ("There's a hurricane on the way"), I too may feel worried; but even so, I feel my worry and you feel yours. There are two worries going on here, yours and mine, and I can't experience yours any more than you can experience mine. In fact, it would seem to be a necessary truth that I can't experience your experiences and you can't experience mine.

But is it a necessary truth? Suppose that the laws of physiology were different, and that we consider two persons, A and B. When A is cut with a knife, B feels pain, and when B is cut, A feels pain. Wouldn't that be a case of A feeling B's pain, and B A's pain? We might *say* that it is; if "my pain" means "the pain felt in my body," the answer would be yes. But in another sense the answer would be no. A might feel pain when B's body is injured, and B might feel pain when A's body is injured; this would be a very peculiar kind of world: I might say to you, "Don't get hit over the head today; I don't want to have that headache again." Still, wouldn't I be having *my* pain—but feeling it when your body was injured— just as you would still be feeling your pain when my body was injured? The causal conditions of having pain would be different in such a world, but I would still have my pain and you would have yours. "My pain" is *the pain I feel*—regardless of the causal conditions under which it was felt; even if I feel the pain when your finger is cut, it would still be my pain, because I am the one who *has* the pain.

It seems, then, that "I feel your pain" and "You feel my pain" are not just empirically impossible—that is contrary to biological laws—but logically impossible; it would involve saying that I feel a pain that is not mine but yours. Experiences, including pains, are essentially private; I could not have your pain any more than a circle could be square. In that case, however, I cannot possibly *verify* that you are in pain; I can verify only what your facial expression is and, if necessary, supplement that with a lie-detector test and a brain scan. But I cannot feel your pain myself. By such means I may be able to discover what thoughts or feelings you are having— even to know (at least in the weak sense of "know") *that* you are feeling so-and-so. But knowing *that* you are having a certain feeling is not at all the same as feeling it myself. If I know you well I may be able to say truly, "I know just what you're going through," but that's not the same thing as feeling it myself. I may empathize strongly with you and even feel pain when you are in pain, but the pain I feel is still mine and the pain you feel is yours.

Can I verify the proposition that you are feeling pain? Not if verifying means having all the evidence, or even the best possible evidence, which would be feeling it. At best I can verify that you behave in a certain way, respond in a certain way to a lie-detector test, and so on.

Perhaps then all I mean by saying that you are in pain is that you behave in a certain way and respond to lie-detector tests and so on. But this view is absurdly implausible. If you have just cut yourself badly and I see your agonized behavior, do I, in saying that you feel pain, mean only that you behave *as if* you felt pain? Surely I mean that your behavior is an *indication* that you feel pain—and when I say that you are in pain I mean to say exactly the same thing about you that I am saying about myself when I say that I am in pain. The only difference between "I am in pain" and "You are in pain" is the personal pronoun. *What* I am saying about me and about you is exactly the same in the two cases. The question is, How can I verify the pain in your case, as I can do so immediately in my own?

"Well, at least I can *confirm* that you are feeling pain." Surely the fact that you cry out after having been cut is a good *confirmation* to me that you are in pain. Sometimes when you cry out you may be play-acting, but with careful observation I can confirm that too.

Many would be content with confirmation rather than verification. But a skeptic can pursue the question further: how do I know that you have pains or any other experiences at all? How do I know that you experience pain or pleasure or have sensations or thoughts or feelings of any kind? Could you not be a cleverly rigged-up automaton, wound up like a top every morning to go through certain complicated motions every day, but all the while experiencing nothing at all? True, you give answers to mathematical questions faster than I do; but so do computers when they have been programmed to do so. How do I know that you are not a fancy computer, having no more feelings or thoughts than the computers scientists build? If you were one, programmed to go through just the motions that you do, how would I ever know the difference? You would do the same things, say the same things, every bit of your behavior would be the same—so how could I tell? I can tell that you feel pain only from the symptoms from which I make the inference—but what if the symptoms were the same? If I don't believe that a computer has feelings, and if you behaved just as a computer does (the computer too can exhibit pain behavior and even say that it is in pain), what reason would I have for saying that you experience pain but the computer doesn't? Your behavior is all I can confirm, and I have no evidence that there is anything else beyond that.

To counter this alarming possibility, the *argument from analogy* is often invoked. When my finger is cut (A), I feel pain (B); therefore, I infer that when your finger is cut (A′), you feel pain (B′). That doesn't confer certainty on the statement that you feel pain, but doesn't it make it quite probable? After all, you behave as I do when I feel pain; you too are composed of skin, bones, nerves, and blood vessels—just as I am. So can't I infer by

analogy (similarity) that if I feel pain when cut, so do you?

The trouble is that as an argument from analogy, this seems to be weak. Suppose I see a set of boxes stored in someone's garage. I open one box and find that it is full of books. I don't open any of the rest, but I say, "Since all the boxes look pretty much alike, I infer that they all contain books." Admittedly this wouldn't be a very safe inference, and you wouldn't bet much on it. The boxes might contain anything—trinkets, papers, children's toys. If you open only one box, you're not in a very good position to say that they all contain books. Your position would be much better if you had opened all the boxes but one, found that they contained books, and then inferred that probably the last box would contain books also. An argument from analogy based on only one case is a pretty poor argument.

But isn't that exactly the position we are in with regard to other minds? In my own case, I have (1) my behavior; and (2) my feeling pain. But in every other case, I have only the behavior to go by. So am I not in the position of the person who concludes that all the boxes contain books on the slender basis of finding that one box contains books?

Yet I am much more confident that you feel pain when your finger is cut than I am that all the boxes contain books after examining the contents of only one box. Why is this? Is this just an irrational conclusion, a prejudice? Or is it my belief that you have feelings based on something other than a weak argument from analogy?

Consider the following three statements:

1   I ask you, "Where is the book I lent you?"
2   You understand my question and think for a moment.
3   You utter the words, "I'm sorry–I forgot it. I left it at home."

The first statement is a report of words emanating from my mouth; these I not only utter but can hear myself uttering. The third statement is also something I can hear; your lips move, and you utter the words. The problem is with the second statement. How do I know it is true, since I can't experience your thoughts? John Stuart Mill wrote,

> I conclude that other human beings have feelings like me because, first, they have bodies like me, which I know in my own case, to be the antecedent condition of feelings; and because secondly, they exhibit the acts, and other outward signs, which in my own case I know from experience to be caused by feelings. . . . In the case of other human beings I have the evidence of my senses for the first and last links of the series, but not for the intermediate link. I find, however, that the sequence between the first and last is as regular and constant in those other cases as it is in mine. In my own case I know that the first link produces the last through the intermediate link, and could not produce it without. Experience, therefore, obliges me to conclude that there must be an intermediate link; which must either be the same in others as in myself, or a different one; I must either believe them to be alive, or to be automatons; and by believing them to be alive, that is, by supposing the link to be of the same nature as in the case of which I have experience, and which is in all other respects similar, I bring other human beings, as phenomena, under the same generalizations which I know by experience to be the true story of my own existence.[1]

I ask someone a question and then from that person's lips emanate words that answer the very question I asked. How would this be possible if the other body doesn't have a mind that understands the question? To understand the question must he not have con-sciousness like me? Surely, the belief that he has consciousness like me is *the best explanation* of his ability to answer my questions.

Many would rest content with this answer, believing the problem of other minds to be solved. But there are a few bothersome questions that have been raised about this account.

1. How did we ever learn to use words like "pain" and "anger"—and other words we use—in talking about our "inner states"? As children we learned to use words by having them uttered by our parents, accompanied typically by acts of pointing: "That's a chair," "That's a car." But of course you can't point to pain or anger. So how does the child learn to use the language of sensations and feelings? How did we ourselves learn to use the words correctly? How did words like "pain" become part of a *public language*?

Suppose you have some special feeling whenever you see, say, a mountain gorge. You might give a name to that peculiar sensation, and use it again if you had that same peculiar sensation another time. But thus far the name would not be part of a public language; you could use it only in "communing with yourself." You might try to communicate this special feeling to others, but others might be quite uncomprehending as to what you meant. But the word "pain" is not the same. You learned to use that word from hearing your parents and other people use it, and to use it correctly you didn't need to feel their pains, or even to feel pain yourself. It was only necessary to observe the occasions on which they used the word—what their behavior was like when they used it, and by doing so you became able to use it yourself. If your father cut his finger and said that it hurt, and later you cut your finger, you could say the same thing of yourself—and presumably the feeling you had when this happened would be one you would identify as "pain."

[1]John Stuart Mill, *An Examination of Sir William Hamilton's Philosophy,* 6th ed. (London: Longmans Green, 1889), pp. 243–244.

This is not to say, then, that you have no "inner episodes" such as sensations of pain, but that you can learn to identify something as pain only by observing behavior that accompanies the use of the word. The child did not begin with her own case, as the argument from analogy seems to assume. She learned it as she learned any word in a public language, by observing the contexts in which other people used it. Thus, you could learn the meaning of "dread" even if you haven't felt it yourself.

2. Can you know even that *you* are having a certain kind of experience? We have already seen in Chapter 2 how we often misreport an experience by including elements in the description that go far beyond the experience itself. But with something as elemental as pain and pleasure, it would seem that the probability of such an error would be minimal: surely if someone sticks a knife into your flesh while you are fully conscious, you know that you are feeling pain, don't you? But even this has been questioned:

Suppose that an encephalograph was constructed to test whether your reports that you are in pain are true; the machine is designed to test your pain level. What if you sincerely report that you are in pain, but this report conflicts with the evidence of the encephalograph? Should it be concluded that you are not telling the truth when you say you are in pain?

"Not at all," you might well exclaim, "I *know* whether I feel a pain. If the machine says I'm not, then it's the machine that's making the mistake. After all, *I* know whether I have a pain or not—I feel it! The machine only provides an indirect test—one that can be mistaken if the machine malfunctions."

However good the evidence may be, such a physiological theory can never be used to show the sufferer that he was mistaken in thinking that he had a pain. . . . The sufferer's epistemological authority must therefore be better than the best physiological theory can ever be.[2]

But wait: how does Jones know that he is using the word "pain" correctly? Has he any *criteria* for the use of the term? He feels what he feels, but perhaps he is misdescribing what he feels in calling it a pain. Or perhaps he can describe it rightly once it is recognized for what it is, but he doesn't recognize it for what it is, in much the same way that a person may think she sees someone else in the room when she is only seeing her image in a mirror.

The encephalograph says that the brain-process constantly correlated with pain-reports occurs in Jones's brain. However, although he exhibits pain-behavior, Jones thinks that he does not feel pain. . . . Now is it that he does not know that *pain* covers what you feel when you are burned as well as what you feel when you are stuck, struck, etc.? Or is it that he really does not feel pain when he is burned? Suppose we tell Jones that what he feels when he is burned is *also* called "pain." Suppose he then admits that he does feel *something*, but insists that what he feels is quite *different* from what he feels when he is stuck, struck, etc. Where does Jones go from here? Has he failed to learn the language properly, or is he correctly (indeed infallibly) reporting that he has different sensations than those normally had in the situation in question?[3]

If the certainty of a sincere pain report is thus cast in doubt, some alarming skeptical possibilities now confront us. Would one sincere pain report—if at odds with the machine report—be enough to break down at

[2]Kurt Baier, "Smart on Sensations," *Australian Journal of Philosophy* (1962), p. 47.
[3]Richard Rorty, "Mind-Body Identity, Privacy, and Categories," *Review of Metaphysics*, vol. 19 (1965), pp. 24–25.

one blow well-confirmed scientific theories? Can our certainty about our pains possibly be shaken by such questions as "Does she really know which sensations are called pains?" and "Is she a good judge of whether she is in pain or not?" Can the truth of a pain report *never* be overridden by evidence from other sources?

Consider another kind of case. You say, "It's hot in this room." But you look at the thermometer and it reads 55°; you check other thermometers, and they all say the same. Are you sure you are right and the thermometers wrong? In this case we say the thermometers are right and that it isn't hot in the room, you just *feel* hot; perhaps you have a slight fever. Here we trust the thermometer and not your individual judgment. Why not do the same in trusting the encephalograph rather than your individual pain report?

"But this is different," you might say. Instead of saying it's hot in the room, you should say that you *feel* hot. No one will dispute that; it's just that this time your heat experience doesn't correspond to the actual temperature. But in the case of the pain report, how can we deny that the person is feeling pain? If *you* are the one who has the pain, won't you say without hesitation that the encephalograph is mistaken? Aren't *you* the final judge of whether you feel pain? Isn't this one case that's absolutely clear and unshakable?

But some philosophers have questioned even this. We learn the word "pain"—like other words—in certain behavioral and environmental contexts; that's how we come to recognize pain when we feel it and to name it correctly. However,

now suppose that these public criteria (for "knowing how to use 'pain' ") change as physiology and technology progress. Suppose, in particular, that we find it convenient to

speed up the learning of contrastive observation predicates (such as "painful," "tickling," etc.) by supplying children with portable enchephalographs-cum-teaching-machines which, whenever the appropriate brain-process occurs, murmur the appropriate term in their ears. Now "appropriate brain-process" will start out by meaning "brain-process constantly correlated with sincere utterances of 'I'm in pain' by people taught the use of 'pain' in the old rough-and ready way." But soon it will come to mean, "the brain-process which we have always programmed the machine to respond to with a murmur of 'pain.' " . . . Given this situation, it would make sense to say things like "You say you are in pain, and I'm sure you are sincere, but you can see for yourself that your brain is not in the state to which you were trained to respond to with 'Pain,' so apparently the training did not work, and you do not yet understand what pain is." In such a situation, our "inability to be mistaken" about our pains would remain, but our "final epistemological authority" on the subject would be gone, for there would be a standard procedure for overriding our reports.[4]

The question is, however, whether such first-person reports can be overridden in this way. The person reporting the experience may be lying or may be misreporting the experience by using words incorrectly. But if neither of these things is taking place, how can the person be mistaken? Some would contend that the first-person report is not coherent with the physical evidence, and that if the physical evidence is considerable, the first-person report, lacking coherence with the other propositions, must be rejected. But others would contend that if the physical evidence is not coherent with the first-person report, then it is the physical evidence that should be rejected and the first-person report that should be maintained.

[4]Ibid., p. 25.

Can Computers Be Conscious?

Computers can spew out more information, and many times faster, than any human mind can. We say that the computer can "figure things out" and that it "knows the answer" to the questions we put to it. Can't we say then that computers are also conscious: they do the work of minds, and often much more, so why can't we say that they *have* minds? Or should we say that they don't know in the same sense that people do—that they can give us the answer but are not aware of their ability to do so?

Imagine that a computer of the future can not only answer questions we put to it, but writes poetry and shows envy when it is outdone by a person or by another computer (such as the one in Stanley Kubrick's *2001: A Space Odyssey*). If we didn't know that it was a computer, and judged it entirely by its performance, wouldn't we have the same reasons to say it was conscious that we now have in saying that other people are conscious?

"But the computer isn't made of flesh and blood, but tubes and computer chips. If we open it up, that's what we would find, and wouldn't that keep us from saying that it's conscious?" "No, not so," one may reply, "what does its *origin* have to do with it?" It's manufactured, not born, but if it can do the work that conscious beings do, why not believe it *is* conscious? Isn't it just "racial prejudice" to deny this possibility?

No, say others. We can talk in the abstract about computers being conscious or having minds, but let's talk about specifics:

> Consider specific mental states and processes—being thirsty, wanting to go to the bathroom, worrying about your income tax, trying to solve math puzzles, feeling depressed, recalling the French word for "butterfly." . . .
> Let's program our favorite PDP-10 computer with the formal program that simulates thirst. We can even program it to print out at

the end "Boy, am I thirsty!" or "Won't someone please give me a drink?" etc. Now would anyone suppose that we thereby have even the slightest reason to suppose that the computer is literally thirsty? or that any simulation of any other mental phenomena, such as understanding stories, feeling depressed, or worrying about itemized deductions, must therefore produce the real thing? . . .

> So, let us imagine our thirst-simulating program running on a computer made entirely of old beer cans, millions (or billions) of old beer cans that are rigged up to levers and powered by windmills. We can imagine that the program simulates the neuron firings at the synapses by having beer cans bang into each other, thus achieving a strict correspondence between neuron firings and beer-can bangings. At the end of the sequence a beer can pops up on which is written "I am thirsty." Now . . . does anyone suppose that this Rube Goldberg apparatus is literally thirsty in the sense in which you and I are?[5]

2. THE RELATION BETWEEN THE PHYSICAL AND THE MENTAL

Thus far we have two sets of things, or two sets of qualities, the physical and the mental. There are in the physical world certain motions of molecules, and there are also states of consciousness. They are not the same thing, but they are clearly closely related.

It has seemed obvious to many philosophers that the physical and the mental causally *interact*. Don't we all know that the physical causes the mental? Eating certain foods may cause you to feel abdominal pain, hearing a fire engine may cause you to feel anxious, being arrested on a false charge may cause you to feel angry, listening to a teacher's lecture may cause you to have certain thoughts, and so on. These are familiar

---

[5]John Searle, "The Myth of the Computer," *New York Review of Books*, 1982; reprinted in G. Lee Bowie, Meredith Michaels and Robert Solomon, eds., *Twenty Questions* (Fort Worth, TX: Harcourt Brace, 1992), pp. 209—210.

examples that could be multiplied indefinitely. Similarly, isn't it a fact of experience that the mental also causes the physical? You feel hot and uncomfortable in a smoky room, and the discomfort causes you to go out into the fresh air. You feel fearful, and as a result your heart beats faster. You decide to take a walk, and your legs move in accordance with your decision. We may not know just how it happens, but don't we know that it does happen? A volition (an act of will) causes your body to move; this is mysterious and yet familiar. And don't we know in general that the mind has a great influence on the body—that if you feel calm and confident and optimistic you are more likely to recover from a serious disease?

The brain seems to be the "point of contact" between the physical and the mental: nothing enters your consciousness except through the brain, and no mental event or condition can have a physical consequence without the brain. But the brain is itself a physical thing like a chair or a tree, with a definite size and weight and position. The "gap" between physical and mental isn't bridged by something that is itself physical. When the final brain event before your awareness of the table takes place, how does this cause the *awareness* to occur? Does motion of molecules result in something that is *not* the motion of molecules?

The connection between the two seems to be quite mysterious. Why, for example, when light of one wavelength impinges on the retina, do we have the peculiar color experience we call "red," and when the wavelength is just a bit shorter, do we have another peculiar color experience we call "orange"? Is there any reason why it should be that way, and not the other way round, or something quite different? Is there any explanation for these mysterious psycho-physical correlations?

There may be similar mysteries within the realm of the physical. A piece of wood is

heated, and finally it bursts into flame. Could anyone have predicted, when first it was heated, that something quite different, namely flames, would result? Perhaps there is some explanation of this; at any rate, this is entirely within the realm of the physical; it's one physical state causing another physical state. The relation between physical and mental, however, seems quite inexplicable. Something happens in the cerebral cortex, and suddenly, presto, a state of consciousness results. Still, it seems, the fact that we know of no explanation of these causal connections in no way proves that they do not occur; indeed, it seems obvious from hundreds of examples every day that they do occur.

Not everyone, however, will go this far. A theory that was made famous by Thomas H. Huxley (1825–1895), called *epiphenomenalism*, holds that mental states never do any causing. Physical states cause mental states, but the causation never goes the other way. The relation of physical to mental is like the relation of the locomotive to the smoke that it produces. The brain, it was sometimes said, produces thoughts just as the liver produces bile. The mental by itself is causally impotent—just as the smoke has no influence on the motion of the locomotive that produces it, and the shadow has no influence on the object that casts it—the shadow is an effect of the object's motion but not a cause. We are, said Huxley, "conscious automata."

But, we say, this is wildly implausible. We have overwhelming evidence that the physical causes the mental; don't we have the same degree of evidence that the mental causes the physical? Doesn't your decision to leave the room cause you to leave the room? Doesn't the depression a person feels sometimes cause her to commit suicide? How can anyone deny that what you feel or think affects how you act?

Epiphenomenalists do deny it. Everything you experience is caused by some state of the body, and the proximate cause (the cause that is the last to occur before the effect occurs) of a mental event is always some complicated state of the brain—about which even today we know very little. No one knows how your brain state when you think about Paris is different from your brain state when you think about London, although there is (must be?) such a difference to cause you to think about the one rather than the other. But thinking about London is not the cause of your subsequent actions, such as taking a map of England off your bookshelf. What does the causing is always the brain state, not the conscious thought itself. The conscious thought "represents" the brain state; the thought by itself is causally impotent, but the brain state that it "reflects" is not: it is a state of the brain that causes you to pull out that map of England.

In the ordinary way of speaking, it is true that placing your hand in the fire causes you to feel pain *and* that the pain you feel causes you to remove your hand from the fire. Contact with the hot stove is communicated through the nerves to what is called the C-fibers in the brain, which cause you to feel the pain; and it is the stimulation of the C-fibers that causes you to remove your hand from the fire. The physical chain of causes and effects is unbroken. The pain does "tell you" to remove your hand from the fire, but it is the pain's "representative" in the physical world, the C-fibers, that affect the efferent nerves and do the actual causal work of removing your hand from the fire.

The mental is, some would put it, a *function* of the physical: the motion of the wheel is different from the wheel itself, but without the wheel there would be no motion of the wheel. The brain is the causal base-of-operation, and the mental is like sparks thrown off by the wheel.

Does the mind, then, never *originate* anything? According to epiphenomenalism, the answer is no. But brain states do originate (through muscles and efferent nerves) motions of the body, like walking out of the room. And the brain is a part of *you.* When we say that the mind affects the body, what we should say, if we are to be accurate, is that events going on in the brain affect the body. And the brain is a part of *you,* isn't it?

"It's a part of you, but not a part that *you* can control," one may say. But that leads us to the deepest question of all in this entire issue, namely, "What exactly is the you?" We shall turn to this question in the next section. Meanwhile, we have not yet finished our survey of the relation of mental states to physical states.

Materialism

The physical-mental distinction, which has seemed obvious to many, has been strongly opposed by others. One view is that there is only behavior, another is that there are only brain states.

Behaviorism. *Methodological* behaviorism is not so much a doctrine or theory as a mode of procedure often used in psychology. When you listen to people's introspective reports, you find that they are often mistaken—not that they're lying, but that they just don't report their experiences accurately. It is more reliable to observe their behavior carefully—their body language, what they do, and what they don't do. As a method for doing psychology, relying on behavior rather than reports of experiences may or may not be desirable: this is for psychologists to say, not philosophers.

Metaphysical behaviorism, however, is a doctrine about reality: there are no "inner episodes," there is only behavior. What we take to be mental events are actually complex tendencies to behave in certain ways.

When we say that glass is brittle, we are saying that it has a certain *dispositional* characteristic: it tends to break easily when it is subjected to forces that are quite small. A piece of glass may never shatter at all, but it is still brittle: it is still true that it *would* break if struck with a hammer and so on, even if it never does. And glass has this tendency because it is in a certain molecular state, which is easily described by chemists.

Similarly, to say that a person is volatile is to say that he is quick to exhibit angry behavior: when someone makes an irritating remark he retaliates with physical violence or incendiary remarks more quickly than most people do. The tendency to behave in this way is doubtless due to some state (perhaps too much adrenalin) of a person's brain. In any case, saying that he is an angry person is to say something about how he is disposed to behave, just as saying that glass is brittle is saying something about what it does when subjected to strain.

Whatever may be said of methodological behaviorism, metaphysical behaviorism doesn't seem very plausible. If a person has a dispositional state (of being easily angered), doesn't this involve saying that he *feels angry* more quickly than most others? And isn't the felt anger an "inner episode" that the person himself has? But the "inner episode"—the felt anger—is not itself behavior, but is (at least sometimes) the cause of behavior: a person throws the cat against the wall because he *feels* angry. Isn't feeling angry a vital part of the whole process?

The identity theory. According to this view, what we call mental states just *are*—are identical with—certain states of the brain. Your having a thought is *nothing but* being in a certain brain state (although only a trained neurologist might be able to say exactly what it is). It is not that thoughts and brain states are uniquely correlated in some way, but that they are *the very same thing*, as being rich is identical with being wealthy. The identity theory is a contemporary version of materialism.

Identity theorists do not say that conscious events are identical with brain states in that they have the same qualities, as two marbles may be identical. In that case there are still two things. They are said to be identical in the strongest possible sense—that they literally *are* the same thing, just as the Morning Star and the Evening Star, which the ancients believed were two different things, are one and the same thing, the planet Venus. What was thought to be two is actually one.

But how can this be? Don't conscious states have different qualities from physical states? If a conscious event has quality A but the physical event does not, how can they be one and the same quality?

How can words describing mental events ("I feel drowsy") and words describing physical events ("My brain is in such-and-such a state") have the same meaning? They do not have the same meaning, says identity theory. When I say that I have an afterimage, I don't *mean* that my brain is in a certain state—I don't even know anything about what's in my brain. But two words or phrases can *refer* to the same thing even though they don't have the same meaning. The phrases "vice-president of the United States" and "president of the United States Senate" denote the same person: by law the same person holds both offices, but I can refer to the vice-president without knowing that he is the same person who is president of the Senate.

The word "lightning" does not mean the same as "electrical discharge," although every flash of lightning is in fact an electrical discharge. This was an empirical discovery, like finding that the Morning Star and the Evening Star are the same object, Venus. "I see lightning" doesn't mean the same as "I see an electrical discharge" (the electrical discharge theory might even be abandoned).

But how can they be numerically identical if there are facts we can know about the one without knowing them about the other?

They can, says the identity theorist. I can know that someone is vice-president of the United States without knowing that he is also president of the Senate. I may know that the object I see is red but not that it is a balloon, yet the red object is in fact a balloon. A person may talk about her thoughts and feelings without knowing that they are actually brain states.

I can also expect A but not B even though A and B are the same thing. I can expect to see a white image on the screen but not expect to be in a certain brain state, although seeing the image *is* being in that brain state. The identity is not a meaning identity between two *words* but a factual (empirical) identity of two alleged things.

But isn't it *logically possible* for an experience to occur but no brain state? It is logically possible, says the identity theorist, but not actually *true*. If there were an experience that is not identical with a brain state, this would disprove the identity theory, which says they are the same—just as the identity of lightning with electrical discharge would be disproved if lightning turned out not to be an electrical discharge.

If two explorers are mapping an area of unexplored wilderness, they may on their return home compare notes with each other. Each one thinks she has discovered a mountain, and each one gives her discovery a different name; but after talking and comparing maps, they realize that what they have discovered is the same mountain, each having come to it from a different direction. The identity theorist says that conscious events and brain states are numerically identical, like the alleged two mountains.

But a critic may object: if the alleged two mountains are really the same mountain, they must have the same characteristics: if the alleged two objects are numerically identical, they must have exactly the same characteristics (otherwise they would be two, not

one). If the Morning Star has characteristics that the Evening Star doesn't have, then of course they aren't the same star.

And, the critic pursues, isn't it plain that they *do* have different characteristics? Brain processes are located where the brain is, in a particular region of physical space. But is consciousness in the brain—not just *dependent* on the brain, but literally *in* the brain? Yet no one has found it there. And if the conscious state is not in the brain, it cannot be numerically identical with what *is* in the brain.

Or again, a brain process is a publicly observable event, like all physical processes—available for inspection by others if the conditions of observation are met. However, says the critic, a conscious state is not. Only you can experience your pain, your sense-data, your hallucinatory red spots. So there is at least one feature that brain events have that conscious states do not.

Pain, says the identity theorist, is (is numerically identical with) the stimulation of C-fibers—just as heat is the motion of molecules. If so, there could never be a stimulation of C-fibers that was not a pain, or vice versa: after all they are, he says, one and the same thing. And there never *is* an example of the one without the other—can you show me one instance?

But wait, the critic says. "Heat = molecular motion" is true only of heat in the physical sense; it says nothing about the *sensation* of heat we get when we touch a hot stove. Saul Kripke writes:

Suppose we imagine God creating the world; what does He need to do to make the identity of heat and molecular motion obtain? Here it would seem that all He needs to do is to create the heat; that is, the molecular motion itself. . . . [But] the mere creation of molecular motion still leaves God with the additional task of making molecular motion into heat. . . . To do this He must create some sentient beings to insure that the molecular motion produces the sensation S in them.[6]

To create this sensation, it would seem that God need only create beings with C-fibers capable of the appropriate type of physical stimulation; whether the beings are conscious or not is irrelevant here. But it would also seem that to make the C-fiber stimulation correspond to pain or be felt as pain, God must do something in addition to the mere creation of the C-fiber stimulation:

> He must let the creatures feel the C-fiber stimulation as *pain,* and not as a tickle, or as warmth, or as nothing, as apparently would also have been within His powers. If these things in fact are within His powers, the relation between the pain God creates and the stimulation of C-fibers cannot be identity.[7]

What is missing in the identity theory? It is, surely, what the thought or feeling *feels like* to the experiencer. We are lacking "the idea of how a mental and a physical term might refer to the same thing . . . and the usual analogies with theoretical identification in other fields fail to supply it."[8]

We have "the view from *inside*": we notice what things look like and feel like—for which we need no assistance from the natural sciences. Poets and novelists explore "the view from inside." But when we take "the view from *outside*" as scientists, we see particles of matter in motion, including those in human brains. That, of course, is a subject of legitimate scientific inquiry, as long as we do not try to reduce the first to the second. We have two types of endeavor, and no overall theory for putting Humpty-Dumpty together again.

What is needed is something we do not have: a theory of conscious organisms as physical systems composed of chemical elements and occupying space, which also have an individual perspective on the world, and in some cases a capacity for self-awareness as well. In some way that we do not now understand, our minds as well as our bodies come into being when these materials are suitably combined and organized. The strange truth seems to be that certain complex, biologically generated physical systems, of which each of us is an example, have rich non-physical properties. An integrated theory of reality must account for this, and I believe that if and when it arrives, probably not for centuries, it will alter our conception of the universe as radically as anything has to date.[9]

3. PERSONAL IDENTITY

Who am I? The easy answer is just to give your name. Well, then, what am I? I am a body—a body with a brain, and thoughts that pervade the universe, and aspirations that rise to the stars. I am, one might say, a body *and* a mind together—but that isn't very helpful if we can't state just how they are related.

I speak of *myself*. But what is this self? David Hume, reflecting on this problem, confessed that he always encountered some specific thought or feeling, but never any "I" (self) over and above these to connect them with each other:

> There are some philosophers who imagine we are every moment intimately conscious of what we call our *self;* that we feel its existence and its continuance in existence. . . . For my part, when I enter most intimately into what I call *myself* I always stumble on some particular perception or other, of heat or cold, light or shade, love or hatred, pain or pleasure. I never can catch *myself* at any time without a percep-

[6]Saul Kripke, *Naming and Necessity* (Cambridge: Harvard University Press, 1978), p. 153.
[7]Ibid., pp. 153–154.
[8]Thomas Nagel, "How Does It Feel to Be a Bat?" *Philosophical Review,* vol. 83, no. 4 (1974), pp. 435–450.
[9]Thomas Nagel, *The View from Nowhere* (New York: Oxford University Press, 1986), p. 5.

tion, and never can observe anything but the perception.[10]

This is sometimes called "the bundle theory"—there is a bundle of experiences, without any string to tie the bundle together.

What then unites the series of states in the bundle into the history of *this person*? Don't the various items in the bundle require an owner, a "haver"? Thoughts and feelings and wonderings don't float around with no one to have them. Thoughts require thinkers—there are no free-floating thoughts. They belong to someone; they are, surely, ingredients in the history of a self. My experiences throughout life constitute one series; your experiences constitute another series. No part of my bundle is a part of yours. What then is it that ties the items in my bundle together?

Thomas Reid (1710–1796), a contemporary of Hume, said that whether or not we can analyze it further, *ownership* of experiences is a basic fact, which resists attempts to analyze it:

> My personal identity implies the continued existence of that indivisible thing which I call *myself*. Whatever this self may be, it is something which thinks, and deliberates, and resolves, and acts, and suffers. I am not thought, I am not action, I am not feeling. I am something that thinks, and acts, and suffers. My thoughts, and actions, and feelings, change every moment; they have no continued, but a successive, existence; but that *self*, or I, to which they belong, is permanent, and has the same relation to all the succeeding thoughts, actions, and feelings which I call mine. Such are the notions that I have of my personal identity.[11]

---

[10]David Hume, *Treatise of Human Nature* (1739), Book 1, Part 4, Chapter 6.
[11]Thomas Reid, *Essays on the Intellectual Powers of Man* (1785), Essay 3, Chapter 4.

When Is It Still You?

Am I the same person I was ten years ago? I have the same body, although I've changed quite a lot. No cell in my body was there ten years ago; but the replacement was gradual and unnoticed, and the overall structure remains pretty much the same. It's not as if I had suddenly changed, as a tadpole does into a frog. Friends can recognize me after these years; comparing old photos with new ones, a person can tell that it's still the same person.

But you don't have to rely on physiognomy alone. I am still the same intellectually curious person I was then, refusing to assent to something just on faith; I still enjoy engaging in argument, and so on. I have a rather unique way of responding to questions; you might recognize me on the phone by that alone, even if my voice had changed.

But suppose that during those ten years I've been converted to a new cause and a new way of life. I joined a commune and lived a simple life in the hills, with no books. I forswore all previous friendships. I do various exercises and meditate several hours a day. My family might recognize me physically, but even they might say, "He's not the same person as before." Would this be true?

Surely this is a semantic squabble, one might say; in some ways I'm the same person, and in other ways I'm not. If I want to emphasize how different I am now, I say, "I'm no longer the same person." But if I say, "*I* am no longer . . . ," don't I thereby admit that it's still me and not someone else?

Bodily continuity. To many people the problem, so-called, is easily resolved. I am the same person as long as I have the same body—not that the body must look the same as it did years ago, but that there is a body, which I was born with and which exists *continuously* as long as I live. There was not a moment during all that time in which this body did not exist. If a motion picture camera had followed me around during all that time, it would provide a continuous record of my existence—no breaks in the record, no interruptions, no gaps. Throughout all that time, it's still *me,* however much I may change in my appearance, my habits, my interests. Saul renamed himself Paul, but he was still the same person as he was before he had his vision on the road to Damascus.

In the case of other people, I may not be so sure, because I don't see them constantly. I "recognize" you, but didn't know you had an identical twin. If you were one of the townspeople in *The Return of Martin Guerre* (the book or film), you would have reason for being unsure. It looks like the same person, although changed quite a bit after ten years, so it *might* be a look-alike. On the other hand, he tells us many tales that (it seems) no stranger could tell—intimate details known only to him and perhaps his wife; how would he know all this if he weren't Martin Guerre? Here (so says the bodily continuity theory), our knowledge is incomplete, and we may not be sure because we don't know whether the body we saw ten years ago is the same body we see today, and whether it has *continuously existed* during all that time. There may be no sure way to tell, but at least we know what we are after, namely to discover whether the body we saw then and the body we see now are the very same body.

1. Suppose a person is a woman who has amnesia and remembers nothing. That doesn't keep her from being the same person, as long as it's the same body; and an uninterrupted record of a movie camera would show this.

2. Suppose she has sudden personality changes—she is a Dr. Jekyll and Mrs. Hyde. Still, she is the same person because she has the same body—she is still Sarah Smith, al-

though she is subject to sudden and surprising personality changes.

3. Suppose she is a multiple personality: Sarah sometimes calls herself Jane, and when she is Jane, she is hostile rather than her usual friendly self, and she doesn't remember what Sarah has said or done; and sometimes she calls herself Betty, and then she is very different again and doesn't remember anything done by either Sarah or Jane (as in *The Three Faces of Eve*). We can now say, "She has three different *personalities,* but she's still the same person who was born on such-and-such a day and was raised in such-and-such a town, and so on."

4. Even if she has a car accident and becomes a human vegetable without consciousness of anything, she is still Sarah Smith lying there in the hospital bed, although she doesn't know that that's who she is. When someone has a dual or multiple personality, or becomes an unconscious, merely breathing organism, we do sometimes say, "She's not the same person she was," but this can be taken to mean that her personality has altered, not that she is not the person who was born at such-and-such a date and place, and so on; when we say "She's not the same person any more," don't we speak figuratively? It's still the same "she," is it not, and don't we imply this even when we say "She is not the same person any more"?

In all of these cases, bodily continuity has been preserved; and we can (and do) use this criterion to say, "It's still the same person."

Let's turn to some other cases. They may not be actual cases, but (at least they seem to be) logically possible cases. The question here is not "Do they happen?" but "What should we say, and why, if they did?"

Suppose when you awoke this morning your body looked quite unlike your body of yesterday. You now have an extra leg and feathers sprouting all over, and can emit only a few ostrich-like screeches and no words. Of course, nobody recognizes you; everyone thinks you're someone (or something) else. But don't *you* know it's still you, in spite of this unexpected transformation?

Or suppose you watched your body gradually being transformed into that of a wolf or a monkey, like some of the creatures in Dante's *Inferno*. There would still be bodily continuity—at no moment does the body cease to exist. But it is no longer the body of a person but a monkey. There is bodily continuity, but no *human*-body continuity. Are you now a person or a monkey?

In Franz Kafka's story *The Metamorphosis*, the main character, Gregor, is suddenly transformed into a beetle. He can no longer speak (he has no organs of speech), and he can't move about in the way he did before, but isn't he still Gregor in the body of a beetle? He remembers his life before the transformation and tries to communicate with his family, but is almost crushed to death when the housekeeper nearly steps on him. "Well, then, he's no longer a person but a beetle." Still, he has the mind of a person, and remembers his life as a person; surely he's still Gregor.

In the film *Here Comes Mr. Jordan*, a prizefighter is taken to heaven because of a mistake in the heavenly records. His body has been crushed beyond repair in a plane crash, and he demands a new body so that he can continue his career. He is supplied with another body; no one recognizes him, of course, but his own memories are intact, and he fulfills his dream of becoming world champion. All this is fantasy, to be sure—but wouldn't you be as certain as the movie audience that it is still the same person with a different body? And even if you weren't sure, *he* is sure—and he knows, doesn't he?

Suppose a professor lecturing in New York suddenly disappears and mysteriously reappears one minute later in Seattle—same looks, same clothes, same personality, even continuing the same lecture. This would violate the bodily continuity criterion: there's that one minute in which his body did not exist. Did *he* exist during that minute? And if so, where? How did he, or his body, get from New York to Seattle in that minute? Can a body exist, then not exist, then exist again?

Memory.

A: How do I know that you're the same person I was talking with last night? Surely it's because I *recognize* you—you look the same. Even if I only saw your picture, I'd recognize it as you. You look the same.

B: And if I didn't? What if my face had been meanwhile disfigured in an accident? What if I had a make-up job done so that you wouldn't recognize me?

A: I'd still know, at least after a while of being with you, that it was still you—your special kind of sense of humor, your mental characteristics such as your intelligence, your unique empathy, your combination of firmness and tolerance, your individual character traits.

B: But you know these only by seeing my physical organism.

A: That's true, but it's still your mental features that uniquely identify you. Suppose someone has exchanged brains with you. Your body looks the same, but when I start to engage you in conversation, I see that something is radically altered: you no longer know anything about international relations, which we discussed yesterday; you don't speak English; your demeanor is utterly different, more like that of a street thug. Finally I'd have to say that it isn't really *you*, although the body is the same. The person I'm trying to talk with is a stranger to me, a stranger who is in your body. It would be a mistake to say that bodily continuity is everything, that it's still you as long as it's your body. If the mental characteristics are utterly different—say, those of a Portuguese peasant of two centuries ago—I'd have to say that someone else had somehow gotten into your body, or more likely a body exactly like yours. But it wouldn't be a case of amnesia or multiple personality or a sudden characterological change like that of Saint Paul on the road to Damascus.

What mental feature or features might make me call you the same person in the absence of bodily continuity? Some philosophers, such as John Locke and Thomas Reid, have said that the unifying feature, the one that makes you the same person you were ten or twenty years ago, is *memory.*

Why do we say that it's still the same prizefighter, or the same Gregor? Isn't it because the person *remembers* his existence in a different body? The criterion of bodily continuity has not been met, yet we say it is the same person (the same self) continuing to exist, because the person in his transformed state remembers his life in a previous state. It is memory, not bodily continuity (we might now suggest), that determines whether it is the same self. Even without bodily continuity, it's the same person as long as memory survives.

The proper evidence of all this is remembrance. I remember that, twenty years ago, I conversed with such a person; I remember several things that passed in that conversation; my memory testifies not only that this was done, but that it was done by me who now remember it. If it was done by me, I must have existed at that time, and continued to exist from that time to the present.[12]

But this won't quite do either. A person's memory is fallible and intermittent. Didn't lots of things happen to you that you don't remember? Reid cautions us:

It is not my remembering any action of mine that makes me to be the person who did it. This remembrance makes me to know assuredly that I did it; but I might have done it though I did not remember it. That relation to me, which is expressed by saying that I did it, would be the same though I had not the least remembrance of it. To say that my remembering that I did such a thing . . . appears to me as great an absurdity as it would be to say, that my belief that the world was created made it to be created.[13]

If memory alone were sufficient, we would get the curious result

. . . that a man may be, and at the same time not be, the person that did a particular action. Suppose a brave officer to have been flogged when a boy at school for robbing an orchard, to have taken a standard from the enemy in his first campaign, and to have been made a general in advanced life; suppose, also, which must be admitted to be possible, that when he took the standard, he was conscious of his having been flogged at school, and that, when made a general, he was conscious of his taking the standard, but had absolutely lost the consciousness of his flogging. These things being supposed, it follows . . . that he who was flogged at school is the same person who took the standard, and that he who took the standard is the same person who was made a general. Whence it follows, if there by any truth in logic, that the general is the same person with him who was flogged at school. But the general's consciousness does not reach so far back as his flogging; therefore . . . he is not the person who was flogged. Therefore the general is, and at the same time is not, the same person with him who was flogged at school.[14]

[12]Thomas Reid, *Essays on the Intellectual Powers of Man,* Essay 3, Chapter 4.

[13]Ibid.
[14]Reid, *Essays on the Intellectual Powers of Man,* Essay 3, Chapter 6.

Memory, then, can't be the sole criterion for being the same person. Is there anything that's indispensable? Maybe you don't have to have the same body, but it might be suggested that at least you have to have the same *brain*. You can have your appendix or gall bladder removed and still be the same person. You can get artificial limbs and even an artificial heart, and there's no problem about it still being you. You still have the same body, with a few differences. But what about a transplanted brain? If you and I could exchange toes (through surgery) and still be the persons we were before, why do we hesitate if it's suggested that we exchange brains? If you and I exchanged brains, which would still be me?

Suppose that White's brain continues to function normally, but that after a car accident, he is a quadriplegic and much of his body has been destroyed; he isn't given long to live. Brown has a healthy body but a brain disease that will soon kill him. A surgeon removes White's brain, removes Brown's brain, and implants White's brain where Brown's brain was. Who is it that now survives, White or Brown?

The law would probably say that Brown, with a healthy body, is the survivor. The survivor has Brown's fingerprints and Brown's DNA, not to mention Brown's identity cards and other legal paraphernalia. The law would consider White legally dead, and in fact his body would be buried. By the criterion of bodily continuity, it is Brown who is the survivor.

Yet the surviving brain contains all of White's memory traces as well as White's personality, White's habits, and countless memories of White's childhood. So wouldn't it be White who is the survivor?

"It's just a matter of nomenclature—of who you choose to *call* or *stipulate* is the survivor." But will this do? Use a bodily criterion, and Brown is the survivor; use the memory-and-personality criterion, and White is the survivor. Can we just say, "You choose"? Isn't it a matter of fact, not of language or nomenclature, which one it is? If you were White and were told about the coming brain exchange, wouldn't it matter a great deal to you which one would be the survivor? If you were White, would you anticipate dying imminently or living again in another's body, complete with your same memories? It would surely make a lot of difference to *you*, wouldn't it?

Surely, we are inclined to say, White is the survivor. Brown's body has no connection with the life he had before; White is the one who remembers his past, reflects on it, and may even draw lessons from it. As a mind, Brown is dead. But if this is the alternative we adopt, aren't we saying that it *is* memory after all that decides, more at least than the continued existence of a body?

Reincarnation. Many people today claim that they are the reincarnation, or reembodiment, of someone else who lived long ago. Jeffrey Jones, a music student of some ability, claims, with apparent sincerity, that he is a reincarnation of Johann Sebastian Bach. He admits that Bach's body has long since turned to dust. So bodily continuity is out. Does he then have Bach's memories? No, he doesn't remember that either. Of course he has read a lot about Bach, and by playing Bach's clavier music several hours a day, he has some sense of what some of Bach's experiences must have been like. He identifies so strongly with Bach and is so "in tune" with Bach's music that he says that he *is* Bach, only reincarnated.

What sense can we make of this? What is there to connect him with Bach, other than a knowledge of Bach's life that is also available to many other students? If someone said, "Prove to me that you are a reincarnation of Bach and not of someone else," he could give no evidence. He might as well be a reincarnation of Caesar or Nero or the village idiot. It is not as if he *remembered* being any of these people; it is not as if he had been in Rome in the first century B.C. or in Germany in the eighteenth century A.D. He was born in 1980, after all.

The claim, it seems, is empty. Consider two statements: (1) Bach was born in 1685 and died in 1750, and Jeffrey Jones was born in 1980; (2) Jeffrey Jones has no memory of being Bach but is a reincarnation of him. What is the difference between these two statements? Isn't the second statement just a poetic but utterly misleading way of describing the first?

Let's change the example a bit. A man appears in your town who looks much like Abraham Lincoln in his last year of life. You remark on the resemblance, and he says he *is* Lincoln. Oh, you say, Lincoln didn't really die in 1865? No, he admits, this did happen; he remembers being shot in Ford's Theater and then became unconscious, and that's all he remembers until he awoke this morning in a strange town.

Suspecting another reincarnation impostor, you tend to dismiss him but decide to test him anyway. So he tells you many details of Lincoln's life, but you've already read many of them in books about Lincoln. Yet although you are something of a Lincoln scholar, many things he says are things you have never heard. You don't know whether they are all true, but some of them can be checked. He describes a diary that he buried in a metal case in a certain oak tree near Springfield in 1837. You go there and find the diary. You consult historians—it's news to them all. But they examine it with interest and say it's authentic. Handwriting experts assert unanimously that it's Lincoln's handwriting. Chemical dating tests all agree that the date is genuine. We give the man polygraph tests, and he passes them all. He gives us details of his daily life during the Civil War

that no historian has written, but, when we are in a position to test them, all his claims pass the test. And we do the same with many other details of Lincoln's life.

What shall we say now? We may put it down to coincidence—he just happened to get it right about the diary, and so on. But when this happens a hundred times without fail, the coincidence claim becomes a bit ragged. There is *some* connection between this guy and Lincoln; you just don't know what it is.

"Maybe he doesn't really remember it; he only *seems* to remember it." This is indeed a problem about memory; you can seem to remember what didn't happen. If your mother tells guests often enough about things you did as a baby, you may get to the point that you actually "remember" it happening. So perhaps the alleged Lincoln only seems to remember.

But if he only seems to remember, how is it that he is always right? His claims pass every test, and we obtain much new knowledge from what he says—at least from those claims of his that we can verify. Won't we at this point have to conclude *something*? But what shall it be? Isn't it plausible to conclude that this is Lincoln, that his mind and memory are very much alive, although he now "inhabits" a different body from the one that was buried in Springfield in 1865?

We would be reluctant, on inductive grounds, to come to such a conclusion. It would contradict some of our most cherished beliefs—that a person cannot successively inhabit different bodies and that the existence of a person might be intermittent. Still, wouldn't the evidence now suggest that we abandon, or at least question, these beliefs?

Since you are only an outside observer of this Lincolnesque drama, you can't be sure. "There are more things in heaven and earth, Horatio," said Hamlet, "than exist in your philosophy." But there may also be many things in one's philosophy that exist neither in heaven nor on earth. But if *you* remembered being president of the United States from 1861 to 1865, and remembered nothing since then until you awoke this morning, wouldn't *you*, having an inside view, be justified in saying that you are the very same man? And might that not be what we could justifiably call "reincarnation"?

Reconstitution. Suppose that

> a machine is built that will, when a person enters it, record the type and position of each molecule in his body and then disintegrate him. The process takes only a few seconds and ends with a pile of atomic debris lying on the floor of the recording chamber. The tape which contains the information about the molecular structure of the individual's body can then be fed back into the machine; and after the requisite raw materials are added, the machine will fabricate a person who not only looks and talks exactly like the one who entered the machine in the first place, but also believes that he is that person.[15]

This example violates the bodily continuity criterion, although no more than the one about the professor who suddenly finds himself not in New York but in Seattle. In each case there is a momentary interruption in which, presumably, the body did not exist. This would be disturbing, as it would be even if we found that the existence of this table were interrupted even for a moment. ("What happened in between?" we would ask.)

Still, every atom of your body, including your brain, was duplicated precisely, and what more could you ask for? You remember everything that happened prior to your stepping into the machine. And only a few seconds have passed—far less than the length of

time your life is interrupted every day by sleep. It would be a bit eerie, wouldn't it? But then, you might get used to it, just as the people in the starship *Enterprise* got used to being reduced to atoms and being reconstituted again on some faraway planet.

> Scientists tell you that instead of having to travel by rocket, which would take many years, you can step into their machine here on earth and (so they claim) step out of a similar machine on the colonized planet a few hours later. What the machine does is conduct a complete scan of the state of every cell in your body, recording all this information on a computer (the nature of the scan being such that the cells are all destroyed by the process). The information is then transmitted in the form of a radio signal to a machine on the colonized planet, which will build a replica of you which is exact right down to the last detail.[16]

The body that emerges on the distant planet has all your personality features and all the memories of life on earth that you had when you stepped into the machine. The atoms that constituted your body on earth have been left behind and were replaced by different ones on the distant planet. So the body is a new one; no material is transmitted by the machine. Also, there is a gap in continuity—for several hours, it seems, you didn't exist at all. Still, isn't it you? Isn't it your memory again that bridges the gap? Your existence on the new planet seems to be just a continuation of your life on earth; you may even fulfill some of the plans you had on earth. Again, surely it is you that survives—isn't it?

Let's try one more complication. You step into the machine, and it scans every cell in your body, transmitting the information to a machine on the distant planet—all as before. But now suppose the machine duplicates *two*

[15]Charles B. Daniels, "Personal Identity," in Peter A. French and Curtis Brown, eds., *Puzzles, Paradoxes, and Problems* (New York: St. Martin's Press, 1987), pp. 49–50.

[16]Peter Carruthers, *Introducing Persons* (Albany: State University of New York Press, 1986), pp. 191–192.

of you: two identical bodies, with two sets of identical memories. Which of them is you? Or are they both you? Can there be *two* of *you*? Can you have two minds, two identical sets of memories? Could you, after the duplication, run across yourself, converse with yourself, leave and come back again and encounter yourself? And if the machine could duplicate your body twice, why not three times, why not a hundred? Each one has your memories. But could they all be you?

Or perhaps none of them will be you. But in that case, what happened to you? Did you die? When? One duplication, all right—but more than one duplication, and you're dead? Should you think that duplication is as bad as death?

> If we can imagine duplicate selves, what about memories? Can you have other people's memories? No, we say, you can have only your own; your inner states are private. But consider this scenario:
>
> Jane has agreed to have copied in her brain some of Paul's memory-traces. After she recovers consciousness in the post-surgery room, she has a new set of vivid apparent memories. She seems to remember walking on the marble paving of a square, hearing the flapping of flying pigeons and the cries of gulls, and seeing light sparkling on green water. One apparent memory is very clear. She seems to remember looking across the water to an island, where a white Palladian church stood out brilliantly against a dark thundercloud.[17]

She has seen this church in photographs; it is San Giorgio in Venice. She knows that she has never been to Italy. But Paul goes to Venice often. She knows that she has received copies of some of Paul's memory-traces. Perhaps she is remembering some of *his* experiences in Venice?

"She doesn't remember, she only seems to remember." But her apparent memory checks with the facts. Besides, she has some of Paul's memory-traces in her brain. That would explain it. But what if she didn't, and still had the same memories, or apparent memories. What should we say then?

To complicate matters still further, what if I can divide into two?

> My body is fatally injured, as are the brains of my two brothers. My brain is divided, and each half is successfully transplanted into the body of one of my brothers. Each of the resulting people believes that he is me, seems to remember living my life, has my character, and is in every other way psychologically continuous with me. And he has a body that is very like mine. . . . What happens to me?
>
> Perhaps I shall be one of the two resulting people. The objection here is that, in this case, each half of my brain is exactly similar, and so, to start with, is each resulting person. Given these facts, how can I survive as only one of the two people? What can make me one of them rather than the other? . . .
>
> Suppose we admit that the two "products" are, as they seem to be, two different people. Could we still claim that I survive as both?[18]

Where can we rest in all this madness? The more ingenious we make our examples, the more we seem required to alter or revise the conceptual apparatus with which we began. Meanwhile, what of reality? We might speculate on logical possibilities forever, but what is there in all this that is in the slightest degree plausible?

Immortality. Most religions have some concept of immortality, of the same person continuing to live after bodily death. If one believes in posthumous survival because one's religion teaches it, then of course one's belief in immortality stands or falls with one's religious belief.

---

[17]Derek Parfit, *Reasons and Persons* (Oxford: Clarendon Press, 1983), p. 220.

[18]Ibid., pp. 254–256.

There are many accounts of survival in some form quite apart from religious belief. For example, a man sees an apparition of his father some months after the father's death. In it the father reveals to him the existence and location of a second will, which is then found exactly as described. Or a traveling salesman is writing up his orders in his hotel room, when, he says, "[I] suddenly became conscious . . . that someone was sitting on my left, with one arm resting on the table. Quick as a flash I turned and distinctly saw the form of my dead sister." She had died nine years before. He tells his parents what has occurred, mentioning that in the apparition there was a bright red line or scratch on the right hand side of the sister's face. "The mother, in a state of shock, trembled to her feet and declared that she herself had made the scratch accidentally after her sister's death, and, pained at the disfiguration, had immediately obliterated all trace of it with powder and had never mentioned it to anyone."[19]

One is inclined to dismiss all such cases. After all, people want to survive their death and will grasp at any seeming evidence that what they want to believe is true. Still, there is a host of these alleged cases, whose cumulative impact makes it difficult to put them all down to coincidence or chicanery or wishful thinking.

Some questions, however, may be in order. It is repeatedly alleged that someone saw a phantasm. What kind of entity is this? If it is the "spirit" of the departed, what kind of being is this supposed to be? Does it exist continuously, or just for a few fleeting moments? If continuously, where was it before and after

its appearance? If not continuously, whence did it "pop into" existence? Presumably it has no mass and no bodily organs, nor does it eat or drink; how exactly does it exist? Without a tongue, how can it speak, as it is often alleged to do? Does it see, or is it only seen? One would like to know, if such apparitions occur, exactly what it is that does the appearing. But in the absence of any account of what these alleged beings are, what is one to say? It's not that the allegations are false, but that the concepts used in the reports aren't very clear, and suggest many questions that the reports do not answer.

Such "indirect evidence of survival" is conceptually unclear and empirically quite inconclusive. In general, people do not come back from the grave and tell us what life is like on the other side. But what of a more direct avenue? If you want to know whether you will survive your bodily death, *wait and see*. If you survive, you will know that your hopes were realized; if you don't survive, you will not live to find out.

If you remember lying in a hospital bed, hearing physicians say that you are dying, and then you awaken in a totally different environment, perhaps surrounded by white clouds and choirs of angels, then surely you would know that you had survived your bodily death. You remember your life on earth, and the scene in the hospital, and wondering whether this would be your last experience—and now it turned out that it was not. All this seems quite easy to imagine. You may not know whether it's true, but you know what kind of conditions would have to be fulfilled to be able to say "It *is* true." But again, if you don't survive, you'll never know.

Still, there are questions to be asked. What kind of survival is this? And how do you get from here to there?

1. *Survival in a new body.* This is the kind of survival that most people imagine. The old body turns to dust in the grave, so survival re-

---

[19] These and numerous other examples are given in C. J. Ducasse, *A Philosophical Scrutiny of Religion* (New York: Ronald Press, 1953). See also, among others, C. D. Broad, *Lectures on Psychical Research;* R. H. Thouless, *Experimental Psychical Research;* and Gardner Murphy, *The Challenge of Psychical Research.*

quires a new body. How do we obtain this new body? Presumably this is a direct action of God; how else could one expect a dead body to be replaced by a new and better one? It is no accident that belief in immortality is almost always tied to belief in God.

When people imagine themselves as surviving their bodily death, they usually imagine themselves as having a body that is somehow perfect, but still enough like their former body to be recognizable by others. The prospect of survival as some invisible incorporeal spirit—perhaps indistinguishable from nothing—is not very attractive to most people. They want to be reunited with the friends and family they knew.

The woman whose husband has suddenly been killed in a car accident imagines meeting her husband in the hereafter. She looks forward to seeing him and talking with him again, and surely, she believes, she would be able to recognize him. Perhaps he won't look just as he did here; if he was overweight, surely he won't be overweight in heaven. If he lost a leg in the accident, he won't be without the leg in the hereafter. If he had scars on his face, surely these will no longer be there (even if the scars were attractive to her?). Would he still have the same habits, the same likes and dislikes, such as sitting on the porch after dinner and eating his steak rare? This would be most unlikely: there may be no earthly scenery in heaven, and one would hardly kill animals there for food. Would he still have digestive organs? Would he wear clothes? Would he desire sex? She could hardly imagine him without that—but would there be male or female at all in the hereafter? If he died at age sixty, would he have the body of a sixty-year-old in heaven, or hopefully that of a thirty-year-old? And would he retain the same appearance forever? As she reflects on it, less and less of what was her husband would seem likely to survive. The picture becomes cloudier the

more she tries to imagine it, and perhaps by now she isn't sure that she even likes it. What is the "him" that she can now look forward to meeting again?

2. *Disembodied existence.* Perhaps one might do better to imagine surviving without a body. We have already noticed some problems with ghost life and apparition life, but these at least contained some aspects of body, such as visual appearance. Let's try now to eliminate body altogether and imagine a purely mentalistic existence.

You go to bed one night and go to sleep, then awaken some hours later and see the sunlight streaming in the window, the clock pointing to eight, the mirror on the other side of the room, and you wonder what you will do today. Still in bed, you look down to where your body should be, but there isn't any. The blankets and bed sheets are there, but there is no body under them. Startled, you look into the mirror, and see the reflection of the bed, the pillows, the blankets, but no reflection of your face or body. "Perhaps I have become invisible like H. G. Wells's *The Invisible Man.*" The invisible man could not be seen, but he could be touched. You try to touch yourself, but there is nothing there to be touched. A person coming into the room would be unable to see or touch you—people could run their hands over the entire bed without ever coming into contact with a body. You are now thoroughly alarmed, thinking that now no one will know that you still exist. You try to walk forward to the mirror, but you have no feet. You might have the visual experiences you would have if you were approaching the mirror, but of course, not having a body, you are unable to walk.

Have we now succeeded in imagining existence without a body? Not at all. There are hidden references to body even in this description. You see—with eyes? But you have no eyes. You look toward the foot of the bed—but how can you look in one direction and then another if you have no head? You can't touch your body because there is no body there—and what would you touch it with? Did you reach out with your fingers? But of course you have no fingers—nor hands, nor arms, nor anything else. What would it mean, without a body, to even *try* to touch? You move, or seem to move, toward the mirror—but what is it that moves or seems to move? Not your body; you have none. Things seem to be getting larger as you approach them—approach them with what? your feet? Your body seems to be involved in every activity we try to describe, even though we have endeavored to imagine existing without it.

Is the problem just that we are accustomed to thinking of ourselves as having bodies and can't get out of the habit? The difficulty seems to be not just the inability to imagine; we can be very ingenious at imagining. The difficulty seems to be conceptual: how can we have a concept of moving when there is nothing to move, or touching when there is nothing with which to touch, and so on.

"But a person can imagine visual sense-data even if she has no eyes; surely she can imagine the visual data even if she lacks the sense organ, the eyes, with which in our present world she sees." But can she? Try it for touch—to touch is to be in physical contact with something, and how can one be in physical contact without a body? Even the idea of seeing without a body doesn't really survive analysis:

> What shows a man to have the concept seeing is not merely that he sees, but that he can take an intelligent part in our everyday use of the word "seeing." Our concept of sight has its life only in connection with a whole set of other concepts, some of them relating to the physical characteristics of visible objects, others relating to the behavior of people who see things. I express exercise of this concept in such utterances as "I can't see, it's too far off—now it's coming into view!" "He couldn't see me, he didn't look round," "I caught his eye," etc., etc. . . .
>
> And the exercise of one concept is intertwined with the exercise of others; as with a spider's web, some connections may be broken with impunity, but if you break enough the whole web collapses—the concept becomes unusable. Just such a collapse happens, I believe, when we try to think of seeing, hearing, pain, emotions, etc., going on independently of a body.[20]

Is there anything left of the concept of disembodied existence? Descartes believed himself to be a mind, a "center of consciousness." The body is only the external trapping, said Saint Augustine, which is discarded at death. There are thoughts, and since thoughts cannot exist without a thinker, there is a thinker. And what is that thinker, and how can he/she/it be distinguished from anything else? Can one try to imagine it, perhaps in a community of other minds or spirits? Without a body, how could such a spirit have even the most elementary interaction with the world? (How could one even distinguish he or she from it?) And how could these disembodied minds *do* anything? Is such a description even intelligible? Whether it satisfies anyone's conception of personal immortality is surely open to question.

EXERCISES

1. Can you replace the word "mind" in the following expressions?
  a. You didn't really see it—it's all in your mind.
  b. She has too many silly ideas in her mind.
  c. This strange idea kept cropping up in the back of her mind.
  d. She was a scatterbrain—her thoughts just went flitting this way and that through her mind.
  e. Having so many responsibilities put too much pressure on his mind.

---

[20]Peter Geach, *Mental Acts: Their Content and Their Objects* (London: Routledge, 1963), pp. 112–113.

f. He changes his mind so frequently that no one knows what he really believes.

2. Evaluate each of the following assertions:
a. Mental events are nothing but brain events.
b. What I see is always something going on in my own brain.
c. Mental events and physical events are logically interconnected.
d. If mental telepathy is a fact, I can experience your pain directly.
e. If mental telepathy is a fact, one's experiences are not really private, for other people can share them.
f. Mental events are not really private even now (without telepathy), since I can share your experiences (such as your suffering) by being with you and empathizing with you.
g. It is true that no surgeon, on opening someone's brain, has ever found any mental events, but perhaps that's because she has never looked hard enough.

3. "It is not the mind that survives death, it is the *soul* which survives death." What could be meant by "soul" if the word is not synonymous with "mind"? Is the soul a substance? a mental substance? Would a theory of the soul be different (and if so, how) from a theory of the mind?

4. Do you consider each of the following logically possible? Why or why not? In each case, try first to describe a situation that would count as an instance of the kind of thing mentioned.
a. For one mind to affect another mind without the intermediary of matter
b. For a mind to exist without a body
c. For a mind to touch a body
d. For one person to have two bodies
e. For one person to have two minds
f. For one mind to control two bodies directly (e.g., by willing it to raise its arm)
g. For one body to be controlled by two minds

5. Do you believe that your dog or cat
a. Has desires?
b. Has wishes?
c. Has fears?
d. Ever worries about anything?
e. Dreads anything in the future?
f. Thinks of you when you're absent?
g. Wonders where you are?
h. Loves you?
i. Appreciates the food you provide?
j. Has any concepts?
k. Has any beliefs?
l. Knows any propositions to be true?

Give reasons for your answer in each case.

6. Consider these two claims: (1) "Napoleon had a stronger power impulse than most people do." (2) "No, it's not that he had a greater desire for power, it's that he had much *less* of a desire than the rest of us do for everything else." Is there any way to tell which is true? Is there a difference?

7. If you anticipate being touched by a very hot object, you expect to feel a burning sensation—and you *do,* even if what touches you is ice. What does expecting to feel a burning sensation cause—a false belief, or a burning sensation?

8. "This desk before me would not be the desk it is if it were not made of wood; if it were of a different size and shape; if it didn't have just this particular scratch on it; if it didn't have just these books which are on it at this moment. Every property of this desk is necessary to its being this desk. Similarly, you would not be the person you are if you had been born at a different time; if you had been born a different sex; if you didn't have the color eyes you do; if you didn't have the parents you do; and if you weren't reading just the book you are reading now." Discuss.

9. Is it logically possible to witness one's own funeral?[21]

---

[21]See two articles on this by Antony Flew: "Can a Man Witness His Own Funeral?" *Hilbert Journal* (1956); and "Sense and Survival," *The Humanist* (1960).

10. What would you say about personal identity if the existence of the body were *intermittent*? Two minutes out of every three there is a body—you see it moving and hear words coming from its lips—and the other minute there is nothing there at all: nothing that can be seen, touched, photographed, or x-rayed, nothing fulfilling any of the tests for a physical object. What meaning (if any) would you attach to the hypothesis that the person existed during the one-minute intervals? What (if anything) would entitle us to say that what reappeared after the one-minute disappearance each time was *the same* person as the one who had existed before the disappearance? (Would he have to reappear in the same place, or have the same physical characteristics that he had had prior to his disappearance? By what criteria would you decide whether it's "really the same person"?)

11. Which of the following ways of speaking would you find preferable, and why?
a. "I am a mind" or "I have a mind."
b. "I am a body" or "I have a body."
c. "I am a mind that has or is associated with a body" or "I am a body that has or is associated with a mind."
d. "I am a person who has a mind and a body" or "I am a person who is both a mind and a body."

12. Would you still say "It's the same person" if
a. She loses her memory, completely and permanently, but her body persists
b. She turns into a monkey, but retains her memories as a human being
c. She turns into a monkey, and also loses her memories as a human being
d. Her body disintegrates before your eyes, but her voice (or one that sounds exactly like hers) continues to speak
e. After her body disappears before our eyes, it (or another body just like it) returns ten years later, complete with the woman's memories and personality traits

13. Defend one of the following views:
a. That you can know that others have pains and can give evidence
b. That you can have well-founded belief that others have pains, but belief short of knowledge
c. That you do not have even well-founded belief in this matter

14. If someone you had conversed with many times died, and if his skull were posthumously opened—revealing not bones and tissue but plastic tubes and electric wiring—would this discovery lead you to believe or suspect that he had never been a conscious human being at all but a mindless automaton? Why or why not? (If someone opened *your* skull and found only plastic tubing and complicated circuits, would that person be entitled to say that you had been an automaton without conscious states all along?)

15. Can computers feel pain? Assuming that they can present some of the same responses that human beings do, including saying that they're in pain, would this incline you (or disincline you) toward saying that computers can feel pain? Is pain necessarily a response to tissue damage in one's body, or is this only a contingent fact, which might be otherwise?

16. How would you go about finding out whether creatures from another planet, appearing on earth, felt pain? They don't withdraw their hands from the fire—but then perhaps fire doesn't hurt them as it does us.

17. Suppose that instead of one man with Lincoln's memories, six men, all look-alikes of Lincoln, turned up, and each one could produce some piece of evidence like the diary in the tree, and thus each had an equal claim to be the real Lincoln resurrected. Would you say there were six genuine Lincolns now? Are they all the same person, all impostors, or what?

18. A man disappears suddenly from the chair opposite you where he was sitting; you can neither see nor touch him, but his voice continues to converse with you as before. Would you say he still exists? Only as long as the voice continues? If sight and touch are the means by which we recognize something as a physical object, what happens when we have neither sight nor touch but only sound? Would you say that the person still exists or that only the sound of the voice still exists? (Lewis Carroll's smile without the Cheshire cat?)

19. Try to describe being conscious but having no body. Is consciousness without a body impossible, in your opinion, or is it that our powers of imagination are insufficient for the task?

SELECTED READINGS

ARMSTRONG, D. W. *A Materialist Theory of Mind.* London: Routledge, 1964.

AYER, ALFRED J. *The Concept of a Person and Other Essays.* London: Macmillan, 1964.

BITLER, JOSEPH. "Of a Personal Identity." In Butler, *The Analogy of Religion.* 1736. Many editions.

BORST, C. V., ed. *The Mind-Brain Identity Theory.* New York: St. Martin's Press, 1970.

BROAD, C. D. *The Mind and Its Place in Nature.* London: Routledge, 1925.

CARRUTHERS, PETER. *Introducing Persons.* Albany: State University of New York Press, 1986.

DAVIDSON, DONALD. *Actions and Events.* Oxford: Clarendon Press, 1980.

DENNETT, DANIEL. *Brainstorms.* Cambridge: MIT Press, 1978.

DENNETT, DANIEL. *Content and Consciousness.* London: Routledge, 1986.

EWING, A. C. "Ryle's Attack on Dualism." In H. D. Lewis, ed., *Clarity Is Not Enough.* London: Allen & Unwin, 1963.

FEYERABEND, M., and GROVER MAXWELL, eds. *Mind, Matter, and Method.* Minneapolis: University of Minnesota Press, 1966.

FLEW, ANTONY, ed. *Body, Mind, and Death.* New York: Macmillan, 1962.

FOSTER, JOHN. *The Immaterial Self.* London: Routledge, 1991.

FULLERTON, G. S. *A System of Metaphysics.* Part 3. New York: Macmillan, 1904.

GLOVER, JONATHAN. *The Philosophy of Mind.* London: Oxford University Press, 1976.

GRAHAM, GEORGE. *Philosophy of Mind: An Introduction.* Oxford: Blackwell, 1993.

HIRSCH, ELI. *The Concept of Identity.* London: Oxford University Press, 1982.

HODGSON, DAVID. *Consciousness and Choice in a Quantum World.* London: Oxford University Press, 1991.

HOOK, SIDNEY, ed. *Dimensions of Mind.* New York: New York University Press, 1966.

KENNY, ANTHONY. *The Metaphysics of Mind.* London: Oxford University Press, 1990.

KOESTLER, ARTHUR. *The Ghost in the Machine.* New York: Macmillan, 1967.

KRIPKE, SAUL. *Naming and Necessity.* Chapter 3. Cambridge: Harvard University Press, 1972.

LEVIN, MICHAEL. *Metaphysics and the Mind-Body Problem.* London: Oxford University Press, 1970.

LOCKE, JOHN. *An Essay Concerning Human Understanding.* 2nd ed. 1694. Book 2, Chapter 27.

LOCKWOOD, MICHAEL. *Mind, Brain, and the Quantum.* Oxford: Blackwell, 1991.

McGINN, COLIN. *The Problem of Consciousness.* Oxford: Blackwell, 1993.

MALCOLM, NORMAN. *Memory and Mind.* Ithaca: Cornell University Press, 1977.

NAGEL, THOMAS. *The View from Nowhere.* New York: Oxford University Press, 1986.

ORNSTEIN, JACK. *The Mind and the Brain.* The Hague: Nijhoff, 1972.

PARFIT, DEREK. *Reasons and Persons.* London: Oxford University Press, 1983.

PERRY, JOHN. *Personal Identity.* Berkeley: University of California Press, 1975.

POPPER, KARL. *Knowledge and the Mind-Body Problem.* London: Routledge, 1964.

PUTNAM, HILARY. *Mind, Language, and Reality.* New York: Cambridge University Press, 1975.

REID, THOMAS. *Essays on the Intellectual Powers of Man.* 1785.

RORTY, AMELIE, ed. *The Identity of Persons.* Berkeley: University of California Press, 1976.

ROSENTHAL, DAVID, ed. *The Nature of Mind.* New York: Oxford University Press, 1991.

RYLE, GILBERT. *The Concept of Mind.* London: Hutchinson, 1949.

SHAFFER, JEROME. *Philosophy of Mind.* Prentice Hall, 1968.

SHOEMAKER, SIDNEY. *Self-Knowledge and Self-Identity.* Ithaca: Cornell University Press, 1963.

STRAWSON, P. F. *Individuals.* London: Methuen, 1959.

STRAWSON, P. F. *Studies in Thought and Action.* London: Oxford University Press, 1968.

UNGER, PETER. *Identity, Consciousness, and Value.* London: Oxford University Press, 1992.

VESEY, GODFREY. *Body and Mind.* London: Allen & Unwin, 1964.

VESSEY, GODFREY. *The Embodied Mind.* London: Allen & Unwin, 1965.

WARNER, RICHARD, and THOMAS SZUBKA. *The Mind-Body Problem.* Oxford: Blackwell, 1994.

WILLIAMS, BERNARD. *Problems of the Self.* Cambridge: Cambridge University Press, 1973.

WISDOM, JOHN. *Other Minds.* Oxford: Blackwell, 1949.

WITTGENSTEIN, LUDWIG. *Philosophical Investigations.* Translated by Elizabeth Anscombe. Oxford: Blackwell, 1953.

7 *What Else Is There?*

THE PHILOSOPHY
OF RELIGION

The word "religion" does not always carry the same meaning. Some people use it to mean belief in God (or gods); by this meaning, a person who does not believe in God or gods has no religion. For others, religion means total commitment or total dedication to something, not necessarily God. In this sense, a person who is totally dedicated to some humanitarian project is said to be religious, and the cause to which he dedicates himself is "his religion." "That's his religion," one may say, of someone who devotes his life to Marxism or to the preservation of endangered species. A person's religion has even been defined as "whatever a person does with his leisure time." The variations on the use of the word are virtually endless. A person may have a religion in any one of these senses, but it only follows from the first sense that the person has a belief in God.

Even a person who believes in God is not necessarily said to be religious. A person may give a kind of *pro forma* assent to belief in God: if asked whether she believes in God, she will say yes, but the belief occupies no part in her life, and she seldom or never thinks about it or acts upon it. To be religious, as opposed to professing a religious belief, involves such matters as prayer, membership in a religious organization, thought and meditation about spiritual matters, dedication to a way of life, and emotional involvement in the religious ideal—although not necessarily all of these.

Many aspects of religion are of no concern to us as philosophers. We are not concerned here with the psychology of religious believers or matters of ecclesiastical organization; we are concerned, as philosophy always is, with the *justification of belief*. By what arguments, if any, can religious belief be defended or attacked? Moreover, we shall narrow this question to belief in God or gods, saying nothing about religions such as Buddhism that have ethical beliefs but profess no belief in God, although Buddhism is almost always counted as a religion.

What kind of belief is belief in God? Belief in God is belief in a supernatural being, we might say. But what is meant by "supernatural being"? "Supernatural" means literally "above nature." But the word "above" cannot here be taken literally. The universe includes all space, so there is nothing literally above it. The believer in God holds that in addition to the material universe of planets and stars and galaxies, in addition to atoms and energy and the entities observed or hypothesized by the physical sciences, there is something else—a power (or powers) that created or sustains the universe, and that created the laws of nature and can suspend these laws at will, although this power did not necessarily do all of these things. In ancient Greek religion the gods did not create the universe but only gave it new form; and according to *deism* God does not sustain the material universe but only created it and thereafter lets it run by itself like a piece of machinery. According to *theism,* on the other hand, God both created and sustains or guides the universe. (Christianity, Mohammedanism, and Judaism are all theistic.) According to most religions, this power has *human* characteristics—it is a personality with qualities such as benevolence, love, or vengeance. But there are also religions that believe in a supernatural power possessing virtually none of these human characteristics other than the *power* to issue commands and punish those who disobey. In every case, however, there is believed to be something in reality *other than* the universe of matter and energy studied by physics and other sciences—perhaps a supernatural mind, a "cosmic consciousness"—but at any rate, a power that exists in addition to the universe perceived with the senses or investigated by science. A person who denies that any supernatural being exists is an *atheist;* one who withholds judgment either way is an *agnostic.*

A religion that holds there is only one such supreme power is called *monotheism*—for example, Mohammedanism, Christianity, and Judaism. A religion that holds there are many such powers is called *polytheism*—exemplified by the numerous gods of the ancient Greeks (Zeus, Apollo, Minerva, Poseidon, and so on) as well as of most ancient religions.

Is belief in God (or gods) justified? Perhaps the most obvious place to begin in considering this is the claim to direct experience of God. If I experience God, God must exist as the object of that experience.

1. RELIGIOUS EXPERIENCE

A: If I have an experience of something, that something exists. I have an experience of God, therefore God exists. It's as simple as that. Why do we have to go through elaborate proofs?

B: Because just having an experience won't do. Believers say that their experience points to something *beyond* the experience, something that really exists out there, not merely in the believer's mind. And going from a subjective experience to an objective entity in reality requires proof, or at least evidence.

A: I feel God's presence in myself. That is a direct experience that I have.

B: And how do you know that it is God's presence that you feel?

A: The same way that I know that this is a table that I now see.

B: This is going to be a rather long story. First of all, what is to count as a religious experience? A Buddhist monk devotes years to meditation and the "oneness" of himself with the universe, but doesn't claim that there is a God "out there." A Catholic priest does claim this, prays numerous times every day, and, inspired by Jesus' words about humility, goes into the slums to help tend the poor. Tribal members, intoxicated, dance frantically about, preparing themselves for the human sacrifice of one of their number. Others participate in the "divine essence" through magical rites and incantations. A Christian evangelist preaches to adoring crowds, claiming that she is directly inspired by God in addressing the multitudes against illicit sex and alcohol. If all these are religious experiences, it seems clear that religious experiences vary enormously from person to person and from culture to culture.

A: Let's admit that they do. What makes them all religious experiences? Surely it's that they all claim to be experiences of God or the gods.

B: That lets the Buddhists out, for they make no such claim.

A: In that case theirs are not religious experiences. A religious experience is an experience of God.

B: That presents a problem. If all religious experiences are experiences of God, what do you do when their beliefs in God contradict one another? The experiences themselves don't contradict one another, they just differ from one another; but their beliefs do contradict one another. According to a recent survey, some 40 million Americans say that they have direct experience of God through Christ. Others say that they have direct experience of the God of the Old Testament but not of Christ. Still others claim direct experience of Allah. Surely these beliefs do contradict one another.

As a rule, each religion claims that its deity is the one and only true one, and that the others are mere pretenders, or that their devotees are sincere but deluded. Christianity says that salvation is possible only through Christ, and this contradicts Muslims, who say that salvation comes only through Allah. They can't both be right. So you see, if religious experience proves God, it proves too much: an experience can't prove both X and not-X. Which of these competing claims is religious experience supposed to establish?

A: A Christian could say that only Christians have genuinely religious experiences—that the experiences that people in other religions have are not genuinely religious, or that others have religious experiences, but of illusory objects.

B: How do you tell which are illusory? Devotees of other religions have the same devotedness, the same impulse to worship, the same awe and sense of mystery and of human powerlessness in the face of cosmic forces, as the devotees of one's own religion. Surely the difference is less in the experiences themselves (varying as they are) than in what they take the experiences to show: that the other religions worship false gods.

The experience of these false gods is like the experience of having a hallucination: someone hallucinating sees something that isn't there. The other religions, one might say, claim deities that aren't there. But that presents the problem: how do you distinguish the true claims from the false ones?

A: Not through religious experience alone, but through revelation—a voice from on high or (preferably) a sacred text that all can read and follow.

B: But other religions also have their sacred texts, and they too claim that their sacred text is divinely inspired and that the other ones are not. Each group claims a monopoly of religious truth.

A: Suppose I say that the essential truth lies in all of them, some kernel of truth that they all contain—and that the religions differ only in their historical manifestations: some say Yahweh, some say Jesus, some say Allah. Perhaps we could glean some truth from all of them, something they all have in common, and then accept that.

B: I don't think that will work. (1) In the first place, each religion denies this: belief in the divinity of Jesus and his resurrection from the dead is essential to Christianity—it is not a mere "historical accompaniment" of the religion. Take it away and whatever you have left, it isn't Christianity. (2) Besides, what could it be that they all have in common? What do Christianity and Buddhism, which celebrate love, have in common with the

Aztec religions involving torture and human sacrifice? These are the very antithesis of each other. The only thing they have in common is belief in the *power* of their deities—power to create the world, to suspend laws of nature, and to smite them dead if they chose. The gods of primitive religions distribute their power, but what they have in common is still belief in the power of the gods.

A: I think it's all a difference in interpretation. Different conceptions of divinity arise in different cultures. They all "see through a glass darkly," and it's only in the "dark" parts in which they contradict one another.

B: That depends on which parts you choose to call "dark." Look: the same being can't have contradictory attributes. If you believe in a god of love, you can't also believe in a god of hate. If you say God has attribute A and another says God has not-A, one has to choose: at least one of them must be mistaken. Christians and Jews who read in the Old Testament about the god Baal, who demands the sacrifice of each couple's first-born child on a fiery altar, are right to say, "That's not the kind of God *I* believe in!"

A: So much of religious experience is a matter of interpretation. We tend to "read into the script." A man says he sees a spaceship when all he really sees is a light in the night sky. We all conceptualize our experiences in different ways. One person taking a Rorschach test interprets a pattern of shapes as beetles, and others interpret the shapes as bats. Which of them is correct?

B: There is no "correct interpretation" of the shapes on the Rorschach. They are designed so that you can see in each of them what you want to see, or perhaps whatever your unconscious motivation leads you to see. That's why this test is re-

vealing. It's deliberately ambiguous. Are you comparing this with religious experience?

A: Yes—in that each person can interpret the experience in his or her own way.

B: Are you suggesting that one person can interpret her religious experience as that of the god Baal and that another could interpret an identical experience as that of the God of Christianity? However you describe or interpret them, A can't be not-A, and something can't be both A and not-A. You can't get round the Law of Noncontradiction. If it's A you're seeing or thinking about, it isn't also at the same time not-A that you're seeing or thinking about. If you said, "Both A and not-A—you're both coming for dinner and not coming for dinner," what you say is simply unintelligible, and no one would know what you were asserting.

A: Do you attach no significance to the fact that religion is virtually universal among human beings—that however variously they may describe the object of their experience, they all have some kind of religious belief?

B: Not at all. People in all times and places feel insecure in a harsh world and would like protection against the "slings and arrows of outrageous fortune." This is our human condition, and it's only natural that people seek something that provides relief from this condition, either in answering their prayers in the here and now or in providing a better life for them in the hereafter. Belief in magic and witchcraft is almost universal, but I don't buy into it because of that. Human error is universal too.

A: So the fact that at all times and places people believe in a divine being or beings doesn't strike you as evidence that such a being exists?

B: No more than the fact that people are hungry proves that they will always have food. No more than the fact that people believe in ghosts proves that there are ghosts. If you believe they do, provide some *evidence* for them or stop repeating your claim.

A: But the evidence lies in the experience itself.

B: Here we go again. Epistemologically you have to fish or cut bait. You say that you directly experience God and therefore require no evidence. But you don't provide the evidence. If what you believe in is something *over and above* the experience itself, as all religions claim—then what is it and by what criteria do you justify your claim?

　　A traveler in the desert claims to see an oasis; but later he retracts that judgment on the basis of subsequent experience (he can't see it any more, can't touch it, and so on). He made a claim to objectivity—that an oasis really exists out there—and the claim didn't pass the test. I would say exactly the same for people's claims about God. Religious belief is more deep-seated, more primordial, and so on, and let's say more meaningful, than belief in oases in the desert. But epistemologically they are on a par. The fact of having an experience doesn't by itself guarantee that anything at all exists beyond the experience itself.

　　If you want to talk about evidence, very well—that's what the traditional arguments for God are all about, that's what "natural theology" is all about; it's about what basis there can be for such an inference. That's what we're about to go into. But you can't short-circuit the complex issue of evidence by trying to get your knowledge "on the cheap." I say that no experience by itself, however worthwhile we take it to be, proves anything beyond itself; and if we do take the mere fact of such experiences as proving something beyond themselves, then we'll have to admit every cockamamie claim that any lunatic or village idiot finds himself able to concoct. We can't just take the quick way out.

We turn then to the traditional *arguments* for the existence of God.

2. THE ONTOLOGICAL ARGUMENT

According to Saint Anselm (1033–1109), God is that than which nothing greater can be conceived. We can conceive of a unicorn although unicorns do not exist in reality (they exist, said Anselm, "in the understanding only"). Can't we similarly conceive of God as not existing? No, said Anselm, God, unlike the unicorn, necessarily exists: God is the being than whom nothing greater can be conceived, and if God did not actually exist, our concept of God would be the concept of a being less great than of one who does exist, and it is the latter idea that we do possess. Therefore, God exists.

　　One obvious rejoinder is, "You can't define anything into existence." I can define a unicorn as a horse with a horn protruding from its forehead, and thus I have the concept of a unicorn; but from this it doesn't follow that unicorns exist. If it did, I could populate the world with thousands of creatures just by imagining them. Saint Anselm of course is aware of this; but the case of God, he says, is different, for God, being the greatest possible being conceivable, must exist *in order to be the greatest*. If God lacked existence—existed only "in the understanding" like unicorns—then God would not be as great as if he *did* exist, and thus would not be the greatest being conceivable.

It is not entirely clear what "greatest" means: greatest in power? in love? in justice? But it doesn't really matter for the argument. The point is that that which is the greatest conceivable being requires existence, else it would lack one necessary element of greatness and not be the greatest after all.

Yet, one may ask, what does this prove? Can't I imagine a perfect island—an island so perfect (in whatever respect one chooses) that no possible island could be more perfect? And by the same argument, might one not say that such a perfect island must exist, because if it did not exist it would not be as perfect as if it did? But again Saint Anselm says no: you can imagine an island than which no greater (more perfect) *island* is possible; but there may be many things greater than, even more perfect than, this "perfect" island (such as an imperfect human being). And the idea of God is the idea of something *than which nothing greater,* of any kind, is conceivable; and for that perfection to occur, actual existence is necessary. Between a maximally great God existing only in the understanding, and a maximally great God existing in reality *as well as* in the understanding, the latter is without doubt greater.

One could question, however, whether existence is a property that is essential to greatness or perfection. If something is perfect if it has properties A, B, and C, is it any more perfect if it has A, B, C, *and* exists? Isn't it the same "something" we're thinking of in both cases? This was the point of Immanuel Kant's criticism of the ontological argument: Kant declared that *existence is not a property.* When you say that a unicorn is a horse with a horn, and then you add that such a creature actually exists, are you adding anything to the list of the unicorn's properties? Not at all, said Kant. You are not adding a property to the list, you are only say-

ing that something which has all these properties *exists.* But to say that X *exists* is something of a different order from saying that X has certain *properties.* A perfect circle has the property of all points on its circumference being equidistant from the center, but it doesn't follow that any such figure exists anywhere; and if it did, this fact would add no properties to the circle already described. The question of *whether X exists* is one thing; the question of *what properties X has* is another. Kant held that the ontological argument made the mistake of assuming that existence is a property, and accordingly he rejected the argument.

3. THE COSMOLOGICAL ARGUMENT

There are various forms of the *cosmological* argument, but they all have their starting point with familiar facts of experience: that things exist in the universe, events occur, causes operate, and they all require a cause or an explanation. And, it is argued, the only thing that can provide this is God.

Saint Thomas Aquinas (1225–1274) and Samuel Clarke (1675–1729) were among the chief proponents of the cosmological argument. Of Aquinas's five arguments for the existence of God, the first three are versions of the cosmological argument. (He rejected the ontological argument.) The first of his five arguments attempts to explain the existence of motion: how did anything in the universe get moving? But this presupposes that "the natural state of things" is rest, and Sir Isaac Newton's view that motion was as "natural" a state as rest has made Thomas's first argument less acceptable today. Things already at rest tend to continue at rest, and things already in motion tend to continue in motion; why does motion require explanation any more than rest?

The Causal Argument

The most popular form of the cosmological argument has always been Thomas's second one, the *causal* argument. Everything that happens, it is said, has a cause. (The causal argument assumes this proposition to be true.) But if everything has a cause, the universe too must have a cause, and that cause is God.

It is events, happenings, comings-to-be that have causes. It is not strictly speaking a thing that has a cause, but the coming-into-being or transformation of that thing, namely an event or process. And the universe, of course, is not an event or process; in fact it is not even a thing. It is, one might say, the entire collection of things and events and processes that occur; "the universe" is a collective term for all of them together. Let's assume, then, that each of the events in the universe had a cause; does it follow that the universe as a whole had a cause? One might suggest that there are as many causes as there are occurrences, each with its own cause.

But still the question persists: doesn't there have to be a first cause to set the entire series of other causes in motion? Didn't there at least have to be a first event? God, however, is not usually referred to as a first event, but rather as an enduring being who created the material universe and thus *caused* its first event to occur. In either case we face the same question—whether a first event or a first being, isn't God required to start the entire series of causes and events that constitute the history of the universe?

There is one very elementary consideration that is fatal to the causal argument as stated. If everything has a cause, then God too has a cause; and what caused God? Many children ask this question, to the embarrassment of their parents. But the question can-

not be dismissed. If everything without exception has a cause, doesn't that include God too?

"But God is the cause of everything else, and he himself has no cause." But if this is so, then the argument's original premise—that everything has a cause—is false. As it stands, the conclusion of the argument ("God has no cause") contradicts its own premise ("Everything has a cause"). If the premise is true, the conclusion cannot be, and if the conclusion is true, the premise cannot be; they contradict one another. Most people do not see this because, as Arthur Schopenhauer (1788–1860) remarked, they use the causal argument the way they use a taxi; they use the taxi to get them where they want to go, and they don't care what happens to the taxi after that. They use the causal principle to get them to God, and take no thought of the fact that if the causal argument is true it applies to God also.

Let us then amend the statement to read that everything *except* God has a cause. God is the cause of everything, without being the effect of anything, that is, without himself being caused. But if God had no cause, was he the cause of himself? And how could that be—if X is already there, X doesn't need to be caused, and if X is not already there but doesn't yet exist, how can it cause anything? What does *causa sui* (cause of itself) come to? Is it more than just a meaningless phrase?

"But we have to stop somewhere; causes can't continue backward forever; so why not stop at a first cause, God?" But other philosophers have turned the question back on the questioner: "*Why* stop there? If you want to go further, and say that God too was caused, then what was the cause of God?" And so on. Or, if you want to stop the process, why not stop at the physical universe, and say that *it* had no cause?

If we stop, and go no farther, why go so far? Why not stop at the material world? How can we satisfy ourselves without going on ad infinitum? And after all, what satisfaction is there in that infinite progression? Let us remember the story of the Indian philosopher and his elephant. It was never more applicable than to the present subject. If the material world rests upon a similar ideal world, this ideal world must rest upon some other; and so on, without end. It were better, therefore, never to look beyond the present material world. By supposing it to contain the principle of its order within itself, we really assert it to be God; and the sooner we arrive at that Divine Being, so much the better. When you go one step beyond the mundane system, you only excite an inquisitive humor, which it is impossible ever to satisfy.[1]

Some philosophers have pointed out that we are here misusing the word "cause," carrying it outside the realm in which it has a meaning. Our knowledge of causes lies entirely within the realm of spatio-temporal things, processes, and events. Beyond that, we have no reason to speak of causes at all, for experience tells us nothing about any such causality. To extend the principle into some transempirical realm is to desert the empirical world in which all known causes occur. Indeed, one might well ask what *meaning* the word "cause" has apart from any references to events and processes going on in the universe. Kant wrote, "The principle of causality has no meaning and no criterion for its application save only in the sensible world. But in the cosmological proof it is precisely in order to enable us to advance beyond the sensible world that it is employed."[2]

Even if successful, however, the causal argument gives us only a first cause. It does not give us any of the deities of traditional religions. (And the same is true for the other arguments: For example, the ontological argument only gives us a that-than-which-nothing-can-be-greater, not the God of traditional religions.) But in most religions God is a personality, having human characteristics such as goodness and power and mercy, only in far greater degree. There is a pervasive human tendency to identify the first cause with a person whose volitions cause the universe and all that is in it. And yet if we are to go by the empirical evidence we have of causes, there is no evidence that mind or volition goes back that far in the history of the universe. John Stuart Mill pointed out the following:[3]

1. Many movements of matter, such as arranging pieces of wood into a house, are indeed the result of will, and without volition they would never occur.

2. But in no case are we entitled to say that the will *creates*, or brings into being, the matter; it merely changes the position of particles of matter which already exist.

3. The will does originate motion, for example when a bodily movement follows upon an act of will; but it does so only by means of innumerable brain events, in which one form of energy is converted into another (energy of motion); physical energy itself the will does not create. Far from creating energy, the behavior of the brain particles (which must occur if consciousness is to occur at all) is itself an instance of the Law of Conservation of Energy. In all cases of which we have experience, energy is prior to volition and not the other way around; volition (or its bodily concomitant, depending on one's theory of mind) is just one of thousands of manifestations of energy. So volition is hardly in a position, in an empirical argument, to be an ultimate cause.

---

[1]David Hume, *Dialogues Concerning Natural Religion*, Part 4.
[2]Immanuel Kant, *Critique of Pure Reason*, trans. Norman Kemp Smith (London: Macmillan, 1933), p. 511.

[3]John Stuart Mill, "Nature," in Mill, *Three Essays on Religion* (London: Longmans Green, 1874).

4. It seems quite certain that volition did not come into being for countless ages—during all of which the Law of Conservation of Energy was nevertheless in operation—until during the long evolutionary process it finally arose. Energy is, so far as we know, eternal; volitions are not, for we can trace their beginning in time.

None of this, of course, proves that the mind—a conscious being who makes decisions—is not the first causal factor to have operated in the universe. One might say, "It could well have happened that way, only we have no empirical means of knowing it now." A conscious being, let us assume, caused the entire series of events and processes to begin; presumably this being not only created the material universe but also the laws of its operation. But now another question confronts us: did this act of divine volition that created the universe occur at a certain point in time, or did it not?

Suppose we say that God created the universe at a certain point in time. The Bishop of Usher determined from Old Testament genealogies that the universe was created in 4004 B.C., and many nineteenth-century Bibles contained marginal notes to this effect. Today, of course, the date has been pushed much further into the past. The origin of the earth alone apparently dates back more than 4 billion years and that of the galaxies more than twice that far. But the actual date doesn't matter. The question is, *was* there such a date? Some advocates of the Big Bang theory allege that the first bang—the formation of the universe, followed by its explosive expansion to an area measuring billions of light years—was the first event; prior to that *there were no events.* Theologically minded scientists add that before this first *material* event there was God, who willed the Big Bang to occur. But in either case, did this first event occur at the first moment of time? Was there a time *before which* there was time?

And what would it mean to say this? "There was time all right, but no material universe." But how can there be time with "nothing in it," so to speak? What would it mean to say that for a million years there was no time and then suddenly time started? How could time *start*? Couldn't we always ask, "*When* did it start?" Was there time before the start?

However, it may not be necessary to posit a first moment of time. Perhaps, like the number system, time is infinite, with no beginning and no end. And if the series is infinite, where does God fit into the picture? God is no longer "first cause," for there was no first cause. If the universe has always existed, then God did not create it at a certain point in time. The universe had no *origin,* since the question "When did it originate?" is apparently the same question as "When did it begin?"—and according to the view now being considered it had no beginning at all. It was "always there"—a discomfiting phrase. We can speak of the number series as infinite because we can always get a higher number by adding one; but is infinite time like that? Can we really conceive what it means to say, "The universe didn't begin 12 billion years ago with a Big Bang; it didn't even begin with a divine act of creation; it was *always* there"?

Was it "always" there? Or did the universe have a beginning, before which there was nothing—not even time? (And did time, then, have a beginning *at a certain time?*) Physicists and astronomers now seem fairly well agreed on the Big Bang theory of the universe's origin, but it still leaves many questions.

On the far side of the Big Bang is a mystery so profound that physicists lack the words even to think about it. Those willing to go out on a limb guess that whatever might have been before the Big Bang was, like a vacuum, unstable. Just as there is a tiny chance that virtual particles will pop into existence in the midst of subatomic space, so there may have been a tiny chance that the nothingness would suddenly be convulsed by the presence of a something.

This something was an inconceivably small, inconceivably violent explosion, hotter than the hottest supernova and smaller than the smallest quark, which contained the stuff of everything we see around us. The Universe consisted of only one type of particle—maybe only one particle—that interacted with itself in that tiny, terrifying space. Detonating outward, it may have doubled in size every 10^{-35} seconds or so, taking but an instant to reach literally cosmic proportions.

Almost no time passed between the birth of the Universe and the birth of gravity. By 10^{-43} seconds after the beginning the plenum was already cooler, though hardly hospitable: every bit of matter was crushed with brutal force into every other bit, within a space smaller than an atomic nucleus. But the cosmos was cool enough, nonetheless, to allow the symmetry to break, and to let gravity crystallize out of the unity the way snowflakes suddenly drop out of clouds. Gravity is thought to have its own virtual particle (the graviton), and so the heavens now had two types of particles (carriers of forces and carriers of mass), although the distinction wasn't yet as clear as it is in the Universe today.

At 10^{-35} seconds the strong force, too, fell out of the grand unified force. Less time had passed since the Big Bang than it now takes for a photon to zip past a proton, and yet the heavens were beginning to split. Somewhere here, too, the single type of mass-carrying particle became two—leptons and quarks—as another symmetry broke, never to be complete again. The Universe was the size of a bowling ball, and 10^{-60} times denser than the densest atomic nucleus, but it was getting colder and thinner rapidly.

One ten-billionth of a second after the Big Bang, the firmament reached the Weinberg-Salam-Glashow transition point, and the tardy weak and electromagnetic forces broke away. All four interactions were now present, as well as the three known families of quarks and leptons. The basic components of the world we know had been formed.[4]

---

[4]Robert Crease and Charles Mann, *The Second Creation* (New York: Macmillan, 1986), pp. 405–406.

The foregoing narrative describes what is believed to be the first events in the history of our universe. But it may be that we have been treading the wrong road in this whole question. Perhaps we should not ask whether we need to posit God as first cause of the series of events, but rather we should posit God as an *explanation* of the fact that there *is* a series at all.

The Argument from Dependency

In Saint Thomas's other formulation of the cosmological argument, he argues from contingency to necessity. The universe contains countless contingent beings. But, it is argued, a contingent being presupposes a necessary being; you can't have a series, ending or unending, of contingent beings.

The language sounds somewhat strange to modern ears; we speak of necessary *propositions* ("Dogs are dogs") and contingent propositions ("Dogs have four legs"), but what would be a necessary or contingent *being*? It is easier to come to grips with the argument by speaking of *dependent* versus nondependent beings. Every person, every animal, every object in the world is a dependent being; it depends for its existence on something else without which it would not have existed. But how can you have a chain of dependent beings without, somewhere (at the end of the line?) having a being that does *not* depend for its existence on anything else? There must, it is argued, exist a nondependent, "self-existent" being; it relies for its existence on no set of conditions outside itself—and this being is God. The existence of a nondependent being is explained wholly from within ("from the nature of") that being itself.

But what is it that requires explanation—each dependent being or the whole collection? There is a difference between explaining *one* occurrence and explaining an entire group or collection of occurrences. If we have explained why each of five people is where he or she is at a certain time, haven't we done all the explaining we need to do?

> Suppose I see a group of five Eskimos standing on the corner of Sixth Avenue and 50th St. and I wish to explain why the group came to New York. Investigation reveals the following stories: Eskimo No. 1 did not enjoy the extreme cold in the polar region and decided to move to a warmer climate. No. 2 is the husband of No. 1; he loves her dearly and did not wish to live without her. No. 3 is the son of Eskimos 1 and 2; he is too small and too weak to oppose his parents. No. 4 saw an advertisement in the New York Times for an Eskimo to appear on television. No. 5 is a private detective engaged by the Pinkerton Agency to keep an eye on Eskimo No. 4.
> Let us assume that we have now explained in the case of each of the five Eskimos why he or she is in New York. Somebody then asks: "All right, but what about the group as a whole, why is *it* in New York?" This would plainly be an absurd question. There is no group over and above the five members and if we have explained why each of the five members is in New York, we have ipso facto explained why the group is there. A critic of the cosmological argument would claim that it is just as absurd to ask for the cause of the series as a whole, as distinct from asking for the causes of individual members.[5]

As Bertrand Russell once remarked, the fact that every human being had a mother doesn't show that the human race in general has a mother.

But the argument persists. Don't we also need an explanation for *the whole series* of dependent things? Don't we still need a nondependent being to explain why the whole collection of dependent beings exists? Doesn't dependency have to be somewhere grounded in nondependency? Dependent

[5]Paul Edwards, in Paul Edwards and Arthur Pap, eds., *A Modern Introduction to Philosophy* (New York: Free Press, 1959), p. 380.

beings require an explanation outside of themselves. Aquinas believed that the universe could not exist as a succession of dependent beings, and that the only alternative to saying that something requires explanation outside itself is to believe that it is explained *by itself alone,* or is its own explanation.

1. But this conclusion too has been challenged. Some philosophers have held that there are "brute facts" in the universe—facts that cannot be explained by means of anything else. For example, it may be just a "brute fact" that when light waves of a certain frequency strike my eyes, I see that particular shade of color I call yellow; I know of no explanation why I should have just *that* kind of sensation when just that physical stimulus occurs. It may be that certain laws of nature are also "brute facts," though we may not know which they are. We can explain laws of thermodynamics by means of laws of mechanics, and we can explain the laws of chemical combination by means of atomic theory. But there are other laws for which we know of no explanation. Perhaps gravitation is an example, although a "unified field theory" may yet explain gravitation in terms of something more fundamental still. But then that more fundamental law or theory would be a "brute fact"—unless, that is, it in turn was explained by something else. However far such explanations may go, don't we sooner or later end up at the level of "brute fact"—something that explains other things but is not itself capable of explanation? If we reach that stage (and we may never know whether we've reached it), don't we just have to say, "That's the way things are," and then end the inquiry?

2. But other philosophers have insisted that the very request for an explanation at this stage is meaningless. To explain something is to place it within a broader context of laws and theories; and when there is no

longer any such context, the request for explanation is meaningless, although we can of course keep on uttering the *words*. I can't tell you how a car runs without explaining it in terms of some laws of mechanics; nor can anyone explain the occurrence of gravitation without a wider network of laws or theories by which to explain it. But when that wider network is absent, because the question is about the whole network itself, hasn't the request become meaningless?

"Why is there a universe?" one may ask; even children ask, "Why is there anything at all?" Almost everyone feels a sense of wonderment, and the question exerts a powerful psychological effect. But hasn't the rug been pulled out from under us in the attempt to answer such a question? "I want you to explain X, but the necessary conditions of explanation are absent"—isn't this what it comes to? To explain something is always to explain in terms of something else—but when there is no "something else" by means of which to do the explaining, what happens to the concept of explanation? Hasn't it lost its meaning, just as the concept of being above something else has lost its meaning light-years away in the midst of empty space when there is no star or planet as a reference point for determining whether something is above something else? It's not that explanation comes to an end when we hit "brute facts," but that the very term "explanation" has lost its meaning when it is torn out by the only context in which it has any meaning.

4. THE ARGUMENT FROM MIRACLES

One argument for belief in God—or gods—that has had great popular appeal is the argument from *miracles*. According to this argument, miracles have occurred at various times in human history. And the occurrence of miracles is a proof of the existence of God, for only God could cause miraculous events to occur.

What exactly is required for an event to be miraculous? Suppose you throw a solid iron bar into water and it floats, or you hold a loaf of bread in your hand and it disappears before your eyes, or you pour someone a glass of water and it turns into wine. Are these events, assuming them to occur, miraculous—and by what criterion?

1. We might agree that a miracle must be an unusual event; something that happened all the time or even once a year would not be considered miraculous unless we extended the word to include such uses as "the miracle of sound," "the miracle of the new Chrysler," and so on. But a miracle can hardly be just any unusual event. The earth passing through a comet would be an unusual event, but it would not be considered miraculous as long as it could be accounted for (as it could) by known laws of nature. Perhaps an object may drop from an airplane and in falling strike a telephone wire outside your window and sever the wire, and the segment of wire on its way to the ground may strike a passing cat and electrocute it. This is surely unusual—"it wouldn't happen again in a million times"—but it would not be considered miraculous, since everything that occurred in this unusual sequence of events is explainable by known laws.

2. It would seem, then, that no event would be called a miracle as long as it is an instance of some known law or laws of nature. But is this enough? Suppose that an event occurred that could not be accounted for on the basis of any *known* laws of nature. Would it then be a miracle? Probably it would make us suspect that there were some laws of nature we did not yet know, or that some of those we were already familiar with had been inaccurately formulated and must be revised or qualified in such a way as to admit the new occurrence. When it was first no-

ticed that photographic plates were exposed although they had been in complete darkness all the time, this could not be accounted for on the basis of any known law of nature; but people soon came to realize that there were other laws they had never suspected which did account for this curious phenomenon, and in so doing the science of radioactivity was founded. When comets' tails were found to be repelled by the sun, it was not assumed that the universal attractive power of matter stated in the law of gravitation had gone berserk; other laws were discovered which accounted for cases like these.

3. Under what conditions *would* an event be considered miraculous? We cannot now say, "When it isn't an instance of any *known* law"; shall we say, "When it isn't an instance of *any law at all,* known or unknown"? This at least escapes the objection to the previous view. On this conception of a miracle, however, we could never definitely state that any event was miraculous. How could we ever know that the event in question could never, even in millions of future years of scientific investigation, be explained on the basis of some law or theory, however complex and elusive? If we could not, we could never know an event to be miraculous. If the iron bar suddenly floated, we would indeed be surprised; but who knows after all exactly what complicated sets of circumstances may cause matter to behave as it does? We judge what is probable or improbable by the kind of behavior nature has exhibited in the past; but there may be a good many springs in nature's depths that only occasionally, or under very special conditions, bubble up to the surface. The surprising behavior of the iron bar might turn out to have something to do with the moisture in the air, or some law of radioactivity not now known, or even the mental state of observers. Such things would be unexpected because they are not in accordance with the way nature generally works

(as far as our present knowledge goes), but they would certainly not be without precedent in the history of science. It was a surprise to learn that profuse bleeding could result from a mental condition and not from any of the physiological causes so earnestly sought for, or that a perpetual hand tremor could result from a forgotten aggressive act committed in early childhood in which no physiological damage was done. Many persons are still suspicious of such phenomena because they feel that "nature just doesn't work that way"; but it may be more likely that nature has a few tricks up her sleeve that we never suspected, and that will certainly seem strange as long as we judge "how nature ought to behave" by laws that are already familiar to us.

On this definition of "miracle," then, we could never be sure that any event, no matter how bizarre or unusual or contrary to the regular course of our experience, was a miracle; we could never know that the event could not be subsumed under some laws. However, let us *suppose* that we could be absolutely sure that some such event was *not an instance of any law at all, known or unknown.* Would this show that God must be invoked to account for it? The answer seems inescapable: of course it wouldn't; it would only prove that some events are not instances of laws. But to establish this and to establish the existence of God are, of course, two entirely different things.

4. According to others—for example, John Stuart Mill—an event cannot be considered a miracle no matter how strange it is, if it would occur again if the same set of conditions were repeated. In order to constitute a miracle, an event must take place *without* having been preceded by a set of conditions that are sufficient to make it happen again. The test of a miracle is: were there present conditions such that whenever these conditions recur the event will recur? If there

were, the event is no miracle. Once again, we could never be sure that an event was a miracle in this sense—we could never know for sure that if the same conditions were to recur, the "miracle" would not recur; at best we could only know that when the conditions were the same as *far as we knew*, the allegedly miraculous event did not occur. But there might always be other conditions that never occurred to us to consider, which were yet causally relevant, and if added to the set of conditions to be repeated, the event *would* occur.

Suppose that somehow we *could* know that we had all the relevant conditions and that they were all the same, but the event did not recur; what would this prove? Only that two identical sets of conditions may be followed by nonidentical events—that is, indeterminism. This might be a surprise, but, one might ask, why shouldn't the universe be indeterministic (at least sometimes) rather than deterministic? Need indeterminism be considered evidence of the miraculous?

5. Some events, it is said, are so vastly improbable that their occurrence must be miraculous. According to the biblical account, when Joshua's trumpet caused the walls of Jericho to fall, the sun stood still in the sky for several hours. Today we realize that for the sun to stand still in the sky, the earth would have to stop revolving on its axis, causing countless objects on its surface to fly through the air, as the objects in a speeding car do when the car comes to a sudden stop. This effect would occur over the entire earth, far beyond the bounds of Jericho. It is difficult to believe that the earth really stopped rotating on that occasion. But a believer in this miracle would of course believe that all this really happened, although no one (outside the biblical account) apparently reported the event. However, said David Hume in his essay "On Miracles," it is more probable that those who wrote that the sun stopped in its tracks were deluded, or imagined it, or lied, than that the event really occurred. The same applies to allegations that water was turned into wine, that a few fishes and loaves of bread were suddenly multiplied into thousands, that Lazarus was raised from the dead, and so on. "No testimony," wrote Hume, "is sufficient to establish a miracle unless the testimony be of such a kind that its falsehood would be more miraculous than the fact which it endeavors to establish."[6]

That people are sometimes deluded or tell tall tales to impress others, that rumors spread and are wildly exaggerated when they have traveled even a small distance from their source, and that people will believe almost anything when it is something they very much want to believe and are already conditioned to believe it—all these, said Hume, are well-known facts that require no miracles for us to believe. Most alleged miracles were reported by people in times long past, so we can no longer check their claims—people who were not well trained in reporting what they saw without adding anything to the observed facts. It is easy to see how all these things could have occurred; each religion has its own stock of miracles to bolster its claim to authenticity.

None of this, however, proves that the miraculous events did not occur. We are rather in the position of a Sherlock Holmes who has to solve a crime that was committed centuries ago and in which most of the clues that were once available have now vanished. The miracle is firmly believed chiefly by those people who are already believers, and the claims of the miraculous are used to add credibility to a belief that they already have.

---

[6]David Hume, "On Miracles," in Hume, *An Enquiry Concerning Human Understanding*, Section 10.

Belief in miracles depends not nearly as much on the evidence in a particular case—in most cases we have none—as on our antecedent beliefs. If a person already believes that the lives of people who have terminal cancer are saved through prayer, she is more likely to believe that a man was raised from the dead and that the sun stood still in the sky.

Many people, including those of deep religious conviction, are repelled by tales of the miraculous because they believe that these alleged miracles are somehow unworthy of an omnipotent being. If God wanted people to believe, why perform a few "parlor tricks" in a remote area where few people could witness them? Instead of healing a few people of their disease, why not cure everyone? Instead of a vision of the Virgin Mary at Fatima, Portugal, in 1917, why not put an end to the enormous slaughter of World War I, which was raging all around at the time? Or, if this is tampering with people's free will, why not do something that would save many human lives, such as stopping the earthquake in Lisbon that killed thirty thousand people as they were gathered in their churches to worship (an example repeatedly cited by Voltaire in his *Candide*)?

Many people even today are quick to accept as a miracle an event that goes contrary to probabilities, as long as it works *in their favor*. A hundred people are killed in an airplane accident, but one person survives. "It's a miracle!" says the survivor and his family. What of the families of those who did not survive? Now suppose, instead, that there is an airplane accident in which one person dies but a hundred survive. The family of the one nonsurvivor doesn't say, "It's a miracle!" although the survival of a hundred when one dies is no more or less unusual than the survival of one when a hundred die. It is not called a miracle unless it has a result that

they desire. The sudden death of all one's family and friends is not something that would be likely to be called a miracle. And the saving of hundreds of lives in an earthquake in some remote region of the world would not usually be called a miracle by people far away who never heard of them and don't particularly care about them. Apparently God works to protect *you*, not the multitudes of other people in the world who might seem equally entitled to protection.

Suppose, however, that there was some super miracle that we could all observe and could not explain away. Suppose that at this moment we all heard a voice coming from somewhere in the sky, simultaneously intelligible in all languages, announcing that from this moment on whoever knowingly kills another person will be struck dead with a thunderbolt on the spot, and suppose that from that moment on this actually happens—every killer is immediately killed by a thunderbolt. Wouldn't that be proof of the miraculous?

We would at first want to disprove some obvious suspicions: that it was not some clever auditory trick, and so on. And if it was understood in all languages, in what language would it be transcribed on your tape recorder? And from what point in the sky would the sound originate? Would the tape recording become louder as you approached a certain point (perhaps as recorded in a high-flying plane)? And so on. We might have to change the description of some of the conditions; how, for example, could it be in all languages at once? But even if it were spoken in one language—say ancient Sanskrit or Hebrew—there are enough scholars around to translate it for us and tell us what the announcement said. And if all killers were thenceforth executed by thunderbolts in accordance with the announcement, this would still be mightily impressive. "There's something out there we hadn't figured on," we might say, or more likely, "There's *someone* out there, a personality, a mind, someone with sufficient power to carry out threats." It would certainly be evidence for the existence of "a powerful being out there"—perhaps not a being who was omnipotent, or infinitely wise, or the cause of the universe, or a "necessary being"—but at least something for whose existence we had thus far had no direct evidence. But no alleged miracle in history has thus far presented us with anything like this kind of evidence.

This example, however, brings out a point about the allegedly miraculous. Even a very extraordinary event, one contrary to known laws of nature, will not impress people as a candidate for the miraculous nearly as much as will occurrences with a "personal touch"— that appear to be the work of a will, a personality of some kind. Water changing into wine in a cellar would not be as impressive as someone standing before a crowd and changing it (assuming it could be tested as water beforehand and as wine afterward), or publicly multiplying five loaves and two fishes into enough to feed thousands. Even raising someone from the dead might not be found particularly impressive—physicians have revived people after thier heartbeat and brainwaves have stopped; it would more likely be thought of as a medical triumph than a miracle. But suppose posters in various languages started to fall mysteriously from the skies announcing that the Antarctic icecap will be made to melt (thus raising the sea level and flooding coastal cities around the world) unless all nations remained at peace with one another; then suppose a war broke out and immediately the entire Antarctic ice sheet melted. This might well be counted as miraculous, not merely because of the event itself, but because of the prior warning from the clouds: it would be a manifestation of a *will*, backed

up by *power*, both of which are universally considered to be distinctive features of a deity.

6. One could, of course, *define* a miracle as an intervention of God into the natural course of events. Assuming this definition, if one is asked whether miracles prove the existence of God, the answer of course would be yes—an intervention of God logically entails the existence of a God that is able to intervene. But this definition, of course, begs the whole question. The question would now become "*Are* there any miracles in this sense? Does this definition apply to anything in reality, or is it like 'unicorn', which is easily defined but nothing in the world exists for the definition to apply to?" We can define as we like, but the question is whether the definition applies to anything. The existence of unusual events, events that instantiate no laws, and so on, would not prove it. No matter how many iron bars were seen to float on water, such an occurrence would not establish the miraculous in this sense.

5. THE TELEOLOGICAL ARGUMENT (THE ARGUMENT FROM DESIGN)

Of all arguments, the one with widest appeal is the teleological argument (from the Greek *telos*, or "purpose"), or argument from design. More than any other it appeals to empirically observable features of the universe and attempts to infer from these that God exists—not necessarily God the creator, or God the first cause, but God as cosmic designer. Observe the world carefully, the argument runs, and you cannot help coming to the conclusion that it contains abundant evidence of order and design—evidence that a "master architect" has been at work. Not blind chance but order and purpose govern the universe, and evidence of purposiveness permeates it. And when there is purpose, there must be a purposer; where there is design, there must be a designer.

What kind of being must the designer of the cosmos be? Is he (or she, or it?) a person—a personality with intelligence, wisdom, and other human qualities? The advocate of the teleological argument replies in the affirmative: design presupposes intelligence. But what *kind* of designer? Does the designer have unlimited power? Is he benevolently disposed toward the creatures he has designed? Although the usual answer given to these questions is yes, opinions, as we shall see, are divided on these last two questions. In all versions, certain features of the universe are taken as evidence for a designer, and presumably if the universe were very different from what it is, it would *not* provide such evidence (or would provide evidence for a different kind of designer). To that extent at least the argument has an empirical base.

If successful, the argument does not establish the existence of a necessary being, a first cause, or even a creater-of-the-universe-out-of-nothing; it attempts to establish only the existence of a being with sufficient intelligence and power to shape the materials of the universe in accordance with a plan or purpose. The first-cause argument, had it been successful, would have yielded us only a first cause; the contingency argument would have yielded only a necessary being; the teleological argument—if successful—will yield us only a cosmic designer. Traditionally the name "God" has been given to all these things; but this assumes that that which is a necessary being or a first cause is also a cosmic designer. We should not insist that all of these must be the same being because we use the same word, "God," for each. When Plato discussed the hypothesis of a designer (or artificer) in his dialogue *Timaeus,* he never assumed—nor did any of the ancient Greeks—that the cosmic designer created the universe

from nothing, as people usually interpret the biblical account; in Plato, the cosmic designer took materials already present and shaped them in accordance with a plan, much as a builder takes materials already in existence and uses them to design and build a house.

Let us see, then, what forms the teleological argument can take, what kind of designer it can make a case for, and what evidence it can adduce. When we have done so, we shall examine the general structure of the argument in its varying forms.

The universe, the argument begins, is *orderly,* and order is the result of design. The millions of stars in the heavens behave in an orderly manner, all exhibiting certain physical laws that hold equally for all of them; and so do the millions of species of life on the earth. How could all these things have come into existence except as the result of design? Pieces of clay do not come together of themselves to make bricks, or bricks to form a house; this requires the designing activity of human beings. In the same way, particles of matter cannot come together of themselves to form living cells, or cells to form the complex living organisms that inhabit the earth; such a result can be brought about only by a designer who fashions the materials in such a way as to form them.

But such arguments are subject to several objections:

1. The word "order" is not very clear: that which seems orderly to one person will not seem so to another. A painting that appears orderly to one observer will appear chaotic to another.

2. Nor is it clear that the universe is orderly in any specific sense. If galaxies are orderly, but drifting nebulae in the universe are not, then it must be pointed out that there are many nebulae in the universe; and so on for anything that might be considered not to be orderly. Yet if *anything* that the uni-

verse contains is orderly, no matter what, then what are the limits on the term "orderly"? What could count *against* a thing or arrangement of things being orderly? If you throw a bag of marbles on the floor, they must fall out in *some* order or other. In this sense, every arrangement of things must be orderly, so the statement that *this* universe is orderly tells us nothing distinctive about it.

3. Most important, what is the guarantee that order is always the result of design? Some examples of order are indeed the result of design, as in the case of mechanical objects (watches, wrenches, automobiles); we know this because we ourselves (or other human beings) have taken the materials and put them together in certain ways to form objects that we can use and enjoy. The order is there as a result of designing minds—*ours*. But as Hume said, order is evidence for design *only* to the extent that order has been *observed* to result from design. And the order we find in plants and animals has *not* been observed to result from design. We have never seen any beings who form plants or animals, or for that matter stars, as a result of their design, and therefore we are not entitled to conclude that these things do exist as a result of design.

"But that's just the point," the defender of the teleological argument replies, "We have never *seen* plants and animals being designed the way architects design buildings and watchmakers design watches, but we must *infer* that they were designed, for how else could we account for their existence? Once again, stones don't come together on their own to form cathedrals, and neither can particles of matter come together to form organisms. This requires intelligence, and since the intelligence in the case of organisms is not human, it must be divine."

This comment, however, invites still another objection. What if the phenomenon in question can be explained without assuming the existence of a cosmic designer? Then we shall not, strictly speaking, have disproved the hypothesis, but we shall have shown that it isn't required in order to account for the facts. Can this be done, specifically in the case of organisms, which are the most striking example of order that invites the hypothesis of design?

In a universe composed chiefly of inorganic matter, the existence of life and mind seemed a mystery that could be explained only on the hypothesis of a cosmic designer. But for many thousands of years there have been theories of organic evolution attempting to explain the existence of organisms without recourse to the hypothesis of a designer. The early Greek philosopher Anaximander (611–547 B.C.), for example, argued that organisms originally sprang from the sea and evolved into land creatures. But no comprehensive theory with the full weight of detailed and painstaking empirical observation behind it arose until the publication of Charles Darwin's *On the Origin of Species* in 1859. Darwin set forth a hypothesis according to which organisms gradually evolved, from the simplest amoebas to the most complex primates, through the struggle for existence and the survival of the fittest. As a result of his pioneering and the work of many biologists since, the hypothesis of organic evolution has become so well confirmed as to be quite universally accepted among biologists.

It did not, to be sure, explain everything: it explained why certain species survived, but not how the first species originated. But this gap too has been gradually closing, beginning more than a century ago with the synthesis in the laboratory of uric acid (the first organic compound to be produced from inorganic ones) to the latest feats of genetic engineering. Gradually, by bits and pieces, the genesis of life (under conditions occurring during the Precambrian era of the earth's history) has come to be explained without any recourse to design.

The designer hypothesis has not thereby been shown to be false, however. If a person believed in design before, she could do so after Darwin as well as before, even accepting all of Darwin's conclusions. She could say that, whereas it had previously been thought that God had created all the species instantaneously, she now believed that God had chosen the slow and gradual process of evolution as a means of executing his design. The method of design would have changed, but not the fact.

Nevertheless, the teleological argument has lost most of its currency (among scientists, at any rate) since Darwin—not because Darwin disproved design, for he did not, but because there no longer seemed to be any necessity for having such a hypothesis. If you once believed that a knock on your door was caused by the ghost of a departed spirit, you no longer need to believe this if you find that the knock was caused by a salesman making a call (although it is still possible for you to believe that the knock was caused by the salesman *and* a departed spirit).

But the impact of Darwin's theory cut deeper: it did not refute design in general, but it did appear to refute, or at any rate seriously to impair, belief in a *benevolent* design—yet the belief in a benevolent designer, one who cared about his creatures and did not wish them to suffer, has always been the mainspring of belief in design. People would not be so likely to be attracted to the argument from design if they thought that the cosmic designer was malevolent. Yet it was precisely the belief in a benevolent designer that was difficult to sustain in the face of belief in the evolutionary process, for the evolutionary process is a scene of continuous and endless strife, pain, and death. Life is a struggle for existence, in which many species die out and every individual inevitably dies—

most often in agony, through starvation, cold, disease, or being eaten alive by animals. The individual life is expendable; millions of individuals of every species die every day (usually before they have lived out a full life), but life continues through their offspring, who in their turn die in pain and suffering.

Does the designer inflict all this suffering merely to preserve the species, at the expense of the individual? If so, it is not much consolation to the individual; and of what value is a species if all the individuals in it must live a life of constant threat and insecurity and finally die in misery? Nor does nature appear to be any more careful of the species or type than of the individual; thousands of species have perished through starvation, changes in climate, attacks from other animals, or the appearance of some new mutation that was swifter or more adaptable. Nature seems indifferent to individual and species alike.

> "So careful of the type?" but no.
> From scarped cliff and quarried stone
> She cries, "A thousand types are gone:
> I care for nothing, all shall go."
>
> . . . .
>
> [Shall] Man, her last work, who seem'd so fair,
> Such splendid purpose in his eyes,
> Who roll'd the psalm to wintry skies,
> Who built him fanes of fruitless prayer,
>
> Who trusted God was love indeed
> And love Creation's final law—
> Tho' Nature, red in tooth and claw
> With ravine, shriek'd against his creed—
>
> Who loved, who suffer'd countless ills,
> Who battled for the True, the Just,
> Be blown about the desert dust,
> Or seal'd within the iron hills?[7]

-----

[7]Alfred, Lord Tennyson, *In Memoriam,* LVI.

Through countless ages innumerable species of creatures evolve; those that are able to adjust themselves to changing conditions to find sufficient food, drink, shelter, and safety survive for a time; the rest are blotted out in the struggle for existence. Most living things, including all the carnivorous animals, can continue to live only by catching other living things as prey and devouring them as food. Even when they are successful in this (at the expense of the creatures they kill), the environmental conditions are so undependable, and the life of the organism so dependent on a vast multitude of conditions (they can live only within a narrow range of temperature, moisture, and nutritional supply), that even a comparatively small change in the environment or disorder in the functioning of the organism may cause their extinction. If nature is designed, the plan of the designer does not appear to be benevolent:

> In sober truth, nearly all the things which men are hanged or imprisoned for doing to one another, are nature's every-day performances. Killing, the most criminal act recognized by human laws, Nature does once to every being that lives; and in a large proportion of cases, after protracted tortures such as only the greatest monsters whom we read of ever purposely inflicted on their living fellow-creatures. . . . Nature impales men, breaks them as if on the wheel, casts them to be devoured by wild beasts, burns them to death, crushes them with stones like the first Christian martyr, starves them with hunger, freezes them with cold, poisons them by the quick or slow venom of her exhalations, and has hundreds of other hideous deaths in reserve, such as the ingenious cruelty of a Nabis or a Domitian never surpassed. All this, Nature does with the most supercilious disregard both of mercy and of justice, emptying her shafts upon the best and noblest indifferently with the meanest and worst; upon those who are engaged in the highest and worthiest enterprises, and often as the direct consequences of the noblest acts; and it might almost be imagined as a punish-

ment for them. She mows down those on whose existence hangs the well-being of a whole people, perhaps the prospects of the human race for generations to come, with as little compunction as those whose death is a relief to themselves, or a blessing to those under their noxious influence.[8]

We find young lions and young antelopes appealing, and we don't want to see them suffer or be killed. But they will spend most of their lives killing and trying to avoid being killed. For them life is far from beautiful. The lions who do not continue to kill, die of hunger or disease or drought or cold. Nature gives not a snap of its fingers for a creature's survival after it has contributed to its gene pool. Would any creature, knowing the odds and the outcome, wish to be born into such a world? Could any being who designed such a world be deemed benevolent? There is

> a perpetual war amongst all living creatures. Necessity, hunger, want, stimulate the strong and courageous; fear, anxiety, terror, agitate the weak and infirm. The first entrance into life gives anguish to the new-born infant and to its wretched parent: weakness, impotence, distress, attend each stage of that life: and 'tis at last finished in agony and horror.
>
> Observe too . . . the curious artifices of nature, in order to embitter the life of every living being. The stronger prey upon the weaker, and keep them in perpetual terror and anxiety. The weaker, too, in their turn, often prey upon the stronger, and vex and molest them without relaxation. Consider that innumerable race of insects, which either are bred upon the body of each animal, or flying about infix their stings in him. These insects have others still less than themselves, which torment them. And thus on each hand, before and behind, above and below, every animal is surrounded with enemies, which incessantly seek his misery and destruction. . . .
>
> Look round this universe. What an immense profusion of beings, animated and or-

---

[8]Mill, "Nature," pp. 28–30.

ganized, sensible and active! You admire this prodigious fecundity and variety. But inspect a little more narrowly these living existences. . . . How hostile and destructive to each other! How insufficient all of them for their own happiness! How contemptible and odious to the spectator! The whole presents nothing but the idea of a blind nature, impregnated by a great vivifying principle, and pouring forth from her lap, without discernment or parental care, her maimed and abortive children![9]

The Problem of Evil

The principal objection to the teleological argument, if that argument is intended to prove the existence of a *benevolent* designer, is the problem of evil. In ancient times Epicurus (342–270 B.C.) put the problem as follows: "Is God willing to prevent evil, but not able? Then he is not omnipotent. Is he able, but not willing? Then he is malevolent. Is he both able and willing? Then whence evil?" Hume put the argument in the form of a dilemma: "If the evil in the world is from the intention of the Deity, then he is not benevolent. If the evil in the world is contrary to his intention, then he is not omnipotent. But it is either in accordance with his intention or contrary to it. Therefore, either the Deity is not benevolent or he is not omnipotent."

The problem arises only if the hypothesis is that of a designer who is both omnipotent and benevolent. If he is not omnipotent, then the evil in the world can be attributed to the fact that he doesn't desire it but is unable to prevent it. If he is not benevolent, then the evil can be said to arise from the fact that he is able to prevent it but doesn't wish to. But if he is both benevolent and omnipotent (which most religions say that he is), then the problem arises in full force: why evil?

Hume's dilemma is valid, as every student of elementary logic can work out for himself. But are its premises true? There have been a number of attempts to escape from it by questioning one or more premises in some way.

1. *There is no evil in the world.* One might deny that there is any evil at all and thus undercut the presupposition of the problem. But this solution is so implausible that it would take considerable gall to suggest it. People may not entirely agree on what things are evil (it would require a long excursus into ethics in order to become clearer about this), but they do agree that some things are. Ordinarily, for example, we believe that pain and suffering are bad, and we exhibit this belief in our practice when we try to avoid them or to minimize them as much as possible; for example, we try to alleviate the pain of those who suffer from diseases. Nor is the suffering illusory; people do not merely *think* they are suffering; they *are* suffering. The fact of such suffering is, indeed, one of the principal reasons many persons find it difficult to believe in a God who is both all-powerful and benevolent. *We* would alleviate these sufferings if we could; yet God, who is all-powerful and benevolent, fails to do so.

2. *Evil is a negative thing.* Saint Augustine advanced the idea that evil is not a positive thing but a lack, a privation, a negative. There is no evil, but only the comparative absence of good; evil is simply nonbeing. Sometimes it is added, as Augustine did, that to be real is to be perfect, and thus only God can be wholly real; his creation, being necessarily finite and limited, must necessarily involve incomplete goodness, and thus involve evil to some degree or other.

But to say that evil is negative seems to be primarily a play on words. Is war negative, the absence of peace, or is peace negative, the absence of war? Whichever way we classify it, the one is as real as the other—there is

---

[9]Hume, *Dialogues Concerning Natural Religion*, Parts 10 and 11.

war, and there is peace; there is happiness, and there is suffering; there is good, and there is evil. The facts of reality are not changed by being classified as negative or positive. Suffering exists, and is not alleviated in the slightest by the consideration that "It is only negative."

> It may console the paralytic to be told that paralysis is mere lack of motility, nothing positive, and that insofar as he *is,* he is perfect. It is not clear, however, that this kind of comfort is available to the sufferer from malaria. He will reply that his trouble is not that he lacks anything, but rather that he has too much of something, namely, protozoans of the genus *Plasmodium.*[10]

3. *Evil is necessary for the greatest good.* "Granted that there is evil in the world. But there *has* to be, since that is the only way good can be achieved. We are all familiar with instances of this: you cannot get back to full health without painful surgery, but you undergo the surgery (which is not as good when considered by itself—that is, you wouldn't do it *except* thereby to achieve recovery) to attain a goal. The pain and suffering incurred are worth it as long as they are the only means by which you can achieve recovery. And so on for countless situations. Even war is sometimes the only way a better world (or the prevention of a worse one) can be attained. Thus, though there *is* evil in the world, it is compatible with the goodness of God, since the evil that there is is the least possible required to get the greatest possible good. This is not a perfect world, but it is the *best* of all *possible* worlds."

People do often have to suffer pain in order to recover health, our medical knowledge being what it is, and the laws of biology being what they are. But this consideration,

which to most people would justify a physician in inflicting pain on a patient in order that the patient may recover, applies only to limited beings who can achieve the end *in no other way.* Once we suspect, however, that the physician could achieve the goal *without* inflicting suffering on her patient, and that she is inflicting it anyway, we call her a cruel and sadistic monster. God, unlike the physician, is omnipotent and could bring about a recovery without making the patient go through the excruciating pain. Why then does he not do this?

"But this would require a miracle, and it would upset the orderliness of nature to continually perform miracles." But surely the laws of nature could have been set up so that no miracle would be required in each case. After all, who is the author of the laws of nature? Why did God set up the causal order in such a way as to require creatures to die in agony? There is not the excuse in the case of God that there is in the case of the surgeon, who can bring about his patient's recovery *only* by causing suffering; for God, being omnipotent as well as benevolent, could easily bring about the recovery without such means; indeed, he could have kept the patient from being sick in the first place. What would we think of a surgeon who first infected his child's leg and then decided to amputate it, although a cure was within his power to give and the infection was of his own giving to begin with? But this would be the position of an omnipotent God. A physician who is benevolent but not omnipotent can be excused for causing suffering only because the end can be achieved in no other way; but this is not the case with an omnipotent God, for, being omnipotent, he does not need to use evil means to bring about a good end.

Indeed, is it not a mistake to use means-end terminology in talking about omnipotence at all? An omnipotent being could bring about the end directly, without em-

---

[10]Wallace I. Matson, *The Existence of God* (Ithaca: Cornell University Press, 1965), pp. 142–143.

barking upon means to do it. Means toward ends are needed only by beings who cannot achieve their ends directly.

> When I was in India, I was standing on the veranda of an Indian home darkened by bereavement. My Indian friend had lost his little son, the light of his eyes, in a cholera epidemic. At the far end of the veranda his little daughter, the only remaining child, slept in a cot covered over with a mosquito net. We paced up and down, and I tried in my clumsy way to comfort and console him. But he said, "Well, padre, it is the will of God. That's all there is to it. It is the will of God."
>
> Fortunately I knew him well enough to be able to reply without being misunderstood, and I said something like this: "Supposing someone crept up the steps onto the veranda tonight, while you all slept, and deliberately put a wad of cotton soaked in cholera germ culture over your little girl's mouth as she lay in that cot there on the veranda, what would you think about that?"
>
> "My God," he said, "what would I think about that? Nobody would do such a damnable thing. If he attempted it and I caught him, I would kill him with as little compunction as I would a snake, and throw him over the veranda. What did you mean by suggesting such a thing?"
>
> "But John," I said quietly, "isn't that just what you have accused God of doing when you said it was His will? Call your little boy's death the result of mass ignorance, call it mass folly, call it mass sin, if you like, call it bad drains or communal carelessness, but don't call it the will of God. Surely we cannot identify as the will of God something for which a man would be locked up in jail, or put in a criminal lunatic asylum."[11]

Of course, if God too is limited in power, as the physician is, then the outcome may be the result of his inability to do better in spite of his good intentions. But such a defense is not available in the case of a God who is both benevolent and omnipotent.

> Did I show you a house or palace, where there was not one apartment convenient or agreeable; where the windows, doors, fires, passages, stairs, and the whole economy of the building were the source of noise, confusion, fatigue, darkness, and extremes of hot and cold; you would certainly blame the contrivance, without any further examination. The architect would in vain display his subtlety, and prove to you that if this door or that window were altered, greater ills would ensue. What he says, may be strictly true: the alteration of one particular, while the other parts of the building remain, may only augment the inconveniences. But still you would assert in general, that if the architect had had skill and good intentions, he might have formed such a plan of the whole, and might have adjusted the parts in such a manner, as would have remedied all or most of these inconveniences.[12]

A good architect would have designed the house in such a way as to avoid these disadvantages, so that one would not have to choose between a design that was bad and one that was worse. And if an architect was so incompetent that he could devise no such house, perhaps he should refrain from any further attempts at architecture. If the best universe that a designer could bring about is one as full of pain and suffering as this one, perhaps she should have chosen instead some activity in which she had greater skill.

4. *Good often comes out of evil.*

A: Out of hardship and adversity comes achievement. Out of suffering comes appreciation of the feelings of others. Out of poverty comes thrift. And so on. How else can these things come about?

B: In the first place, if God could not bring about any other outcome, he is not om-

---

[11]Leslie D. Weatherhead, *The Will of God* (Nashville: Abingdon Press, 1944), quoted in Harold Titus, *Ethics for Today*, 3rd ed. (New York: American Book Co., 1953), p. 539.

[12]Hume, *Dialogues Concerning Natural Religion*, Part 11.

nipotent. *We* perhaps cannot bring about another outcome, conditions being what they are, and the laws of nature being what they are; but an omnipotent God could.

In the second place, the good that comes out of evil is often hardly sufficient to justify it. The causal order is so complex that there is probably no disaster to one person that does not work to the advantage of another. A hurricane kills a hundred people and destroys a thousand buildings, but it provides work for builders. Is it worth it? If you were God, would you be justified in bringing about all this death and destruction in order to provide this work? Don't you consider the destruction of a city in an earthquake evil, in spite of the fact that some old buildings are destroyed, thus enabling new and better ones to be built on their site? Would *you* be justified in destroying a city to bring about this result?

In the third place, if good sometimes comes out of evil, evil also sometimes comes out of good—probably just as frequently. For everything we thought evil at the time and later changed our minds about in the light of later developments, there is probably another event we thought good or beneficial at the time that in the light of later events we now consider disastrous or regrettable. The fact is that the most usual tendency is for good to produce more good and evil to produce more evil.

Health, strength, wealth, knowledge, virtue, are not only good in themselves but facilitate and promote the acquisition of good, both of the same and of other kinds. The person who can learn easily, is he who already knows much; it is the strong and not the sickly person who can do everything which most conduces to health, those who find it easy to gain money are not the poor but the rich; while health, strength, knowledge, talents, are all means of acquiring riches, and riches are often an indispensable means of acquiring these. Again, *e converso*, whatever may be said of evil turning into good, the general tendency of evil is towards further evil. Bodily illness renders the body more susceptible of disease; it produces incapacity of exertion, sometimes debility of mind, and often the loss of means of subsistence. All severe pain, either bodily or mental, tends to increase the susceptibilities of pain for ever after. Poverty is the parent of a thousand mental and moral evils. What is still worse, to be injured or oppressed, when habitual, lowers the whole tone of the character. One bad action leads to others, both in the agent himself, in the bystanders, and in the sufferers. All bad qualities are strengthened by habit, and all vices and follies tend to spread. Intellectual defects generate moral, and moral, intellectual; and every intellectual or moral defect generates others, and so on without end.[13]

5. *The purpose of evil is not to make us happy but to make us virtuous.*

A: The world is a moral training ground for the building of character. Evils are put there to discipline and improve us rather than to punish us.

B: But the order of nature is such as to frustrate the goal of making people virtuous as much as or even more than the goal of making people happy. Here is a person who, we believe, needs to know what suffering is like, so that he will not be so insensitive to it in others; and what happens? He is never made to experience it; but a person who already is borne down by the weight of suffering only has more of the same heaped upon her—the person who already has one disease, let us say, contracts another. This is the way of things in the actual world. Sufferings seem to occur hit-or-miss: they miss the

---

[13]Mill, "Nature," pp. 35–36.

person who (if anyone) should have them, and come constantly to others who already have more than they can bear, rendering them miserable and perhaps embittered for life. This is quite inconsistent with the behavior of a being who is both omnipotent and benevolent. Here is a man who drives his car carelessly so as to be a danger to others on the highway. Short of changing his nature, the best way to make him more careful would be to have him involved in an accident in which he was slightly injured, just enough to scare him; but what actually happens, more often than not, is that he escapes scot-free while others are injured or killed, until that one last time when he himself is killed in an accident, when it is too late to improve him. If moral improvement were the aim, any reasonably intelligent fifteen-year-old who was benevolently disposed and had the power could effect a better distribution of good in the world than now exists.

If the Creator of mankind willed that they should all be virtuous, his designs are as completely baffled as if he had willed that they should all be happy; and the order of nature is constructed with even less regard to the requirements of justice than to those of benevolence. If the law of all creation were justice and the Creator omnipotent, then in whatever amount suffering and happiness might be dispensed to the world, each person's share of them would be exactly proportioned to that person's good or evil deeds; no human being would have a worse lot than another, without worse deserts; accident or favoritism would have no part in such a world, but every human life would be the playing out of a drama constructed like a perfect moral tale. . . . The world we live in is totally different from this; insomuch that the necessity of redressing the balance has been deemed one of the strongest arguments for another life after death, which amounts to an admission that the order of things in this

life is often an example of injustice, not justice. . . . Every kind of moral depravity is inflicted upon multitudes by the fatality of their birth: through the fault of their parents, of society, or of the uncontrollable circumstances, certainly through no fault of their own. Not even on the most distorted and contracted theory of good which ever was framed by religious or philosophical fanatacism, can the government of Nature be made to resemble the work of a being at once good and omnipotent.[14]

6. *God's goodness is different from ours.* But now a different solution may be suggested: "Perhaps what we call evil is really good; what seems evil to us is in fact good when seen from the vantage point of omniscience. The goodness of everything is perceived only by God, but he after all sees everything while we see very little: that everything is good is seen by his infinite intelligence but is beyond our finite comprehension."

Considering the spectacle of the world as we find it, said Mill, there is no judgment of which we are more certain than that it is not perfectly good. If we distrust this judgment, we have no reason to trust *any* moral judgment, including the judgment that what is evil to us is good to God. Even if everything we think is evil is really good, the fact is that we still *think* it is evil—and this would be an error, an error hiding from us the perfect goodness of the universe. And since it would surely be better if we did not commit this error, the existence of this error would be an evil.

The world we inhabit is full of pain and suffering, cruelty and death, wars, plague, floods, earthquakes, and other disasters. If there is a powerful being who considers all this to be good, what view must we take of the morality of such a being? What would we think of a physician who wanted to alleviate the extreme pain and suffering of a patient?

[14]Ibid., p. 38.

Perhaps she was willing but not able: to help the patient was beyond her powers. We exonerate her because although willing, she was not able. But no such consideration would excuse a divine being who wanted to alleviate the patient's condition *and* was able to do so. A physician who both wanted to help the patient and was able to do so but did not would be considered to be a cruel sadist; would not the same have to be said of a deity? Should our attitude be different toward him than the physician? Yet we are asked to believe that a God who could prevent needless suffering and yet refused to do so is good.

> When I am told that I must believe this, and at the same time call this being by the names which express and affirm the highest human morality, I say in plain terms that I will not. Whatever power such a being may have over me, there is one thing which he shall not do: he shall not compel me to worship him. I will call no being good, who is not what I mean when I apply that epithet to my fellow creatures, and if such a being can sentence me to hell for not so calling him, to hell I will go.[15]

So many of the things we are supposed to attribute to God are incompatible with anything we call goodness that people often try to shift the meaning of "good" to accommodate the discrepancy. We are told that God is good, but infinitely good, and that of course we can not understand infinite goodness. But, of course, the same argument could support the view that either God or the world is infinitely *bad:* if some things look to us as if they were good, never fear, in the light of infinite knowledge we could see that they are all bad after all—the universe is the perfect epitome of evil. This argument is ex-

actly on a par with the view that, although it sometimes seems evil, everything is really good.

Moreover, if God is infinitely good, the fact remains that infinite goodness must still be *goodness,* just as infinite space must still be space:

> Among the many who have said that we cannot conceive infinite space, did anyone ever suppose that it is *not* space? that is does not possess all the properties by which space is characterized? Infinite space cannot be cubical or spherical, because these are modes of being bounded; but does anyone imagine that in ranging through it we might arrive at some region which was not extended; of which one part was not outside another; where, though no Body intervened, motion was impossible; or where the sum of two sides of a triangle was less than the third side? The parallel assertion may be made respecting infinite goodness. What belongs to it as infinite I do not pretend to know; but I know that infinite goodness must be goodness, and that what is not consistent with goodness, is not consistent with infinite goodness.
>
> If in ascribing goodness to God I do not mean what I mean by goodness; if I do not mean the goodness of which I have some knowledge, but an incomprehensible attribute of an incomprehensible substance, which for aught I know may be a totally different quality from that which I love and venerate . . . what do I mean by calling it goodness? and what reason have I for venerating it? If I know nothing about what the attribute is, I cannot tell that it is a proper object of veneration. To say that God's goodness may be different in kind from man's goodness, what is it but saying, with a slight change of phraseology, that God may possibly not be good? To assert in words what we do not think in meaning, is as suitable a definition as can be given of a moral falsehood.[16]

The power of the deity, by contrast, is always interpreted in a completely human way.

[15]John Stuart Mill, *An Examination of Sir William Hamilton's Philosophy* (London: Longmans Green, 1865), p. 131.

[16]Ibid., p. 101.

It is never thought to mean that we could not be killed or punished, in spite of the fact that the power of the deity is conceived of as far greater than ours. Greater power means more of the same thing that we call "power." Does not the same remark apply to "good"? But divine goodness is often spoken of, unlike divine power, as incomprehensible, perhaps because so many of its manifestations conflict so strongly with anything we would ever call goodness.

7. *Human freedom as the cause of evil.* "The evil in the universe is caused by human wickedness. Human beings are free, which means free to do evil as well as good. Even an omnipotent being could not make human beings free and yet not free to do evil. Evil is thus an inevitable consequence of humankind's freedom."

This is probably the most often cited attempt to get round the problem of evil. There is a distinction, however, between *natural* and *moral* evils. Natural evils are those that occur in the course of nature without human intervention: earthquakes, volcanic eruptions, floods, hurricanes, plagues, and so on. These catastrophes are not caused by human activity. Moral evils, however, are those inflicted by people upon other people, such as mental and physical torture, plunder, killing, and war. The latter is the only class of evils that could be said to be the result of human freedom. Even if the argument is a valid one with regard to moral evils, it does not explain the existence of the natural evils.

But let us now concentrate on the moral evils:

A: Human beings, you will surely agree, are created free beings, which means that they are free to choose good or evil. Their often choosing evil, then, is the result of their freedom. There is no way for persons to be free except by having choices open to them, and the moment choices are open a person may choose the worse instead of the better alternative. From this fact very great evils may indeed follow: one person in a position of power may order millions of other people to be killed in concentration camps. But all this is a part of human freedom; once you grant that human beings are free, you must go along with it *all the way.* If they are free, they are free, free to perpetrate the most extreme miseries upon other human beings.

B: But if this is so, is their freedom worth such a price? If one person's freedom involves the power to have millions of other people exterminated, I'm quite sure the victims would wish the freedom of the dictator to be somewhat more limited. In order that *he* may have his freedom, *they* must be massacred. Isn't that putting rather too high a premium on *his* freedom, since his freedom requires that they give up not only their freedom but their lives? Is it any comfort to them, as the gas in the chamber is turned on, to reflect that this is the price they are paying for the dictator's freedom of decision? Could not that freedom be possible at a lesser price?

A: No, it couldn't. If people are free, they are free to commit evils. Otherwise freedom is a delusion.

B: But there are many things that human beings are not free to do now, such as fly like a bird or digest sticks and stones. I don't see why a few further limitations would not be beneficial. For instance, people might have a protective shell so that they would be immune to attack by other people, thus making murder impossible. People would still be free to make countless decisions, and they would still have many choices open to them, but at least they would not be free to take away the lives (and with them the freedom) of *other* people. There would still be many choices available that did not carry in their train the destruction of other free agents. One of the greatest areas in which people can exercise their choice is in scientific or artistic creativity. There would be a large area of free choices here, without choices going so far as to involve murder. I would think that that would be a much better basis for the exercise of choice than we have now, for as things are now one person's choice may involve another person's destruction. And I would remind you that if God could *not* devise a system without evil in which human beings are free, then God is not omnipotent.

A: I dispute this. God's omnipotence does not imply that God can do what is logically impossible. God could not make a square circle, for example, because if it is a circle it isn't square. Nor could God make what *has* happened *not* have happened; the past is what has occurred, and no one, even God, could make what has occurred not have occurred. Omnipotence is the ability to do anything that is logically possible, such as suspend laws of nature.

B: I agree that saying God is omnipotent doesn't mean that God can do what is logically impossible. But what's logically impossible about creating human beings so as to give them choices, and yet limit those choices in some ways—as they already are in other ways? If people can't fly like birds, why should they be able to (for example) kill and maim other people so easily? There are certainly plenty of other ways in which free choice could be exercised besides taking away life (and with it the possibility for any free choices in the future) from other human

beings. There's surely nothing self-contradictory about *that*.

A: The logically possible choices are limited:

> A creator who is going to create humanly free agents and place them in a universe has a choice of the kind of universe to create. First, he can create a finished universe in which nothing needs improving. Humanly free agents know what is right, and pursue it; and they achieve their purposes without hindrance. Second, he can create a basically evil universe, in which everything needs improving, and nothing can be improved. Or, third, he can crate a basically good but half-finished universe—one in which many things need improving, humanly free agents do not altogether know what is right, and their purposes are often frustrated; but one in which agents can come to know what is right and can overcome the obstacles to the achievement of their purposes.[17]

I suggest that God chose the third alternative, because only in such a universe could there be beings who through their decisions and actions can form their own character and be responsible for their own actions. It is *logically* impossible for God to *impose* a character on the beings he creates, and at the same time leave them *free* to develop their own characters by their own choices. Imposing a character on them would take away the creatures' power to develop their own. It's either-or; you can't have their actions guaranteed good because God created them so, and at the same time have them free to choose between good and bad alternatives. Their ability to act freely is *logically* incompatible with their characters being "set in advance" by God. The logical impossibility here is just as gen-

---

[17]Richard Swinburne, "The Problem of Evil," in Stuart C. Brown, ed., *Reason and Religion* (Ithaca: Cornell University Press, 1977), pp. 81–102.

uine as the impossibility of changing the past.

B: By the command of Stalin in the 1930s, 7 million people in the Ukraine were systematically starved to death, and thus deprived forever of *their* freedom. Is Stalin's freedom to perpetrate such acts so precious as to be worth the destruction of the freedom of his 7 million victims? You are certainly placing a higher value on *his* freedom than on *theirs*. And you are saying seriously that without this freedom people would not be free agents but only programmed automata?

A: Yes. To the extent that a creator predetermines a person's character, to that extent the person is not free to develop it himself or herself. You can't have it both ways. When it comes to moral decisions, a person must be free all the way—even free as Stalin was to condemn millions of people to death. That's a part of human freedom; you can't have moral freedom and not include the possibility of choosing evil, even a monstrous evil like this one.

B: Then I don't think the freedom you describe is worth it. Nor would I choose to create a universe in which such incalculable suffering could be inflicted by some persons upon others. If I did knowingly create such a world, I would be a cruel tyrant. I would refrain from world-making if the only kind of world I could make would be a world like *that*. If I couldn't control the causal laws of my world (although as an omnipotent being, I could), I would at least perform a few miracles and have Stalin die of a heart attack before he could do these things—or better still, never let him be born.

A: You *say* that human freedom wouldn't be worth it. But the things you condemn are inextricably connected with the ones you applaud. It is only if there are prob-

lems that they can be solved, only if there is conflict and difficulty can there be triumph over them, only if there is risk can risk be surmounted, and only if there is danger of defeat can there be victory.

Suppose, contrary to fact, that this world were a paradise from which all possibility of pain and suffering were excluded. The consequences would be very far-reaching. For example, no one could ever injure anyone else: the murderer's knife would turn to paper or his bullets to thin air; the bank safe, robbed of a million dollars, would miraculously become filled with another million dollars (without this device, on however large a scale, proving inflationary); fraud, deceit, conspiracy, and treason would somehow always leave the fabric of society undamaged. Again, no one would ever be injured by accident: the mountain-climber, steeplejack, or playing child falling from a height would float unharmed to the ground; the reckless driver would never meet with disaster. There would be no need to work, since no harm could result from avoiding work; there would be no call to be concerned for others in time of need or danger, for in such a world there could be no real needs or dangers.

. . . [In] such a world . . . our present ethical concepts would have no meaning. . . . If, for example, the notion of harming someone is an essential element in the concept of a wrong action, in our hedonistic paradise there could be no wrong actions—nor any right actions in distinction from wrong. Courage and fortitude would have no point in an environment in which there is, by definition, no danger or difficulty. Generosity, kindness, the *agape* aspect of love, prudence, unselfishness, and all other ethical notions which presuppose life in a stable environment, could not even be formed. Consequently, such a world, however well it might promote pleasure, would be very ill adapted for the development of the moral qualities of human personality. In relation to this purpose it would be the worst of all possible worlds.[18]

[18]John Hick, *Philosophy of Religion* (Englewood Cliffs, NJ: Prentice Hall, 1962), pp. 44–45.

B: An omnipotent God could still create human beings in such a way as to have them develop moral qualities without massacring one another. It's true that the moral qualities are very valuable, the world being what it is *now:* courage is valuable when one goes to war, but wouldn't a world without war be better? And couldn't human virtues still be exercised in other ways, for example, in the self-discipline required to complete some worthwhile creative activity? Besides, we have already seen (pages 224–225) that the world is not a very efficient training ground of moral virtues—that if *that* is God's purpose, the purpose is as much frustrated as if it were to make people happy. Many of the things we call virtues now are so only because of the evil of the world we live in, and I would gladly do without them if the world were ever so much better—then we wouldn't need them. Those virtues that are contingent upon having an evil world we could well do without if the world were no longer evil.

Besides, the *distribution* of these evils is far from what justice would demand. If the moral evils of the world are a punishment for humanity's wickedness, what of the innocent victims? The aggressors sometimes get away with what they do, but the victims never. For what is a child being punished when she is left alone in a room and burns to death on a hot stove, or when she is stricken with poliomyelitis or spinal meningitis? For what is a whole people being punished when their country is invaded by a powerful foreign army and thousands of their citizens die to repel the invader? Is *this* your idea of a justly governed universe?

A: You can't know whether it's unjust until you see the whole scheme of things— and that includes the hereafter, in which all injustices are rectified.

B: The fact that there are injustices in this world doesn't prove, of course, that another world exists to correct them—any more than the fact that people are hungry proves that they will always have food. But let's grant a hereafter; how can that possibly cancel out the evils of the present? A person slowly wastes to death of a debilitating and painful bone disease; does a happy hereafter really "make it up" to this person? In one of Dostoyevsky's many examples of the evil inflicted on human beings by one another, he considers a sadistic army officer who has a child torn to pieces by wolves. Maybe the officer will suffer in hell. But what good does hell do, since the child has already been tortured? That evil *has* occurred, and even omnipotence cannot make what has happened *not* have happened. Nothing that could ever happen in the future would be just recompense for this act. It remains a stain, a blot, on the history of the world, a blot that *nothing* can remove not even eternal punishment for the person who committed the deed. The world is put together in such a way that this thing not only could have happened but *did* happen. Nothing that ever *will* happen can make it otherwise.

The "freedom argument" remains the most persistent attempt to circumvent the problem of evil. Whether it is successful will depend largely on how much value is attributed to the faculty of human choice over the range of choices that human beings now have.

Alternative Design Arguments

Meanwhile, there are other versions of the teleological argument that do circumvent the problem of evil.

1. *An omnipotent being who is malevolent.* This view has not been as popular as the belief in a benevolent being, perhaps because one's desire for justice to be done in an afterlife is not fulfilled by belief in a malevolent being. Such a being would be like a powerful but tyrannical dictator, different only in that he is all-powerful and one would be completely and forever in his clutches. Many critics of Christian fundamentalism have believed that the Christian God is something like this in that he has devised hell—a place of never-ending torment for nonbelievers. Even the most hardened prisoner in an earthly jail may be released or paroled, but not so with the God who punishes his creatures forever without any hope of reformation, pardon, or parole. Such punishment would seem to be utterly pointless, since it could never lead to any good result, and, one might wonder, what crime could possibly deserve *endless* punishment?

Imagine a Satan who is omnipotent, and then the prevalence of evil in the world would be no surprise: it would be just as Satan designed it. Support for this devil-hypothesis would be found in the very facts that were difficulties for the view that God is both benevolent and omnipotent: the prevalence of human misery and suffering, the fact that living things can survive only by killing and eating other living things, and so on. If thousands of people slowly suffer and die, caught between underground rocks after an earthquake, this is just the sort of thing a malevolent being would delight in. What is a problem for traditional theology is "par for the course" in the devil hypothesis.

2. *A benevolent but not omnipotent designer.* There might be a cosmic designer who was benevolent but limited in power, like human beings only less so. On this view, there is no problem of evil; there is evil because God is limited in power and cannot help the evil that there is—he has to work with material over which he lacks complete control. It has

sometimes been suggested that God is merely a fellow worker with human beings in the attempt to minimize the evil in the universe. This view not only encounters no problem of evil but also has inspired many persons to work for the elimination of evil, since it is now partly up to them; their efforts can make a difference.

Yet the view has not been very popular, perhaps because people want a God who can present them with certain guarantees—for example that if they deserve their reward he will be able to deliver it and that there will be no hitches in his plan. They want security more than incentive. (One problem for this view: if there is but one God, who or what could limit his power? Whence would come the competition?)

3. *Ditheism.* Since ancient times it has sometimes been suggested that there are two cosmic intelligences, each planning and executing his plans in the world, but whose plans work at cross-purposes. Obviously neither is omnipotent (if one were, the other would not be God), but one is benevolent and the other not. The ancient Zoroastrians and Manicheans argued that the world is a battleground for conflicting deities, not the work of a single designer; that is why some things in the world really are good and others really are bad (they do not merely appear to be so). Nor is there any problem of evil; the evil is easily explained by the existence of the evil deity. In the Manichean view, the physical universe was designed by the good god and human beings were designed by the bad one—a doctrine perhaps better in accord with observable facts than any other we have encountered.

Sometimes, in Christian theology, it is as if there were two gods, Jehovah and Satan. But Christianity is not ditheistic, since one of the two is all-powerful. The conflict between them is a sham battle, since Jehovah created Satan in the first place, and could destroy him any time if he so desired (which raises the question why this has not happened). In a genuine religious ditheism, both deities must be limited in power, and the outcome of the struggle genuinely in doubt.

4. *Polytheism.* If two, why not more than two? Why not revive the polytheism of the Greeks, who believed in many gods, each with its separate sphere of influence, and each interacting with the rest? To be sure, Zeus was the kingpin; but he was by no means omnipotent, for his best-laid plans could be thwarted by other gods, and particularly by his wife Hera. Since the laws of nature operate uniformly and impartially, there must be a certain degree of cooperation among the gods, or perhaps Zeus reigns supreme in one department; but there is still much room for diverse influences, even for gods working at cross-purposes. Why, indeed, should there be only *one* cosmic planner? In the cases of design known to human beings, a plan usually was devised in a rather crude form by one person, then certain rough edges were removed by someone else, and further improvements made by a third, and so on through many generations, as in the case of shipbuilding:

> If we survey a ship, what an exalted idea must we form of the ingenuity of the carpenter, who framed so complicated, useful, and beautiful a machine? And what surprise must we feel, when we find him a stupid mechanic, who imitated others, and copied an art, which, through a long succession of ages, after multiplied trials, mistakes, corrections, deliberations, and controversies, had been gradually improving? Many worlds might have been botched and bungled, throughout an eternity, ere this system was struck out; much labor lost; many fruitless trials made; and a slow, but continued improvement carried on during infinite ages in the art of world-making.[19]

And, one might add, even at the present moment the art of world-making has been far from perfected; perhaps if the cosmic world designers pooled their efforts and got at the job more conscientiously, a world might be brought about that is a considerable improvement over the present one.

5. *A cosmic organism.* Thus far we have considered only teleology in the form of design, or plan, in the mind of a designer. A being possessing a mind plans and carries out his plan; this is the most familiar type of teleology known to us, since it goes on in ourselves; we design something, and it comes into existence as a result of our plan. But organisms also exhibit teleological behavior. The sunflower deepens its roots in the life-giving soil and turns its face to the sun, thereby making its continued existence possible. True, the sunflower does not consciously do this *in order* to preserve its existence, but its behavior is teleological nonetheless (see pages 115–117): it acts in such-and-such a way, thereby making it possible for a condition (such as survival) to occur that would not have occurred without this activity. Instead of saying, then, that the universe is the result of a plan in a mind, why not say instead that the universe is the result of purposive activity on the part of a huge cosmic organism?

> In like manner as a tree sheds its seed into the neighboring fields, and produces other trees; so the great vegetable, the world, or this planetary system, produces within itself certain seeds, which, being scattered into the surrounding chaos, vegetate into new worlds.[20]

Or why not consider the ancient Brahmin hypothesis

> that the world arose from an infinite spider, who spun this whole complicated mass from his bowels, and annihilates afterwards the whole or any part of it, by absorbing it again, and resolving it into his own essence. Here is a

---

[19]Hume, *Dialogues Concerning Natural Religion*, Part 5.

[20]Ibid., Part 7.

species of cosmogony, which appears to us ridiculous; because a spider is a little contemptible animal, whose operations we are never likely to take for a model of the whole universe. But . . . were there a planet wholly inhabited by spiders (which is very possible), this inference would there appear as natural and irrefragable as that which in our planet ascribes the origin of all things to design and intelligence. . . . Why an orderly system may not be spun from the belly as well as from the brain, it will be difficult . . . to give a satisfactory reason.[21]

"But this is ridiculous!" we may exclaim. Aren't these hypotheses absurd? Are they *all* wildly improbable? Must we admit them all as possibilities, and a thousand others like them? "What wild, arbitrary suppositions are these? What *data* have you for such extraordinary conclusions? And is the slight, imaginary resemblance of the world to a vegetable or animal sufficient to establish the same inference with regard to both?"[22] But this, says Hume, is just the point. They *are* all wildly improbable; there is no justification for believing any of the versions of the teleological argument:

We have no *data* to establish any system of cosmogony. Our experience, so imperfect in itself, and so limited both in extent and duration, can afford us no probable conjecture concerning the whole of things. But if we must needs fix on some hypothesis, by what rule, pray, ought we to determine our choice? Is there any other rule than the greater similarity of the objects compared? And does not a plant or an animal, which springs from vegetation or generation, bear a stronger resemblance to the world, than does any artificial machine, which arises from reason and design?[23]

Argument from analogy. All the arguments in this group are arguments from analogy. An analogy is simply a comparison, and an argument from analogy is an argument from

[21]Ibid.
[22]Ibid.
[23]Ibid.

comparison. We begin with a comparison between two things, X and Y, which are alike in certain respects, A, B, and C, and conclude that they are also alike in another respect, D, in which they have not been observed to resemble one another. For example, a person (X) and a dog (Y) are alike in numerous respects; they have hearts that pump blood, they consume and digest food, and so on (A, B, and C). Therefore, it is concluded, since a person has a liver (D), the dog will also have a liver. (Assume that the argument is presented before it has been discovered through dissection of dogs whether they have livers.) Since the human being and the dog are alike in numerous respects, the argument runs, it is likely that they will resemble one another in the other respect in which no such similarity has yet been discovered.

Arguments from analogy, of course, are never conclusive. That two things are alike in numerous respects never shows that they will also be alike in other respects. They may be, but even if they are, the argument from analogy does not prove it; only an investigation of the two things will enable us to discover whether they are alike in the new respect. If the two things are very similar in a large number of respects, it may be more likely that they are similar in the new respect; since lions and leopards are very similar in most respects, a characteristic of lions is quite likely to be true also of leopards—but not all characteristics; if all of them were the same, lions would be indistinguishable from leopards. Even in cases where the two things are very similar, the argument from analogy is still inconclusive.

The teleological argument in its various forms has usually been presented as an argument from analogy. Thus, there is a watch and a human eye. They have the same characteristics in common—for example, the same apparent adaptation of means to ends. If we came across a watch without knowing what it was for, we would conclude that it had been designed by someone, for every part is linked to every other part in such a way as to fulfill one function, that of keeping time. Similarly, in the human eye there is the same complex interconnection of parts, all serving one function, that of seeing. Since the watch is the result of design, we infer that the eye is also the result of design:

> There is precisely the same proof that the eye was made for vision, as there is that the telescope was made for assisting it. They are made upon the same principles; both being adjusted to the laws by which the transmission and reflection of rays of light are regulated. . . . These laws require, in order to produce the same effect, that the rays of light, in passing from water into the eye, should be refracted by a more convex surface than when it passes out of air into the eye. Accordingly we find that the eye of a fish, in that part of it called the crystalline lens, is much rounder than the eye of terrestrial animals. What plainer manifestation of design can there be than this difference?[24]

The analogy between the eye and a manufactured object like a watch or telescope is fairly obvious. In both cases there is a complex structure that fulfills a function. (We must say "function" and not "purpose," for to say that the eye fulfills a purpose would assume the point at issue; opponents of the teleological argument would say that the eye, while it fulfills a function, seeing, was not the result of design, and hence not of a designer's purpose.) But in the case of the eye, as well as of organisms in general, no designing activity has ever been observed, whereas in the case of manufactured objects it has; and in addition, there is considerable other evidence that the eye, along with the entire organism of which it is a part, is the result of a slow and gradual process of evolution. Moreover, eyes are often defective.

To discover that certain forms and formations are adjusted for certain action has nothing to do with design. None of these developments are perfect, or anywhere near so. All of them, including the eye, are botchwork that any good mechanic would be ashamed to make. All of them need constant readjustment, are always out of order, and are entirely too complicated for dependable work. They are not made for any purpose; they simply grew out of needs and adaptations; in other words, they happened.[25]

What people do with the teleological argument depends largely on which features of the world they start with. If we start with ships instead of watches, we get the hypothesis that the universe was the result of many centuries of accumulated experience in world-making. If we start with desert wastes, we get the hypothesis that besides being sloppy and inefficient, the designer did not have human well-being in mind. The universe contains so many things, each with so many different properties, that there is virtually no argument from analogy that we cannot construct, depending on which features we select at the outset. That is why Hume concluded that argument from analogy provides no basis for *any* conclusions concerning a designer, or for that matter multiple designers, "cosmic organisms," or (in Hume's words) "any system of cosmogony."

6. ANTHROPOMORPHISM AND MYSTICISM

Anthropomorphism

Most people, when they think of God or gods, conceive of him (or them) in a highly anthropomorphic manner: they "conceive of

[24]Bishop William Paley, *Evidence of the Existence and Attributes of the Deity* (1802), quoted in Paul Edwards and Arthur Pap, eds., *A Modern Introduction to Philosophy*, p. 412.

[25]Clarence Darrow, "The Delusion of Design and Purpose," in Darrow, *The Story of My Life* (New York: Charles Scribner's Sons, 1932), p. 413.

God in the form of man" (*anthropos,* man, and *morphe,* form). People say that God is wise, benevolent, powerful; that he commands, hears our prayers, desires our welfare, forgives our trespasses. And when primitive people thought of God or gods, they thought of a "bigger and better" human being out there somewhere in the sky or on a mountaintop, watching us, issuing commands, rewarding those who obeyed. Such gods were physical organisms, presumably having sense organs not entirely unlike ours. Having fashioned Eve out of Adam's rib, God met with Adam and Eve in the cool of the evening.

Virtually all religions, for example, refer to God as "he"; do they really believe that God is of the male sex—perhaps a saintly old man in flowing white robes wielding a scepter? If one says that God is not literally male, is one then to refer to God as "she"? But that would be to describe God as belonging to the female sex. (Perhaps calling God "he" is a relic of the days when the man was the undisputed head of the household.) The word "it" is impersonal—referring usually to inanimate objects—and seems to fit no better than the other two, because God is still conceived of as a person with a personalty (benevolent or vengeful, forgiving or unforgiving, and so on). Yet "he," "she," and "it" are the only singular personal pronouns we have.

As religions became less anthropomorphic, they ceased to think of God as a physical organism occupying physical space; instead, God was a mind, a personality, with human qualities like love and wisdom. There are problems, as we have seen, of conceiving of a mind without a body; but let us ignore these for the moment and see what features a mind must have. A person thinks of A at time t-1 and of B at time t-2; a person deliberates, chooses, acts, sometimes changes his mind, and regrets previous decisions. To think of God as a mind places God directly in the time stream. God does this and then does that. To attribute these human characteristics to God is still anthropomorphic, although there is an attempt to do without any crude physical anthropomorphism. Yet to say that God does things like create or design worlds, hear and answer prayers, and reward some persons and punish others, is still anthropomorphic. It is incompatible with saying, as some do, that God is nontemporal, not existing in time but *timeless,* having no history at all, like the number 2 (one cannot meaningfully say, for example, that the number 2 was a year old yesterday). A mind might be everlasting but not timeless; to have a mind involves doing things like thinking, willing, feeling, deliberating—all of which are processes that take place in time. (The word "eternal" is ambiguous: it can mean *timeless*—having no history—or *everlasting*—existing throughout all time.)

> A mind, whose acts and sentiments and ideas are not distinct and successive; one, that is wholly simple, and totally immutable; is a mind which has no thought, no reason, no will, no sentiment, no love, no hatred; or in a word, is no mind at all. It is an abuse of terms to give it that appellation.[26]

But if we speak of a mind *without* thoughts, feelings, volitions, and other events in its history, and yet call it a mind, is this not to take away with one hand what we give with the other? It doesn't help to say that it is still a mind, but a mind of a very different kind from ours, such that we cannot really conceive of it; for if we cannot conceive of it, what entitles us to call it a mind at all? What entitles us to say that it is a *mind* rather than something else? It is much as if we were told that there exists a very special and unusual kind of book that has no pages, no cover, no print—in fact, it is a red liquid. But whatever

---

[26]Hume, *Dialogues Concerning Natural Religion,* Part 4.

it is, this is not what we mean by "book" when we use the word; it cannot be a book, since it lacks the defining characteristics of books. Just as surely, it would seem does "timeless mind" lack a basic defining characteristic of mind.

Moreover, many of the traits people attribute to God are inconsistent with other traits they attribute to him. God desires—but how can a being who has everything desire anything? God changes his mind—he "repented himself" that he had made human beings. "God created the world to glorify his name"—which, Mill said, is to attribute to God "one of the lowest of human attributes, a restless appetite for applause." As we have seen, if God is omnipotent he need not adopt means to achieve ends; he can achieve the ends directly and therefore need never do one thing in order to achieve another (such as tolerating evil in order to promote good). To say such things about God is almost as crudely anthropomorphic as to say that God is a physical organism having bodily organs.

Nonliteral use of terms. But perhaps when we call God benevolent, wise, and so on, these terms should not be taken literally; perhaps we should not mean them, in describing God, in the same sense in which we mean them when we refer to human beings. Perhaps when we say God is just we should not mean justice in any literal sense; perhaps we should use such terms only in a figurative sense. When people speak of God as powerful, however, they always seem to mean power in its most literal sense, the power to save or destroy, the power of life and death.

We constantly use words in figurative senses. As we saw in Chapter 1, when we call a man a weasel, we do not imply that he has four legs and fur, but that he has some characteristics of a weasel—at any rate, characteristics popularly (although often falsely) attributed to weasels—such as deceitfulness.

The popular definition of an assistant dean, "A mouse training to be a rat," doesn't purport to be a biological description. We may call a person on various occasions a lion, a bear, a snake, an insect, a walrus, a toad. But in calling a person any of these names, we have certain descriptive characteristics in mind which we could name if asked. "What do you mean by calling him a snake?"—and we could easily answer such a question. The figurative term is simply a quick, shorthand way of referring to a group or collection of familiar characteristics. We can easily translate these figurative expressions into literal ones. But what happens in cases where we can't do this?

> Suppose I am told of a new theological discovery, namely that Brahma wears a hat. And then I am told that it is a divine hat and worn infinitely, since Brahma has neither head nor shape. In what sense then is a hat being worn? Why use *these* words? I am told that God exists but in a "different sense" of "exists." Then if he doesn't exist (in the plain sense) why use *that* word? Or that God loves us—but in a wholly special sense of "love." Or God is a circle whose center is everywhere and circumference nowhere. But this is then to have neither a center nor a circumference, and hence not to be a circle. One half of the description cancels out the other half. And what is left over but just noise?[27]

Some theists have suggested other avenues, however. One is that of "symbolic truth." The truth about God, it is said, if far beyond any human powers of description, and words we use function not as descriptions but as *symbols* of a truth that is beyond our reach. Suppose someone says, "God is a hot fire," not meaning thereby that God is characterized by a high temperature; the

---

[27]Arthur C. Danto, "Faith, Language, and Religious Experience," in Sidney Hook, ed., *Religious Experience and Truth* (New York: New York University Press, 1962), p. 137.

phrase "hot fire" is only a symbol for a quite different property that we cannot express in words.

There are problems, however. If the true property is unknown, how do we know that the words we use as a symbol correctly expresses it? Why is one word or phrase used rather than another one? Why is "God is a hot fire" preferable to "God is a cold sweat"? If it is, isn't this because *some* resemblance is believed to exist between the properties of God and the properties of fire? Why else would the one phrase be more apt than the other?

Still another gambit consists of saying that words do apply literally to God, but with an enormous difference in *degree*. The dog loves its master; the person loves God; God loves all human beings. The love that a dog can experience, while genuine, is only a pale shadow of the love that human beings can experience, yet there is enough similarity between the two so that the word "love" can be used in preference to other words. Similarly, God's love, although so great as to be incomprehensible to us, is still more aptly called love than anything else—we somehow "get closer to it" by calling it that than by using any other term for it. As a dog's love is to a person's, so a person's love is to God's. But in attributing love to God we are only hinting at something we cannot fully conceive and cannot adequately express in words.

Mysticism

A: I see that anything I might say about God is going to be subject to your criticisms. I suggest that the way out is *mysticism*. According to mysticism, there are no words we can use that accurately describe God. God is beyond any concept we have or can devise. It won't do to say that God is powerful or omnipotent or even loving

or merciful, because God's nature transcends all such distinctions: when you say that God is A (whatever quality you please), you limit God by saying that God is not also not-A. This applies even to the most complimentary things we might say; God transcends those too.

B: So then what *do* you say about God?

A: Nothing at all. No words are adequate. As Wittgenstein said, "Whereof thou canst not speak, thereof thou must be silent."[28]

B: But you're not entirely silent. You still say it's God you are experiencing. If you can't describe God, what makes you say it's God you are experiencing and not something else?

A: Yes, even calling the object of my experience God is already to conceptualize: to say it's not both God and not-God, and therefore not to transcend *that* distinction.

B: And how do you get around that problem?

A: I don't. God is beyond all description, but I do want to say that it's God and not something that's not-God.

B: You have to say that much in order to tell me what it is you believe you are experiencing. But how do you know that it's God you're experiencing and not something else?

A: What can I say? I can't give you any objective criteria. I can only try to make you meditate in a certain way, and prepare the ground for you to have the experience for yourself.

B: And suppose you did that; what would it prove?

A: There are experiences one can have only under certain special conditions—not the conditions of normal living, which

[28]Ludwig Wittgenstein, *Tractatus Logico-Philosophicus* (London: Routledge and Kegan Paul, 1922).

involve planning for the day and eating and driving to work. Under certain conditions, immersed in meditation, I have the experience that I call being one with God. I have to be in a special frame of mind to have that experience.

B: That's true of many experiences. But that doesn't show that anything exists beyond the experiences. When a person is depressed, she has a certain feeling, but there's no depression-out-there that the experience is *about*.

A: Yet mystics can share their experiences with one another. Each can know that another is having similar experiences, even though they can't describe them.

B: How then can they know that the experiences are similar?

A: Suppose we found various persons, scattered in different places around the world and at different times in history, all uttering the same words when they were in a state of meditation—let's say the words are "square circle," which is nonsense to us. But when they utter these words to each other, their eyes light up as if someone else is understanding them for the first time. What they say seems gibberish to us—we are outsiders. We aren't on their wavelength. We don't know what they are experiencing, but we can see that they do share the experiences and seem to understand one another. What would you say? If it happened regularly you couldn't put it down to "just coincidence." Surely you would conclude something.

B: I would conclude, yes, that they were all having similar experiences. But I wouldn't know what the experiences were *of*, or even if they were of anything at all. Perhaps, like depression, they signify nothing beyond themselves.

A: And perhaps they do—but you will never know it.

Religious Hypotheses

The mystical experience establishes no divine source of experience. But perhaps nothing that we can discover can establish it, or even give any hint of it, one way or the other. Is that not a possibility?

If gods were conceived as human beings, only bigger and better, then we should be able under certain circumstances to perceive them, and their existence would be an ordinary empirical hypothesis like the view that there are insects under that rock. If the Greek gods lived on Mount Olympus, one would only have to scour Mount Olympus for a long period of time to conclude that Zeus, Hera, Poseidon, and the rest do not reside there or anywhere else in or around Greece. But of course we no longer believe in gods with physical bodies. Many people do believe, however, that God has (or is) a mind—thinking, willing, deciding, blessing—but a mind without a body. In that case, however, God's existence cannot be detected by means of the senses, or for that matter by instruments such as x-rays, microscopes, and radar.

But aren't there many entities that scientists believe in which cannot be detected by the senses or even by instruments? Quarks and leptons can't be seen, touched, or even seen in microscopes; they are, as we say "known by their effects." You can't see them, but their existence does make a difference. The entities themselves may be entirely inferences from experience, but scientists believe they are entitled to make the inferences, citing certain observable phenomena that, they say, would not have occurred unless the existence of these entities is assumed. Similarly, we "know God through his effects" in the world. We can't see God but we are entitled to infer God's existence from what we do observe in the world—just as with electrons. The teleological argument, for example, starts out with citing certain observable things and processes in the universe, and concludes that these are the effects of God's creative endeavor. Now perhaps the teleologist's inference is unwarranted—perhaps we can account for what we see without invoking a designer. A bad scientific theory is still a theory within the domain of science—like the once-respected theories regarding ether or phlogiston. But scientists don't consider the existence of God a scientific theory at all—neither a good theory nor a bad one, but something not even within the domain of science. Why the difference?

One might say that this is because, with the God hypothesis, you can always reinterpret the evidence to get the conclusions you want. You can always posit some characteristic of God to reconcile his existence with the events you see occurring in the physical world. Ten thousand people are killed in an earthquake, yet God is perfectly benevolent and omnipotent; how can this be? Well, he has a plan greater than anything we can discern; or, his goodness is different from ours; or, these deaths are means toward some greater end. And thus we try to reconcile whatever facts there are—however unfavorable to our theory—with the view of God we want to preserve. We claim to go by the facts wherever they may lead, but in fact we tend to interpret the facts in such a way as to reconcile them with the theory we want to hold. In science, it is said, we can't do this; we have to respect the observable facts regardless of whether they may spoil our favorite theory.

But "saving a theory at all costs" is something that is familiar in science also; witness the lengths scientists were wiling to go to in order to preserve the principle of no action at a distance or the conservation of matter. In the end, of course, the theories had to go; but one could go a long way in preserving them as long as one was willing to pay the price of abandoning other theories.

But let's suppose that this defect is corrected. Suppose we take our stand (for example) in favor of an omnipotent and benevolent designer, and if the evidence goes against us we abandon the hypothesis; we don't try to think of ways to circumvent it. If X happens, our hypothesis is confirmed; if Y happens, it is disconfirmed; and if Y (for example, the facts brought forth when discussing the problem of evil) is what occurs, then we abandon the omnipotent-benevolent designer hypothesis. If we did this, would the teleological argument then be a scientific hypothesis?

Even so, the answer appears to be no. A scientific theory is accepted only if it can be made to "fit in" (be coherent) with the huge interlocking network of laws and theories that constitute science. It must have explanatory power (the more the better). And from this explanatory power must arise some ability to predict future occurrences on the basis of the theory. But the God hypothesis is not connected with any body of laws and theories; it stands quite apart from them, apparently unrelated to any part of the network. Nor does it have any predictive power; no matter what happens, one can always say God willed it or it was a part of God's plan. If a thousand people die, then that was part of his plan; but if they do not, then it was part of his plan to keep them alive. We can predict nothing but can only say "after the fact" what the plan was. Such assertions of course are scientifically quite useless.

"But that doesn't disprove God's existence. There may indeed be a God who has the power to create or design the universe, and whose plan we cannot fathom, and therefore cannot predict what He will do. We might believe there is one God who created and also sustains the universe (theism), or one who, having created it, leaves it alone (deism). Maybe we aren't in a position to know which is true, but one or the other may *be* true just the same."

The ancient Epicureans believed that there were many gods but that they had nothing to do with human life—they sat in the garden and chatted and drank ambrosia, but they eschewed all contact with human beings, so the fact of their existence made no difference to human experience. If human beings had wished to devise the hypothesis that such beings existed, and then looked to experience for confirmation of the hypothesis, they would have found none, since the gods had left no traces in the world. Still, one could urge, they might exist even though people looked in vain for traces of their existence.

A contemporary philosopher, John Wisdom, has presented a story that could be called "the tale of the invisible gardener":

Two people return to their long neglected garden and find among the weeds a few of the old plants surprisingly vigorous. One says to the other, "It must be that a gardener has been coming and doing something about these plants." Upon inquiry they find that no neighbor has ever seen anyone at work in their garden. The first man says to the other, "He must have worked while people slept." The other says, "No, someone would have heard him and besides, anyone who cared about the plants would have kept down these weeds." The first man says, "Look at the way these are arranged. There is purpose and a feeling for beauty here. I believe that someone comes, someone invisible to mortal eyes. I believe that the more carefully we look the more we shall find confirmation of this." They examine the garden ever so carefully and sometimes they come on new things suggesting that a gardener comes and sometimes they come on new things suggesting the contrary and even that a malicious person has been at work. Besides examining the garden carefully they also study what happens to gardens left without attention. Each learns all the other learns about this and about the garden. Consequently, when after all this, one says, "I still believe a gardener comes," while

the other says, "I don't," their different words reflect no difference as to what they have found in the garden, no difference as to what they would find in the garden if they looked further and no difference about how fast untended gardens fall into disorder. At this stage, in this context, the gardener hypothesis has ceased to be experimental, the difference between one who accepts and one who rejects it is now not a matter of the one expecting something the other does not expect. What is the difference between them? The one says, "A gardener comes unseen and unheard. He is manifested only in his works with which we are all familiar," the other says, "There is no gardener" and with this difference in what they say about the gardener goes a difference in how they feel towards the garden, in spite of the fact that neither expects anything of it which the other does not expect.[29]

There is no difference in what they expect to observe in the garden, no matter how long or how thoroughly they look. But there may be a difference of another sort in what they expect: they may have differing expectations about a life after death:

Two men are traveling together along a road. One of them believes that it leads to the Celestial City, the other that it leads nowhere; but since this is the only road there is, both must travel it. Neither has been this way before; therefore, neither is able to say what they will find around each corner. During their journey they meet with moments of refreshment and delight, and with moments of hardship and danger. All the time one of them thinks of his journey as a pilgrimage to the Celestial City. He interprets the pleasant parts as encouragements and the obstacles as trials of his purpose and lessons in endurance, prepared by the king of that city and designed to make of him a worthy citizen of the place when at last he arrives. The other, however, believes none of

[29]John Wisdom, "Gods," *Proceedings of the Aristotelian Society,* vol. 44, (1944–45); reprinted in Antony Flew, ed., *Logic and Language,* first ser. (Oxford: Blackwell, 1952), pp. 192–193. Also reprinted in John Wisdom, *Philosophy and Psychoanalysis* (Oxford: Blackwell, 1949).

this, and sees their journey as an unavoidable and aimless ramble. Since he has no choice in the matter, he enjoys the good and endures the bad. For him there is no Celestial City to be reached, no all-encompassing purpose ordaining their journey; there is only the road itself and the luck of the road in good weather and in bad.

During the course of the journey, the issue between them is not an experimental one. They do not entertain different expectations about the coming details of the road, but only about its ultimate destination. Yet, when they turn the last corner, it will be apparent that one of them has been right all the time and the other wrong. Thus, although the issue between them has not been experimental, it has, nevertheless, been a real issue. They have not merely felt differently about the road, for one was feeling appropriately and the other inappropriately in relation to the actual state of affairs. Their opposed interpretations of the situation have constituted genuine rival assertions, whose assertion-status has the peculiar characteristic of being guaranteed retrospectively by a future crux. . . . The theist and the atheist do not (or need not) expect different events to occur in the successive details of the temporal process. They do not (or need not) entertain divergent expectations of the course of history as viewed from within. However, the theist does and the atheist does not expect that when history is completed it will be seen to have led to a particular end-state and to have fulfilled a specific purpose, namely, that of creating "children of God."[30]

If the theist is right, we shall not know until we die and live again which of the expectations is correct. All we have to do to discover which expectation is justified is to *wait and see*.

But there is still a problem. God is not the same as immortality, even if it is only God who could guarantee immortality. If we regained consciousness after dying and remembered our life on earth, that would be proof of immortality. Would it also be proof

of God? What *would* be proof of God? Would we *see* God? And what would seeing God be? Seeing someone in white robes? Is God visible at all, or otherwise accessible to the senses? What exactly would we be experiencing if we were experiencing God? What exactly is it that the believer in God is believing in?

The principal challenges to religious belief are: (1) what exactly is the object of the belief?; and (2) how are we to discover whether such an object-of-belief exists? H. L. Mencken asked:

What has become of Sutekh, once high god of the whole Nile Valley? What has become of:

Resheph	Isis	Dagon
Anath	Ptah	Yau
Ashtoreth	Baal	Amon-Re
Nebo	Astarte	Osiris
Melek	Hadad	Molech?
Ahijah		

All these were once gods of the highest eminence. Many of them are mentioned with fear and trembling in the Old Testament. They ranked, five or six thousand years ago, with Yahweh Himself; the worst of them stood far higher than Thor. Yet they have all gone down the chute, and with them the following:

Arianrod	Iuno Lucina
Morrigu	Saturn
Govannon	Furrina
Gunfled	Cronos
Dagda	Engurra
Ogyrvan	Belus
Dea Dia	Ubilulu
U-dimmer-an-kia	Diana of Ephesus
U-sab-sib	Robigus
U-Mersi	Pluto
Tammuz	Vesta
Venus	Zer-panitu
Beltis	Merodach
Nusku	Elum
Aa	Marduk

[30]Hick, *Philosophy of Religion*, pp. 101–102.

Sin	Nin
Apsu	Persephone
Elali	Istar
Mami	Lagas
Zaraqu	Nirig
Zagaga	Nebo
Nuada Argetlam	En-Mersi
Tagd	Assur
Goibniu	Beltu
Odin	Kuski-banda
Ogma	Nin-azu
Marzin	Qarradu
Mars	Ueras

Ask the rector to lend you any good book on comparative religion: you will find them all listed. They were gods of the highest dignity— gods of civilized peoples—worshiped and believed in by millions. All were omnipotent, omniscient and immortal. And all are dead.[31]

The bottom-line question is: how are the live ones to be distinguished from this mass of dead ones?

The Utility of Religion

Does religious belief lead a person to live a better life?

To answer this question one would first have to know what is meant by the phrase "a better life." Does it mean being truthful and reliable, paying one's debts and being careful about incurring them, being caring of friends and strangers alike—and how much else? Does being immoral include only harming others, or something more than that, and if so what?

Once it was agreed what kinds of actions are to count as moral, one would then conduct a sociological survey to determine how these actions are affected by religious belief.

---

[31]H. L. Mencken, "Memorial Service," in Norman Bowie, Meredith Michaels, and Robert Solomon, eds., *Twenty Questions* (Fort Worth, TX: Harcourt Brace, 1992), pp. 80–81.

Do unbelievers engage in more immoral actions than believers do? One would also have to distinguish various religious beliefs: perhaps Christians are better than non-Christians in some kinds of acts, but not as good as orthodox Jews or Muslims, or less good than believers in Norse or Aztec gods.

Even if all this could be settled, what would it show? Not that the belief in question was *true,* and that is what arguments for God's existence are all about. Surely, you should believe *p* because *p* is true. If belief in ghosts made people live better lives, this wouldn't make belief in ghosts true. The *effects* of a belief are a different issue from the *truth* of a belief.

There is another problem as well: can you really believe something, sincerely, because believing it is useful, or ennobling, or has certain other effects? When you believe it, don't you believe it as something that is *true*? When religious belief is taught, must it not be taught as a belief that is *true*? Would the plea "It may not be true, but I want you to believe it anyway" be effective, even on children? Can you sincerely believe what you are not convinced is true?

Once a belief has been shown to be true, whether it is useful, has good influences, and so on is a *separate* question. That many biological innovations can be achieved with recombinant DNA is true, but much argument continues about its effects, even its morality. The question whether religious belief is useful, uplifting, and so on would hardly be likely to take place if there were not already some doubt about whether it was true, or could be shown to be so. As Mill said:

> An argument for the utility of religion is an appeal to unbelievers, to induce them to practice a well-meant hypocrisy, or to semi-believers to make them avert their eyes from what might possibly shake their unstable belief, or finally to persons in general to abstain from expressing any doubts they may feel, since a fabric of

immense importance to mankind is so insecure at its foundations, that men must hold their breath in its neighborhood for fear of blowing it down.[32]

And in our own day, Bertrand Russell has said:

I can respect the men who argue that religion is true and therefore ought to be believed, but I can feel only reprobation for those who say that religion ought to be believed because it is useful, and that to ask whether it is true is a waste of time.[33]

Many persons, indeed, have been much concerned to disengage morality from any dependence on religion. They have felt that it is a dangerous thing for religion and morality to be closely intertwined in the public mind, the survival of morality being made dependent on the survival of religion; for in that case, if the religious belief should ever collapse, the morality that has been made dependent upon it may collapse with it.

Suppose you knew, or had very good reason to believe, that a certain religious belief was false; but suppose that believing it, and having it taught to children from an early age, made people more secure, more moral, more honest in their dealings with others, and that those who didn't have the belief had much less of these desirable qualities. Do you think that those around you should have these beliefs and be taught them at home or in school, perhaps to make your streets safer? This of course is a question in ethics, not in religion. Presumably we want to do what makes the world better; but should we do this even if it involves compromising the truth? And if the truth is repeat-

edly compromised in the interests of social betterment, where might *that* lead?

EXERCISES

1. Would the following events, if they occurred, confirm the existence of the God of Christianity? Why or why not?
 a. If Christians lived on the average twenty five years longer than non-Christians.
 b. If prayers of Christians were usually answered but those of non-Christians were not.
 c. If the accounts written by Matthew, Mark, Luke, and John turned out to have been eyewitness reports rather than writings of a generation or so later.
 d. If children started to quote the Bible as soon as they learned to talk, without having learned any of the statements in the Bible.
 e. If Christians had fewer neuroses and psychoses than non-Christians.
 f. If water were turned into wine at a ceremony in Jerusalem every Easter.
 g. If professing Christians, after their death, disappeared from their coffins and flew upward through the air until they vanished from sight.

2. Evaluate the following assertions:
 a. God was the first event.
 b. God caused the first event.
 c. There was no first event, but God is the explanation of why there was a first event as well as any subsequent events.
 d. God was present before time began.
 e. God created time.
 f. God created time, then the world.
 g. The universe came from God.
 h. First there was a conscious being (God), a mind without a body, who then created matter (including bodies).
 i. God created space before creating the matter that would occupy the space.
 j. Only if one believes in God can one solve the mystery of why anything exists at all.
 k. If you don't believe in a God who created and designed the universe, you must believe that everything that happens and ever has happened is one vast *accident*.

[32]From Mill's essay "The Utility of Religion" in his *Three Essays on Religion*, p. 70.
[33]Bertrand Russell, *Why I Am Not a Christian* (London: George Allen & Unwin, 1957), p. 172.

3. "Since the innocent often suffer and the guilty go unpunished in this life, there must be another life in which these wrongs are righted and each person is judged by an impartial God according to his or her deserts." Evaluate this argument.

4. Describe the kind of universe (if any) that would make each of the following hypotheses probable.
   a. There are two gods (one good, one evil) fighting for control of the world.
   b. There are many gods, each with his own sphere of influence.
   c. Everything in the universe tends toward good.
   d. Everything in the universe tends toward evil.
   e. Everything that appears to be bad in the world will in the end turn out for the best.
   f. Everything that appears to be good in the world will in the end turn out for the worst.
   g. There is one God, both omnipotent and benevolent.
   h. There is one God, omnipotent but not benevolent.
   i. There is one God, benevolent but not omnipotent.

5. Are there any occurrences, or series of occurrences, that, if they were to happen, would lead you to say, "It's a miracle"? If so, describe them and indicate why you would label them miracles.

6. "My sick child recovered, and I take this fact as evidence for a benevolent God." "But my sick child did not recover, so I take this fact as evidence that there is not a benevolent God." Does either alleged fact confirm the hypothesis for which the fact is given as evidence? Justify your answer.

7. "Two hundred years ago the average human life span was only half what it is now. This increase is directly traceable to the advances in medical science. Medical science, not God, is the cause of the greater longevity today." "No, the facts you cite equally con-

firm another hypothesis: that God used medical science (perhaps even implanting ideas in the minds of medical experts) to fulfill his plan, that of lengthening the span of human life." Discuss.

8. We all know what it is to create a poem, or a disturbance, or an idea. But what is it to create out of nothing? Imagine yourself a conscious being, and no material universe exists. You say, "Let there be stars," and suddenly stars come into existence where there were none. How would you know that your uttering these words was what brought the stars into being? (You take the medicine and feel better, but how do you know that taking the medicine is what caused you to feel better?)

9. Which of the following statements could be taken, in your opinion, as literally true? When words or phrases in them cannot be taken literally, try to translate the sentences in which they occur into sentences that can be taken literally. Examine those than can be taken literally for internal consistency.
   a. God is above the stars.
   b. God is above human concerns.
   c. God existed before time began.
   d. "And God said . . . ."
   e. God exists throughout all space and all time.
   f. The earth is God's footstool.
   g. God caused the world.
   h. God is love.
   i. God is truth.

10. Discuss the criteria for the use of the word "exist" with reference to each of the following:
   a. Tables exist.
   b. Headaches exist.
   c. Magnetism exists.
   d. Ghosts exist.
   e. God exists.

11. "God does not really possess the properties we attribute to him (masculine gender, existing in time, having will and intellect and feeling, and so on), but he possesses something *like* each of these things; the words we use to characterize God apply only *analogically*." Evaluate this view.

12. Which of the following would you accept, which would you reject, and why?
  a. There is an elephant in this room, invisible and intangible.
  b. There are radio waves in this room, invisible and intangible.
  c. There are atoms in every bit of matter, invisible and intangible.
  d. There is a God in the world, invisible and intangible.

13. If the following events were to occur, what would they show? Would they establish (or render probable) the existence of a supernatural being?
  a. Someone who is about to kill another human being suddenly dies of a heart attack.
  b. Every adult human being in the world is simultaneously stricken with paralysis in one leg. In time people discover that if they read a few versus from the Gospel of Saint Luke (concerning the miraculous healing of the sick), the paralysis of the person who reads it suddenly and permanently disappears.
  c. You die and then wake up with a different body but all of your memories of earthly life. You see around you a city of gold, a radiant sky, and white creatures with wings flying about. Someone in a long white robe approaches you and says, "You are in heaven now."
  d. Someone appears on earth and says, "God is invisible, but I, who am visible, am God's representative." To show his credentials he changes water into wine and raises people from the dead.

14. Assume that you are creating a world, including human beings, and that you want to minimize or eliminate pain and misery but at the same time want to preserve people's freedom of choice. (1) What laws of nature or human nature would you change? (2) Without changing any laws, to what extent would you permit pain and misery in order to preserve freedom of choice? Consider the following cases:
  a. A man regularly provokes his wife into fits of jealous rage. Her response amuses him. "I like to play with people's minds," he says. "That's my freedom."
  b. A man who has raped and mutilated a girl later repents his deed. "I would never do such a thing again," he says. "But it was the only way I could learn."
  c. By repeatedly distorting the news and suppressing items he dislikes, the head of a news-gathering agency provokes a dangerous international crisis. "We are all free to express our views," he says. "Whatever the cost, freedom is worth it."
  d. Human beings have freedom of choice; no other animal does. In the interests of promoting maximum freedom for human beings, it is accordingly permissible to kill animals for food, for their hides, and for sport, and to use them for purposes of medical experimentation and to satisfy intellectual curiosity. The sacrifice of animals is a small price to pay for enhancing human freedom and increasing the range of human choices.

15. Should the teleological argument be considered a scientific theory? Doesn't it have empirical consequences that can be confirmed or disconfirmed?

16. "Whereof thou canst not speak, thereof thou must be silent" (Ludwig Wittgenstein). Must the mystic, to be consistent, remain completely silent?

17.
A: The religious impulse is as much a part of human nature as is the scientific impulse. As such it is equally worthy of respect.
B: Too bad then that religion doesn't yield the uniform results that science does. The claims of various religions contradict one another.
A: So do the claims of various scientists.
B: Yes, but there is a way of deciding which of the contending parties is right: vacci-

nation works and magical incantation does not.

A: But you assume that the same "scientific method" that yields results in physical science is also appropriate for religion. You are trying to use a method that works well in one area and export it to another area where it doesn't belong.

B: Well, then, describe some other method that does. Give me some alternative method by which we can distinguish the true from the false.

Take the discussion up from here.

18. "Mystics may be in very different (abnormal?) mental conditions when they have their experiences of God. They are on a very different wavelength from the rest of us. And what's wrong with that? Perhaps some truths can be discovered only when those persons are in a very special mental condition that the rest of us aren't in or can't be in, and that's why we don't discover the truths that they do." Comment.

19.

A: If prayers are answered, isn't that evidence for a God who hears and answers prayer?

B: Sometimes people get what they pray for, sometimes they don't. How does that show that they get what they want because they pray for it?

A: But what if they get what they want more often than not?

B: Then I'd say that they've probably asked for things which they would get anyway, prayer or no prayer.

A: Sometimes, but what if you made a point of asking for something you wanted very much . . .

B: Look, God is not your lackey who serves your whims. Is he supposed to change his mind because of what you ask? Do you

really believe you know what should be done better than he does? Come now, this is anthropomorphism in spades!

A: If you ask for material things, then perhaps—but what about courage to face a loss or to face the future? Praying often helps then.

B: Certainly, it may help your own psychological state. In that case, keep on praying.

A: But praying to whom? I realize that believers tend to have fewer heart attacks and strokes (see *Time*, June 27, 1996, pp. 62–64), but how do I make myself into a believer? Do you want me to pray insincerely?

Continue or conclude the dialogue.

SELECTED READINGS

ADAMS, MARILYN, and ROBERT M. ADAMS. *The Problem of Evil.* New York: Oxford University Press, 1991.

ALEXANDER, SAMUEL. *Space, Time, and Deity.* 2 vols. London: Macmillan, 1918.

ALSTON, WILLIAM. *Perceiving God.* Ithaca: Cornell University Press, 1993.

ALSTON, WILLIAM, ed. *Religious Belief and Philosophical Thought.* New York: Harcourt Brace, 1963.

ANGELES, PETER, ed. *Critiques of God.* Buffalo: Prometheus Books, 1976.

AQUINAS, SAINT THOMAS. *Summa theologica.* 1266–73, Many editions.

BLANCHARD, BRAND. *Reason and Belief.* New Haven: Yale University Press, 1975.

DAVIES, BRIAN. *An Introduction to the Philosophy of Religion.* New York: Oxford University Press, 1993.

DAVIS, CAROLYN. *The Evidential Force of Religious Experience.* New York: Oxford University Press, 1989.

DEWEY, JOHN. *A Common Faith.* New Haven: Yale University Press, 1934.

FLEW, ANTONY. *God and Philosophy.* London: Hutchinson, 1966.

FLEW, ANTONY, and ALASDAIR MACINTYRE. *New Essays in Philosophical Theology.* London: SCM Press, 1955.

GEACH, PETER. *God and the Soul.* New York: Schocken Books, 1969.

GEACH, PETER. *Providence and Evil.* Cambridge: Cambridge University Press, 1977.

GEIVETT, DOUGLAS, and BRENDAN SWEETMAN, eds. *Contemporary Perspectives on Religious Epistemology.* New York: Oxford University Press, 1992.

GUTHRIE, STEWART E. *Faces in the Clouds.* London: Oxford University Press, 1993.

HICK, JOHN. *Faith and Knowledge.* Ithaca: Cornell University Press, 1957.

HICK, JOHN. *Religious Experience and Faith.* New York: New York University Press, 1961.

HOOK, SIDNEY, ed. *Religious Experience and Truth.* New York: New York University Press, 1962.

HUGHES, GERALD. *The Nature of God.* London: Routledge, 1995.

HUME, DAVID. *Dialogues Concerning Natural Religion.* Edited by Norman Kemp Smith. Edinburgh: Thomas Nelson & Sons, 1935. Originally published 1776.

KENNY, ANTHONY. *What Is Faith?* London: Oxford University Press, 1992.

LEWIS, C. S. *The Problem of Pain.* New York: Macmillan, 1962.

MACPHERSON, THOMAS. *The Philosophy of Religion.* Princeton: Van Nostrand, 1965.

MACTAGGART, J. E. *Some Dogmas of Religion.* London: Edward Arnold, 1906.

MATSON, WALLACE I. *The Existence of God.* Ithaca: Cornell University Press, 1965.

MILL, JOHN STUART. *An Examination of Sir William Hamilton's Philosophy.* London: Longmans Green, 1865. Chapter 7.

MILL, JOHN STUART. *Three Essays on Religion.* London: Longmans Green, 1874.

MUNITZ, MILTON. *The Mystery of Existence.* New York: Appleton Century Crofts, 1965.

PETERSON, MICHAEL, et al. *Reason and Religious Belief.* New York: Oxford University Press, 1990.

PIKE, NELSON. *Good and Evil.* Englewood Cliffs, NJ: Prentice-Hall, 1964.

PLANTINGA, ALAN. "The Free-Will Defense." In Max Black, ed., *Philosophy in America.* London: Allen & Unwin, 1965.

STACE, WALTER T. *Religion and the Modern Mind.* Philadelphia: Lippincott, 1952.

STACE, WALTER T. *Time and Eternity.* Princeton: Princeton University Press, 1952.

SWINBURNE, RICHARD. "The Problem of Evil." In Stuart C. Brown, ed., *Reason and Religion.* Ithaca: Cornell University Press, 1977.

WARD, JAMES. *Naturalism and Agnosticism.* 2 vols. London: Black, 1899.

WISDOM, JOHN. "Gods." In Antony Flew, ed., *Logic and Language,* 1st ser. Oxford: Blackwell, 1952.

WISDOM, JOHN. *Philosophy and Psychoanalysis.* Oxford: Blackwell, 1965.

The Is and the Ought

PROBLEMS IN ETHICS

"It would be so good of you if you did that." "Reimburse him, of course. That's the only fair thing for you to do." "It's not right that he should do such a thing to you." Our daily discourse is peppered with value judgements like these. People often disagree with one another about whether a particular judgment of value is true or false, justified or unjustified.

But first of all don't we have to know what they mean? When someone says, "It's wrong to take a bribe," what is the meaning of this sentence? What information is the speaker giving when he or she utters it? What kind of meaning do words such as "good" and "right" and "just" have? This is the subject of meta-ethics.

1. META-ETHICS

Maybe sentences like these don't have any meaning—at least not in the sense of conveying information, what is often called "cognitive meaning." If I tell you that I am six feet tall, or that this house is haunted by ghosts, or that I have three sisters, what I say may not be true—it may not contain information— but at least we all know what these sentences mean. But if someone says, "Cannibalism is wrong," what information is he giving about cannibalism? And how would one discover whether what he says is true?

Some philosophers have held that there are ethical sentences—sentences containing ethical terms like "good" and "bad" and "duty" and "right" and "wrong" and so on— but that these sentences *express no propositions,* that they contain nothing that could be called true or false. Rather, it is said, they are expressions of one's feeling or attitude toward something, just as interjections like "Alas" and "Whoopee" express attitudes and feelings but don't state anything, and are neither true nor false.

"Isn't that true of many sentences we utter?", we might ask. "She's gorgeous," "She's scrumptious," and so on—we are reacting in a certain way to her, but what are we really saying about her? And if someone says, "He's scum," the listener surely can infer how the speaker feels toward the person he's talking about, but what exactly is he saying about him? Doesn't what he says tell us more about *how he reacts* to the person than what the person is really like?

According to the *emotive theory of ethics,* there are no moral truths; sentences containing moral terms like "good" express no propositions at all, and we don't see this right away because these sentences have the same *grammatical form* as other sentences that do express propositions. "Promise-breaking is bad" looks very much like "Promise-breaking is a frequent occurrence," but the second is an empirical statement that we can all confirm for ourselves without much trouble, whereas the first is not. According to the emotive theory, you are asserting no proposition but only registering your disapproval of, or antipathy toward, the practice of breaking one's promises. When you say to Smith, "You did a good thing, rescuing him from his burning car," you are not stating any fact about Smith's action when you call it good; you are not even *stating* the fact that you approve of it; you are only *expressing* your approval of it,—and sometimes also attempting to *evoke* an attitude of approval in others as well.

Do sentences containing "good" and other ethical terms never give information? They do—indeed, most of the time they do:

1. If the third-grader is asked, "How much is 6×8?" and she replies, "68," the teacher may say, "That's the wrong answer," but the word "wrong" in this sentence has nothing to do with morality. "That's a good sports car" is an empirical statement about a car—what it says is that this car possesses to a high degree the features used in judging sports cars: it is powerful, it can perform at high speeds, it has a snazzy appearance.

2. Often the word "good" is used in an empirical statement about what *means* will achieve a given *end*. "That's a good way to get to Knoxville"—that is, it will get you there faster or more easily than other routes. "That's a good way to get rich" is also about means, although it may not be easy to discover whether it's true: that is, it's not easy to discover any sure road to riches. But whether riches itself is good, or whether it's good to acquire it or possess it, is another question. That seems to be a moral issue, not an ordinary empirical one like whether something is an efficient means toward a given end. Some philosophers have suggested that "good" and related words have meaning (cognitive meaning, that is) only if we're talking about the means to an end, not the ends themselves. They would say, for example, that "That's a good way to commit a murder" is meaningful (it's a testable empirical statement) but that "Murder itself is good/bad" is not.

3. One could also allege that the sentence "He's a good man" does have a cognitive meaning, but that the meaning *varies* from one context to another: when his friends say it, they mean that he is affable, good company, and pleasant to be with; when his employer says it, she means that he is reliable, punctual, and efficient at his job; when his girlfriend says it, she means that he's sexy and a great lover. Doesn't the meaning vary depending on who says it and the circumstances in which it's said?

This last suggestion, however, is not very plausible. Does the *meaning* of the word "good" vary from case to case? Does the meaning of "good" constantly vary whereas the meanings of "chair" and "stone" do not? Is the word "good" then multiply ambiguous? Do you really attach one meaning to the word on one occasion and a different meaning on another occasion? True, the word "good," is *applied to different things* on different occasions, just as the word "chair" is (the chair in your office, the chair in my office). But does it have a different meaning each time? If it did, *how could we ever learn* all these different meanings? Don't all these different alleged meanings of "good" have something in common?

The word "good," says the dictionary, is the most general term of commendation or approbation in the language. To say that someone is good, or a good X (good husband, good employee, good driver) is at least to put one's stamp of approval on that person. It's the use of the word to *commend* that they all have in common. A Viking may say that a good man is one who is brave and fearless, ready to kill anyone who stands in his way. A pacifist may say that a good man is one who is meek and humble, never lifting his hand against another person. These are rather opposite characteristics. Do different people use "good" as a label for these very different characteristics? Shouldn't we say instead that the word "good" always has pretty much the same *meaning,* but that it is used to *refer to* different characteristics, depending on what one approves? Both the Viking and the pacifist use the word as a term of approbation or commendation, but *what* they commend are very different qualities.

If this is so, there is no single cognitive meaning that "good" always has—unlike "chair" and "stone." The single meaning it has is its favorable emotive meaning—"the aura of feeling that hovers around a word"—and not any quality it refers to. The quality varies depending on who is speaking and what qualities the speaker is commending. In this respect "good" is like "stool pigeon" rather than like "communist" (see pages 25–26), except that "stool pigeon," besides always having an unfavorable emotive meaning, has a definite cognitive (descriptive) meaning besides—it is used to refer to police informants. Is there anything analogous to this that is shared by all uses of the word "good" and other ethical words?

Defining Ethical Terms

The ancient Greeks thought of some person or thing as good based on whether it fulfilled a *function.* A good pilot is one who guides his ship well to its intended destination; a good physician is one who is skilled in healing. In general, a good X is an X that fulfills (to a fairly high degree) the function of X's, whatever that function may be.

Today we speak of mechanical objects as good or better than something else, or as bad or worse than something else, depend-

ing on how well or ill they serve a certain purpose or function. A good alarm clock is one that keeps accurate time, goes off at the correct time, has a luminous dial, and so on. We say that to do or to have these things is the function of an alarm clock. Why? Because we—not you or I, but human beings—have *constructed* alarm clocks with this use in mind. This is an alarm clock's function, because we have made it so as to serve that function.

We also speak of animals as having certain functions, depending on what use we assign them. A horse is for riding or for drawing a wagon. A dog may be good as a watchdog but not as a companion, or vice versa. However, if someone said, "That's a good armadillo" we would be puzzled: what purposes do armadillos serve? Armadillos are not like machines, they weren't constructed by human beings to serve a purpose—they just appeared on the scene through a long evolutionary process; they aren't here for a purpose, they just *are.* (If they do serve a divine purpose, we don't know what it is.) We might use a few armadillos to stock a zoo, and then perhaps a good armadillo would be a healthy young specimen of the species. It would depend on what we used it for. And if it had no use, the question would have no meaning. If someone said, "Seven, that's a good number," we might respond in jest, "What's good about it?" Good, how? Good, by what criterion?

Can we say that someone is a good man if he fulfills the function of a man? But what *is* the function of a man? Man is not a manufactured object like a clock or a hammer. Men, like armadillos, appeared on the scene, but unlike clocks they have no function that we know of. We can say that man is created (manufactured?) by God just as clocks are manufactured by men, and that the function of man is to serve God or glorify God's name. And in that case, man, like a clock or hammer, does have a function. But we can say this only in a theological context. (Remember our discussion of purpose on pages 116–117.)

If we can't define "good" in terms of function—except in the case of mechanical objects—where shall we look for a definition? It is not difficult to define ethical terms as long as we employ *other* ethical terms in the definition. For example, one can say, "Good is that which we ought to seek." This is a definition "good" by means of another ethical term, "ought." Or we could say, as some moral philosophers do, "Right acts are those that maximize good," thus defining "right" in terms of "good." The question is, can we define any ethical terms entirely by means of *non*ethical ones? Can we define an ethical term by using no other ethical term in the definition?

Some philosophers have endeavored to do so. Here a few of the simpler examples:

1. Suppose someone says, "When I say it's good, I just mean that I like it." But did the speaker never consider anything good that she didn't like, or like anything that she didn't consider good? Does being a "good boy" mean doing as you like?

Or suppose we say, as one of Ernest Hemingway's characters did, "Good is what I feel good after and bad is what I feel bad after." "Feeling good" is not an ethical term at all; it merely describes some aspect of one's conscious state at the time. (Nor is "I have a bad taste in my mouth" an ethical use of the word "bad"; it is not used to condemn but only to describe an ineffable felt quality, like a color or a smell.) You can feel good after a hot bath, but this is hardly a statement about anything in ethics. It is much more plausible to link "good" with approval than with liking.

2. "When I say it's good, all I mean is that I approve of it." We consider integrity good without particularly liking it, but if we consider it good, surely we at least approve of it.

(On this definition, calling something good is not *expressing* approval of it, as in the emotive theory, but it is *stating that you feel* approval toward it. This is cognitive meaning, used to inform others not that X has a certain quality but that you have an attitude of approval toward X.)

Adopting this definition, however, has some serious consequences that may not at first occur to us. To know that something is good according to this definition, all I would have to do is introspect and be able to tell myself sincerely that I approve of it. And if you introspect and find that what I approve of is not what you approve of, then the thing or quality in question is good-for-me (because I approve it) and not-good-for-you (because you don't approve it)—just as I may say that calculus is interesting (because it interests me), and you may say that it is not (it doesn't interest you); both statements are true, the one a truth about me, and the other a truth about you. I approve of X and you don't, and that's the end of the matter—nothing remains to be discussed, unless I believe you are lying when you say you don't approve X, in which case I will say, "But you *do* approve of X; you just say you don't."

Moreover, if all I mean when I say that it's good is that I approve of it, and all you mean by saying that it's not good is that you don't approve of it, we are *not* really disagreeing; for you don't deny that I approve X, and I don't deny that you don't approve it, so what is (according to this definition) left to argue about?

When we argue ethical matters with one another, we don't say things like "X must be good, because after all you approve of it." We may say that "X is good" means that we all *ought* to approve X, but that is, once again, defining an ethical term by means of another ethical term, and there's little point in doing that if you don't already know what the other ethical term means.

3. Or we could say that the good is the same as the *desired*. But desired by whom? and when? Is everything that Smith desires good, by definition? Aren't some desired things bad?

Instead of saying that "X is good" means that X is desired, couldn't we rather say that it means that X is *desirable*? But again "desirable" is an ethical term: it doesn't mean that something *is* desired, but that it *ought to be* desired.

4. Or we could say that "X is good" means that *most people* approve of X. But again this will hardly do. Can you discover whether something is good just by taking a poll? If you know that most people approve of X, does that really tell you whether X is good? Why should what most people think be decisive in ethics any more than in mathematics or physics? Can't the majority be ignorant, mistaken, or uninformed? At one time most people approved of slavery; did that make it good or desirable?

5. There is a more promising possibility: "good" means what God commands. What God commands is good, by definition. If God says it's good, it is, and if God says it isn't, it isn't.

By this definition, unbelievers could not have any views about good; but surely they do, even though their views might be incorrect. Unbelievers have as strong convictions about what should be done to make the world better as believers do. And *they* don't mean "God commands it" when they say "It's good."

Besides, people in different times and places have very different conceptions of God (or the gods), and what the god of one religion commands people to do may be quite opposite of what the gods of other religions command (such as keeping the Sabbath or making human sacrifices).

There is still another objection to the definition. Does a believer have to say that what

God commands is "the very meaning" of the words "good" and "ought"? Socrates, in Plato's dialogue *Euthyphro*, considered whether "good" meant the same as "pleasing to the gods." But, he asked, might not something be good whether or not the gods approve it? Perhaps it's not that it's good because the gods are pleased by it, but that the gods are pleased by it because it's good. If it's good, the gods commend it to us, but that's not what's meant by saying it's good; rather, the gods see that certain things are good and accordingly command us to do them. In that case, being good is logically independent of the gods' commands: honesty would be good even if the gods did not tell us to be honest.

In his classic work *The Methods of Ethics*, the nineteenth-century philosopher Henry Sidgwick concluded that no definition of ethical terms entirely by means of nonethical ones is possible, any more than we can define mathematical terms by nonmathematical ones:

> What definition can we give of "ought," "right," and other terms expressing the same fundamental notion? To this I should answer that the notion which these terms have in common is too elementary to admit of any formal definition. . . . The notion we have been examining, as it now exists in our thought, cannot be resolved into any more simple notions; it can only be made clearer by determining as precisely as possible its relation to other notions with which it is connected in ordinary thought, especially those with which it is liable to be confounded.[1]

The British philosopher G. E. Moore employed what he called the "open question technique." Take whatever property (call it P) you care to and say that that's the meaning of "good"; you can always meaningfully

[1]Henry Sidgwick, *The Methods of Ethics* (London: Macmillan, 1878), p. 23.

ask the following question: "I grant that X has that property, but nevertheless, *is X good?*" For example, I know that person X is honest but I can ask without contradiction, *is* honesty good? (Even if it *is* always good, I can still ask that question.) Of any property P, one can always ask whether having that property is good.

But in that case, says Moore, "good" cannot be defined as possessing any nonethical property. To speak of something or someone as good is to speak of some *further* characteristic beyond the ordinary empirical ones we are accustomed to attributing to things; and if a person attempts to define the ethical term by means of nonethical ones, she is guilty of what Moore called the *naturalistic fallacy.* There are many other words that are not definable (other than ostensively), words like "yellow" and "pleasure," and Moore attempts to show that the same considerations apply to "good":

> Suppose a man says, "I am pleased"; and suppose that it is not a lie or a mistake but the truth. Well, if it is true, what does that mean? It means that his mind, a certain definite mind, distinguished by certain definite marks from all others, has at this moment a certain definite feeling called pleasure. "Pleased" *means* nothing but having pleasure, and though we may be more pleased or less pleased, and even, we may admit for the present, have one or another kind of pleasure; yet in so far as it is pleasure we have, whether there be more or less of it, and whether it be of one kind or another, what we have is one definite thing, absolutely indefinable, some one thing that is the same in all the various degrees and in all the various kinds of it that there may be. We may be able to say how it is related to other things: that, for example, it is in the mind, that it causes desire, that we are conscious of it, etc., etc. We can, I say, describe its relations to other things, but define it we can *not.* And if anybody tried to define pleasure for us as being any other natural object: if anybody were to say, for instance, that pleasure *means* the sensation of red, and were

to proceed to deduce from that that pleasure is a color, we should be entitled to laugh at him and to distrust his future statements about pleasure.

> Well, that would be the same fallacy which I have called the naturalistic fallacy. That "pleased" does not mean "having the sensation of red," or anything else whatever, does not prevent us from understanding what it does mean. It is enough for us to know that "pleased" does mean "having the sensation of pleasure," and though pleasure is absolutely indefinable, though pleasure is pleasure and nothing else whatever, yet we feel no difficulty in saying that we are pleased.[2]

But to compare "good" with "yellow" also has its problems. We can pretty well agree on what objects are yellow; even color-blind people can agree on this (see pages 27–28). But if people disagree on what is good, where can we turn to obtain agreement? What if one person says that the nonnatural quality of goodness belongs to a certain action or motive or state of affairs, and another person denies it? Is there any rational recourse here? Or do we resort again to "Then ends the argument and begins the fight?"

Meta-ethics is the subject that deals with the meanings of ethical terms. In spite of many thousands of pages in books and scholarly periodicals in which meta-ethical issues are discussed, not much agreement on these issues has resulted. *Normative ethics* is the subject that deals with substantive issues such as what ends are *good,* what acts are *right,* what policies are *just,* and for what actions a person should be held *responsible.* People who may be deadlocked on meta-ethical issues are often in agreement on issues of normative ethics. It is to normative ethics that we now turn.

---

[2]G. E. Moore, *Principia Ethica* (London: Cambridge University Press, 1903), pp. 12–13.

2. THE GOOD

David Hume remarked on the many treatises he had read in which the author began with a description of some fact or situation, and after a "therefore" or "we may conclude that . . .", came to a conclusion about what should be or what one ought to do. How, he wondered, did the author bridge the gap between the first assertion and the second? How did the writer get from the is to the ought, from how things are to how they ought to be?

We constantly refer to people and things as having value or being good or worthwhile. In what kind of situation do such terms arise?

1. *Good as pro-life.* Ethical concepts, wrote Ayn Rand (1905–1982), arise only in the context of actions required to sustain life. Imagine an immortal robot, a being who does not face the alternative of life or death, who requires no action to sustain itself: "an entity which moves and acts, but which cannot be affected by anything . . . which cannot be damaged, injured or destroyed."[3] There is nothing that it could act *for* or *against*. What goals could it have? And what could place them in jeopardy?

To an indestructible entity, nothing can have a value. Only beings who are capable of being destroyed and are able to prevent it have a reason to act. Only living organisms face the alternative of life or death.

Plants and animals behave instinctively to sustain their lives. They do not choose their goals. They may die from floods or droughts or other conditions beyond their control, but within the limits of their ability they act to sustain their own existence. They can be destroyed, but they do not pursue their own destruction.

The goals of human beings, by contrast, are not implanted by instinct; they have to be *chosen* by the individuals themselves.

A being of volitional consciousness has no automatic course of behavior. He needs a code of values to guide his actions. "Value" is that which one acts to gain and keep, "virtue" is the action by which one gains and keeps it. . . .

There is only one fundamental alternative in the universe, existence or non-existence—and it pertains to a single class of entities, to living organisms. The existence of inanimate matter is unconditional, the existence of life is not; it depends on a specific course of action. Matter is indestructible, it changes its forms, but it cannot cease to exist. It is only a living organism that faces a constant alternative: the issue of life or death. Life is a process of self-sustaining and self-generating action. If an organism fails in that action, it dies; its chemical elements remain, but its life goes out of existence. It is only the concept of "life" that makes the concept of "value" possible. . . .

A living entity that regarded its means of survival as evil, would not survive. A plant that struggled to mangle its roots, a bird that fought to break its wings would not remain for long in the existence they affronted. But the history of man has been a struggle to deny and to destroy his mind.

Man has been called a rational being, but rationality is a matter of choice—and the alternative his nature offers him is: rational being or suicidal animal. Man has to be man—by choice; he has to hold his life as a value by choice; he has to learn to sustain it—by choice; he has to discover the values it requires and practice his virtues—by choice.

A code of values accepted by choice is a code of morality.[4]

Throughout history men have engaged in self-destroying actions, but the effect may not be immediate. A person may do something that is instantly fatal, such as mistaking a poisonous snake for a nonpoisonous one. One may also take actions that endanger

[3]Ayn Rand, "The Objectivist Ethics," in Rand, *The Virtue of Selfishness* (New York: New American Library, 1964), p. 17.

[4]Ayn Rand, *Atlas Shrugged* (New York: Random House, 1957), pp. 1012–1013.

one's health, but this may not be evident for some time. One may act in response to destructive situations (father was a sadist, mother was a crack cocaine addict) in self-destroying ways, such as isolating oneself from all human contact or belonging to an armed gang (and being shot to death at age twenty-five), even though these are protective mechanisms at the time they are chosen.

To live long-range, one must think and plan long-range. When we act on impulses that are "range of the moment," they often turn out to be destructive of our life and our well-being.

A person's survival cannot be ensured by instinct; with instincts alone human beings would die. Survival must be consciously pursued by actions every day of one's life. "Morality is the instruction manual in regard to proper care and use that did *not* come with man. It is the science of human self-preservation."[5]

A person cannot survive as an animal; if one tried to live by one's inborn instincts, one would soon die. Someone can survive only as a rational being charting one's own course of action. "Man's survival *qua* man (i.e., as a rational being)" means "the terms, methods, conditions, and goals required for the survival of a rational being through the whole of his life span, in all those aspects of existence which are open to his choice."

One risks one's survival if one does not think for oneself but instead depends on the thinking of others, which may or may not be correct. One risks one's survival if one thinks only range-of-the-moment. One risks one's survival if one "fakes reality," submitting to wishful thinking (a reality substitute that exists only in fantasy) and risking destruction by some unwelcome bit of reality that one later confronts. People who live on wishes

and fantasies risk having these wishes and fantasies exploded as surely as those who live on a flood plain and ignore the danger or believe that God will always protect them risk huge losses in a flood.

> [Man] cannot provide for his simplest physical need without a process of thought. He needs a process of thought to discover how to plant and grow his food or how to make weapons for hunting. . . . No percepts and no "instincts" will tell him how to light a fire, how to weave cloth, how to forge tools, how to make a wheel, how to make an airplane, how to perform an appendectomy, how to produce an electric light bulb or an electronic tube or a cyclotron or a book of matches. Yet his life depends on such knowledge—and only a volitional act of his consciousness, a process of thought, can provide it.[6]

The importance of the mind for human survival is dramatically illustrated in this passage:

> Stand on an empty stretch of soil in a wilderness unexplored by men and ask yourself what manner of survival you would achieve and how long you would last if you refused to think, with no one around to teach you the motions, or, if you chose to think, how much your mind would be able to discover. Ask yourself how many independent conclusions you would have reached in the course of your life and how much of your time was spent on performing motions you learned from others. Ask yourself whether you would be able to discover how to till the soil and grow your food, whether you would be able to invent a wheel, a lever, an induction coil, a generator, or an electronic tube.[7]

For a living organism, the good is that which promotes the survival and flourishing of that organism. What is good is what is pro-life. This is only the beginning of a very long story. But let's start once more:

[5]Leonard Peikoff, *Objectivism: The Philosophy of Ayn Rand* (New York: Dutton, 1991), p. 214.

[6]Rand, "The Objectivist Ethics," p. 17.
[7]Rand, *Atlas Shrugged*, pp. 1048–1049.

2. *Good as fulfillment.* We begin again with the indestructible robot that can distinguish things in its environment but cannot be endangered by anything. Richard Taylor writes:

> it is only because man has a will—that is, because he has desires, passions, wants, inclinations, or in short, because he pursues ends or objects of desire—that any distinctions of good and evil ever arise in the first place. The original goodness of something consists simply in its being desired, and the evil of any state of affairs consists simply in its frustration of desire. Were it not for this desiderative aspect of human nature, everything would be on a dead level, nothing would even matter. Things would acquire the status of being good or evil only if someone—anyone—cares about them one way or the other. . . .
>
> Reason, by itself, can make no distinction whatever between what is good and what is not. Reason can only, and within limits, see what is so, and can never declare whether it ought to be so.
>
> What is significant about a man is that he wills certain ends. From one sunrise to the next, this is what gives his life meaning; indeed, it is the very expression of life itself. Human reason employed almost exclusively in discerning the means whereby those ends, which are the product of the will, can be achieved.[8]

Reason tells us what means we can best use to achieve our ends, but the ends themselves are determined by the will. Reason tells us what the alternatives are and how to achieve them, but it is the will that decides to *do* them. "It is more obvious that men are . . . conative beings, than that they are rational ones. There are men whom one might genuinely doubt to be rational, but it is doubtful whether anyone has ever seen a living man whom he suspected had no needs, desire, or wants."[9]

---

[8]Richard Taylor, *Good and Evil* (New York: Macmillan, 1970), p. 14.
[9]Ibid., p. 120.

What, then, is the good? Fulfillment. What is bad? Frustration, lack of fulfillment. There is a complication, however: some fulfillments get in the way of others. If I am to finish medical school, I will have to sacrifice other things I would also find fulfilling, like having more time for rest and relaxation; some of those fulfillments will have to be frustrated if my longer-term fulfillment, of becoming a doctor, is to be possible. Or, if I want a fulfilling career, I may along the way have to take a part-time job I dislike. Indeed, if life were nothing but fulfillments, there would be no frustrations along the way, and some of these may be necessary if I am to become the kind of sympathetic human being I would like to be. All these must be weighed against each other, but the ideal remains: the more fulfillments, the better. (We could also append this to the Randian view by saying that without rationality, including the ability to foresee whatever possible implications of our actions it is humanly possible to see, long-term fulfillment itself would not be possible.)

One could also believe—and many philosophers have believed—that the maximum possible *happiness* is the ideal, and should be the goal of human action. But happiness and fulfillment are inextricably intertwined, and an abundant employment of our rational powers is required to determine wherein our long-term happiness or fulfillment will lie.

3. THEORIES OF CONDUCT

None of these considerations, however, get us very far in telling us what specifically we should *do.* Let's say we should aim at happiness: happiness, said Aristotle at the opening of his *Nicomachean Ethics,* is that at which all human beings aim. But one question confronts us at the outset: *whose* happiness? whose fulfillment? Should I aim at the maximum possible happiness for myself? or for myself and my family and friends? or for everyone—the whole human race? If we say that X (happiness, for example) is good—good as an end in itself, not as a means to something else—what should be our next step? If happiness (or fulfillment, etc.) is good no matter who has it, shouldn't I aim at *everyone's* happiness? On the other hand, even if happiness is good no matter who has it, does it follow that I should aim at everyone's? Why not aim at my own, and you aim at your own? At this point there is a sharp cleavage in normative ethics.

Egoism

There are various versions of ethical egoism. According to the ancient Epicureans, we should live a life of placid contemplation and not interfere in the affairs of the world, or even form close relationships with other people, because in the long run we will be rendered unhappy by these activities. You form a close relationship and the person dies or deserts you; you fight for political causes, only to lose and emerge embittered; you form expensive habits now, only to find later that having to do without expensive things is harder on you than the indulgence in them was pleasing.

The ancient Stoics thought that the most satisfactory life could come only through the suppression of wants and desires, since you could never become accustomed to what you didn't have, and if you kept your distance from everyone, you could never be hurt or disappointed. If happiness is determined by what you have divided by what you want, most people are unhappy because their wants keep increasing, whereas the Stoics advised people to keep their wants to a minimum so that their desires would never exceed their wants.

Does the egoist advocate that you should lie, cheat, and kill in order to gain your ends? Not many egoists have thought so. To do so would be like walking in a field filled with land mines; one would soon be maimed or killed. If you don't deal honestly with other people, they will cease to deal honestly with you. If you are not concerned for your friends or family, they will not be concerned for you, even when you need their help. If you commit crimes, you may be caught and imprisoned, and even if you aren't, you will fear and mistrust others, not knowing who will be the one to turn you in—your relations with everyone will be soured. If you adopt the motto "Kill or be killed," as a way of settling disputes, you may not be killed the first time or even the tenth, but your chances of dying will be much greater than if you had not adopted this motto. Talking things out with people, airing your grievances, and arriving at a mutually accepted solution, even if it is a compromise, is usually a much safer course than resorting to violence every time you have a grievance.

Should you deceive, steal, and kill if you know you can get away with it? (Not that you ever can be sure, of course.) According to the egoist Thrasymachus in Plato's *Republic,* the answer is yes. You should do what you can to promote your interests, even if this means trampling on the interests of others. The man who seeks political power and achieves it does just that: as soon as he has the army on his side and his commands will be obeyed by others, there is almost no limit to what he can do to gain wealth and power at their expense.

Plato concludes, however, that he will not thereby achieve the goals that he himself seeks. The tyrant will never know who his friends are or even whether he has any; he will never know which of them may be plotting to kill or unseat him; he will never be at peace, wondering who will join forces with others to plunder or murder him. Using this and other examples of "rampant egoism," Plato concludes that such a life leads only to misery and frustration. The egoist whose motto is "Kill or be killed" or "Cheat or be cheated," is creating only misery for himself. If your country is attacked by a tyrant who would enslave or massacre you and your fellow citizens, then you have to choose either to fight or to be enslaved; but in that case it is in your own egoistic interest to fight rather than be enslaved—to fight, even if there is a considerable probability of dying, is preferable to enslavement or "death with dishonor."

It is not egoism itself that Plato attacks but the means by which so many people pursue it. They think that what they do will be for their own long-term self-interest, but it is not; people constantly *miscalculate* on the vital matter of what will bring them happiness or peace of mind. They want to be happy, but they just don't know how to go about it.

To put the issue in more modern terms, most people would agree that when they drive on the highway there should be certain "rules of the road." I should drive on the same side of the road except when passing other vehicles; I should have my lights on when driving at night; I should not go more than so fast in certain areas; I must not run through stop lights or ignore road signs; and so on. It may be that I am not particularly interested in the other drivers along the highway—I don't know them, and I may not much care about them; but *I* want to get to my destination safely, and if I ignore the rules of the road, I am more likely to be involved in an accident. It is in my own self-interest to obey the rules of the road.

There are also rules (the egoist would continue) we should obey when traveling along the highway of life. Some of these rules should have the force of law, because unless force is threatened against those who would ignore the rules, there would be widespread violation of them. Rules against murder, robbery, and rape should have the force of law. Other rules should be voluntary rather than mandatory, such as rules about the habits to be instilled in children. In any case, it is in one's own interest to have these rules. They are "good to have around."

For example, you may sometime be so angry at someone that you want to kill him or set fire to his house, and to refrain from such an act may be extremely difficult. But the rule that prohibits you from harming others also prohibits others from harming *you*. You lose something by having the rule (not being permitted to do what you want), but you also gain something—in this case, greater safety and security—and what you gain is much more than what you lose.

Most people can't be happy for long without love and friendship. But if the other person is a genuine friend, not someone you use to get what you want and then drop, you want her to be happy because you take pleasure in the thought that she is happy. Moreover, you want to be the object of the same kind of concern that you are showing for her. When she doesn't show this degree of concern, the friendship tends to cool off. The aim, in every case, is to do what produces for you the greatest long-term happiness or fulfillment.

Altruism

Whatever they may have done in practice, most people believe that they should do some things that benefit others more than themselves. Out of countless possible examples, let's consider two:

1. You are a French citizen under the Vichy regime, after Germany's victory over

France in World War II. You know that Hitler's henchmen are scouring every village in search of Jews, and that whoever they find will be shipped to concentration camps and be put to death in gas chambers. You may save your Jewish neighbors' lives by hiding them, as in the Anne Frank case. But, if you shield them, they may be caught anyway and you will be sent to a prison or concentration camp yourself (along with your whole family) for the crime of hiding them. It is hardly in your self-interest to give them shelter; but wouldn't it be right to do so? In fact may it not be morally incumbent on you to do so?

2. You are a worker in a Soviet office, and a fellow worker says something mildly critical of the government. By law, anyone who hears another worker criticize the government is required to report this fact, and as a result the accused person will probably be sentenced to twenty years or more in an Arctic labor camp, a sentence he will probably not live long enough to serve. So you decide not to report his remark. But if a member of the secret police were present he could later have you arrested for saying nothing—so for your own sake you should report it.

> You, who had bent your back beside him for twenty years at the same desk, now by your noble silence . . . had to show how hostile you were to his crimes. (You had to make this sacrifice for the sake of your own dear family, for your own dear ones! What right had you not to think about them?) But the person arrested had left behind him a wife, a mother, children, and perhaps they at least ought to be helped? No, no, that would be dangerous: after all these were the wife of an enemy and the mother of an enemy, and they were the children of an enemy—and your own children had a long education ahead of them.[10]

---

[10]Aleksandr Solzhenitsyn, *The Gulag Archipelago* (New York: Harper & Row, 1979), Vol. 3, p. 637.

While it would be safer for you if you reported his remarks to the police, many would say that in spite of this you should keep silent, even if it could mean your own destruction—although the case is complicated by the fact that your family would be destroyed along with you.

The view that you ought to perform actions to help others, even if doing so involves great loss to yourself—even loss of life—is called *altruism*. Altruism, however, takes various forms.

Altruism—concern for the welfare of others—is the opposite of egoism—concern for one's own interests. A *pure* altruist doesn't consider her own welfare at all but only that of others. If she had a choice between an action that would produce a great benefit for herself (such as enabling her to go to college) and an action that would produce no benefit for herself but a small benefit for someone else (such as enabling him to go to a concert this evening), she should do the second. She should be *selfless*, considering herself not at all: she should face death rather than subject another person to a minor discomfort. She is committed to serving others only and to pass up any benefits to herself.

Such pure altruists would not remain alive for long. They would have to eat and drink and sleep in order to stay alive, but if their own interests don't count at all, they would have to do without the food if thereby others could have it—and before long they would starve to death. Indeed, a world consisting only of altruists would be impossible: if one person were offered food she would have to say, "No, you take it; I serve your interests and not my own." If the person offering it to her then offered the food to someone else, that someone else, as an altruist, would have to say, "No, you take it; my own well-being counts for nothing." And so on for everyone to whom the food was offered. An altruist would have to allow her own needs to count for something, however little, in order to stay alive and be an altruist tomorrow.

"Love Your Neighbor"

In the famous precept of Jesus, you are not told to ignore your own needs entirely; you are not even told not to love yourself; but you are told to love you neighbor *as much as* you love yourself. And who is your neighbor? Not just your family, not just the person living next door, not just your townspeople and countrypeople, but every human being that exists. Everyone in the world, just by virtue of being human, is your neighbor.

What then does "Love your neighbor" command you to do? Are you supposed to earn money to support your neighbors and their children as well as your own? Are you supposed to be as concerned that an unknown person ten thousand miles away receive lifesaving medicine as that you yourself or some member of your family should receive it? If you are a physician, should you be as eager to save the life of a tribesman in New Guinea as you are to save your own life or that of your spouse or parents? Is this psychologically even possible?

In what way are you supposed to love everyone? The ancient Greeks had three words for love: *eros* (erotic feeling), which you can have toward only a very limited number of people; *philein* (friendship or fellow-feeling), which you can have for only a few people you have come to know and with whom you share values that are important to both of you; and *agape* (total dedication), which you feel toward God. None of them, it would seem, can encompass the entire human race.

Presumably the commandment does not demand of us what is psychologically impossible—a benevolent attachment to everyone. It is less concerned with how we should *feel* than with what we should *do*. Even if we can't love the distant tribesmen with the same intensity that we love our family, perhaps we can act as if we had an equal concern for them. But what would such actions be? To work as hard for the well-being of distant tribesmen as we do for ourselves and our children? You work hard to sustain your family; should you work just as hard to sustain everyone in the world who needs it? And isn't that as impossible to do as to feel love toward everyone?

And whether possible or not, is this something you ought to try to do? An egoist will contend that the whole enterprise is misconceived:

> You *owe* nothing to your neighbor. If you want to help him—that is another matter. Then the determining factor is *your desire*—not his need. It is then a favor to him—*not* his rightful due.
>
> Now, *must* you always want to help him? Is it morally desirable that you should? No. Here is where the real issue comes in: you may (morally) wish to help him only when such help does not involve the sacrifice of your own interests. Example: you may loan money to a friend in need, if you really like him and can spare the money; but if you give him money which you need yourself for a major purpose of your own—I say you are positively *immoral*. . . . If your friend needs money for food, and you pass up buying a new dress and give him the money—that is all right. But that is *not* a sacrifice, because you actually wanted him to have food more than you wanted a new dress. But if that money was required to finance your education, or career, or wedding, or even if you wanted that dress for a date with your sweetheart—then you would be immoral if you gave that money away. You cannot place the interests of another man *above* yours, nor on an *equal* basis with yours. Yours must come first. (Always remembering that *his* come first for him.) That's the only way men can live together at all.[11]

In our personal relations with others we find that if we are to help others we must be

---

[11]*Letters of Ayn Rand*, ed. Michael S. Berliner (New York: Dutton, 1995), pp. 344–345.

selective. If you help someone who is in a jam, are you sure that that person isn't in a jam because of her own past habits? Perhaps, unlike you, she never got up at 6:00 A.M. to report to a job; perhaps she didn't take the precautions necessary to continue—perhaps she didn't bother to keep her car in good working order, and after several breakdowns and repeated lateness to work, was fired, which is why she is now in need. Perhaps she needs a job because she wasn't willing to do what you were willing to do, such as take a job you didn't like until you obtained one that you did like. If you help her, may you not be encouraging indolence? There are many people who would rather take hand-outs than work, people for whom, as the saying goes, "Theft is easier than honest labor." You soon learn that helping people who are always in need, people for whom everything that happens is a dire emergency because they haven't planned ahead, is a losing game: your good will and good intentions bankrupt you without helping them. Perhaps you are just an "enabler,": your action, designed to help them, doesn't change the bad habits that got them into their present plight and only encourages them to be more dependent in the future, counting on handouts from people who can be made to feel sorry for them, or from the government that merely classifies them as "disadvantaged" and doles out money to them from the taxes levied on the rest of us because we work.

If, in our everyday contacts with people, we have to *know individually* the people we are helping if we are to avoid harming them more than we help them, how should we react to the prescription that we should love everyone *as we love ourselves*? Without knowing anything of their individual nature or their individual problems, how can we possibly know which actions of ours would help them? Perhaps, as Hamlet said, "I must be cruel only to be kind."

The Golden Rule

"As you would have others do unto you, so should you do unto them," says the Golden Rule of Jesus. You should do as you would be done by. You should treat others the way you would want to be treated. If you want others to help you when you are in trouble, you should help others when they are in trouble. If you want others to be considerate of you, you should be considerate of them. If you wish others to tell you the truth, you should also tell the truth to them.

But this precept invites several comments. (1) Is that the reason you should be truthful to them—that you want them to be truthful to you? If they aren't, then is it all right to lie to them? (2) Does how you should treat them really depend on how you would *want* to be treated? But not everyone wants to be treated in the same way. Some people want to be treated not with kindness but with indifference, even cruelty; should you therefore treat them cruelly because that's how *they* want to be treated? Here is a masochist who likes to be beaten up; should you therefore beat him up, because that is how he likes to be treated? Or, here is someone who prefers not to be helped—"I'll take care of myself, thank you, and you take care of yourself." Should we be indifferent to her plight when she is in trouble, because that is how she said she wants to be treated? According to the Golden Rule, what we should do depends on what the other person *wants*. Should what the other person wants be the criterion for what *I* should do in my dealing with her?

Universalizability

Immanuel Kant was dissatisfied with the Golden Rule, partly for the reasons just given: it depends on what the other person happens to want. Rather, before you do a certain action, consider what would happen if everyone did it. You may want to steal an item from a store, but what if everyone did this? Conducting a business would be impossible, and nothing would be available for sale. Or, before you tell a lie, consider a world in which everyone lied and no one's word could be relied on. Kant said: "I can by no means will a universal law of lying; for by such a law there could properly be no promises at all. . . . My maxim, as soon as it was made a universal law, would be bound to annul itself."[12]

A maxim is a rule about what an individual should do. When you lie you act on some such maxim as "I may lie when it is convenient to do so." What Kant is pointing out is the result of universalizing that maxim, that is, turning it into a universal rule of human conduct. In some cases, the rule would self-destruct: universal lying would eliminate statements; who would bother to make them if no one believed them anyway? The rule could be sustained only as long as there were people who believed them to be true.

Similarly, if someone borrows money, knowing that he will not be able to pay it back, Kant asks:

> How would things stand if my maxim can never rank as a universal law? I then see straightaway that this maxim can never rank as a universal law of nature and be self-consistent, but must necessarily contradict itself. . . . It would make promising, and the very purpose of promising, itself impossible, since on one would believe he was being promised anything, but would laugh at utterances of this kind as empty shams.[13]

In other cases, however, the universalization of the maxim would not be *inconsistent* but only extremely *undesirable*. If everyone committed suicide, there would be no human race. There would be no contradiction in this, but many (not all) persons would find this state to be very undesirable. Or, if no one helped anyone else in trouble, we would have no inconsistency (each person helps no one but him- or herself) but perhaps (although not everyone would agree) a highly undesirable state of affairs. We would then be without the help of others when we need it. But, one might ask, why nevertheless couldn't this be a universal law of human conduct?

Similarly, if no one developed individual talents the world would be a sorry place in which to live; but isn't it possible to will indolence rather than industriousness—and even to prefer it as a universal rule of human conduct, even if it meant that one wouldn't have any of the conveniences of life, medication for disease, warmth from freezing cold, and so on? There has been endless discussion of which maxims one would wish to be universal rules of conduct, but at least we can distinguish maxims that *could* not be made into universal rules of human conduct from those that could be but, for various reasons, should not be.

Utilitarianism

But why should one want to universalize certain maxims? The most popular answer has been "Because society—or, each individual in it—would be better off if certain rules of behavior were practiced." Better off how? The most usual answer is that they would be happier. Happiness is conceived of as the ultimate good. We may wonder what we want money or fame for, but not what happiness is for. It need serve no purpose at all. Happiness may have various sources—some will be happier if they have more money, others will not; some will be happier if they are famous, others will not. But whatever the *sources* of

[12]Immanuel Kant, *Groundwork of the Metaphysics of Morals* (New York: Harper & Row, 1964), p. 59.
[13]Ibid., p. 44.

happiness, it is happiness that is worth having, not as a means to something else, but for its own sake.

What we should aim at, according to utilitarianism, is the achievement of the greatest happiness possible—not for oneself, but for everyone. Every person counts for one and only one, and you are to count yourself as only one among all the others. If your happiness is increased by +10 (however one may count the units) by doing a certain act, but the happiness of others is increased by +100 if you do something else, the second is to be preferred to the first, even if you yourself get little out of it. But if you would benefit more (+25) and others less (+15), you should do the first, not because it is you who would benefit (this is irrelevant), but because the highest total amount of happiness is achieved in that way. What matters in every case is that the maximum possible happiness be achieved, rather than who has it: better have +40 for one person than +30 distributed equally among fifteen people. I should not do something that produces *less* total good if by my action I could produce more.

Although I should act to promote the greatest possible good, it is difficult, often impossible, to know which action will achieve this; consequences of acts are far-flung, complex, and often unpredictable. You may think you're doing someone a favor by driving her home, but a drunken driver hits your car and injures you both. The right act cannot be the one that *does* in fact produce the most good, nor even the one that the agent *thinks* will produce the most good (a person may think that using snake-oil medicine or facing the full moon will cure cancer), but the act that *probably* will produce the most good, judging by the best evidence available at the time. The evidence is that facing the moon will not cure cancer, although some persons may believe it. The mother believes her child should take Ritalin

for attention-deficit disorder, since it helped the neighbor's children, and if a pill can provide the quick fix, why not? But what if this child is not helped by taking the medication? Most people (utilitarians often remind us) don't think a problem through before they act.

Even if they do think, it's fatally easy to consider just one kind of probable consequence when there are many. A person may consider the consequence of an action on his own family, but ignore its effect on others and the precedent it sets for subsequent behavior. If you break a promise to your employer to be at the office by a certain time, you may say that your own date is much more important and that the boss can go fly a kite. But perhaps it was very important for the whole business enterprise for you to be there on time; and even if not, when you are once known to break you word, you are much less likely to be believed in the future, even when it is a life-or-death matter for you. Once gone, your reputation for honesty is very difficult to restore. This fact is among the many things to be considered when you do something that "breaks the rules." Perhaps rules like "Always tell the truth" and "Never knowingly injure another" have exceptions, but the rules are there because of centuries of experience of what happens when they are broken. Short-sighted utilitarianism in practice can have catastrophic effects in the long run.

Utilitarianism in practice is quite demanding. If you should always act so as to promote the maximum possible good, that good includes everyone. If by contributing a few dollars you could save the life of someone ten thousand miles away, shouldn't you do it, according to utilitarianism? The expense to you would be quite small, and the benefit to the recipient would be enormous: a matter of life and death. But now there is a second person who is also starving, and your donation of $25 would save her life; shouldn't you give, again, for the same reason? And so on for millions of people who are living on the brink of starvation. But of course you couldn't possibly help them all; you'd soon run out of money, and you'd be giving up what you had worked for years to earn—and if you did so there would still be an endless array of people in want, standing in line (as it were) to receive a handout. Can you really be under a moral obligation to help them, or as many of them as you can, until you have nothing left? Is this (almost) pure altruism again?

Perhaps you're trying to help in the wrong way. Perhaps you should (or should encourage others to) introduce some technical innovation into that country (a drought-free strain of rice, for example) or start a business there that would enable people to work and receive wages instead of handouts. Isn't productive labor the cure for poverty? If the people of that country are to be helped, it's important to give them a jump-start by introducing new enterprises that will produce more goods and services at lower prices. Otherwise the poverty will be unending, and no amount of effort from the outside could possibly succeed in eradicating it. In other words, giving handouts in not the best *means* for maximizing human welfare, prosperity, and happiness. Unending handouts may be an example of misplaced utilitarianism.

Because degrees of happiness and unhappiness, pain and pleasure, enjoyment and distress, cannot be quantified with any precision, utilitarianism is extremely difficult to apply in most everyday situations. The most we can do is to consider pros and cons. "She will be much happier if I tell her a flattering lie—but on the other hand, if she later discovers the truth she will be very unhappy; better if I tell the truth in the first place," and so on. Even if psychological states could be quantified, it is impossible to foresee the

long-term consequences of one's actions: what will happen if I do A? Will B result, leading in turn to C, or will D result, with a long train of consequences of its own? But the utilitarian will respond that this is not the fault of the theory but of the world in which the consequences of one's actions are so complex and far-flung that often we can't reasonably expect one outcome rather than another.

There are not only problems of application but an ambiguity within the theory itself. Suppose that you were in a position to choose between two alternative policies for the human race. In policy 1, you would encourage people to have more children; there would soon be overcrowding and even malnutrition as more and more people competed for less and less food. Even so, however, if there were twice as many people in the world, and each one had only a little more than half as much total happiness as they have now, it would be worth it: the total quantity of happiness would be greater than it is now because there would be so many more people. In policy 2, you would limit the population of the world; there would be more happiness per person but fewer people to enjoy the happiness. A utilitarian who held strictly to the greatest-total-quantity formulation would favor the first policy, but one who opted for the highest-average-good would favor the second policy.

The conclusions arrived at by Kantians and utilitarians would often agree, but the reasons would not be the same. Both would agree, for example, that one should not cheat on exams. Suppose I say that this is because if the professor found out that I had cheated, he would give me an F; or because, if the practice became widespread, there would be no point in having exams at all, since they wouldn't test what they were supposed to test. But these are utilitarian reasons. Kant held that even if *no one* else cheated, cheating would still be wrong, and the more prevalent it became, the more the rule against it would become self-defeating. You could not will cheating to be a universal law of conduct. If you violate the rule, you are (as it were) destroying the capital that others have accumulated by their honesty.

Kant did not argue against lying by saying that if I lie, others will lose confidence in me and won't believe my promises any more (a utilitarian reason), or that my lie will contribute to the general practice of telling lies, which will lead to a breakdown of trust (another utilitarian reason). He meant that lying violates the fundamental premise of a society that is based on mutual trust: it treats others in a way that they would not conceivably consent to be treated.

Human Rights

One should always, said Kant, treat other human beings as ends, not as means toward your or other people's ends. When I deal with you I should realize that you are, like me, a volitional being with abilities, needs, and desires just as I have—and that I should treat you with the same respect with which I myself wish to be treated. I am not an instrument for serving your ends, nor are you an instrument for serving mine.

The concept of *human rights* is closely related to this Kantian precept. When I assert that I have a right—to my life, for example—I am laying a claim to a certain bit of "moral space," just as a settler is laying claim to a certain piece of land. If I have a right to my life, this means that others may not forcibly interfere with it—they may not kill me, assault me, or otherwise harm me without my consent. If I have this right, other people have the duty (or responsibility) not to violate it.

But of course they also have a right to life, which means that I and everyone else have a duty not to violate that right. A right of A implies an obligation of B, C, D, etc., not to violate A's right; and a right of B implies a duty of A, C, D, etc., not to violate B's right; and so on.

Rights may sometimes work counter to utility. If I have a right to do certain things, I have that right even if it may not maximize the amount of good in the world or contribute to "the greatest happiness of the greatest number." Maybe more total good would be achieved if I were killed so that five people in need of bodily organs could have my heart, liver, lungs, etc., transplanted into them, thus saving their lives. But if I have a right to my life, this option is out, regardless of what maximizes utility.

Or, if I have bought my house and paid for it, I have a right to live in it, even though more good might be achieved if I were forced to share it with a dozen homeless people. The concept of rights has the effect (in some cases) of reinforcing egoism against any mass sacrifice on the altar of the greatest good. Rights place a limit on what I must suffer from others, as they also place a limit on what I may do *to* others. In general, having rights helps me to be a master of my own fate and not merely a pawn in the hands of others. My life does not belong to other people, for them to do with as they choose, any more than their lives belong to me, for me to do with as I choose.

Suppose that I am engaged in some project that is important to me, such as studying the structure of galactic systems; but another person is engaged in another project, such as providing a vaccine for a tribe in Patagonia, which will produce far more good for more people than my project will. A utilitarian would say that I should abandon my project, and should be made to do so by force if necessary, if thereby the greatest good for the most people would be achieved. Of course, I may not want to join that project and may be bored by it, but I am only one of many and my objections don't count for much in the whole system of utilitarian calculation.

But if I have a right to engage in my project—it's a peaceful project and perhaps even a useful one, and my pursuit of it doesn't violate anyone else's rights ("I'm not *bothering* anybody," as we say)—then surely I have a right to pursue it. If I have a right to pursue it, then no one has a right to stop me forcibly. My right takes precedence over utility. Or suppose that each of a hundred people would derive enormous pleasure from kidnapping me and torturing me to death. Even if such an action were happiness-maximizing, giving them far more total enjoyment than I would be suffering misery, it would still be wrong because it is a violation of my right to life.

Slavery is always a violation of human rights, since it involves the forced subservience of one person or group to another person or group, without the subservient person's consent.

It is different if I consent to work for you for a certain period; if I consent, my rights are not violated, any more than my right to my television set is violated if I voluntarily give it to you as a gift. But slavery, of course, is not by mutual consent: the one party is forced to labor for the other without the first party's consent. The central feature of human rights is "Other people's lives are not yours to dispose of." (And of course, yours is not theirs to dispose of either. It goes both ways. No one is anyone else's master, nor is anyone another's slave.) Slavery is condemned not because it doesn't maximize happiness. It doesn't, although there might be isolated cases in which the benefit to the slaveowner greatly outweighs the suffering of the slave. But that is not the reason for condemning slavery, which is that it is a violation of human rights.

Thus far, we have considered only what are called *negative* rights. If I have a right, others have a duty or obligation; but their duty is only of a negative kind: not to interfere with the exercise of my right. They do not have to *do* anything; they have only to *forbear* from any rights-violating action. The right to life, liberty, and the pursuit of happiness expressed in the Declaration of Independence means that the government is to *refrain* from forcible interference with our peaceful activities, such as pursuing our life goals.

Various thinkers have asserted that we also have *positive* rights—such as the right to three square meals a day, to shelter, and to other necessities of daily life. If human rights are rooted in human needs, shouldn't we also have a right to these basics? The problem here is not that they are not needs but that other people are being asked to supply them. If I have a right to food, others cannot honor that right without providing me the food. To honor it, then, requires not merely noninterference on their part but a positive action: providing me with the food.

It is true, of course, that people cannot live without food. But there are some problems with saying that people have a *right* to it, problems that do not arise with the right to life and liberty. For example:

1. If I provide food for myself, why shouldn't others provide food for themselves? Why must I redouble my efforts to provide it for myself *and* others?

Perhaps the person is *unable* to provide it for herself. Then of course others must provide it if she is not to starve to death. Surely those who can provide it for themselves do not have a right to *take* it from others; but perhaps those who cannot provide it for themselves have this right.

2. If everyone has a positive right, who is to fulfill it? What if there are not enough re-

sources to fill the need? If everyone has a right to three square meals a day, what happens when there is a drought or the nation is not productive enough to grow that much food?

The right to life (the right not to be harmed) can be honored no matter how many people there are in the world: all that is required of others is "hands off." But the right to food depends on how many claimants there are in relation to the number of people who can supply it. A government could enforce "subsistence rights" to food only by compelling others to supply it—at least until the supply runs out. (The supply of course *will* run out sooner if people lack the motivation to produce it for themselves or to sell it—they will soon say, "Why should I produce at all, when others only consume what I have produced?")

Can the right to food be a universal human right, if not everyone can claim it? "Well, only the poor can claim it." But now a host of other questions arises: how poor is poor? Who is to decide this? What committee should decide, and by what criteria, who gets what? How can any committee know the situation of each person, whether he is unable to survive without outside help or whether he just prefers not to exert much energy and to allow other people to exert it for him? And by what right does one person or group forcibly take away from them what others by their labor have produced? If other people have a right to the food, what happens to *your* right as producer of the food to use it (and distribute it if you wish) in accordance with your own choices rather than the choices of others?

3. Can there be a right to violate rights? If the right of one person can be fulfilled only by violating the equal rights of others, can both be a right? If others must coerce me in order to fulfill their right, what has meanwhile happened to my right? What must we

say of an alleged right of one person that cannot be honored without violating the equal rights of another?

Justice

A: Should she receive an A on the course?
B: No, she hasn't done the work, she doesn't know the material, and she doesn't deserve an A.
A: But she'd be much happier if you have her an A. And it might bother you for a little while, but you'd soon forget about it. There would be more happiness all around.
B: Yes, but it wouldn't be fair; it would be *unjust.*

Or:

A: Should he be sentenced to prison?
B: Of course not; he is innocent.
A: But he's a public nuisance, and it would be easy to convince people that he's guilty. The public would believe that the police are doing their job, and they'd feel safer.
B: But sending him to prison for what he didn't do would be unjust. I don't care how many good effects it may have, it's still an injustice.

Justice is another concept in the arsenal of ethics. Sentencing the man might have good effects, but it's still wrong because it is unjust—he doesn't deserve the sentence. Justice is *treatment in accordance with one's deserts.*

Deserts are *individual.* One student deserves an A and another does not; one lawbreaker deserves a prison sentence and another may not. You don't add all the student's scores, divide them by the number of students in the class, and give every one the result. That would be *collectivism;* treating all the members of a group as if they were alike, instead of considering their individual differences. Since people do differ from one another, it is unjust to ignore these differences and treat them as if there were no differences. If a member of a certain tribe is murdered by a member of another, her family may take revenge on everyone in the other tribe. This is an example of the injustice of collectivism.

A frequently encountered form of collectivism is *racism.* A racist looks on all members of a certain racial or ethnic group (other than his or her own) as if they were all alike. Of course this assumption is false: some members of a group are brilliant, some stupid; some are friendly, some hostile; some are generous, others not. In every group there are many individual differences. Taking into account these individual differences is *individualism*—treating each person on the basis of his or her own merits or demerits (qualifications for a job, admission to a college, etc.).

The difference between justice and utility is most clearly seen if we examine various theories of punishment. A man has committed a murder, and the question is not "Should he be punished?" but "Why should he be punished? What is the *rationale* for punishment?"

1. Some say that the aim of punishment is to *rehabilitate* the offender—to transform him into the kind of person who will not repeat his crime. That is what the "correctors" in the film *A Clockwork Orange* did by administering compulsory behavioral modification with electric shock treatments and so on, so that the subject was no longer violent: in fact, just after his release he was assaulted by a street gang and was so conditioned to hate violence that he was unable to defend himself.

But is rehabilitation what punishment is all about? It doesn't work very often, and even when it does it is very expensive to administer. And does the state have the right to change a person's personality against his will? (What if he says, "I committed the crime and I'll do my time, but you have no right to play with my personality and turn me into the kind of person I don't want to be"?) Moreover, if rehabilitation is successful, should the murderer be released at once without doing the rest of his time?

2. Others say that the aim of punishment is *deterrence.* Criminals should be punished in order to deter them and others from committing crimes in the future.

Deterrence, however, is uncertain. If we knew that a certain punishment didn't deter anyone, should we then not punish the person who committed it? Besides, deterrence depends on the degree of publicity a certain crime receives—an unknown person rotting in prison for life is not likely to deter anyone, since others don't know about it. And deterrence can be achieved even if the wrong person is punished, as long as the public never hears about it. Moreover, as Kant remarked, to punish a man in order to deter others from crime is to use him as a means toward an end (society's end), not to treat him with the respect that is due all rational beings.

3. Others say that the aim of punishment is to *protect* the rest of us against those who would be dangerous to our safety if they were allowed to go about freely among us.

Not everyone will agree on who is dangerous, to what extent, and why. (Should we be protected against "dangerous ideas"?) We are protected against serial killers as long as they remain in prison. Is their dangerousness what justifies us in imprisoning them? What if we could establish that a certain man who had committed murder was not a danger to anyone and would never commit a crime again (most murderers, after all, are one-timers)? Should we release him from prison as soon as we are sure that he is no longer a danger to anyone?

These three justifications of punishment are all utilitarian; they differ only in which consequences they emphasize, but they all defend punishment for the good results it is alleged to produce (or the bad results it is alleged to avoid). The punishment is always done *in order to* achieve some result. In the *retributive* theory (the deserts theory), on the other hand, punishment is always done *because of* an act committed in the past. What justifies the punishment is that the person has committed an act against another person for which he *deserves* to be punished. People can differ on exactly what punishment a person deserves—whether the murderer deserves life imprisonment or capital punishment, for example—but they agree on the principle: punishment is permissible only if it is deserved, not because he or society is improved by it or because we are all safer as a result; these may be desirable consequences of punishing, but they are not the reason for punishing. Suppose that punishing someone would make him a better person, deter others from crime, and protect society against a perennial nuisance, but that *he* is not guilty; does anyone really believe that he should be punished just the same?

A retributivist rejects all three utilitarian justifications for punishing:

A: Neither rehabilitation nor deterrence nor protection of society has anything to do with what the offender *deserves* for what she has done. I say that if two persons are exactly similar to each other and are in exactly the same circumstances, it would be unjust for the one to be treated better or worse than the other—for one to be given five years in jail and the other a suspended sentence, for example.

B: Why do you say that they have to be exactly alike and in identical circumstances?

A: Because many things can make a difference to one's desert. Let's say that one of them killed another by accident or in self-defense and the other killed on purpose; surely that would make a difference—one doesn't deserve to be punished and the other does. Or suppose that one of them grew up in a normal home environment and the other in a crime-infested area where murder was a daily thing, and that she had no father and her mother was a crack addict. Some (not all) would say that *that* factor made a difference in her desert, because to some extent at least the second person couldn't help, or had less control over, what she was doing. If there were a difference between the two in their nature or circumstances, that *might* make a difference in what they deserve. Any difference in the circumstances could make a difference in desert; that's why I say that only when the two persons and circumstances are exactly the same, it would be unjust to give them different punishments. Justice implies similar treatment for similar cases.

B: That's fine, but it doesn't tell us *which* similarities or dissimilarities of persons or circumstances should be taken as the basis for a dissimilarity of treatment. Two men each knowingly and deliberately kill some innocent victim; should the first man be given a lighter sentence because he came from a crime-infested slum?

A: I could say that if they both (1) killed intentionally, and (2) not in self-defense, then they should be given the same punishment. The law should treat them the same, because the circumstances were similar.

B: Not similar enough. If the criminal environment in any way made it less likely that one of them had control over his actions or that he couldn't have avoided doing what he did, then that might well make a difference in what punishment he deserves.

A: Then if one of them couldn't help what he did—literally did it entirely from an uncontrollable inner compulsion—then he didn't deserve to be punished at all!

B: If it was entirely a matter of inner compulsion, then that's true; then he is not responsible for his act and doesn't deserve to be punished for it. That's why we sometimes admit insanity pleas.

A: And suppose that both of them acted from inner compulsion and couldn't help what they were doing, then neither of them deserves to be punished?

B: *If* neither of them had any control over what he was doing. But that isn't the case. Nobody was holding a gun to their heads, and their actions weren't determined (at least not entirely determined) by inner compulsion. So the concept of desert is applicable to both cases.

A: But if *none* of us can ever help what we do, then none of us deserve punishment?

B: Of course, but most of us, most of the time, *can* help what we do.

A: But if we couldn't, then none of us should ever be punished for committing a crime?

B: Not on the basis of desert. Punishment would then be a case of "social engineering"—"They can't help what they're doing but we have to put them away anyway for our protection, or recondition them so that they won't repeat it." But in such a world there would be no desert, either good or ill.

A: I just wanted to extract that admission from you. OK, let's proceed. The punishment should depend on the desert. And identical persons in identical circumstances have the same desert, therefore they should have the same punishment (whatever it is). Now the next question: what should that punishment be? What principles of justice are we to use to decide this?

B: Since some crimes are more serious than others, we have to have some principle of *proportionality*. A man who kills another deserves a more severe punishment than one who has merely stolen from another. A man who has robbed you at gunpoint deserves a more severe punishment than one who has peacefully stolen your television set from you while you were not at home. And so on.

A: Should the punishment then depend on how badly the victim *feels,* how much she has suffered because of the crime?

B: No, there is no way of estimating that, and anyway most persons will grossly overestimate the amount of pain or discomfort they experienced. There must be some objective standard of loss: if someone stole your car, you deserve to have your car back (or its market value) plus something more for your pain and discomfort. It should depend on the amount of loss, not on how the loss made you feel.

A: There are many variables here. A family heirloom may be worthless at a pawnshop but extremely valuable to you for sentimental reasons. Should you recoup more because of that fact?

B: Perhaps, but you're changing the subject: how much the victim should recover is one thing, how much punishment if any the lawbreaker deserves is another. What she deserves depends on *her* situation: did she commit the crime knowingly? deliberately? did she want to kill the other person? Did she do it in self-defense? Did she think the gun wasn't loaded, and if so did she *reasonably* think this? All these things make a difference, and once we believe the killing was accidental, we change our view of what punishment is deserved.

A: All these things make a difference. But even more important, and much more controversial, are factors like the following: if his father skipped out when he was two and his mother was a crack addict, does this entitle us to say that "He couldn't help what he did" (he had no control over his aggressive impulses, etc.)—or at least was *less able* to control what he did—than if he had been brought up in a normal middle-class family? You see, if he really couldn't help it, it would be pointless to punish him—not only pointless but immoral according to the retributive theory: if he doesn't deserve the punishment, it is unjust to punish him. We may try to rehabilitate him and deter him and others from doing such things, but desert is something else again. Punishment, as opposed to these other things, presupposes ill desert. What possible excuse would we have for putting someone in prison for years at a time, unless he deserves it?

B: I'm not at all convinced that people should be imprisoned because of ill desert. They are imprisoned because they're dangerous and because we need to be protected against them. Some people are like mad dogs—the mad dog may not deserve to be shot, but we shoot him so he won't do any more damage.

A: So the serial killer doesn't deserve the punishment he gets?

B: I don't know. I doubt whether anybody knows. I only know that we are not safe having him around. He can no longer be permitted to walk among us. Our own safety is at stake.

Justice and compensation. Whatever we may conclude about justice in punishment, we also speak of justice in other contexts—particularly compensation, such as for damages inflicted or work performed. Let's consider a few examples.

Case 1. If a drunken driver has run into my car and damaged it, I deserve compensation; after all it is my loss. Perhaps I can afford the loss; perhaps more total good would be achieved if the driver gave the money to someone else or to a charitable organization. Still, justice requires that I be compensated; for the money to go to someone else (at least without my consent) might have some utility, but it would nevertheless be an injustice.

Case 2. I don't deserve an A in the course: I did poorly on the tests and I seldom went to class. But I would be much happier if I did get an A. That undeserved grade might even make the difference between being admitted to graduate school and not being admitted. As for you, the teacher, you might feel uncomfortable at first about giving me the undeserved grade, but you have many other students and you'd soon forget about it; your happiness might even be increased a bit if I gave you $500 to give me the A and tell no one.

There's still another consideration, of course: the effect of undeserved grades on the whole grading system. Grades are supposed to tell graduate schools and future employers how well a student has done, and misgrading gives a distorted picture of a student's record to whoever needs to know what that record is. Still, one bit of misgrading will have no effect on the grading system in general (millions of grades are assigned every week), and if nobody talks, no one will ever know that it happened. Of course, the misgrading might have an effect on the future employer or graduate school: an incompetent person might be admitted and a more competent one refused admission as a result; lives might even be lost if the student becomes an incompetent doctor. But this is not very likely; if the student was on the whole a good one, and the poor record in this course was the result of illness or a family crisis, the undeserved grade would have no bad effects at all. Still, it would be an injustice, would it not?

Case 3. Consider this much more controversial example:

A: She deserved a higher wage than he did: she worked much harder than he did in the same office. She was tireless and always gave her best effort.

B: But with all that extra effort she didn't accomplish any more. She was a bit clumsy at the job and made lots of mistakes, so that extra effort didn't add any productivity to the company—others' time had to be spent correcting her mistakes. Effort by itself doesn't mean much if it is not accompanied by ability or achievement. Why should an employer pay an employee for trying hard if that effort yields no result? The employer pays for an employee's achievement, just as the teacher gives an A to the student who has achieved the most in the course, whether the student has spent a thousand hours on the course or only a hundred.

A: If the employees get paid by the hour, both should get the same as per the contract (although the employer might not wish to renew hers), and it is just for them both to get the same. But if payment is for doing a certain job, and he finishes the job more quickly than she does, then they should both be paid the same even though he took less time doing it.

B: But suppose that they each got half of what they are now being paid—wouldn't that be an unjust wage?

A: I don't know what an unjust wage is— lots of people think they are worth fifty bucks an hour for working in a car wash—other than whatever an employer is willing to pay. If an employee feels she is being underpaid, she can try another company that might reward her abilities more than the present one does. After all, we don't feel we are being unjust as consumers if we shop around for the best bargains; nor is the employer treating employees unjustly if she gets the most service she can at the lowest wages. If she paid twice as much, her company might not be profitable and might even have to close. Of course, "you get what you pay for"—if she pays them little, her best workers will soon leave and go somewhere else.

B: That's what usually happens, but in the meanwhile she *is* underpaying them, isn't she? Suppose that as an employer she is guilty of racial discrimination: she pays minority workers less even though they do the same amount of work. Surely that is an injustice to the workers who are discriminated against.

A: Of course, because the two workers are not compensated equally for doing the same work. That's like having unequal punishments for the same crime. Such discrimination, whether for reasons of race or gender, is always unjust, because it is done on the basis of something that is utterly irrelevant to one's performance at a job, namely the color of one's skin, rather than on the basis of achievement or work performed.

Case 4. Which is the most just (or least unjust) system of taxation—one in which everybody is taxed the same amount, one in which everybody is taxed the same percentage of income, or one in which those with the most income are taxed a higher percentage of income (progressive taxation)?

B: If everyone is equally protected (of course in practice they aren't), then everyone should pay an equal amount in taxes—equal protection, equal payment.

A: But the poor have less ability to pay, so they should pay less.

B: The poor pay the same as the rich for an item in the supermarket; both get the same value for the same money. So it should be with protection afforded by the law.

A: But the rich get more protection—they have more property to protect.

B: The rich could afford to buy their own protection. The poor get more protection in proportion to the money they expend on it. The police keep trespassers off the little old lady's yard even though she has no assets except her house and yard.

A: Anyway, justice requires that we consider ability to pay. Those better off should pay more.

B: That seems to me a formula for *in*justice, not justice. Why should someone pay more for the same goods or services that are available to others for less? You seem to assume that equalization of incomes is all or part of what we mean by justice.

A: Well, it is. It is unjust for some to have more while others have less.

B: No matter what they do or don't do to deserve it? This person works hard and is creative on the job, that person shows up late or drunk and finally quits the job entirely, and you say that the one shouldn't have more and the other less?

A: I'm saying that until everyone has bread, no one should have cake.

B: That's a way of guaranteeing that no one will ever have cake; the cake will never be produced under those conditions. If the rich are taxed for most of what they earn, the economy will stagnate and unemployment will continue. Lower the taxes on the rich, and new businesses will start, more consumer products will be manufactured, and more people will be employed in the new enterprises. There will then be more people gainfully employed, and fewer people dependent on others for welfare payments. There will be greater prosperity and a higher standard of living whenever the government doesn't eat up more and more in taxes. You want to equalize incomes— which means you want to kill the goose that lays the golden egg. You want to sustain the poor, which can be done only out of the surplus of productive enterprises, but you want to make sure that the would-be employers have no surplus left that they can use to create the jobs or manufacture the products! I want everyone to have bread *and* cake—a prosperous economy with everyone who is able to work gainfully employed—but your mania for income equalization would make the prosperity impossible, the very prosperity required to provide for the poor in the first place.

A: We can do without some of the prosperity in order to provide a nearer approach to equality of income.

B: Why don't you let people make that choice for themselves, instead of forcing those who are most economically successful to part with most of their earnings, with the result that many who would otherwise be employed are *not* employed? What gives you (or your legislator) the right to force that situation on them?

A: If we disagree on the empirical facts, how are we ever going to agree on the ethical issues that depend on those facts?

Case 5. Assume a society of five persons—actually 5 million or 50 million—but make it five for purposes of illustration. The government takes away from everyone all the money they have earned beyond a certain amount and gives to everyone who has earned less. Those who earned more than $25,000 last year must surrender to the government everything over $25,000, those who earned $10,000 are given $15,000, and those who earned nothing at all are given the entire $25,000.

A: I take it you would not think highly of such an entirely egalitarian society, at least as far as income is concerned—the income pattern is 5-5-5-5-5.

B: No—it's a "one-shot deal": those who worked hard and had a large income during the year would discover that all but the minimum amount was taken away from them—so why bother to earn anything at all when Redistribution Day comes around? At the other end of the scale, those who earned nothing wouldn't have any incentive to find a job—they'd get the income anyway. The result would be that nobody would work: everyone would freeload off of someone else, and of course there would soon be no one left off of whom one could freeload. Universal parasitism cannot be sustained. When the income pattern is 0-0-0-0-0, everyone starves.

So instead of 5-5-5-5-5, let's try a society in which each person can keep the reward for his or her labor. People would compete with one another to produce, knowing that whatever they earned they could keep. Some people would become

wealthy: 5,000 or even 10,000. Those who worked for these entrepreneurs would be better off than they were before, but not as well off as the entrepreneurs themselves, although they would be free to become entrepreneurs themselves if they chose, with all the risks of failure that go with it. So the pattern might be 0-5-15-100-1,000, or something like that.

A: This capitalistic (free market) society would have too much inequality to suit me. For example, there are still people with zero income.

B: Yes, but the society would be rich enough to sustain the nonworkers, either through private charity or government welfare benefits (if the percentage of the nonworkers wasn't too high). So no one would end up starving (zero income). But the society would be a very prosperous one, with new enterprises springing up whenever people thought they might profit from them, and many more people being productively involved in these enterprises. What could destroy such a society is *envy*: the person who earns $25,000 a year would envy the person who made $250,000, saying, "She doesn't work any harder than I do, and look at her with her fancy house and cars! Let's take it away from her!" And laws would be passed taking more and more away from those who have, to give to those who (for whatever reason) have not. And at last, if no one succeeded in stopping the process, we would once again have a state of "splendidly equalized destitution."

A: We needn't go as far as an equality of zero. We have to stop short of that. But I think your infatuation with maximizing material prosperity carries you too far in the direction of inequality. Poverty is bad, but inequality is also bad—we have to balance the one against the other.

B: You may be repelled by the idea of radical inequality because you believe that one person who is well-off is the cause of someone else being worse off—that the first one has *harmed* the second in some way. And sometimes of course this is true: Jones stole Smith's assets and got away with it. But in a market economy the entrepreneur's wealth is not the cause of the comparative poverty of others: quite the opposite. He creates the jobs, and others are free to decide whether they want to accept the job offered rather than continuing to do whatever they were doing already. He doesn't cause poverty, he creates choices—and chances to rise in the world—which they wouldn't have but for him.

A: I agree that poverty is bad and should be avoided if possible, but that inequality is also bad. You don't want poverty but don't mind inequality. Where do we go from here? Do we just have conflicting ethical intuitions?

B: I think that what you are seeking is an equality of *outcomes*—that somehow everyone will end up equal or nearly equal (economically). And this is a mistake. Some people try, but some don't; some people are born at the wrong place or time; some people try and are struck down by death or disease. The world is not a level playing field. And you believe it ought to be—or at least that we should do whatever we can to make it so.

A: You believe that what I should be advocating is equality of *opportunity*, not equality of income. And I do advocate that. Some people who fail to achieve their goals never had a chance to achieve them: they were handicapped, or they

weren't smart enough, or they didn't have the money that others had to start with, or they had parents who didn't care.

B: And I don't see how you can ever get rid of such inequality. We can handle poverty to some extent, trying to make sure that no one is in dire want (but that is possible only in an affluent society that can afford to give out of its surplus). But what do you do with bad parents? Do you take children away from such parents (assuming we can agree on who they are) and put them in foster homes, where they might well be much worse off? The problem is really insoluble. I can see no satisfactory solution to this problem, nothing that doesn't make things still worse. Yet how a person turns out as an adult has much more to do with what kind of parents she had than with how much money they had. Equality of conditions is impossible to achieve. And of course it is equality of *favorable* conditions that we want, not equality of destitution.

A: Well, there we are. Life is better than death. Rationality is better than irrationality. Fulfillment is better than frustration. Happiness is better than unhappiness. Satisfaction is better than misery. These are basic premises in ethics, just as the Law of Identity and the Law of Noncontradiction are basic in all discourse. We can juggle these around and rate some as higher on balance than others, and try to decide what to do when one of them can be achieved only at the expense of one of the others. And we can clarify our terminology and make sure we aren't confusing one concept with another. Do we really know, for example, what "equality of opportunity" means when it comes to concrete cases? If one child is dull and another one bright, do you provide equality of opportunity by giving more time to the dull child because she needs it more, or to the bright child because you can accomplish so much more in an hour with her? Or do you give them each equal time regardless of such considerations? I don't think that as philosophers we have worked out these concepts very clearly; we use the *words,* especially when they have a nice ring to them or sound somehow noble, but we—neither ordinary people nor trained social workers—are not very good at tracing the implications of the views we profess, or even at clarifying our differences. We have our work cut out for us!

B: There are other areas of ethics that require extended discussion: for example, the concept of a good society, not merely a good individual, as well as good government, a good economic system, and so on. There's another fascinating subject that's just coming into its own: the treatment of animals. Do animals have rights? Should we try to preserve them no matter how harmful they may be to us (such as cobras)? Should we be more concerned about endangered species than about common ones? Should we be more concerned with our pets than with animals in the wild? Should we refrain from killing animals for food, for medical experiments, or to preserve a native species against a population explosion of imported animals (such as rabbits in Australia), which if left unchecked would exterminate most native species? Should we check human population so as to leave more room for wild animals, who are now facing extinction from loss of their habitat? There are many questions of this kind in normative ethics.

A: I'm afraid we will have to save all this for another occasion.[14]

EXERCISES

1. "What does it matter whether ethical theories use the word 'good' and other ethical words as they are used in ordinary discourse? In the sciences, when we find a word vague, we give it a special, technical meaning; we do that in physics with such words as 'energy,' 'resistance,' and 'work'. Why not do this in ethics too and get rid of the vagueness and the overlapping meanings?" Comment.

2. Which of the following are empirical statements? Explain.
  a. Broccoli is good for you.
  b. It was good of you to come to visit me.
  c. Tangerines taste good.
  d. Holding your breath is a good way to cure the hiccups.
  e. I value your friendship.
  f. You may not value reliability, but you will find that it will be a valuable trait for you to have.
  g. I have a bad taste in my mouth.

3. Evaluate the following:
  a. Happiness is good independently of who has it. We should work to achieve the good. Therefore, I should work to achieve your good as well as my own.
  b. "Why is it immoral to produce a value and keep it, but moral to give it away? And if it is not moral for you to keep a value when you give it, are they not selfish and vicious when they take it? Does virtue consist of serving vice?"[15]

4. Do the following rules, in your opinion, have exceptions? If so, under what possible conditions? Explain.

---
[14]See John Hospers, *Human Conduct* (Fort Worth, TX: Harcourt Brace, 1996), Chapter 8.
[15]Rand, *Atlas Shrugged,* p. 1031.

a. "One should never use force against another." "But it's all right to use force in self-defense, when others attack you." "All right then, the rule should be: Never *initiate* the use of force against others."
b. Never cheat a customer, even if the boss threatens to fire you for not doing so.
c. A defendant who is known to be innocent should never be punished.
d. When two applicants are equally qualified, the minority candidate should always be chosen.
e. I should always act so as to preserve (and if possible increase) the liberty of others.
f. There are times when a person should be executed without a trial.

5. Much in ethics depends on how an act is classified. Should the following be classified as murder or attempted murder?
a. Your father is terminally ill and in great and incurable pain; you help him die painlessly by administering a quick-acting poison.
b. A intends to shoot B but by mistake shoots and kills C.
c. Some men dynamited a prison wall to get a prisoner out, but other prisoners were killed in the blast.
d. The villagers offered to give the pilgrims to Mecca a boat ride across the Red Sea for a fee, but after they had collected the money they dumped the pilgrims on a deserted island where there was no food or water, and they died.
e. The policeman is about to arrest the driver of a truck. The driver starts the motor and accelerates rapidly, and the policeman falls off the fender and is killed in the oncoming traffic.
f. A man jumps out of the twelfth story of a burning building, knowing that the fall will kill him. Was it suicide? (According to the Catholic doctrine of "double effect," it was not suicide if his intention was only to escape the flames but not to kill himself.)
g. He lied to her by telling her, before they had sex, that he didn't have AIDS. She contracted AIDS and died.
h. She failed to tell him that the car's brakes weren't working. On the first downhill stretch of road, he crashed into a wall and was killed.

6. "It's not that we want to see people suffer; it's just that we want to be protected against dangerous predators. If we could parachute all the serial killers onto a remote South Seas island (assuming it wasn't already inhabited), that would get rid of them just as well as a stretch in prison. Who cares how much of a good time they'd have, as long as they don't bother other people any more?"

"There is an ingredient missing from that picture: they *deserve* to suffer because of what they have done. They have snuffed out other human lives, and for this they should pay the penalty. Punishment achieves that, and exile on a South Seas island does not."

Continue the conversation, or discuss the example.

7. A Nazi who was responsible for the deaths of several hundred prisoners in a death camp has been found in Argentina. Now he is the head of a factory and has led an impeccable life since coming to Argentina. Should he be tried and punished for his crimes of fifty years ago, or should we forget about it, saying, "It's too long ago now" or "Punishing him wouldn't do any good"? Which theory of punishment are you defending in giving your answer?

8. When some act is (1) unjust to someone; or (2) a violation of someone's rights, does that settle the matter? Does it follow that you should never do it? Or are violations of rights sometimes permissible? (How about in war?)

9. Does a defendant deserve punishment for abusing his child less because he himself was abused as a child? Does someone deserve punishment less because a friend persuaded her to join in the robbery when she was intoxicated and not fully aware of what she was doing (and certainly not of its consequences)?

10. Is it unjust (unfair) if an officer selects a soldier for a dangerous mission because: (1) he dislikes the man and doesn't want him to come back alive, or (2) the man was deemed most capable of doing the job?

11.

A: What you should do or not do depends on your circumstances. In a desert society, where wasting water could cost lives, you should not waste water, but in a water-affluent society it's OK. Ordinarily we shouldn't eat our comrades, but when there's no other way to fend off starvation after a plane crash, it's OK. In your circumstances, it would be desirable to get a divorce: you have no children and you're better off separate; but in my circumstances, where there are children and we might be able to patch things up, we should not obtain a divorce. In situations of dire poverty some things may be permissible that would not be permissible in a wealthier society—such as taking partially eaten food from someone's plate and using it again. It all depends on the circumstances: what is right in one set of circumstances may not be in another; what is desirable in one place or time is often not so at another.

B: But there are acts, or types of acts, that are wrong under all circumstances. These are the special concern of ethics.

In your opinion are there any such acts? Discuss.

12. Would your prescriptions for a good society be the same as or similar to those you would prescribe for a good person?

13.

A: You may *say* that your services are worth one hundred dollars an hour, but if no one will pay you that, there is no reason to keep saying it. Your services are worth only what the highest bidder will pay; what other criterion can there be of what your services are "really worth"?

B: We pay millions today for a single painting by Van Gogh. Nobody would pay him even one hundred dollars at the time it was painted. But surely his works were worth a lot more, even then; it's just that nobody appreciated their true worth. The same is true about the value of my services at McDonald's.

Discuss.

14. Should we apply the parts of the ethics we use (or profess) about our relations with other human beings ("Do not kill," "Do not cause needless pain," "Do not use as a means to your end," etc.) to our treatment of animals?

SELECTED READINGS

ARISTOTLE. *Nicomachean Ethics.* Many editions.

BENTHAM, JEREMY. *Principles of Morals and Legislation.* 1789. Many editions.

BLANSHARD, BRAND. *Reason and Goodness.* London: Allen & Unwin, 1961.

BRANDT, RICHARD. *A Theory of the Good and the Right.* New York: Oxford University Press, 1979.

BROAD, C. D. *Five Types of Ethical Theory.* London: Routledge, 1935.

CLARK, STEPHEN. *The Moral Status of Animals.* Oxford: Clarendon Press, 1977.

DANCY, JONATHAN. *Moral Reasons.* Oxford: Blackwell, 1993.

DUFF, R. A. *Intention, Agency, and Criminal Liability.* Oxford: Blackwell, 1990.

EDEL, ABRAHAM. *Ethical Judgment.* New York: Free Press, 1955.

EWING, ALFRED C. *The Definition of Good.* New York: Macmillan, 1947.

FEINBERG, JOEL. *Doing and Deserving.* Princeton: Princeton University Press, 1970.

FOOT, PHILIPPA. *Theories of Ethics.* London: Oxford University Press, 1967.

FRANKENA, WILLIAM. *Ethics*. Englewood Cliffs, NJ: Prentice Hall, 1963.

GEWIRTH, ALAN. *Reason and Morality*. Chicago: University of Chicago Press, 1978.

GLOVER, JONATHAN. *Causing Death and Saving Lives*. Baltimore: Penguin, 1977.

HARE, R. M. *Freedom and Reason*. Oxford: Clarendon Press, 1963.

HARE, R. M. *The Language of Morals*. London: Oxford University Press, 1961.

HARMAN, GILBERT. *The Nature of Morality*. New York: Oxford University Press, 1977.

HARTLAND-SWANN, JOHN. *An Analysis of Morals*. London: Allen & Unwin, 1950.

HAZLITT, HENRY. *The Foundations of Morality*. Princeton: Van Nostrand, 1964.

HOSPERS, JOHN. *Human Conduct*. 3rd ed. Fort Worth, TX: Harcourt Brace, 1996.

HUME, DAVID. *A Treatise of Human Nature*. Book 3. 1739. Many editions.

KAGAN, SHELLY. *The Limits of Morality*. London: Oxford University Press, 1989.

KANT, IMMANUEL. *Fundamental Principles of the Metaphysics of Morals*. New York: Harper & Row, 1964. Originally published in 1783.

MACHAN, TIBOR, ed. *The Great Debate*. New York: Random House, 1987.

MACKIE, J. M. *Ethics*. Baltimore: Penguin, 1977.

MCINTYRE, ALASDAIR. *After Virtue*. Notre Dame, IN: Notre Dame University Press, 1983.

MIDGLEY, MARY. *The Ethical Primate: Humans, Freedom, and Morality*. London: Routledge, 1994.

MILL, JOHN STUART. *On Liberty*. London: Longmans Green, 1859.

MILL, JOHN STUART. *Principles of Political Economy*. London: Longmans Green, 1865.

MILL, JOHN STUART. *Utilitarianism*. London: Longmans Green, 1863.

MOORE, GEORGE E. *Ethics*. London: Oxford University Press, 1912.

MOORE, GEORGE E. *Principia Ethica*. London: Cambridge University Press, 1903.

NAGEL, THOMAS. *Moral Questions*. Cambridge: Cambridge University Press, 1979.

NOWELL-SMITH, PATRICK. *Ethics*. Baltimore: Penguin, 1954.

NOZICK, ROBERT. *Anarchy, State, and Utopia*. New York: Basic Books, 1974.

PAUL, ELLEN, et al. *Human Rights*. Oxford: Blackwell, 1984.

PLATO. *Apology; Crito; Euthyphro; Philebus; Republic*. Many editions.

QUINTON, ANTHONY. *Utilitarian Ethics*. LaSalle, IL: Open Court, 1988.

RAND, AYN. *The Virtue of Selfishness*. New York: New American Library, 1964.

RASHDALL, HASTINGS. *Theory of Good and Evil*. 2 vols. London: Routledge, 1924.

RAWLS, JOHN. *A Theory of Justice*. Cambridge: Harvard University Press, 1971.

ROSS, WILLIAM D. *The Right and the Good*. London: Oxford University Press, 1931.

RUSSELL, BERTRAND. *Human Society in Ethics and Politics*. London: Allen & Unwin, 1955.

SCHEFFLER, SAMUEL. *Human Morality*. London: Oxford University Press, 1992.

SIDGWICK, HENRY. *The Methods of Ethics*. London: Macmillan, 1877.

SINGER, PETER. *A Companion to Ethics*. Oxford: Blackwell, 1993.

SMART, J.J.C., and BERNARD WILLIAMS. *Utilitarianism: For and Against*. Cambridge: Cambridge University Press, 1973.

SMITH, ADAM. *Theory of the Moral Sentiments*. 1759. Many editions.

SPENCER, HERBERT. *The Principles of Ethics*. 2 vols. Indianapolis: Liberty Press, 1979. Originally published 1897.

STACE, WALTER T. *The Concept of Morals*. New York: Macmillan, 1937.

STERBA, JAMES, ed. *Justice: Alternative Approaches*. Belmont, CA: Dickensen, 1979.

STEVENSON, CHARLES L. *Ethics and Language*. New Haven: Yale University Press, 1943.

TAYLOR, RICHARD. *Freedom, Anarchy, and the Law*. Buffalo: Prometheus, 1973.

TAYLOR, RICHARD. *Good and Evil*. New York: Macmillan, 1970.

VON WRIGHT, G. H. *The Varieties of Goodness*. London: Routledge, 1963.

WARNOCK, GEOFFREY. *The Object of Morality*. London: Metheun, 1977.

WHITE, MORTON. *What Is and What Ought to Be Done*. New York: Oxford University Press, 1988.

WILLIAMS, BERNARD. *Ethics and the Limits of Philosophy*. Cambridge: Harvard Universtiy Press, 1985

Index